Interviewing for Solutions

THIRD EDITION

PETER DE JONG
Calvin College

INSOO KIM BERG
Brief Family Therapy Center

BROOKS/COLE
CENGAGE Learning™

Australia • Brazil • Japan • Korea • Mexico • Singapore • Spain • United Kingdom • United States

BROOKS/COLE
CENGAGE Learning™

Interviewing for Solutions, Third Edition

Peter De Jong, Insoo Kim Berg

Acquisitions Editor: Dan Alpert

Development Editor: Tangelique Williams

Assistant Editor: Ann Lee Richards

Editorial Assistant: Stephanie Rue

Technology Project Manager: Julie Aguilar

Marketing Manager: Meghan McCullough

Marketing Assistant: Teresa Marino

Marketing Communications Manager: Shemika Britt

Project Manager, Editorial Production: Christy Krueger

Creative Director: Rob Hugel

Art Director: Vernon Boes

Print Buyer: Linda Hsu

Permissions Editor: Robert Kauser

Production Service: Aaron Downey/ Matrix Productions Inc.

Copy Editor: Kate Petrella

Cover Designer: Brenda Duke

Cover Image: © Nic Miller/Getty Images

Compositor: Integra Software Services

For product information and technology assistance, contact us at **Cengage Learning Customer & Sales Support, 1-800-354-9706**.

For permission to use material from this text or product, submit all requests online at **www.cengage.com/ permissions**. Further permissions questions can be e-mailed to **permissionrequest@cengage.com**.

Library of Congress Control Number: 2006934702

ISBN-13: 978-0-495-11588-5
ISBN-10: 0-495-11588-6

Brooks/Cole
10 Davis Drive
Belmont, CA 94002-3098
USA

Cengage Learning is a leading provider of customized learning solutions with office locations around the globe, including Singapore, the United Kingdom, Australia, Mexico, Brazil, and Japan. Locate your local office at **international.cengage.com/region**

Cengage Learning products are represented in Canada by Nelson Education, Ltd.

For your course and learning solutions, visit **academic.cengage.com.**

Purchase any of our products at your local college store or at our preferred online store **www.ichapters.com**.

Printed in Canada
2 3 4 5 6 7 11 10 09 08

Contents

Preface

This is a book about how to interview clients. It offers a set of skills for basic interviewing in the helping professions. In most respects, these skills are unique. First, they are intended to assist the client in developing a vision of a more satisfying future. Second, they direct both client and practitioner toward a deeper awareness of the strengths and resources that the client can use in turning vision into reality. These skills are based on the belief that it is essential to work within each client's frame of reference.

We have chosen to call this way of interviewing clients *solution building,* in contrast to *problem solving* embedded in most other interviewing approaches. In problem solving, practitioners gather information from clients to assess the nature and seriousness of client problems, and design interventions that will solve or alleviate problems. Problem solving relies heavily upon professional expertise for its assessments and interventions.

Our students and workshop participants who are making the change from problem solving to solution building have told us that this change is similar to the switch from doing things with your right hand to doing them with your left hand; it takes some getting used to. They also report that understanding the differences between the two approaches in theory is easier than effectively putting the skills into practice. Consequently, we wanted to produce teaching materials primarily aimed at enhancing practice skills.

The purpose of this book, then, is to teach you, the reader, how to build solutions with clients. We devote most of the book to describing and illustrating the requisite skills. Because solution building occurs through the words that pass between practitioners and clients, many dialogues from our actual interviews with clients are included. They are quoted at sufficient length to give you a clear sense of the ways in which solution-building conversations unfold; such conversations tend to be full of starts and stops and twists and turns.

To complement this book, a DVD and Instructor's Resource Manual are available. While these materials and the book are designed to be an integrated learning package and are cross-referenced, each also could stand on its own. The supplementary materials are organized around the belief that those new to solution building will learn it most quickly and effectively by practicing it. The materials include demonstration interviews, instructional ideas, class (or work-shop) exercises, exercises for practice outside of class, sample test items, and tools for solution building with clients.

The DVD includes 22 clips from six interviews originally recorded for the second edition. The clips are sequenced according to the presentation of skills and types of interviewing situations addressed in our book. The first clips illustrate basic skills in situations in which clients come voluntarily; later clips add additional skills for working in involuntary situations (with children, adolescents, dyads, and mandated clients) and crisis situations. The interviewers are a student and ourselves; the clients represent a diversity of age, gender, socioeconomic status, and ethnicity. Clips are cross-referenced to the book by identifying specific clips where given skills and types of solution-focused conversations may be found. You should be aware that the DVD is organized more around different types of interviewing situations than around particular skills. Therefore, although we have chosen to point readers to Clips 1–7 as examples of the basic skills, you will find these skills used throughout all the clips.

The third edition's DVD offers clips in two formats. The first is a section of "Uninterrupted Clips" in which all 22 clips are available for viewing straight through. Learners have told us watching clips in this format is useful in conjunc-tion with related reading in the book as illustration of various solution-focused skills. New to the third edition is the DVD's section of "Guided Exercises," which learners can use to improve their skills on their own outside of a class or workshop setting once they have a beginning familiarity with the skills. In this section, learners work more intensively with selected clips from the original 22 clips. The primary guided exercise invites the learner into the recorded inter-views through a set of pre-programmed stops and requests for their interviewing questions and responses. More specifically, for a given clip, the recorded inter-view plays partway until the client has shared some information; then the DVD automatically pauses with instructions to the learner to write out what his or her response and next question would be, were the learner the interviewer. Once the learner has decided on a response, he or she resumes the clip and listens to the interviewer's response and next question. The clip then pauses again and instructs the learner to compare and write down which response and next question—the learner's or the interviewer's on the clip—was more useful from a solution-building point of view. This guided exercise requires learners to listen, absorb client perceptions and language, and formulate responses and next questions "in the moment" much as they would in actual interviews. The request for a comparison between their responses and next questions and those of the inter-viewers on the clips encourages the type of solution-focused thinking required of practitioners who wish to build solutions with clients.

Unlike the first and second editions of *Interviewing for Solutions*, there is no workbook with this third edition. Instead, there is a companion website for the book that provides an Instructor's Resource Manual for the learning materials as well as a place for learners to record their responses to the DVD's guided exercises. The responses to the exercises are then e-mailed to instructors for review. Substituting the companion website for a workbook reduces costs for the learning package. For those who wish to use a hardcopy workbook learners, an electronic copy of a third edition workbook will be available for downloading from the Brief Family Therapy Center in Milwaukee (BFTC) (www.brief-therapy.org). Users may reproduce and use this workbook at their own expense.

The companion website's Instructor's Resource Manual (IRM) is available for viewing and downloading by those who adopt the learning package. While revised for the third edition, the IRM continues to include (1) learning activities for class or workshop settings related to the concepts and skills included in the book, (2) more description of how to use the DVD to enhance learners' interviewing skills, including details about having learners use the companion website to complete the guided exercises on the DVD, (3) role-play scenarios of different interviewing situations that learners can use to practice solution-focused skills in different interviewing contexts, (4) sample test questions on the book, and (5) solution-building tools to enhance practice and learning. The IRM (minus the sample test questions) is also available for viewing and downloading at BFTC's website (www.brief-therapy.org).

The chapters in *Interviewing for Solutions* are organized as follows. First, two chapters provide a context for the skills. In these chapters, we explain that the problem-solving approach to helping clients may be traced to the rise of modern medicine and its impressive accomplishments. We outline concerns about the assumptions of problem solving as applied in the helping professions, and describe solution building as an alternative. Second, in Chapters 3–10, we present the skills used in solution building. The sequence of presentation reflects the order in which the skills are used in first and later sessions of solution building; in other words, their presentation follows the process of solution building from beginning to end and from what are generally thought to be simpler to more challenging interviewing situations (voluntary to involuntary to crisis). This organization, we believe, will make it easiest for learners to eventually apply the skills to their own practice. Third, in Chapters 11–15, we give information that relates more generally to the place of solution building in agency practice and the helping professions. We present outcome data and address the extent to which solution building reflects the most cherished values of the helping professions, including a commitment to diversity-sensitive practice. We provide examples of adaptations of the approach to small group and organizational practice. There is a chapter about the many program applications to which solution-focused concepts and skills are now being put. Last, we discuss the theoretical implications of these skills and clients' responses to them.

For those familiar with our first and second editions, you will notice that the major change to this edition is the new chapter on applications (Chapter 14). The major development in solution-focused practice since the second edition has been the application of solution-focused thinking and techniques to different practice contexts. We wanted to familiarize readers with a sampling of these applications to illustrate how innovative and widely applicable the approach has become. The chapter is composed of eight different program applications whose settings include schools, mental health therapy rooms, hospitals, prisons, child welfare settings, and organizational planning groups, and whose levels of application include individual, family, group, and organizational practice. The descriptions of the eight program applications are written by those who invented and refined them. These innovators each describe what led them to think solution-focused practices might be useful in their contexts, what steps they took to introduce the practices, which practices they use and description of typical cases, what differences the innovations made for clients and practitioners, and a summary of any qualitative and quantitative outcome data they have collected so far. The diversity of the applications is meant to acquaint readers with current developments in solution-focused practice and to stir their imaginations about how they might apply these practices in their own settings.

In addition to the new chapter, this edition is updated throughout to capture additional changes as the solution-focused approach itself has continued to develop. For example, Chapter 4 and the remainder of the book no longer use the distinctions among customer, complainant, and visitor relationships. While the interviewing challenges that inspired these concepts continue to exist, we and other solution-focused practitioners have come to recognize that paying attention to the extent to which clients have developed goals related to their visions of a preferred future is a simpler and more respectful basis on which to decide what to explore next and suggest to clients than is an assessment of the type of relationship. Additional updating of this edition includes revisions to Chapter 11, on qualitative and quantitative outcomes that reflect the increased research on the approach. Chapter 13 also has been significantly revised to reflect the innovations in recordkeeping, supervision, and other aspects of agency practice that are associated with a shift from problem solving to solution building.

We believe that this book can be useful to a wide audience. Along with the DVD, Instructor's Resource Manual, and companion website, the book can be used to teach interviewing skills to undergraduate and graduate students enrolled in beginning practice courses in counseling, psychology, pastoral counseling, psychiatric nursing, and social work. We also believe that it will be useful to counseling centers, family service centers, mental health centers for children and adults, and other social service agencies interested in training their staff in solution-building skills. We have used this material with a wide range of audiences, who have encouraged us to organize it in the manner described here.

As you will soon discover, the book is written in an informal, conversational style. We have avoided technical words, and we make frequent use of first- and second-person pronouns. When referring to past experiences particular to one of us, we identify the person involved as Insoo or Peter. Informality is more natural to us. This style more accurately reflects the way we work with our clients, students, and workshop audiences, and we believe that it allows us to communicate our experiences and ideas more clearly.

This book offers a map to practitioners who wish to help clients build solutions within their own frames of reference. We believe that clients empower themselves by envisioning alternative futures and working hard to turn those visions into realities; as practitioners, we can contribute to their solution building. When purposefully and meaningfully applied, the skills presented in this book represent the practitioner's contribution to client empowerment. To participate in this process is invigorating and gratifying. Welcome to the exciting world in which clients make something different happen in their lives.

Our thanks to the following reviewers: Cynthia Bishop, Meredith College; Robert Blundo, University of North Carolina at Wilmington; Sherry L. Edwards, University of North Carolina at Pembroke; Diane L. Scott, University of West Florida; and Kim Womack, Jacksonville State University.

We also benefited greatly from conversations with our colleagues: Steve de Shazer, Brief Family Therapy Center; Gale Miller, Marquette University; Cheryl Brandsen, Calvin College; Sarah Rhein, Bethany Christian Services; and Wallace Gingerich, Case Western Reserve University. Our thanks, too, to our students, workshop participants, and clients, whose questions and struggles are the inspiration for much of what is written here.

Peter De Jong & Insoo Kim Berg

About the Authors

Peter De Jong, PhD, is a professor of social work at Calvin College in Grand Rapids, Michigan. He has been an outpatient therapist and caseworker, and has led trainings and consultations with mental health clinics, family service agencies, juvenile corrections programs, and schools. In addition to coauthoring (with Insoo Kim Berg) two earlier editions of *Interviewing for Solutions* (now translated into several languages), he has written several articles and book chapters on solution-focused therapy. Peter continues to develop new practice tools and training materials, and to conduct research on practice and how new practitioners acquire a solution-focused outlook and skills.

Insoo Kim Berg, MSSW, was a codeveloper of the solution-focused approach and, until her unexpected death in 2007, was the director of the Brief Family Therapy Center, Milwaukee, Wisconsin. Many of her 10 books and more than 35 papers have been translated into 14 languages. Among her books are *Family Based Services*; *Working with the Problem Drinker* (coauthor Scott D. Miller); *Building Solutions in Child Protective Services* (coauthor Susan Kelly); and *Children's Solution Work* (coauthor Therese Steiner). For three decades, Insoo lectured across North America, Europe, and the Pacific Rim, and consulted with organizations and government agencies.

About the Chapter 14 Contributors

Steve de Shazer, MSW, was the codeveloper of solution-focused brief therapy and for many years the director of research at the Brief Family Therapy Center in Milwaukee, Wisconsin, where solution-focused brief therapy was originally developed. He is known for his groundbreaking work in brief therapy and admired for his ability to simplify complex problems into manageable ways of viewing issues and persons. He is the author of several books including *Keys to Solution in Brief Therapy; Clues: Investigating Solutions in Brief Therapy; Putting Difference to Work;* and *Words Were Originally Magic.* These books and his many articles in professional journals are widely recognized as defining works in solution-focused therapy. He died in September 2005 while on a teaching tour in Europe.

Luc Isebaert, MD, is a psychiatrist, psychotherapist, and trainer in systemic brief therapy and Ericksonian (hypno)therapy. He is also the founder of the Bruges Model in psychotherapy and addiction therapy. He directs the Bruges Group of Training Institutes (Korzybski Institutes of Belgium, France, and the Netherlands). He is author (with M. C. Cabie) of *Pour une Therapie Breve* and *Drink Wijzer.* (e-mail: luc.isebaert@azbrugge.be)

Mo Yee Lee, PhD, is a professor at the College of Social Work, The Ohio State University, Columbus, Ohio. Her professional interests are the utilization and evaluation of a solution-focused/strength-based approach for social work treatment, particularly in the area of domestic violence. In addition, her current work includes the integration of Eastern philosophy and practices in social work treatment using a mind–body–spirit holistic perspective. (e-mail: lee.355@osu.edu)

Teri Pichot, MAC, has developed and implemented innovative treatment programs for court and other mandated substance-using adults and adolescents in the Denver, Colorado, area. She is currently the program manager of the Substance Abuse Counseling Program at the Jefferson County Department of Health and Environment, where she developed and implemented the department's current treatment model, which incorporates solution-focused therapy. In addition, she has created and implemented an animal-assisted activities and therapy program at the agency, conducts a private practice, and provides trainings and consultations. She has authored several articles and coauthored two books, one with Yvonne Dolan titled *Solution-Focused Brief Therapy: Its Effective Use in Agency Settings*, and the other with Marc Coulter, *Animal Assisted Brief Therapy: A Solution-Focused Approach*. She provides workshops and community presentations, as well as consultation and team building for community organizations. (e-mail: tpichot@jeffco.us)

John Sebold, MSW, is Director of Plumas County Mental Health, Quincy, California. John and Adriana Uken developed the Plumas Project, a solution-focused, domestic violence offender treatment program in 1990. In addition, he developed a solution-focused, wilderness-based treatment program for adolescents, which he has been running for the past 18 years. He provides solution-focused consultation and is currently interested in the application of solution-focused principles to the administrative process. (e-mail: jsebold@kingsview.org)

Lee Shilts, PhD, has taught in the family therapy program at Nova Southeastern University for the past two decades. His professional interests include the application of solution-focused practices to school systems, letter writing in systemic therapy, supervision issues, and hypnotherapy. Dr. Shilts currently supervises graduate students in applying the WOWW Program at a local school in south Florida. He also is currently writing a book on that program with coauthor Insoo Kim Berg. (e-mail: shilts@nova.edu)

Peter Stam, PhD, is the director of Youthcare Drenthe in the province of Drenthe in the Netherlands. His professional passion is to develop a system in which "damaged" children and families have the maximum chance of putting their lives on track to healthy, hopeful, and productive futures of their own design. He is a devoted student of the systemic view of human behavior and its potential for envisioning and remaking patterns of interaction in both families and organizations. (e-mail: peter.stam@jeugdzorgdrenthe.nl)

Mark Stancer, MSc, is the team manager and founder of the Family Solutions program in Children's Services in the London, England, borough of Ealing. A trained systemic therapist and social worker, his professional goal has been to empower all families he encounters professionally. One of his aims in setting up Family Solutions was to make "family therapy" available to people who would not have had access to it before, either because they could not afford it or because their home lives were seen by other professionals as too unstable or unsafe for productive therapy to take place. In using solution-focused therapy with such families and treating families as the experts on their problems and solutions, he has found "they are amazing and can make amazing things happen." (e-mail: markstancer@hotmail.com)

Adriana Uken,   MSW, recently retired after 27 years as a therapist for Plumas County Mental Health, in Quincy, California. She and John Sebold started the Plumas Project, a solution-focused domestic violence treatment program, in 1990. She and her coauthors (Mo Yee Lee and John Sebold) have written a book about their work, *Solution-Focused Treatment of Domestic Violence Offenders*. She is currently working as a consultant and trainer in solution-focused approaches. (e-mail: uken@frontiernet.net)

Lorenn Walker,   JD, MPH, is a health educator and lawyer based in Waialua, Hawai'i, who assists organizations with capacity building. She designs, implements, and evaluates programs focused on violence prevention and reconciliation. Her work incorporates themes and techniques from the fields of cooperative education, reconciliation, and solution-focused therapy. To learn more about her work, contact her at www.lorennwalker.com.

Sue Young,   MEd, is a "behaviour support manager" at Children and Young People's Services in Hull, United Kingdom. While having a particular interest in promoting anti-bullying behaviors, over the last 10 years she also has become an advocate for using solution-focused thinking to encourage success at every level in the school system. Her initiatives include proposing national policies across schools that promote positive behaviors, helping local staff encourage positive behaviors in their students, and giving support to individual children and parents. (e-mail: sue@young.karoo.co.uk)

From Problem Solving
to Solution Building

Assessments include our inferences about the nature and causes of
clients' difficulties, and thus they serve as the basis for the rest of our
work with the client—the goals we set, the interventions we enact, and
the progress we evaluate.
(HEPWORTH, ROONEY, & LARSEN, 2002, P. 187)

The client constructs his or her own solution based on his or her own
resources and successes.
(DE SHAZER, 1988, P. 50)

Cheryl, a colleague of Peter's, who teaches an introductory course to one of
the helping professions, demonstrates to her students, by engaging them in a
role-play exercise, that even before we begin our professional education, we have
preexisting ideas about how to help others. On one occasion, she role-played
Rosie, a character based on one of her clients.

The professor told her students that Rosie is 23 years old and has never
married. She is five months pregnant and has four children: two boys (ages 8 and
6) and two girls (ages 3 and 2). She subsists on welfare benefits, including food
stamps and Medicaid. Cheryl then asked her students to collectively interview
Rosie—that is, to ask the questions they thought necessary to help Rosie.
Following are the questions they asked, along with Rosie's answers.

STUDENT: How do you feel about being pregnant again?

    ROSIE: I don't like it. I'm sick all the time, and I don't have any energy.
I really want an abortion, but I didn't find out about being pregnant
soon enough to have one on Medicaid. Now that I'm five months
along, I can't get a doctor to do one; so I'm stuck with another child.

STUDENT: It sounds like you didn't want to get pregnant again. Were you using birth control?

ROSIE: No, I wasn't. Birth control costs a lot, and I guess I didn't have the money.

STUDENT: Did the baby's father use a condom?

ROSIE: Look, I make some extra money by having men over, and if I asked all of my clients to use rubbers, I wouldn't have any business. Yes, I know I shouldn't have men over, especially with little kids around, but welfare doesn't go very far with four kids. The extra money from the men helps, and besides, I need things too.

STUDENT: What can we do for you here today?

ROSIE: I'm going crazy with all the things I have to do for my kids. I'm always tired, and I'm afraid that my two boys are gonna be put in a foster home again because I have trouble getting them to school in the morning.

STUDENT: How did you feel about your children being taken away?

ROSIE: Terrible! Horrible! I cried a lot.

STUDENT: What was your childhood like?

ROSIE: Terrible. I was oldest of six kids. I had two younger brothers always hanging around the house and trying to get the older boys to carry a beeper and deliver drugs because it pays good. I tell my boys not to get into that, because it won't get them anywhere.

STUDENT: But yet you prostitute yourself for money.

ROSIE: That's different.

STUDENT: How is it different?

ROSIE: [glowering] It just is!

STUDENT: Tell me about the difficulty you have with getting your boys to school.

ROSIE: They don't want to get up in the morning and fix their breakfast. I try to, but I'm not feeling well with this pregnancy. When I do get up before them and make them breakfast, then things go better. But usually they just want to lay around and watch TV. They say school won't do them any good anyway, and that they can earn more working for their uncles—delivering goods.

STUDENT: Did you know that most schools have attendance officers who can come to the house and get your kids for you if they don't show up at school? Maybe that would help. You could get another adult with you to help get them out the door.

ROSIE: Maybe.

STUDENT: Rosie, how motivated are you to help yourself?

ROSIE: I'm motivated, but I'm not sure about how you plan to help me.

STUDENT: Have you ever thought about placing the baby for adoption?

ROSIE: No. If I give birth to it, I'm going to keep it. No way am I going to give it to strangers.

STUDENT: Adoption really isn't like that at all. Wouldn't you be interested in hearing more about how adoption works these days—for your benefit and your child's?

ROSIE: No.

STUDENT: How much education do you have?

ROSIE: I went through the eighth grade. I dropped out when I got pregnant the first time.

STUDENT: How did you feel about having to drop out?

ROSIE: OK. I didn't like school much anyway.

STUDENT: Would you like to go back to finish high school?

ROSIE: Well, um, sure, but who will watch my babies, and how will I get there?

STUDENT: There are programs that offer child care, and you could take the bus. Do you have any people around who could help you, like your neighbors or your parents?

ROSIE: My neighbors are in the same boat as me. I don't know who my father is. My mom is sick, and she is always worrying about her other kids.

STUDENT: Tell me about your relationship with your mother.

ROSIE: It's OK now—better than when I was a kid. My mom used to shout at us and hit us a lot. There was a lot of fighting. I always had to take care of the younger kids. She got real angry at me when I got pregnant and kicked me out of the house.

STUDENT: That must have made you sad.

ROSIE: Yeah, life stinks sometimes. But I can see now how tough it is to take care of kids and why she treated us the way she did.

STUDENT: Do you find that you often make the same mistakes in parenting as your mother?

ROSIE: Yeah, I yell, and sometimes I hit them.

STUDENT: How do you feel when you treat your kids this way?

ROSIE: I feel lousy, OK? But I get tired, and I can't help it.

STUDENT: Have you ever thought about taking parenting classes?

ROSIE: Yeah, it's probably a good idea, but it seems like a lot of work right now.

The interview ended at this point, partly because the students ran out of questions to ask and partly because Rosie did not want to continue.

We would like to make several observations about this interview, especially about the types of questions that the students chose to ask Rosie. These questions reveal how the students assumed they could be most helpful. Undoubtedly, the students were eager to assist Rosie.

First, note that the students chose to ask Rosie many questions, rather than, for example, make observations about her or give her instructions. This focus suggests the students believed they needed more information about Rosie to assist her. What kinds of questions did they ask?

- *Questions about problems.* Some questions zeroed in on possible problem areas in Rosie's life. The students asked Rosie about being pregnant again, prostituting herself, not getting her boys to school consistently, dropping out of school, not having a job, and making mistakes in parenting.

- *Questions about mistakes.* The students also asked Rosie—sometimes directly and sometimes by implication—whether she had taken certain actions. These questions were directly related to the problem areas that the students had identified: "Were you using birth control?" "Did the baby's father use a condom?" "Do you find that you often make the same mistakes in parenting as your mother?" An apparent implication of this type of question is that had Rosie made other choices, she would not be having these problems right now, or the problems would not be as serious.

- *Questions about causes.* We might also think about those questions that searched for Rosie's past mistakes as attempts to get at immediate, practical *causes* of her problems, such as not using birth control and dropping out of school. The interview also contained questions about more remote causes: "What was your childhood like?" "Tell me about your relationship with your mother." The students are acting as though they must know *why* Rosie's problems are occurring before they can help her.

- *Questions about solutions.* A fourth group of questions implied possible solutions. These questions generally came after those that sought to identify Rosie's problems and their causes: "Wouldn't you be interested in hearing more about how adoption works these days?" "Would you like to go back to finish high school?" "Have you ever thought about taking parenting classes?" Given that these questions consistently follow those about problems and their causes, it seems the students are interviewing as though possibilities for solutions will flow from *the interviewers' understandings* of Rosie's problems and their causes.

Reviewing the four types of questions we have identified so far, we can make a few observations. First, two thirds of the questions the students asked fall into one or more of these four categories. Second, the students asked the questions in an identifiable sequence: questions about problem areas, followed by questions about immediate and remote causes, followed by questions about possible solutions. On the basis of these observations, we believe that these students already have absorbed a *problem-solving* approach about how best to help others. One final type of question remains.

- *Questions about feelings.* Most of the remaining questions were about Rosie's feelings: "How do you feel about being pregnant again?" "How did you feel about your children being taken away?" "How do you feel when you treat your kids this way?" These students somehow believed that getting Rosie to express her feelings was an important part of helping her.

HELPING AS PROBLEM SOLVING

The approach to helping implicit in the questions of these beginning students is very similar to the basic approach found in many textbooks about professional practice in counseling, psychology, and social work that frequently organize content around the stages of the problem-solving approach (Hepworth, Rooney, & Larsen, 2002; McClam & Woodside, 1994; Timberlake, Farber, & Sabatino, 2002). The stages of problem solving essentially systematize and elaborate the approach taken by Rosie's interviewers.

The Stages of Problem Solving

Timberlake, Farber, & Sabatino's (2002) formulation includes the following stages:

- *Description of problem(s) and data collection.* Here, the client describes those concerns for which relief is sought. The practitioner asks follow-up questions to obtain a more detailed understanding of the client's problem(s) so that a professional assessment can be made.
- *Problem assessment.* Once the problem is described, the practitioner makes a determination of the nature of the client's problem and its seriousness. The practitioner draws from a profession's acquired knowledge base—its categories, theories, research findings, and practice wisdom—to make the assessment.
- *Intervention planning.* Together with the client, the practitioner develops a list of goals and designs a set of interventions intended to solve or reduce the negative consequences of the problem(s). Again, the practitioner relies on the profession's knowledge base to participate in developing the plan.
- *Intervention.* The problem-solving actions (interventions) intended to alleviate the problem are carried out.
- *Evaluation and follow-up.* As problem-solving actions are taken, the client and professional monitor the consequences. The information from the monitoring is used to decide whether the actions taken have been successful. If not, adjustments in the level of intervention are made or new actions are taken. Once the problem is deemed solved by the client and practitioner, the process is finished, and the client stops services. Often the practitioner and client make arrangements for follow-up contacts to make sure that the problem does not recur.

A Caveat: The Importance of Trust Development

The helping professions are aware that professional helping cannot be reduced to problem solving alone. Practitioners long ago recognized that establishing a relationship of trust with their clients is very important in the helping process. Professionals know that, without trust, clients will be unlikely to contract for services or follow through on recommendations. Consequently, those who write about and teach professional helping commonly add a step to the helping process before problem solving begins. This step is called relationship building or engagement. They also add a final step, named termination. In these steps, the practitioner pays special attention to sensitivity, warmth, and empathy to establish and maintain a trusting relationship with the client.

The Medical Model

Problem solving in the helping professions has been strongly influenced by the medical model (Conrad & Schneider, 1985; Goldstein, 2002; Weick, 1992). This model arose as a result of the impressive achievements in the field of medicine in the late 19th and early 20th centuries. During that period, researchers such as Louis Pasteur discovered that many contagious, life-threatening diseases may be traced to bacteria. This new knowledge led to a practice model of diagnosis and treatment. Physicians tried to help patients by *diagnosing* which diseases were causing their symptoms and then administering appropriate *treatments* (antidotes). By the early 20th century, death rates from contagious disease were falling dramatically. The causes of tuberculosis, cholera, tetanus, diphtheria, and typhoid were known, and hope was running high that the devastating effects of diseases could be controlled. These achievements prompted great confidence in scientific knowledge as a basis for medical practice and also in the medical model of diagnosis and treatment.

Problem Solving: The Paradigm of the Helping Professions

Kuhn (1962) defines a *paradigm* as an overarching model. It guides theory, research, and professional practice in a field. We believe that problem solving has been the dominant paradigm of practice in the helping professions.

During the 20th century, the application of the medical model has not been confined to physical illness. Biomedicine's impressive progress in quelling infectious diseases, where a specific cause could be identified, quickly influenced the way both professionals and the public came to view mental illness, emotional problems, interpersonal difficulties, and social problems. Over the past century, scientists have conducted research about the nature and sources of problems at every level of human existence in the belief that, once we come to understand the causes of these problems, we can better devise strategies to solve and control them. The helping professions now abound with classifications of problems. The psychiatric profession's *Diagnostic and Statistical Manual of Mental Disorders (DSM–IV–TR)* (American Psychiatric Association, 2000) is one such classification.

Others include Freud's (1966) categories of psychopathology, Satir's (1982) categorization of discrepancies between levels of messages in interpersonal communication, and Germain and Gitterman's (1980, 1996) list of psycho-social-environmental stressors.

The helping professions have become highly diversified. They differ in the types of problems that they address, and they prefer different explanations of problems and solutions. Despite their differences, however, the helping professions share some equally important commonalities. These commonalities, which derive from the medical model, together make up the basic features of a problem-solving paradigm. Let us examine these commonalities.

Commonality One: A Problem-Solving Structure   Since the appearance of the medical model, most helpers follow the same basic *structure* when providing assistance to clients.[1] They work from the premise that, before the client can be helped, the practitioner must figure out what the client has. This is true whether the practitioner thinks in terms of assessing problems or diagnosing disorders. The heart of this premise is that there is a necessary connection between a problem and its solution. Because different problems demand different solutions, the practitioner must make an accurate assessment in order to determine interventions that will be most effective in each individual case. It is clear that this premise has found its way into popular thinking. When clients finish describing their problems and symptoms, they commonly ask the practitioner, "What do you think it is? I just can't figure out what it is."

This problem-solving structure is based on the medical model, which prescribes that the physician must diagnose the patient's disease before being able to treat it effectively. Different diseases require different treatments, and each disease has a different cure.

Another aspect of the medical model is the idea that the client's problem and whatever gives rise to it are objectively real, just as organ malfunction, disease process, and bacteria are objectively real. As we have seen, professions have developed extensive categorizations of problems, with associated assessment techniques and intervention techniques, just as modern medicine has generated categories of disease, diagnostic procedures, and treatments. Moreover, for much of the 20th century, the helping professions have regarded the factors that give rise to a client's problem as operating in a linear, cause-and-effect manner, just as bacteria attacking the organs of the body cause a disease.

Although seemingly diverse, most viewpoints within these professions work from the premise that problem and solution are somehow connected. (This is even true of the systems viewpoint, which simply adopts a circular, rather than a linear, model of causation.) They differ mainly in their categorizations of problems, assessment procedures, and intervention techniques. For example, clinical psychologists look for different problems using different assessment procedures than do generalist social workers. Clinical psychologists typically find a problem by psychological testing and proceed to assign it to a category found in the *Diagnostic and Statistical Manual of Mental Disorders*. Generalist social workers, on the other hand, find a problem by means of assessment tools such as genograms and ecomaps and then classify it in terms of system transactions of one sort or another. The problems found and the names given to them are different, but the *structure* of helping remains the same.[2]

Commonality Two: Reliance on Scientific Expertise   The second commonality is an extension of the first. If different problems demand different solutions, then it is important for professional helpers to be knowledgeable about various problems, procedures for assessing them, and techniques for intervening with them. Moreover, as the problems of clients are thought to be objectively real (that is, to have an existence separate from the knower), they can be studied scientifically. Therefore, once science has gained knowledge about them, this knowledge can be taught to professional helpers as the foundation for helping clients. This scientific knowledge about different problems and their different solutions, along with the art of applying this knowledge in professional contexts, is what constitutes the expertise of a helping profession.

HELPING AS SOLUTION BUILDING

The generic structure of problem solving—first determining the nature of the problem and then intervening—influences the content of the interaction between practitioners and clients. Practitioners characteristically ask clients to spend significant amounts of time describing (and sometimes analyzing) the who, what, when, where, and why of their problems to gain sufficient information for accurate assessment of the problems. In this process, clients often fill out long intake forms about themselves, their families, their occupational histories, and other aspects of their lives. They may be asked to list the problems they have been experiencing and complete assessment inventories such as personality tests and family-interaction questionnaires. In employing such assessment tools, practitioners are attempting not only to be as thorough as possible, but also to protect themselves against charges of negligence. Once problems are assessed, most practitioners, again drawing on their expertise about problems and related interventions, shift the interaction toward making interventions. As a result, the interaction between clients and practitioners focuses on problems.

Concerns about the Problem-Solving Paradigm

Increasingly, over the last 30 years, writers are expressing deep concerns about the field's emphasis on problems and scientific expertise. Let us look at some of these concerns.

Client Problems are Not Puzzles   Julian Rappaport (1981) boldly states that many—if not most—of the difficulties brought by clients to helpers bear little resemblance to the diseases for which the medical model was designed. Diseases, which are a consequence of physiological processes such as the workings of bacteria or the effects of environmental contaminants, are more like the scientific problems that natural scientists study than the client difficulties that helping professionals try to address. Diseases and the analytic problems of natural science resemble puzzles. Puzzles can be exceedingly complex when they are made up of many intricate pieces, but because all their pieces exist, solutions can be discovered. This is true whether the solution is discovering a bacterial agent for chicken cholera, unraveling the DNA code, or predicting the precise path of the planets around the sun. Rappaport states that the type of research and reasoning best suited to solving such puzzles *converges* on the solution; that is, over time, increasingly rigorous and ingenious investigations offer various solutions that gradually converge toward the right answer. Experimental research is an example of convergent reasoning and has proved very successful in solving scientific and medical puzzles.

The problems encountered by practitioners in the helping professions are different from puzzles. Most often, these problems do not have a single correct solution. For example, a family may seek professional assistance because it is experiencing parent-children conflict. Perhaps both parents are employed, and the children are getting into mischief after school and seem to want more attention from their parents. The practitioner may be tempted to recommend that one of the parents work fewer hours to devote more time to the children. However, this solution may jeopardize that parent's job performance and, consequently, make the parent more anxious, which, in turn, may have its own negative impact on parent-child interaction in this family.

In thinking about such a case, the practitioner soon realizes that the appropriate solution will depend on the parents' individual needs at this point in their lives, their past experiences with parenting, and their cultural values regarding job and childrearing. Because individual people and their perceptions about life are so diverse, there is no single solution for such a problem. Consequently, Rappaport (1981) maintains that *divergent* thinking is more appropriate in the helping professions. In divergent thinking, the practitioner surveys several different perspectives about the problem and searches for potential workable solutions. With the goal of being useful to clients, divergent thinking gives as much weight to the perceptions of clients as to the expertise of the practitioner.

Focusing on Empowerment and Client Strengths   The mission of the helping professions is to *empower* clients to live more productive and satisfying lives. Blundo (2001), Rappaport (1981, 1990), Saleebey (2007), Schon (1983), and Weick, Rapp, Sullivan, and Kishardt (1989), among others, emphasize that the field's dominant emphasis on client problems and expert solutions detracts from this mission.[3] If practitioners focus on categories of problems or pathology, clients may become discouraged and feel that they are victims of some disease or dysfunction, such as alcoholism or the dysfunctional family syndrome. Empowering clients, on the other hand, "indicates the intent to, and the processes of, assisting individuals, groups, families, and communities to discover and expend the resources and tools within and around them" (Saleebey, 2007, p. 11).

Saleebey calls his version of empowerment the *strengths perspective*. Summarizing the work of several like-minded writers, he identifies the following as its basic assumptions:

1. Despite life's struggles, all persons possess strengths that can be marshaled to improve the quality of their lives. Practitioners should respect these strengths and the directions in which clients wish to apply them.

2. Client motivation is increased by a consistent emphasis on strengths as the client defines them.

3. Discovering strengths requires a process of cooperative exploration between clients and helpers; expert practitioners do not have the last word on what clients need to improve their lives.

4. Focusing on strengths turns practitioners away from the temptation to judge or blame clients for their difficulties and toward discovering how clients have managed to survive, even in the most difficult of circumstances.

5. All environments—even the most bleak—contain resources.

Saleebey's notion of empowerment and the assumptions on which it rests present a clear contrast to the traditional problem-solving approach. Instead of focusing on problems, Saleebey calls for practitioners to discover, in mutual exploration with clients, those personal strengths and resources clients can bring to bear on their concerns. He believes that clients' frames of reference and perceptions about what would be most useful to create more satisfying lives for themselves should count for as much as—if not more than—scientific expertise about problems and solutions. In short, he wants to replace a focus on problems with a focus on client strengths.

> So what is of interest to us is how people have taken steps, summoned up resources, and coped. People are always working on their situations, even if just deciding for the moment to be resigned. As helpers, we must tap into that work, elucidate it, find and build on its promise.
>
> (SALEEBEY, 2007, P. 285)

This is a daunting challenge; the field has long worked and generated practice techniques to fit problem solving. In addition, the literature about empowerment and the strengths perspective has been composed mainly of philosophy, practice principles, and general areas to explore for possible strengths; it has not been rich in techniques. If Saleebey's challenge is to be met, new practice techniques must be developed, taught, and used with clients. That work now has a good beginning. In the past 20 years there has been an accelerating development of competency-based, more collaborative approaches to working with clients (Berg, 1994; Cade & O'Hanlon, 1993; de Shazer, 1985, 1988; Durrant, 1993; Freedman & Combs, 1996; Gilligan & Price, 1993; Greene, 2007; Miley, O'Melia, & DuBois, 2007; W. R. Miller & Rollnick, 2002; Rapp, 1998; Saleebey, 2007; White & Epston, 1990). While there is some difference in the extent to which the techniques of these approaches shed a problem focus and tap into clients' ways of making changes, they all are predominantly directed toward clients' preferred futures and strengths instead of their past problems and deficits.

This book presents one of these approaches and its techniques in detail—the *solution-building* approach. It is an approach to interviewing clients that fosters empowerment by working within clients' frames of reference and one with concrete, learnable, widely applicable techniques.

History of Solution Building

The solution-building approach was pioneered through the work of Steve de Shazer (1985, 1988, 1991, 1994), Insoo Kim Berg (1994), and their colleagues. De Shazer, who has written extensively on solution-focused therapy, has been intrigued throughout his career by the early work on communications by Gregory Bateson (1972; Bateson, Jackson, Haley, & Weakland, 1956) and by the approach to psychotherapy of Milton Erickson (Haley, 1973; Zeig & Lankton, 1988). De Shazer and Berg have spent their professional careers working with individuals, couples, and families to resolve a wide variety of difficulties. They have also trained many other professionals in their procedures at the Brief Family Therapy Center in Milwaukee, Wisconsin, and around the world.

De Shazer and Berg are unusual in that they have always believed that holistically observing and reflecting on the actual process in which they work with their clients will teach them more about how to be effective than will traditional scientific research, which attempts to break down the therapeutic process into components and then gathers and interprets data about these components. They have not been content to accept prevailing ideas about how therapy ought to be conducted. While working at a community agency during the 1970s, de Shazer, Berg, and their colleagues installed a one-way mirror to observe themselves and other therapists at work. Their hope was to make observations about which therapist activities were most useful to clients. The agency, however, was uncomfortable with the mirror and instructed them to remove it. Rather than give up a tool that they believed was necessary to make advances in their understanding of their work, they established their own agency in the mid-1970s. Since then, de Shazer, Berg, and their associates have been innovatively working with their clients, carefully observing the therapy process, researching outcomes, and teaching their procedures to other practitioners.

This brief history highlights a key aspect of the way in which de Shazer, Berg, and their colleagues developed their procedures. They worked *inductively* by observing individual interviews and simply paying attention to what was most useful. In the process, they tried to set aside any preexisting ideas about the nature and origin of client problems. Most other procedures in the field, by contrast, were developed deductively; they were deduced from an existing theory regarding the nature and causes of client problems. De Shazer and Berg have pointed out that they know less about why their solution-building procedures work than they know about what is useful to clients. However, now that the procedures are well developed and their usefulness is being documented, de Shazer and Miller, in particular, are writing more about the nature of therapeutic process (de Shazer, 1991, 1994; de Shazer, et al., in press; G. Miller, 1997).

De Shazer first realized the idea that there is not a necessary connection between problem and solution in 1982, when working with a particular family (Hopwood & de Shazer, 1994). As usual, de Shazer and his colleagues asked, "What brings you in?" In response, family members kept interrupting one another until, by the end of the session, they had listed 27 different problems. Since none of the 27 were clearly defined, de Shazer and his colleagues were unable to design an intervention. Still, wishing to encourage the family members to focus on something different from their problems, de Shazer and his colleagues told them to pay careful attention to "what is happening in your lives that you want to continue to have happen." When the family returned two weeks later, they said that things were going very well, and they felt their problems were solved. According to the assumptions of the problem-solving approach, the family should not have improved so dramatically because the practitioner had not yet been able to isolate and assess the patterns and nature of the problems. Their experience with such cases led de Shazer and his colleagues toward a solution focus in place of a problem focus. De Shazer, his colleagues, and many others (Berg, 1994; Berg & de Shazer, 1997; Berg & Dolan, 2001; Berg & Kelly, 2000; Berg & Miller, 1992; Berg & Reuss, 1997; Berg & Shilts, 2005a, 2005b; Berg & Steiner, 2003; Berg & Szabo, 2005; De Jong & Berg, 2001; de Shazer et al., in press; Dolan, 1991; Durrant, 1995; Furman & Ahola, 1992; George, Iveson, & Ratner, 1999, 2006; Lee, Sebold, & Uken, 2003; Lipchik, 2002; Metcalf, 1995, 1998; G. Miller, 1997; S. D. Miller & Berg, 1995; S. D. Miller, Hubble, & Duncan, 1996; O'Hanlon & Weiner-Davis, 1989; Pichot & Dolan, 2003; Selekman, 1993, 1997, 2002; Sharry, 2001; Turnell & Edwards, 1999; Walter & Peller, 1992, 2000; Weiner-Davis, 1993, 1995) have been continuing to work out the implications of this shift ever since.

NOTES

1. The work of practitioners like Milton Erickson and Steve de Shazer, as well as others, moved in another direction, as we will see later in this chapter.

2. The problem-solving structure has been less readily discernible in some parts of the field than in others. For example, the counseling profession, reflecting the assumptions and goals of humanistic psychology, is less focused on linking diagnosed psychological disorders to particular treatments than is clinical psychology. Counselors work to foster the self-directive, developmentally healthy tendencies of their clients, whom they assume to be essentially normal people. In a general sense, however, the problem-solving structure is still there in their work. When asked about the source of a client's current difficulties, counselors point to developmental issues in the client's past. Also, they regularly ask questions about a client's developmental past; in so doing, they imply that it is important for them and their clients to understand these developmental issues as an aid to treatment.

3. Not all approaches put equal emphasis on expert solutions. The nondirective approach, for instance, deemphasizes such solutions. It relies on unconditional positive regard by the practitioner and self-direction by the client.

2

Solution Building: The Basics

The most useful way to decide which door can be opened to get to a
solution is by getting a description of what the client will be doing
differently and/or what sorts of things will be happening that are
different when the problem is solved, thus creating the expectation of
beneficial change.

(DE SHAZER, 1985, P. 46)

The following presents an overview of solution-building procedures to show
how different they are from problem-solving procedures. Let us begin by
returning to the case of Rosie.

A SECOND INTERVIEW WITH ROSIE

Chapter 1 presented an interview in which Peter's colleague Cheryl role-played a
23 year-old client of hers named Rosie. We saw that, in attempting to help
Rosie, Cheryl's students asked a number of problem-solving questions. In contrast to her students, Cheryl herself had asked several solution-focused questions
in her work with Rosie. To introduce you to the uniqueness of solution
building, some excerpts from Cheryl's first interview with Rosie follow.

CHERYL: How can I be of assistance?

ROSIE: Well, I've got some big problems. First thing—I'm pregnant again. I
already have two babies, two little girls who are 3 and 2 [years old], and
I have two boys who are in school. I'm going crazy with all I have to
do, and I'm afraid that my two boys are gonna be put in a foster home
again because I have trouble getting them to school in the morning.
They don't wanna get up in the morning. They just wanna lay around
and watch TV. They say school won't do them any good, and they can
make more delivering goods for their uncles.

CHERYL: "Delivering goods"?

ROSIE: Yeah, drugs I think. I tell them that is no good and they're gonna get into trouble, but they don't listen to me. I feel better when they're in school, because at least then they can't be with Lamar and Brian [the uncles]. But they won't get up, and I'm so tired because I'm pregnant again.

CHERYL: [empathically] Wow, I can see you really have your hands full. Handling four kids by yourself is really tough to start with, but to be pregnant on top of all that …

ROSIE: Yeah, it is, and I don't want my boys to be taken away again. But they fight me on school, and I'm so tired with everything I have to do and being pregnant.

Rosie continued to give details about her problems, including information about her involvement in prostitution to supplement welfare payments for basic needs and her pregnancy, which may have resulted from unprotected intercourse with a client. Cheryl then moved on to a different area.

CHERYL: So you have several big problems—getting your boys to school, getting enough money, and being pregnant and very tired. Let me ask you a different kind of question about these. It's called the miracle question. [pause] Suppose that you go to bed as usual tonight, and while you are sleeping, a miracle happens. The miracle is that the problems you've been telling me about are solved! Only you're sleeping, and so you do not know right away that they've been solved. What do you suppose you would notice tomorrow morning that would be *different*—that would tell you, wow, things are really better!

ROSIE: [smiling] That's easy. I would have won the lottery—$3 million.

CHERYL: That would be great, wouldn't it? What else would you notice?

ROSIE: Some nice man would come along who has lots of money and lots of patience with kids, and we'd get married. Or I wouldn't have so many kids, and I would finish high school. I would have a good job.

CHERYL: OK, that sounds like a *big* miracle. What do you imagine would be the first thing that you would notice which would tell you that this day is different, it's better—a miracle must have happened?

ROSIE: Well, I would get up in the morning before my kids do, make them breakfast, and sit down with them while we all eat together.

CHERYL: If you were to decide to do that—get up before them and make them breakfast—what would they do?

ROSIE: I think maybe they would come and sit down at the table instead of going and turning on the TV.

CHERYL: How would that be for you?

ROSIE: I'd be happier because we could talk about nice things, not argue over TV. My babies won't start crying over all the fighting about the TV.

CHERYL: What else? What else will be different when the miracle happens?

Rosie and Cheryl went on to explore and develop other parts of Rosie's miracle picture. Cheryl then moved on to questions about a related topic.

CHERYL: Rosie, I'm impressed. You have a pretty clear picture of how things will be different around your house when things are better. Are there times already, say in the last two weeks, which are like the miracle that you have been describing, even a little bit?

ROSIE: Well, I'm not sure. Well, about four days ago it was better.

CHERYL: Tell me about four days ago. *What* was different?

ROSIE: Well, I went to bed about 10:00 the night before and had a good night of sleep. I had food in the house, because I had gone to the store and to the food pantry on Saturday. I had even set the alarm for 6:30 and got up when it rang. I made breakfast and called the kids. The boys ate and got ready for school and left on time. [remembering] One even got some homework out of his backpack and did it—real quick—before he went to school.

CHERYL: [impressed] Rosie, that sounds like a big part of the miracle right there. I'm amazed. How did all that happen?

ROSIE: I'm not sure. I guess one thing was I had the food in the house, and I got to bed on time.

CHERYL: So, how did you make that happen?

ROSIE: Ah, I decided not to see any clients that night, and I read books to my kids for an hour.

CHERYL: How did you manage that, reading to four kids? That seems like it would be really tough.

ROSIE: No, that doesn't work—reading to four kids at the same time. I have my oldest boy read to one baby, because that's the only way I can get him to practice his reading, and I read to my other boy and baby.

CHERYL: Rosie, that seems like a great idea—having him read to the baby. It helps you, and it helps him with his reading. How do you get him to do that?

ROSIE: Oh, I let him stay up a half hour later than the others because he helps me. He really likes that.

Cheryl continued to explore, in detail, what was different about the day that resembled Rosie's miracle and how it happened—especially what Rosie did to make it happen. Then Cheryl asked some scaling questions in order to better understand how Rosie viewed herself in relation to her problems.

CHERYL: I'd like you to put some things on a scale for me, on a scale from 0 to 10. First, on a scale from 0 through 10, where 0 equals the worst your problems have been and 10 means the problems we have been talking about are solved, where are you *today* on that scale?

Rosie: If you had asked me that question before we started today, I would have said about a 2. But now I think it's more like a 5.

Cheryl: Great! Now let me ask you about how *confident* you are that you can have another day in the next week like the one four days ago—the one which was a lot like your miracle picture. On a scale of 0 to 10, where 0 equals no confidence and 10 means you have every confidence, how confident are you that you can make it happen again?

Rosie: Oh, about a 5.

Cheryl: Suppose you were at a 6; what would be different?

Rosie: I'd have to be sure that I always had food in the house for breakfast for the kids.

Cheryl continued to explore with Rosie what else Rosie could do to increase the chances of her miracle happening in the future. She ended this first interview with some final feedback for Rosie, which included pointing out to Rosie what she was already doing to make her miracle happen and suggesting that she do some of the additional things that might make miracle-type days more likely to occur.

SOLUTION-BUILDING INTERVIEWING ACTIVITIES

The questions that Cheryl asked Rosie were intended to assist her in building solutions to her problems. While there is more to the solution-building approach than its interviewing questions, these questions go a long way toward identifying the uniqueness of the approach.

Solution-building interviews are organized, in large part, around two useful activities (De Jong & Miller, 1995). The first is the development of well-formed goals within the client's frame of reference; the second is the development of solutions based on exceptions (de Shazer, 1985). After clients have had an opportunity to describe what in their lives they would like to see changed as a result of meeting with the practitioner, solution building moves on to these two activities.

There are several characteristics of well-formed goals. Among other things, well-formed goals are important to the client, small and concrete, and represent the beginning of something different rather than the end. (See Chapter 5 for more details.) Many of the questions that Cheryl asked were intended to help Rosie develop a sharper vision of what her life would be like when her problems were less serious. Thus, Cheryl asked Rosie the miracle question and related questions to assist her in developing a detailed and vivid picture of a more satisfying life, especially in those areas where she was having problems. With the aid of the questions, Rosie was able to work her way to the point of describing several concrete things that both she and her children might be doing and feeling differently when her problems were solved.

The second solution-building activity that Cheryl used was exploring for exceptions. *Exceptions* are those occasions in clients' lives when their problems could have occurred but did not—or at least were less severe. In solution building, the practitioner focuses on the who, what, when, and where of exception times in clients' lives, instead of the who, what, when, where, and why of problems. In Rosie's case, Cheryl opened up the exploration for exceptions by asking, "Are there times already, say in the last two weeks, which are like the miracle which you have been describing, even a little bit?" Since Rosie was able to identify a specific day that was better, Cheryl went to work exploring, in detail, what was different about the day and what Rosie did that made the day better. The exploration revealed that Rosie already had successes and strengths to her credit; seeing those successes and strengths made her more hopeful that her life could improve.

Solution-building practitioners use information about exceptions to help clients devise strategies that solve or reduce their problems. Ideally, client exceptions should be related to client goals. That is why Cheryl chose to work on well-formed goals before asking about exceptions.

THE STAGES OF SOLUTION BUILDING

Cheryl's work with Rosie reflects the solution-building paradigm discussed in Chapter 1. In particular, it is consistent with de Shazer's observation that clients can usually build solutions to their problems without either clients or practitioners assessing or understanding the nature of the problems. Given this view of problems and solutions, the structure of solution building differs markedly from that of problem solving. The basic stages of solution building are as follows.

Describing the Problem

This step resembles the first step of problem solving in that clients are given an opportunity to describe their problems or concerns. We ask, "How can we be useful to you?" Clients generally respond by describing a problem of some sort, and we ask for some details. In solution building, however, we spend much less time and effort here than is done in the problem-solving approach. We ask for fewer details about the nature and severity of client problems, and we do not ask about possible causes of the problems. Instead, we listen respectfully to clients' problem talk and think about ways to turn the conversation toward the next step, which initiates solution talk.

Developing Well-Formed Goals

Here, we work with our clients to elicit descriptions of what will be different in their lives when their problems are solved. We do this work at the point where a practitioner who follows the problem-solving approach would be conducting assessment.

Exploring for Exceptions

At this stage, we ask about those times in clients' lives when their problems are not happening or are less severe. We also ask about who did what to make the exceptions happen. This step substitutes for intervention planning in the problem-solving approach.

End-of-Session Feedback

At the end of each solution-building conversation, we construct messages for our clients that include compliments and usually some suggestions. The compliments emphasize what clients are already doing that is useful in solving their problems. The suggestions identify what clients could observe or do to further solve their problems. The feedback is based on information that clients have revealed to us in the conversations about well-formed goals and exceptions. It always focuses on what the clients, given their frames of reference, need to do more of and do differently in order to enhance their chances of success in meeting their goals. We construct and give feedback at the point where problem-solving practitioners would be doing the interventions indicated by their prior assessments.

Evaluating Client Progress

In solution building, we regularly evaluate with our clients how they are doing in reaching solutions satisfactory to them. Customarily, this is done by scaling—by asking clients to rate progress on a scale of 0 to 10. Once client progress has been scaled, we work with clients to examine what still needs to be done before they feel that their problems have been adequately solved and they are ready to terminate services.

As with the problem-solving approach, solution building may be thought of as including an engagement step at the beginning and a termination step at the end. In these steps, matters of building a cooperative relationship and reviewing progress are very important. As later chapters show, the two approaches handle these issues in different ways.

THE CLIENT AS EXPERT

As Chapter 1 explains, in the past the helping professions largely committed themselves to working with their clients through the application of scientific expertise—accumulated scientific knowledge about problems and solutions. One consequence of this is, wittingly or unwittingly, the helping professions have encouraged practitioners to believe and act as though their perceptions about their clients' problems and solutions are more important to the helping process than are the clients' perceptions. In fact, the professional literature teaches that clients' perceptions often get in the way of professional practice because they are the source of client resistance, which practitioners must work hard to overcome.

In solution building, by contrast, we insist that clients are the experts about their own lives. We rely on their frames of reference in three ways to move the process of solution building along.

1. We ask them what they would like to see changed in their lives; they customarily answer with a description of their problems. We accept these client definitions of problems and the words (categories) that clients use to describe them.

2. We interview clients about what will be different in their lives when their problems are solved. We listen carefully for, and work hard to respect, the directions in which clients want to go with their lives (their goals) and the words they use to express these directions.

3. We ask clients about their perceptions of exceptions to their problems. We respect these perceptions as evidence of clients' inner resources (strengths) and as sources of information about useful outer resources that exist in the contexts in which they live.

Consequently, in all of this work, we do not view ourselves as expert at scientifically assessing client problems and then intervening. Instead, we strive to be expert at exploring clients' frames of reference and identifying those perceptions that clients can use to create more satisfying lives.

By drawing on clients' frames of reference in these ways, we find that client resistance ceases to be a concern (De Jong & Berg, 2001; de Shazer, 1984). We also find that we can work equally well with diverse clients and with a wide variety of problems. We will return to these topics in the final chapters. Our next step is to examine how we build solutions with clients. This topic is the heart and soul of this book. To begin, we consider how to listen to clients with solution-building ears.

3

Skills for Not Knowing

Curiosity leads to exploration and invention of alternative views and
moves, and different moves and views breed curiosity.

(CECCHIN, 1987, P. 406)

I f, as a practitioner, you wish to put clients into the position of being the experts
about their own lives, you will have to know how to set aside your own frame
of reference as much as possible and explore those of your clients. In other words,
you will have to learn how to adopt the posture of *not knowing*. This useful term
belongs to Anderson and Goolishian (1992), who maintain that a practitioner
never knows a priori (by virtue of an expert frame of reference) the significance
of the client's experiences and actions. Instead, the practitioner must rely on the
client's perceptions and explanations. The best way to do this, they write, is to
take a position of not knowing.

> The not-knowing position entails a general attitude or stance in which
> the therapist's actions communicate an abundant, genuine curiosity.
> That is, the therapist's actions and attitudes express a need to know more
> about what has been said, rather than convey preconceived opinions and
> expectations about the client, the problem, or what must be changed.
> The therapist, therefore, positions himself or herself in such a way as
> always to be in a state of "being informed" by the client.

(ANDERSON & GOOLISHIAN, 1992, P. 29)

Learning how to take and maintain this posture takes commitment and
practice. It is a lifelong process. In this chapter, we will present the basic
communication skills that allow us to be informed by the client. Some of these
skills are unique to solution building. Several are not, but as you will see,
solution building has its own slant on how the practitioner can most usefully
apply them.

BASIC INTERVIEWING SKILLS

Listening

Insoo Kim Berg likes to say that practitioners who are accomplished at solution building have learned how to listen to the client with solution-building ears. They are able to hear the client's story without filtering it through their own frame of reference. Commonly, when we listen to others tell us about themselves, we not only listen, but also react to what they are saying. Suppose you are listening to a 15-year-old who is angry with his parents about a 10 P.M. curfew. He tells you that he called them "old-fashioned jerks" and then stayed out until 3 A.M. While listening to his story, you might think, "Calling his parents names is unlikely to get his curfew lifted" or perhaps, "Developmentally speaking, staying out until 3 A.M. is an immature and unproductive way to handle anger." Such evaluative thoughts come from your frame of reference and interfere with careful listening. First, they interfere because it is difficult to listen and evaluate at the same time. While you are thinking about the first thing the speaker said, it is difficult to absorb the next. Second, such evaluation could easily lead you to premature problem solving, as exhibited by the students who interviewed Rosie (see Chapter 1). Evaluating Rosie's situation from their own frames of reference, they asked Rosie about the possibilities they thought made sense in her situation.

Most of us find it very difficult to suspend our own frame of reference and hear the client's story from the client's point of view. We are used to filtering what others tell us through our own experiences, beliefs, and categories. Education in the helping professions reinforces this approach by its emphasis on listening as a means of gaining assessment information.

To address this problem, Peter De Jong teaches a first course on listening and responding skills in which students develop skills by role-playing. He and his students, who have struggled to discover ways to listen more carefully, find that the most useful place to begin is listening first for who and what are important to the client. As clients describe what assistance they need, they talk about those people, relationships, and events that are significant to them. In the example of the 15-year-old, the important people are his parents, and the important events include the imposition of a 10 P.M. curfew and the night he stayed out until 3 A.M. This example also highlights that who and what are important to clients are not necessarily experienced positively by them. The 15-year-old boy in the example did not appreciate the 10 P.M. curfew or his parents at the moment.

Peter and his students have found that listening for these important players and events has three important consequences. First, it immediately gets the practitioner focused on some important parts of the client's frame of reference; second, it hinders the tendency to evaluate what the client says; and third, it helps prevent early problem solving from the listener's point of view.

DVD   (See DVD Clip 1.)

Formulating Questions

In the most general sense, interviewing clients is a process of formulating and asking a question, listening to the answer, and then formulating and asking another question. In the helping or therapeutic interview, it is the practitioner's job to listen and formulate, and the client's job to answer. As Witkin (1999) has observed, and Chapters 1 and 2 have demonstrated, "Listen to the questions people ask and you get a fairly good idea of what they believe, what they value, and what they hope to accomplish." With Witkin's observation in mind, reflect again on a sampling of the questions that the students asked Rosie:

- How do you feel about being pregnant again?
- Were you using birth control?
- Did you know that most schools have attendance officers who can come to the house and get your kids for you if they don't show up at school?
- Wouldn't you be interested in hearing more about how adoption works these days—for your benefit and your child's?
- Do you find that you often make the same mistakes in parenting as your mother?

Ask yourself: What are the embedded assumptions in these questions about Rosie and how to be helpful to her? By contrast, here are some of the questions Cheryl asked in Chapter 2:

- Suppose . . . a miracle happens. . . . What do you suppose you would notice tomorrow morning that would be *different*—that would tell you, wow, things are really better?
- What else would you notice?
- If you were to decide to do that—get up before them and make them breakfast—what would they do?
- Are there times already, say in the last two weeks, which are like the miracle you have been describing, even a little bit?
- Tell me about four days ago. *What* was different?
- How did all that happen?

What are the embedded assumptions in Cheryl's questions? Most of us can easily see that the two sets of questions are different and represent different ways of thinking about clients and helping. If you are new to solution building, however, you will soon discover, as you begin interviewing, that formulating questions is challenging.

Much of the rest of this book is about how to formulate questions. LaFrance (1992), McGee (1999), McGee, Del Vento, and Bavelas (2005), and Witkin (1999) all state that questions are not simply a way to get information from clients, whether that information is about problems, solutions, or any other topic. Instead, the process of questioning and answering often creates new awareness in the participants and new possibilities for the future. That is a major reason why conversation interests most of us. People in conversation will say, "Oh, I never looked at it that way," "I didn't realize that a job working with people is what I really want," or "I guess I was being a better mom to my kids than I thought." In short, you never know what will come out of a conversation, especially with someone you have not talked with before.

While the questions used in solution-building interviews can be listed and described, reading about them will not guarantee that you will be able to use them effectively in your own interviews. Using them effectively requires practice, just as does artistically performing a Beethoven concerto or a piece of modern jazz. To help you formulate and ask questions, we believe it is most important to emphasize this general principle: Formulate your next question from the client's last or an earlier answer. Cheryl followed this principle throughout her interview with Rosie. See if you can locate examples of it in this excerpt.

CHERYL: OK, that sounds like a *big* miracle. What do you imagine would be the first thing that you would notice which would tell you that this day is different, it's better, a miracle must have happened?

ROSIE: Well, I would get up in the morning before my kids do, make them breakfast, and sit down with them while we all eat together.

CHERYL: If you were to decide to do that—get up before them and make them breakfast—what would they do?

ROSIE: I think maybe they would come and sit down at the table instead of going and turning on the TV.

CHERYL: And how would that be for you?

ROSIE: I'd be happier because we could talk about nice things, not argue over TV. And my babies won't start crying over all the fighting about the TV.

CHERYL: What else? What else will be different when the miracle happens?

This principle is important for two reasons. First, it best puts into action the idea that questions and answers lead to new awareness and possibilities. In other words, solutions are built most readily when interviewers formulate their questions according to this principle. Second, the principle naturally results from working within the client's frame of reference, since that means asking follow-up questions to get more information about what the client has just said. Review Cheryl's questions once more with this observation in mind. Notice how their formulation reveals nothing about what Cheryl thinks Rosie's miracle should be, but only invites Rosie to construct what might be there.

As you become more experienced in formulating questions according to this general principle, you will realize it is the fundamental way in which interviewers make their contribution to solution building. The next section examines more specialized skills that contribute to the effectiveness of putting this principle into action in interviews.

DVD **(See DVD Clips 1 and 2.)**

Getting Details

The French say "God is in the details." The Germans see it differently; they say, "The devil is in the details." Both are probably right. Certainly effective solution building requires getting details, details, and more details.

Clients often make vague statements and sweeping generalizations such as, "Things are going better between my kids and me" or "I will never take another drink." Often, inexperienced interviewers note these statements without asking for clarification. In solution building, interviewers always attempt to clarify statements for both themselves and the client by asking for details; for example, "Oh, things are going better between you and your kids. Congratulations! What has been happening that tells you they are going better?" or "Do you think that's possible, that you will never take another drink?" Usually such a beginning question for details is just the first in a series of several related questions.

Getting details means asking questions about the who, what, when, where, and how of clients' statements. We call this process asking "'wh' and how" questions. These questions are the ones most likely to elicit descriptive clarifications from the client. Notice that "why" questions are not included here. They tend to elicit clients' analyses of possible underlying causes of their behaviors and situations and run the risk of being experienced by clients as confrontational or judgmental. Such analyses and confrontations have not proven useful in building solutions, so you will not see "why" questions used in this book.

Questions asking for descriptive but not analytical details are used throughout the solution-building process. They are used to clarify clients' current situations and to both clarify and amplify clients' goals, strengths, and successes. In the following excerpt from the Cheryl/Rosie conversation, observe how Cheryl skillfully asks whether there are any past successes related to Rosie's miracle picture and, when she finds there has been a success, how she uses "'wh' and how" questions to elicit details.

CHERYL: Rosie, I'm impressed. You have a pretty clear picture of how things will be different around your house when things are better. Are there times already, say in the last two weeks, which are like the miracle you have been describing, even a little bit?

ROSIE: Well, I'm not sure. Well, about four days ago it was better.

CHERYL: Tell me about four days ago. *What* was different?

ROSIE: Well, I went to bed about 10:00 the night before and had a good night of sleep. I had food in the house, because I had gone to the store and to the food pantry on Saturday. I had even set the alarm for 6:30 and got up when it rang. I made breakfast and called the kids. The boys ate and got ready for school and left on time. [remembering] One even got some homework out of his backpack and did it—real quick—before he went to school.

CHERYL: [impressed] Rosie, that sounds like a big part of the miracle right there. I'm amazed. How did all that happen?

ROSIE: I'm not sure. I guess one thing was I had the food in the house, and I got to bed on time.

CHERYL: So, how did you make that happen?

ROSIE: Ah, I decided not to see any clients that night, and I read books to my kids for an hour.

CHERYL: How did you manage that, reading to four kids? That seems like it would be really tough.

ROSIE: No, that doesn't work—reading to four kids at the same time. I have my oldest boy read to one baby, because that's the only way I can get him to practice his reading, and I read to my other boy and baby.

CHERYL: Rosie, that seems like a great idea—having him read to the baby. It helps you, and it helps him with his reading. How do you get him to do that?

ROSIE: Oh, I let him stay up a half hour later than the others because he helps me. He really likes that.

DVD **(See DVD Clips 1, 2, and 3.)**

Echoing Clients' Key Words

The Cheryl/Rosie dialogue presented previously is an excellent example of how the quest for details in solution building reflects the principle of forming the next question from the client's last answer. Another skill that both reflects this principle and leads to more details is echoing clients' key words. Echoing is based on practitioners' awareness that, while it may be meaningful to them, the language clients use to describe their experiences and relationships is often vague to practitioners. One unobtrusive way to resolve ambiguity is to simply repeat or *echo* key words used by the client. Key words are those that clients use to capture their experiences and the meaning they attribute to these experiences. For example, a client might say to you, "My life is a mess." If you wish to know more about what that means to the client, all you need do is to echo "a mess" with a rising intonation or simply ask, "What do you mean by 'a mess'?" The client almost always takes that as an invitation to say more about what is happening in his or her life. We would add that in the process of saying more, the client, as well as the practitioner, often learns more about the meaning of the "mess" being described.

There are some tips to keep in mind when thinking about how to identify clients' key words. Clients often repeat key words. When you notice a client frequently using a word you have not explored, become curious about its meaning. Key words also are often emotionally charged and given special emphasis by clients. The word *mess* in the previous illustration is a good example. Last, an idiosyncratic use of words should raise your curiosity. For example, suppose a client has been having running battles with a coworker at the office and says to you, "The last time I saw him, I kept a small mouth instead of shooting off my big mouth as usual." You should explore what she does differently when she keeps a small mouth.

Language is the primary means by which clients convey their frames of reference. It is crucial to solution building that you listen carefully for and explore each client's choice of words. Exploring the client's words is also an important way of demonstrating respect for the client. In this connection, we believe it is disrespectful and undermines client confidence to reframe the client's key words into professional jargon.

Like any of the basic skills, echoing can be misused by practitioners. In his course on beginning interviewing, Peter notices that at first many students have difficulty picking out key words. In their early interviews, they may demonstrate a thoughtless and mechanical pattern of echoing, or they may echo in a way that suggests they are skeptical or disapprove of what they are hearing. We believe that most of these misapplications arise when the interviewer's frame of reference shapes what he or she hears. Learning to echo effectively can be hard work, but Peter has found that, with role-play practice and feedback, nearly all students learn to do it comfortably and authentically within six weeks of practice.

DVD **(See DVD Clips 1 and 2.)**

Open Questions

As explained earlier, we ask questions throughout the solution-building process. Although we ask some closed questions, we ask many more open questions. As Benjamin (1987) explains, closed questions narrow the client's focus, while open ones widen the client's perceptual field. Closed questions also tend to ask for hard facts, while open ones request the client's attitudes, thoughts, feelings, and perceptions. Last, closed questions more often run the risk of reflecting the practitioner's frame of reference, while open ones are more likely to stay focused on the client's frame of reference. Some examples of closed questions are:

- Do you like your parents?
- Did you ask your parents for a change in your curfew before you decided to break it?
- Do you want to patch things up between you and your parents?

The following are examples of open questions:

- Can you tell me something about your relationship with your parents?
- I'm wondering what happened between you and your parents the night you stayed out until 3 A.M.?
- Suppose things were to get better between you and your parents; what would be different?

Do not confuse open questions with vague questions or questions that do not request specific information. All of the open questions in the examples are intended to elicit specifics from the client. When used with echoing, they provide an effective means of exploring the details of who and what are important to clients, as well as other aspects of solution building.

Open questions (or equivalent statements such as "Please, tell me more about that") are also preferable because they are consistent with a commitment to not knowing. We want to do whatever we can to cast our clients into the role of experts about their own lives. When asked with genuine curiosity, open questions transfer both control and responsibility to the clients. In comparison with closed questions, they give clients more choice about what to say about themselves and how to say it. Using open questions is one way to respect and promote client self-determination.

We ask closed questions at certain points in an interview. For example, Cheryl asked Rosie, "Are there times already, say in the last two weeks, which are like the miracle you have been describing, even a little bit?" We might ask a person who has been abusing alcohol for many years, who says he never will take another drink, "Do you believe that you can do it?" Although these are closed questions, they are asked to set the stage for more open questions about the topic contained in the closed question. Consequently, when Rosie says there was a time four days before that resembled her miracle, Cheryl asks a series of open questions beginning with this question: "Tell me about four days ago. *What* was different?" And to the substance-abusing client who answers "yes" to the closed question about whether he believes he is capable of never taking another drink, the interviewer would turn to a related open question: "What do you know about yourself that tells you that you can do it?"

DVD (See DVD Clip 1.)

Summarizing

Peter teaches the solution-building process to students who have had little or no formal training in professional practice. One of the first skills he teaches is summarizing, which is essential in treating each client as unique. You will use this skill right from the beginning and throughout solution-building work with clients.

In summarizing, you periodically restate to the client his or her thoughts, actions, and feelings. You use this technique after you have obtained a detailed description of a part of the client's story, with the judicious use of echoes and open questions. To illustrate, let us review the case of the 15-year-old at odds with his parents over his curfew. With Tom as the client and Peter as the practitioner, the interview unfolded this way:

PETER: [*open question*][1] How were you hoping that I could help you?

TOM: My parents are such old-fashioned jerks. I can't believe it!

PETER: [*genuinely curious and echoing*] "Old-fashioned jerks"?

TOM: Yeah. Like one thing is that they have this ridiculous rule that I have to be in by 10:00 during the week. They say I need to get to bed on time so I can do well in school, instead of running around with my friends. [cynically] Yeah, right! Just because they're getting old and have to get to bed so early.

PETER: So you don't see it the way they do.

TOM: I sure don't. In fact, the reason they made me come here to see you was because I got mad last week and stayed out past my stupid curfew. [Tom pauses and stares sullenly into the distance, with his arms folded across his chest].

PETER: [*open question*] Can you tell me more about what happened that night?

TOM: [sighing] It was the same old thing. I told them that a bunch of us were going out to the $2 movies and then a fast-food place or to one of my friend's. They told me I had to be home by 10:00 and I said I couldn't, and then we started yelling at each other. They told me my grades were falling and I shouldn't even go. I should be studying. I told them I was doing OK and to chill. They ordered me to stay home, and I got mad and left and stayed at my friend's house overnight after the movie. His parents were gone on vacation.

PETER: [*summarizing*] OK, let me see if I've got this correct. You're here because your parents made you come. You argued with them recently about your curfew, got angry about what they said, and stayed out past curfew without permission by sleeping overnight at your friend's house.

TOM: Yeah, that's right. We fight about this almost every week. They're so old-fashioned. None of my friends have a 10 o'clock curfew like that. You'd think they could get with it!

The summary that Peter gave in this dialogue was intended for both Tom's and his own benefit. The summary reassured Tom that Peter was listening carefully. It also reassured Peter that he had heard Tom accurately. Peter used some of Tom's words and phrases in the summary as a way of respecting the way Tom chose to describe his own experience and as a way of getting as clear an idea as possible of Tom's frame of reference. If they are descriptive and are offered in a spirit of openness, summaries usually have the effect of inviting the client to say more—to correct, revise, and add to the practitioner's summary. Because they are essentially reflective, summaries are an effective way to put clients in control of how to describe their experiences. They also assist the practitioner in formulating the next question based on what the client has just revealed.

Carl Rogers, who is well known among therapists for his role in introducing nondirective therapy techniques, strongly advocates the use of summaries throughout work with clients because they promote an understanding of the other person's frame of reference and block the listener's tendency to evaluate when trying to listen. Summaries also help the listener to remain composed when the speaker is talking about ideas, behaviors, or reactions that the listener would normally find foreign or offensive. To demonstrate the effects of summarizing, Rogers (1961, p. 332) suggests the following exercise.

The next time you get into an argument with your wife, or your friend, or with a small group of friends, just stop the discussion for a moment and for an experiment, institute this rule. "Each person can speak up for himself only *after* he has first restated the ideas and feelings of the previous speaker accurately, and to that speaker's satisfaction."

Rogers points out that successful summarizing requires careful listening, which tends to take heightened emotion out of a discussion or conversation, by making differences among participants more rational and understandable.

DVD **(See DVD Clip 1.)**

Paraphrasing

"*Paraphrasing* feeds back to the client the essence of what has just been said. The listener shortens and clarifies the client's comments" (Ivey & Ivey, 2007, p. 154). Paraphrases are briefer than summaries and do not interrupt the client's train of thought to the same extent. They are very useful in demonstrating to clients that you are really hearing them. In paraphrasing, you offer your clients an invitation to clarify and expand their stories. Paraphrases, like summaries, work best when they include clients' key words.

As an example, let us return to the case of Tom. Instead of summarizing, Peter might have simply paraphrased what Tom had said: "So, you got fed up with your parents' 'old-fashioned' curfew and stayed out all night." Tom would then have had a chance to modify Peter's understanding.

Paraphrasing can be used to move the conversation between you and your clients in a direction you think will be more useful. Chapter 2 demonstrated how, once clients have described their difficulties, we explore what they would like to have different in their lives. Another paraphrase Peter could have used with Tom would be: "So, you're not happy with the way things are going in your relationship with your parents. You want to see something different." This paraphrase would demonstrate to Tom that he was being heard and also serve as an invitation to begin thinking about an alternative, better future with his parents.

Observations of students and workshop participants have shown that as practitioners become more experienced in solution building, they use more paraphrases and fewer summaries. With more experience, they seem to need fewer words to demonstrate that they are listening carefully and to invite clients to move in new directions.

DVD **(See DVD Clip 1.)**

Practitioners' Nonverbal Behavior

Most clients are sensitive to whether practitioners are listening carefully and respectfully. This is especially true at the beginning of our work with them. They seem to come to a conclusion about whether we are listening carefully by watching us, as well as listening to our verbal responses and questions. According to Okun (1997, p. 24), research bears out this observation. Okun states that clients rely on the following nonverbal behaviors of practitioners to judge whether they are being heard and respected:

- A tone of voice that matches the client's voice
- Eye contact
- Occasional head nodding to show that the practitioner is tracking what the client says
- Varying facial expressions in response to what the client says
- Smiling at appropriate points to demonstrate warmth and understanding
- Occasional hand gesturing
- Sitting in close physical proximity to the client
- Using a moderate rate of speech
- Leaning slightly toward the client to indicate interest and concentration

Some practitioners stress the importance of nonverbal skills. Peter has a colleague who instructs students at length about body posture, head nodding, use of smiles, and the forward lean. Although nonverbals are important, we believe that what you choose to say and ask is more important in demonstrating to clients that you are respectfully listening. Moreover, nonverbal skills develop naturally as you learn to quiet your own frame of reference and listen more carefully to who and what are important to clients.

Nevertheless, effective nonverbals can contribute to setting an attentive, respectful atmosphere in a professional interview. Little or no eye contact, inappropriate smiling or facial expressions, unusual gestures, an unpleasant tone of voice, and a rate of speech that is too fast or too slow can all be distracting (Okun, 1997). Consequently, it is useful to make video recordings of your interviews periodically so you can review how your nonverbals are affecting your interactions with clients.

DVD **(See DVD Clip 1.)**

The Use of Silence

Most beginning practitioners are very uncomfortable with silent pauses in interviews. Silences tend to make new practitioners freeze. Freezing, a kind of performance anxiety, is the most common difficulty experienced by those learning interview skills, according to research by Epstein (1985). It seems to be tied to an inner sense of not having the ability to help clients. Epstein states that in such circumstances, the beginner is apt to engage in destructive self-talk: "I can't do it. I'm making a fool of myself. Worse yet, the client knows that I don't know what I'm doing."

What silence means to the client is almost always different from what an anxious practitioner takes it to mean. According to Benjamin (1987), silence may mean the client is sorting out his or her thoughts, is confused or angry about the situation just described, or is simply taking a short breather from the work at hand. Benjamin believes it is important to respect client silences.

The solution-building approach calls for practitioners to increase their toleration of client silences. In Western societies, silence makes people uncomfortable. After five seconds, most people feel pressure to fill a silence by saying something. If that is your tendency and you want to work with a solution-building approach, you have work to do. The questions you will be asking—about clients' experiences, what they want to be different in their lives, and what is already going well—require clients to do some hard thinking before they put their responses into words. Often clients are silent for a time, then say, "I don't know," and then become silent again. If you fill the silence with your observations and suggestions, you will be resorting to the type of questioning the students used with Rosie in Chapter 1. If you tolerate the silence for a while—10, 15, or even 20 seconds—you will be surprised by clients' capacities to construct answers. They often surprise themselves because they really did not know their answer until you asked the question. By remaining silent, you give them an opportunity to work on the answer. Sometimes clients interrupt silences by saying, "That's a tough question" or "I never thought about that." We recommend that you simply respond sympathetically, saying, "Yes, it is. I know I'm asking you some tough questions," and then continue your silence. At times, you can compliment them for their hard work and encourage them to continue working by asking additional questions.

Clients, also, are uncomfortable with silence. You can utilize that discomfort in your efforts to encourage clients' solution building. If you develop your capacity to remain silent, clients will soon learn that you do not intend to answer the questions for them, and they will be more inclined to struggle for their own answers.

There may be circumstances in which allowing the silence to continue is not productive. On occasion, you will do something in an interview that confuses or even offends the client. You might make an odd facial expression or ask a carelessly worded question. In response, the client may remain silent. On other occasions, your client may be an involuntary participant, pressured to meet with you against his or her wishes. Such a client also may be silent, especially at the beginning of the interview. In situations like these, you may wish to use one or both of the following two skills.

DVD **(See DVD Clips 1 and 7.)**

Noticing Clients' Nonverbal Behavior

Most clients measure their practitioners partly by paying attention to facial expressions, gestures, tone of voice, and eye contact. An attentive practitioner will observe the same signals in clients because clients also convey meaning through nonverbal behavior. Clients who respond to a comment by smiling, rolling their eyes, looking off into space, putting their heads down, heaving a sigh, crossing their legs and arms, changing their tone of voice, or falling silent are communicating through these nonverbals as surely as if they were using words (Okun, Fried, & Okun, 1999). When you are in tune with clients, you will notice these nonverbals, the context in which they are used, the various patterns in which different clients use them, and any changes in those patterns. Having noticed such nonverbal signs, you can choose whether or not to mention them and explore their meaning.

Clients tend to use nonverbals in their own individual patterns and, therefore, the meaning of nonverbals must always be discerned in context. According to research, the nonverbals of clients cluster somewhat according to cultural group. Lum (2004) states that not only do people of color differ from the white population in their use of nonverbals such as eye contact and tone of voice, but also that African Americans, Asian Americans, and Latinos exhibit distinctive patterns of nonverbal behavior. It is useful to know these cultural patterns, but when working with specific clients, you need to be aware of the many differences within each cultural group as well. The possible meaning of client nonverbals is best understood within the client's total self-presentation, verbal and nonverbal. Most of us intuitively respond to others in a holistic fashion. That is, we respond on the basis of our interpretation of all their verbal and nonverbal messages. The same is true when we work professionally with clients.

Observing for and openly responding to clients' nonverbal messages is not a major part of solution building. Unlike many other approaches that rely on practitioners' interpretations of client behaviors including nonverbal ones to promote client change, solution building relies on the process of not-knowing questions and answers from the client's frame of reference to create the possibility of change. As you begin to interview, however, pay attention to clients' nonverbal reactions to your statements and questions. These reactions are important indicators of whether your statements and questions are respectful of and working within clients' frames of reference. If, for instance, a client falls silent, slumps down, looks away, or otherwise seems to lose interest, your questions probably are not incorporating who and what are important to the client. When that happens, rather than drawing the client's attention to it and discussing it, asking a question like the following will help you get back on track: "So what needs to be different by the end of our meeting for you to say that our talking together has been useful?" If, by contrast, you observe that, in attempting to answer a question, a client purses lips, narrows eyes, and tightens cheeks in intense and thoughtful effort, you have the nonverbal indicators you need to ask additional, similar questions with confidence.

DVD **(See DVD Clips 1 and 2.)**

Self-Disclosing

As a practitioner, if you employ self-disclosure, you "share your own story, thoughts, or experiences *briefly*" (Ivey & Ivey, 2007, p. 356). Wide variation exists among practitioners in their use of this technique. Some practitioners disclose their own feelings and experiences as a way to motivate and educate their clients. Others shy away from such practices in the belief that they interfere with client self-determination and undermine client self-confidence.

We do not recommend that you tell clients about your own experiences. The notion behind solution building is that the first place, and usually the only necessary place, to look for solutions is within the client's frame of reference and past experiences. However, that does not mean you ought never to reveal to clients what is on your mind. Sometimes it is important to tell clients what you are thinking. For example, if you notice a contradiction in what the client says, you might observe and inquire: "Earlier, you said things were pretty good between you and your mom. Just now, you said you are sick of her. I'm confused. Can you explain to me how those two fit together?" Appropriate use of such self-disclosure can help practitioners understand and clarify clients' perceptions about their lives.

Self-disclosure is best understood to mean using your senses, critical thinking capacities, and thoughts as instruments in the solution-building process. It does not mean telling your clients that, for instance, you too broke curfew as a teenager or you too were sexually abused. Although some practitioners argue that the latter type of self-disclosure enhances rapport, we believe it is unnecessary and impairs clients' ability to build their own solutions. It is also based on the questionable assumption that those who have experienced a particular tragedy can be most useful to clients who are struggling with the same tragedy.

DVD **(See DVD Clips 1 and 5.)**

Noticing Process

As noted in Chapter 1, practitioners in the helping professions have emphasized that the first order of business in working with clients is to establish a relationship of trust. Several authors explain that client trust is tied to perceived practitioner understanding (Benjamin, 1987; Carkhuff, 1987; Kadushin, 1990). Unless clients believe that practitioners really understand what they are trying to say, they are unlikely to believe that the practitioners have their best interests at heart or can be of use to them.

Those authors also emphasize that understanding clients involves grasping both the content and process of client communications. *Content* refers to clients' verbal messages—the information they relate about their struggles and the important people and events in their lives. *Process* refers to the way in which clients express the information, that is, to the affect or feelings that clients convey when they provide information. This affect can be revealed by a client's posture (erect or slumping in a chair), degree of eye contact, pace of speech, use of silence, capacity to stay focused on the subject at hand, facial expression, and tone of voice.

Often client content and process match, and the practitioner paraphrases and summarizes the content for the client, making sure that the two share the same understanding of the client and his or her situation. Sometimes, however, client content and process do not match. For example, a client who is estranged from her husband may say her husband no longer matters to her, but she may have tears welling in her eyes. When practitioners notice such apparent discrepancies between content and process, they can either address them through paraphrasing, summarizing, and self-disclosing or just file them away for the moment, perhaps to be addressed later in the interview. Practitioners' decisions about what to do should always be based on how best to help the client, that is, how to proceed so that the client feels the interview is moving in a constructive direction.

Noticing how a client presents information is important. All clients have their own interpersonal style. Some clients demonstrate impressive clarity and organization of thought, others have sparkle and a sense of humor, and others have a warm and caring manner. When you notice client qualities that might be useful to the client, mention them. This skill is called *complimenting*.

DVD **(See DVD Clips 1 and 2.)**

Complimenting

Clients have personal qualities and past experiences that, if drawn on, can be of great use in resolving their difficulties and creating more satisfying lives. These qualities—such as resilience in the face of hardships, a sense of humor, an organized mind, a capacity for hard work, a sense of caring toward others, the ability to see things from another's point of view, a willingness to listen to others, an interest in learning more about life and living—are *client strengths*. Useful past experiences are those in which the client either thought about or actually did something that might be put to use in resolving the current difficulties. These experiences are the client's *past successes*.

As an example of complimenting, consider the following interview between Peter and a young mother who was at risk of having her children taken from her by Protective Services because of suspected neglect.

PETER: I understand that Protective Services is investigating your home situation to see if they are satisfied that you are taking good care of your children.

ELLEN: That's true, and I'm really scared about it. I have four children: Bill, who is 4; Stacey, who's 3; and my twins, who are 10 months. They are an incredible amount of work.

PETER: I'm sure they must be. It must be difficult for you having four preschoolers.

ELLEN: It is. I feel like I'm buried in diapers and dishes, and sometimes it seems like they all need me at the same time. What makes it even worse is that my husband is just starting out in business and is always gone.

PETER: [*complimenting*] You seem to be a mother who cares very much for her children, trying to get each of them what they need.

ELLEN: [tearfully] I do, but sometimes I just can't keep up, and things get pretty messy. But I try to take a little time with each one separately. Every child needs to know that they're special.

PETER: [*continuing to compliment*] You seem to be working really hard at being a good mother. I'm interested in this idea of yours that each child is special. It seems like an important one to you. Did you figure this out on your own, or did you pick it up somehow from someone else?

ELLEN: My mom had lots of kids, and she got really sick with depression and had to be hospitalized. She never had time for us, much less for each one of us separately. So, I decided a long time ago that it would be different when I got my own children. I was going to pay separate attention to each one of them.

PETER: [*complimenting again*] I can see that you have done a lot of thinking about this. Tell me about exactly what you do when you treat each of your children as a special child.

Complimenting should not be motivated by a desire to be kind to clients. Instead, it should be *reality-based,* in the sense that it is derived from what the client communicates to you through words or client process. As can be seen from Peter and Ellen's conversation, compliments are often used to reinforce in the client's mind what is important to the client.

When complimenting was first introduced at the Brief Family Therapy Center (BFTC) in Milwaukee, Wisconsin, compliments were mainly used at the end of the interview, to draw clients' attention to strengths and past successes that might be useful in achieving their goals. Little by little, practitioners turned to complimenting throughout sessions because the procedure seems to help clients grow more hopeful and confident. In-session complimenting also helps to uncover more information about client strengths and successes. If complimented, a client usually nods in agreement, which tells you he or she shares this perception. You are then in a position to follow up with more questions about what else has happened in the client's life that supports the compliment.

There are several types of compliments (Berg, 1994; Berg & De Jong, 2005). A *direct compliment* is a positive evaluation or reaction by the practitioner in response to the client. An example of positive evaluation is Peter's comment to Ellen in their dialogue: "You seem to be a mother who cares very much for her children." If a client who is struggling to stop drinking tells you that he or she has not had a drink in four weeks, you might exclaim: "Wow! I'm sure that must have been very difficult!" That reaction is also a direct compliment and expresses what MacDonald, Ricci, and Stewart (1998) have called "admiration." Using positive evaluations sparingly and admiration frequently is most effective, but both types of direct compliments work best when used to reflect what the client values.

An *indirect compliment* is a question that implies something positive about the client. One way to indirectly compliment is to ask for more information about a desired outcome stated by the client. For example, Peter might ask Ellen, "How have you managed to make the household so calm?" Another way is to imply something positive through a relationship, that is, the practitioner asks the client to answer a question from the vantage point of another person or persons. Peter might ask Ellen, "If your children were here and I were to ask them what you do to be a good mother to them, what do you suppose they would say?" A third way is to imply that the client knows what is best, as Peter did when he effectively asked Ellen, "How did you know that it is important for you to treat each of your children as though they are special?" Indirect complimenting is preferable to direct compli-menting because its questioning format leads clients to discover and state their own strengths and resources.

Finally, clients may use a *self-compliment*. They might say, "I decided to quit using cocaine because I got smart," or "I decided that, since I was going to school, I might as well do some studying." Your job as a practitioner is to recognize such compliments as possible signs of progress and reinforce them with indirect compliments: "Did it surprise you that you decided to do that?" "Is that new for you?" "Has it been difficult?" "Is that something you can continue to do?"

Many clients accept compliments easily. Others downplay or even reject them. When practitioners begin to give more compliments, they often feel awkward and anxious about how their clients will respond. If you feel anxious, remember that the first goal in giving compliments is for clients to notice their positive changes, strengths, and resources. It is not necessary for clients to openly accept the compliments.

DVD **(See DVD Clips 1 and 3.)**

Affirming Clients' Perceptions

Felix Biestek (1957), a well-known writer on the development of trust, formulated several important principles of relationship building. One principle is the purposeful expression of feelings. Biestek believes that every request for professional help is accompanied by feelings the client needs to purposefully express if he or she is to feel understood and come to trust the practitioner.

Many practitioners have made this principle the centerpiece of their work with clients. Some quotations from basic texts about the importance of under-standing clients' feelings in order to help them follow.

> Underlying clients' words and behaviors are feelings and emotions. The purpose of reflection of feeling is to make these implicit, sometimes hidden, emotions explicit and clear to the client.
>
> (IVEY & IVEY, 2007, P. 178)

> Responding to feelings is the most critical single skill in helping.
>
> (CARKHUFF, 1987, P. 99)

> The skill of reflecting feeling is aimed at assisting others to sense and experience the most basic part of themselves—how they really feel about another person or life event.
>
> (IVEY & IVEY, 2007, P. 189)

Implicit in these quotations is the belief that feelings represent the core aspect of human beings, and clients must come to understand their feelings before they can move on to solve their problems. Practitioners of this persuasion consistently try to tune in to clients' feelings and label them: "You seem angry," or "You seem really scared." Such practitioners also note whether clients can express their feelings with appropriate intensity or whether they repress them. In addition, these practitioners pay attention to whether clients can own their feelings as authentic ways of reacting to the important people and events in their lives or whether they shift responsibility for their feelings to the provocations of others: "My mom makes me so mad because she criticizes all my friends."

Contrary to this view, we have not found that clients regularly need to focus on and own their feelings (especially so-called repressed feelings) in order to feel understood or make progress. They do need to be asked about their perceptions, however, including those related to the nature of their problems, what attempts they have made to overcome their problems, what they want to be different in their lives, what has worked for them already, and what has not worked. *Webster's New World Dictionary* (1988, p. 1002) defines *perception* as follows.

> 1. a) the act of perceiving or the ability to perceive; mental grasp of objects, qualities, etc. by means of the senses; awareness; comprehension b) insight or intuition, or the faculty for these 2. the understanding, knowledge, etc. got by perceiving, or a specific idea, concept, impression, etc. so formed.

So defined, a perception is some aspect of a person's self-awareness or awareness of his or her life. This awareness is achieved through the senses, the person's capacity to think and feel, and his or her intuition.

Perceptions are holistic. They include a person's thoughts, feelings, behaviors, and experiences. Practitioners learn about a client's perceptions by asking the client to describe them in words. Consequently, the client's descriptions of his or her perceptions may be productively thought of as the interplay between the client's experiences and frame of reference (that is, the concepts the client uses to organize and give meaning to his or her experiences).

Clients not only need to be asked about their perceptions in order to feel understood, but they also need affirmation of their perceptions. They need some indication that practitioners can understand how they think, feel, act, or experience life. Insoo had this point dramatically reconfirmed to her on the occasion of interviewing a young prostitute who was dying of AIDS. The woman told Insoo that staff members at the AIDS clinic where she was receiving treatment were pressuring her to confront her brothers for their past sexual abuse of her. On the other hand, she wanted to concentrate on dying well, which meant getting her mother to understand that she was a good person and spending her last days in her own tiny apartment instead of the hospice that the clinic staff preferred. Insoo explored and affirmed the perceptions that led to these wishes and explored with the woman how she could make her wishes happen. Because she was too weak to travel, the woman eventually chose to write her mother a letter, and she stayed in her apartment until she died.

Practitioners can affirm clients' perceptions in several ways. They might simply demonstrate acceptance through nods and short statements ("uh-huh," "sure," "of course"), or they might choose an unmistakable affirmation: "From all you have told me, I can understand why you want to spend your last days in your own apartment."

In reflecting on Biestek's principle of the purposeful expression of feelings, we have come to the conclusion that, although feelings are an important part of client perceptions, they are no more important than client thoughts, attitudes, beliefs, or past behaviors. Rather than separating and labeling any particular aspect of a client's perceptions, we have found it is more useful to ask about and listen to their perceptions as holistically as we can. Once we have grasped their perceptions, we proceed to affirm them as meaningful. We believe that, if you choose to do the same, you will be demonstrating respect for client perceptions, treating each client as an individual, encouraging your clients to value and trust their ways of experiencing their lives, and leading them to trust you and enter into a productive working relationship with you.

Exploring and affirming clients' perceptions, as clients describe them, constitutes a major share of what is done in solution-building interviews. Consequently, almost every interview excerpt in this book illustrates this skill.

The excerpt from Peter's interview with Ellen is an example of how compliments may be used to affirm client perceptions. Notice how Peter continuously asks Ellen to expand on her statements and give more description of both her situation and how she has chosen to deal with it. These requests for more description are a further example of affirming the client's perceptions. By simply asking for a client's perceptions and then accepting them as information, a practitioner affirms their importance. Finally, the examples of empathy in the next section also illustrate how to affirm the client's perceptions.

A question that often arises in our workshops and classes is usually posed this way: "Do you always affirm client perceptions? What if a client is contemplating suicide as a way to escape depression? Or threatening to beat up a romantic rival? Or considering hitting a misbehaving child?" The implication of this question seems to be that the questioner cannot conceive of affirming anything at all related to such client thoughts and would be inclined to immediately use education and confrontation in order to turn the client away from transforming such thoughts into actions. An approach to clients who are contemplating such extreme actions is discussed in Chapter 10, but the basic principle is that, even in such cases, practitioners can proceed from a posture of not knowing. Clients who consider extreme actions, such as suicide, beating up a rival, or hitting, do so within the context of several associated perceptions. When explored and understood, these perceptions help both practitioners and clients to make sense of what is prompting them to talk this way. When meeting with such clients, you can respectfully ask them to provide information about their extreme perceptions. For example, to a client who thinks of hitting a child, you might say, "What's happening in your life that tells you hitting might be helpful in this situation? What else? How would doing that be helpful? Does it work?" You could continue: "If you were to decide to do that, what would be different between you and your child? What would be different between you and your other children? What would be different between you and the courts?"

Such questions serve to make sense of what is driving the client to talk about such extreme actions. When we have heard the client's story, we often find ourselves saying, "After what you have just told me about what is going on around your house, I can understand how you might feel like hitting your child at times, even though you are saying it doesn't work for you." Many practitioners assume that affirming such a client perception will increase the chances of the client taking the action or condone behavior such as hitting a child. Ironically, we have found just the opposite to be true. As clients are respectfully asked about the perceptions that surround possibilities such as suicide and beating or hitting others, they usually are more able to relax, and they turn the conversation toward working on less extreme possibilities.

DVD **(See DVD Clip 1.)**

Natural Empathy

Another principle of relationship building formulated by Biestek (1957) is that the practitioner must be capable of controlled emotional involvement, which Biestek defines as being sensitive to the client's feelings, understanding the meaning of these feelings, and responding appropriately. This principle calls on the practitioner to communicate at the level of feelings as well as thoughts. For example, to a client who has described the ways in which her spouse relentlessly ridicules her for being overweight, the practitioner might say, "His comments must really hurt. They must cut you to the bone." Many practitioners, both beginning and experienced, find developing and using this skill challenging. Some practitioners are never able to connect with clients at that level. This inability is thought by many in the field to be a deficiency.

Biestek's principle comes closest to what other writers (Benjamin, 1987; Egan, 2002; Keefe, 1976;) refer to as empathy. Empathy is an elusive quality. It seems to defy precise conceptualization. (Some authors, including Benjamin, prefer to illustrate its meaning by means of stories.) Empathy is thought to be a consequence of imaginatively entering the client's world of thinking, feeling, and acting. Empathy is not the same thing as sympathy, which means having the same feelings and concerns as the client. Empathy does not mean that the practitioner identifies with the client and becomes lost in the client's world. Rather, the practitioner works to explore and adopt the client's sense of his or her experience, without ever losing the inner sense that he or she is a separate person from the client. According to Carl Rogers (1957, p. 99), to feel empathy is "to sense the client's private world as if it were your own, but without ever losing the 'as if' quality" and "to sense the client's anger, fear, or confusion without getting bound up in it."

Those who write about empathy emphasize that being empathic with another requires practitioners to feel or be moved by the client's story. This brings us back to Biestek's idea of controlled emotional involvement. Practitioners must do more than cognitively comprehend what the client communicates. They must also understand the client's story with all of their being—emotions as well as thoughts.

(Some practitioners refer to empathic statements as "from the heart" statements.) The more practitioners can achieve such empathic understanding, the more natural it will be for them to respond to the client with empathic statements; and the more practitioners are able to use empathic statements, the more the client will feel cared about and fully understood.

Lambert and Bergin (1994, p. 164) state that there has long been virtual unanimity that "accurate empathy, positive regard, non-possessive warmth, and congruence or genuineness" are essential for building a "working alliance" with clients and for client progress in general. However, while research findings continue to confirm the importance of accurate empathy, they are becoming "more ambiguous than once thought" (Lambert & Bergin, 1994, p. 165). The findings do indicate that practitioner empathy is positively related to client satisfaction with the practitioner-client relationship. In addition, findings indicate that empathy is positively related to client progress when progress is measured by clients' estimates of progress. However, when progress is measured by some more objective means—for example, a standardized test or direct observation of client change—practitioner empathy seems less important.

The relative importance of empathy as the practitioner identifies and converses with clients about their emotional responses is becoming a matter of debate among solution-oriented practitioners. Kiser, Piercy, and Lipchik (1993) and Lipchik (1999; 2002) argue that explicit conversation with clients about their emotions fosters empathy and a positive connection between clients and therapists. On the other hand, Miller and de Shazer (2000) imply that such conversations are not necessary to building a cooperative connection between clients and therapists and can represent a subtle form of practitioners imposing their expert interpretations on clients' difficulties and their solutions. They point out that because emotions are embedded in clients' holistic responses to the people and events in their lives, extracting them for special attention, without clients identifying them as something they want changed, can create a conversational context slanted toward viewing clients' difficulties as caused by their emotions. This way of thinking about emotions unnecessarily limits practitioners' approaches to building a cooperative relationship with clients, as well as practitioners' and clients' perceptions of possible solutions.

Bavelas, McGee, Phillips, and Routledge (2000), a team of communications researchers, indirectly lend support to the view of Miller and de Shazer (2000) when summarizing research on different ways to respond to a person telling a story. They describe research wherein active listening with a focus on paraphrasing the storyteller's feelings (for example, "Your husband did not come home for dinner last evening, and you're feeling angry about it.") is compared to irrelevant interrupting (for example, asking for details unrelated to the point of the story: "Does your husband wear a necktie to work?") and to relevant interrupting which is characteristic of untrained, natural listeners (for example, saying "Oh no!" when the storyteller says her husband did not come home for dinner). Among the findings, storytellers themselves and observers of the interactions prefer natural listening (relevant interrupting) to active listening. They view it as a more genuine and more interested way in which to respond to clients and as equally attentive to what the storyteller is saying. Interestingly, the only observers who preferred active to natural listening were the minority who had been trained in active listening. Bavelas et al. (2000) conclude of active listening:

> Norgaard (1990) and Armstrong (1998) both found that the considerable literature on these techniques contains virtually no evaluation studies demonstrating that they are effective with or preferred by clients. . . . We therefore have doubts about these purported communication skills, which continue to be taught as how communication "should be," without systematic observation of how they function in interaction.

We agree with Miller and de Shazer (2000) about emotions not needing to be singled out for special conversation in order to build a cooperative, working relationship with clients. We also agree with Bavelas et al. (2000) that thorough research about communication skills is needed. Based on their work and our experience in working with clients, we recommend using relevant and natural interruptions when you interview. We definitely do not recommend using the type of empathy that is sentimental or tends to amplify negative feelings. For example, we do not recommend repeating statements such as, "You're really hurting now. This seems to be a deeply discouraging time in your life." Such statements tend to drive clients further into those aspects of their lives that are least useful for generating positive change. On the other hand, we are persuaded that a demonstration of natural, empathic understanding is required and helpful on many occasions when clients are describing events and their personal reactions. At these times, such as when a client is describing what is difficult and painful in a particular relationship, empathic affirmation of the client's perceptions is useful; for example, "I can see that things between you and him are not what you want right now." You can then move on to explore what the client might want different in the relationship or what the client is doing to mobilize his or her strengths to get through this difficult time. The exchange between Peter and Ellen earlier in this chapter provides another example of this approach to empathic understanding.

As a practitioner, you can demonstrate empathic understanding of your clients in many natural ways; for instance, by a knowing nod of your head, paraphrases and summaries that convey your understanding of the significance of what the client is saying, respectful silences, and adopting a compassionate tone of voice. Examples of verbal empathic skills are found throughout this book. Nonverbal skills are illustrated on the DVD accompanying this book.

We have discussed empathy as though it is a separate skill. However, its presence or absence in your work with clients is inseparable from the other skills described in this chapter. Your nonverbal responses, paraphrases, and affirmations of client perceptions can all convey a sense of empathy or the lack of it. Empathy, like any other aspect of the client-practitioner interaction, is best thought of as one ingredient existing among many. Client-practitioner interaction is like a cake. Once the cake is baked, we cannot separate the sugar from the flour. The taste of the cake depends on the combination of all the ingredients. Likewise, the taste of the interaction for the client—the client's sense of whether or not the practitioner really understands and is being useful—largely depends on the combination of skills used by the practitioner.[2]

DVD (See DVD Clip 1.)

Normalizing

Clients who are struggling with emotionally charged difficulties often lose perspective. Unable to find satisfactory solutions and caught up in the pain and tension of the moment, they come to think and talk as though their problems are out of control and beyond the bounds of normalcy. For example, parents in conflict with their teenager, or a person who has just discovered that his spouse has been having an affair for the past year, often talk in ways that reinforce a view that their situations are extraordinary. Practitioners can easily get caught up in this intense problem talk and lose their capacity to formulate solution-building questions.

Normalizing involves responding to problem talk by wondering with clients about whether their difficulties are not within the range of ordinary problems of living. It is meant to counter a tendency to see deep-seated problems and personal pathology in life's expected challenges. As a practitioner, there are different ways in which you can normalize. Suppose the parents of a teenage son came to you, as a professional, and said the following.

MOTHER: We've been having huge problems with Tim, our 15-year-old son. He's been skipping classes at school. He'll go to class for the first two periods, then walk right out of school to the parking lot and sit in his car. He's been caught by the attendance officer in his car, smoking, which is against the rules. For all I know he may even be smoking marijuana. He seems so uninvolved in his classes where in years past, he was always interested in his school work. His teachers have reported to me that he refuses to participate in class activities. He just sits there looking sullen. When he's asked a question, he'll refuse to answer or say that he doesn't see why he has to learn the material because it seems worthless to him. Sending him to the principal's office does no good. He just serves his detentions and continues to act out. He seems like a very troubled young man to me, and I can't figure out what to do with him. Maybe he's on drugs. Who knows!

FATHER: What makes it worse is that my wife is an English teacher at the school that Tim attends. She says to me that during her break, other teachers and the attendance officer will tell her all the things that Tim is doing wrong. It makes it very difficult for her to concentrate on her teaching.

One way to normalize would be to ask these clients whether the situation they describe is to be expected, given what they have described to you. You might respond, "You say Tim is a 15-year-old teenage boy, right? So would you say that what he has been doing is normal for a teenager or not?" You could also use a more direct way to normalize, provided the clients seem to have a sense of humor and you are fairly confident you can be direct without the parents taking offense. Here you might say, "Well, after all, he's a teenager! Teenagers get out of line from time to time." Another way of being direct with your normalizations is to use brief statements like "Of course," "Sure," or "Yes, that's understandable." In the preceding example, you might respond to the father's comments in this way.

Normalizing must be done naturally and confidently or clients may feel the practitioner is minimizing their struggles. If you are new to this skill, we suggest you begin by using the more tentative format of asking for clients' views of the normalcy of their difficulties. With experience, it will be easier to use the direct approach. Most important will be how carefully you listen and respond to what your clients say in response to your normalizing. No matter what the response, you will want to listen carefully for clues about what the clients might want different. In the preceding example, the mother may say she agrees that Tim's behavior is troublesome to her but probably normal for a teenager and that she wants to work on developing new, less emotionally charged ways of responding to coworkers when they tell her about Tim's behaviors. Less commonly, she may become even more intense in response to your normalizing, insisting on giving you more details about the extremes to which Tim's behavior can go, as if to persuade you that his is no ordinary problem. When you affirm her perceptions and ask how you can be useful, she will likely respond that she and her husband have to find a way to reach Tim before it is too late. In both cases, formulating your next question around what she wants different will move your conversation in a productive direction. Normalization is useful in solution building because it offers clients a chance to depathologize their difficulties, and it helps both clients and practitioners to clarify what clients want different.

DVD (See DVD Clips 1 and 19.)

Returning the Focus to the Client

Experience at BFTC, and at other facilities where the procedures described in this book are in use, confirms that many clients are able to create more satisfying and productive lives by developing well-formed goals and taking steps to turn these goals into realities. In both parts of this process, the client does the work. Usually, the client needs to do something different from what he or she has done in the past.

Our observations indicate that most clients, when describing their problems and attempting to articulate what they want to achieve through their relationship with the practitioners, talk about what they would like *others* to do differently. They tend to talk as though they are powerless in their circumstances and at the mercy of others. They make statements like these:

- My kids are lazy. They don't want to get up in the morning, and they lay around a lot during the day just watching TV. They don't seem to realize that I need help sometimes.

- I wish my parents would join the 21st century. I'm 15, and they still have this ridiculous curfew that I have to be in by 10 o'clock at night during the week.

- My child is doing very poorly in school. I think a lot of it has to do with the fact that he has special learning needs, which his teachers don't know how to handle.

- If my boss would only stop talking down to me. Sometimes he treats me like I'm a child.

- My husband has a horrible temper, and when he loses it, he hits out. I think it is because he was kicked around a lot when he was growing up. When he gets mad like that, I get really scared because I don't want to get hit.

It is important to listen to and respect these perceptions because they represent how clients view these parts of their lives at the time they are speaking, but in order to move from a sense of powerlessness to a sense of empowerment, clients will have to shift their focus. They will have to focus less on what they do not appreciate about other people and their current circumstances and more on what they want to have happen differently in the situation and how they see themselves participating in a solution.

As practitioners, we can often help clients make this shift. The following are questions you can ask to invite your clients to return the focus to themselves:

- What tells you that your children can be more helpful?

- When things are going better, what will be happening differently? What will others notice you doing differently?

- What's it going to take to make things even a little bit better?

- Suppose your boss were here and I asked him what you could do differently to make it just a little easier for him not to talk down to you. What do you think he would say?

- What gives you hope that this problem can be solved?

- Suppose a miracle happened tonight while you were sleeping and the problem we are talking about was solved by tomorrow morning. Assume that you didn't know that the miracle had happened, because you were asleep. What is the first thing you would notice that would tell you that things were better? What would others notice about you that would tell them you were doing better?

- Are there times already in your life that are like this miracle you are describing?

Some of these questions explicitly ask clients to shift their focus to themselves, while others do so implicitly. Because inviting clients to make this shift is such an important part of what de Shazer (1994) calls the change from problem talk to solution talk, many examples of such questions are presented throughout this book.

DVD (See DVD Clips 1, 2, and 3.)

Noticing Hints of Possibility

Witkin (2000) states: "Noticing involves extracting something from a context." We never notice everything that there is to notice in any given context.

For example, in a conversation, we are more likely to notice and ask about those things the other person says that catch our interest or we believe are important. Noticing reflects the interests, beliefs, and assumptions of the person doing the noticing. Given what we have already written about solution building, we believe that it is very important for interviewers to pay attention to and notice statements clients make that could become the occasion to start a conversation about some aspect of building a solution.

As clients describe their situations, they usually focus on what and who are troublesome and painful to them. It is important to listen to these concerns to orient yourself to their situation, discern who and what are important to them, and let them know they are being heard. However, it is equally important to recognize that getting into countless, repetitive details about their problems can also discourage both them and you about their prospects for solutions. In interviewing, one of the biggest challenges is to not get caught up with clients in detailed conversation about problems. One way to avoid this tendency is to be alert to anything clients say that suggests they might want something different, that they have had a past success, or that they already have tried to improve their situations. These are the hints of possibility all clients include in their conversations with practitioners, although often without being aware of doing so.

Listening for and noticing hints of possibility are key aspects of what it means to be a solution-focused practitioner. What follows is part of an interview with a mother whose children have been removed from her care because of domestic violence and whose husband is under a restraining order to prevent contact between him and his wife or children. As you read it, try to identify the hints of possibility.

> After Children's Protective Services took the children the first time, Ed moved us up north and everything started falling apart as usual. Nothing changed. He still kept drinking. He still had violent moods. He's never hit on me in front of the girls (the two daughters now in foster care) before then. This time was the first time that he has hit me in front of the girls like that. Suzy has seen it all, the whole nine yards. It scares me to death because this is something that I know is going to live with her for the rest of her life. I'll do almost anything to protect her from that. I'll tell her that it's not OK, and I'll guide her through and help her. I know it's going to bother her, and I know she might be having dreams too because I know at the children's shelter she was having dreams.

In this interview, it would be very easy for the practitioner to focus on problems and ask for more details about them. The interviewer might ask about why Protective Services took the children the first time, exactly what fell apart up north, the details regarding Ed's drinking and violent moods, and so forth. It would be more difficult to notice that this mother may want to work with a professional to build ways to help her daughter cope with the consequences of having observed the violence between her parents ("I'll do almost anything to protect her from that") and already seems to have ideas about how to help Suzy ("I'll tell her that it's not OK, and I'll guide her through and help her").

These are the hints that indicate what is worth getting details about. You can do so by first drawing the client's attention to the hint and then beginning a series of questions for details.

- You say you'll do almost anything to protect Suzy from what she has seen. Knowing her and her reactions the way you do, what do you think it will take to protect her? When she gets to the point where she is protected from the bad consequences of what she's seen, what will be different about Suzy that will tell you that now she is protected? What else will you see?

- You also say that you'll tell her it's not OK and you'll guide and help her. It seems like you already have some ideas about what you can do. Is that correct? What are those ideas? Have you done some of those things already? Which have made the most difference? What have you seen already that tells you those things made a difference? What would Suzy say you have done so far that has been most helpful to her?

By beginning the conversation about any hint by restating the client's words or incorporating the client's words into the next question, you invite your client to turn to a conversation about the details of solution possibilities rooted in his or her frame of reference.

DVD **(See DVD Clips 1 and 3.)**

Exploring Client Meanings

Clients often wonder about the meaning of events in their lives and sometimes ask their practitioners for their thoughts about these meanings: "So after my friend died, I lost all my motivation to go out and see people. I wonder what was going on with me." In many approaches, the practitioner offers an interpretation for the client to think about: "Often, people who have had a major loss are struggling to get control of their emotions and isolate themselves from others. Do you think that might have been happening with you?"

In solution building, we do not attempt to interpret clients' experiences for them. We have not found that solutions come from conversations about why events and experiences happen as they do. If a client asks a question like the preceding, for example, at the beginning of our work with the client, we would ask for more information about what is happening in the client's life that indicates to him or her that he or she is "losing all my motivation to go out and see people." As the client describes these events, we would empathically acknowledge the difficulty of the client's situation, listen for what seems important to the client in it, and notice any hints about what the client might want.

This does not mean that we are uninterested in the meanings of client experiences. Rather, as with other aspects of solution building, we rely on client expertise. The meanings that are most useful in solution building are those attached to past successes and future possibilities, not to problems. Two not-knowing questions are commonly used to invite clients to struggle with and construct their own meanings. The first involves asking if something clients did in the past or are contemplating doing in the future might be useful or helpful. For example, a client who is struggling with substance use might tell you that she participated in residential treatment in the past. You might ask her if the treatment was useful and, if she says yes, more specifically what it was about the treatment that was useful. Another way to ask essentially the same question is, "What difference has the treatment made in your life?" The same questions for client meanings can be asked about future possibilities. For example, to a client who is at odds with his boss about his pay level and is thinking about talking to his boss in a way that he has described in some detail, you might ask, "So, suppose you decide to talk to your boss this way, what do you think will be different between you and him?" In working to formulate an answer, the client is constructing the meaning of a possible future action, a meaning that may be useful to him in deciding whether to actually take the action.

There is another thing to notice about the way solution building works with client meanings. Besides asking for meanings associated with client successes and possibilities, we also ask primarily for interactional meanings. Consequently, in the preceding example, in which the client is considering talking to his boss in the different way that he has just described, we would ask, "So suppose you decide to talk to your boss this way; what do you think will be different between you and him?" Our increasing awareness that interactional meanings are those of most use to clients leads us rarely if ever to ask, "So how do you feel about talking to your boss that way?"

DVD (See DVD Clips 1, 2, and 3.)

Relationship Questions

Relationship questions are used in solution building to invite clients to construct descriptions of interactional events as well as their meanings. People live much of their lives in interaction with others, many of whom are tremendously important to them. When clients describe their problems and what they might like to have different in their lives, they regularly include references to their significant others (Mead, 1934): "My problem is that my daughter uses drugs and won't listen to me anymore"; "My husband and I are fighting all the time"; or "I'll know that things are going well when my boss and I can talk man-to-man about a raise." As an interviewer, you must find out who a client's significant others are and weave them into your questions so as to encourage clients to describe their situations, what they want different, and how to make solutions happen in interactional terms. If you do not know who the client's significant others are, it is easy to ask, "Who knows you well?"

To illustrate this way of questioning, suppose a client says that one thing he would like to have different is to talk differently to his daughter when she disobeys, instead of losing his temper and yelling at her. You can invite him to further define this emerging goal in interactional terms by asking, "Suppose you were no longer losing your temper with her and yelling. What would she notice you doing instead?" Assuming the father answers, "I'd be speaking to her more calmly and in a quiet voice," you could continue with, "When she notices that, what will she do?" As described previously, you can also invite the father to construct the meaning of these new possibilities in interactional terms by asking, "So when you are talking more calmly and in a quiet voice to her, what will be different between the two of you?" and "What would your daughter say will be different between the two of you when you are talking this way?" You can elicit more amplification of an emerging solution by asking, "Suppose you were to decide to talk to your daughter more calmly and in a quiet voice more often, what might be different between you and your wife?" "What else might be different between you and others in your house?" "What else might be different in your life?" These additional questions come from a recognition that whatever difference develops in the relationship between the client and his daughter might, in his mind, have implications for his relationships to others, and there-fore influence whether he eventually chooses to do something different in this area of his life. Very often, when the client initiates a positive change in one relationship, a ripple effect leads to positive changes in other relationships. Consequently, when answering such questions, the client tends to reinforce the attractiveness of the original possibility. These questions about clients' interactional contexts, which incorporate clients' significant others, are called *relationship questions*. They are a major way for you to invite clients to amplify their emerging solutions.

DVD **(See DVD Clip 2.)**

Amplifying Solution Talk

Solution talk between client and practitioner addresses what aspects of life the client wants to be different and the possibilities for making those things happen. We have provided examples of questions that invite clients to engage in a conversation around building solutions. Some clients more readily accept the invitation than do others. Clients who are reluctant may insist on returning to problem talk that focuses on what they do not like about their lives and other people. Most clients, however, will begin to participate in solution talk when you lead in that direction. Your task is to notice this switch to solution talk and encourage the client to provide as much detail as possible.

In the following example, Insoo invited a young man to amplify what would be happening differently in his life after his problem of using drugs was solved.

INSOO: So when your problem is solved, what would be different?

KENRICK: I wouldn't do drugs at all.

INSOO: So what would you do when you have these cravings?

KENRICK: Do something constructive so I won't think about it, which is just do anything, play basketball, just run, and just do something just to get it off me, or just go talk to somebody, you know.

INSOO: That helps?

KENRICK: Yeah.

INSOO: [recalling his comment that he was drug-free during a previous stay in the hospital] Is that what helped when you were in the hospital?

KENRICK: Yeah, you know, just make jokes or something.

INSOO: Making jokes helps?

KENRICK: Yeah, when you sit there talking to a bunch of people and everybody is laughing 'cause [of] something you said, you know, it makes you feel good. Then it's like you don't need no drugs to do that.

INSOO: I see. Do you have a good sense of humor?

KENRICK: Yeah.

INSOO: Is that what other people tell you?

KENRICK: Yeah.

INSOO: Really? Have you always been that way?

KENRICK: Yeah.

INSOO: Ah-ha. And you are saying that helps you?

KENRICK: Yeah, it helps me.

INSOO: What else helps you to cope with the cravings?

KENRICK: My kids.

INSOO: Your kids? How do they help you?

KENRICK: 'Cause they remind me of my craving. It's like when I be around them, you know, I be thinking about some dirty stuff to do, to go get some drugs, and my oldest son he talks to me—you know, when these cravings come up—and it's like I look at him and pay attention to him, and then I do something constructive with him and then while we do something it's like ... [silence]

INSOO: Like what? What constructive thing?

KENRICK: We write his name; we do numbers, ABCs, you know.

INSOO: Do you? You teach him how to?

KENRICK: Yeah.

INSOO: Oh, OK. That helps?

KENRICK: Yeah.

INSOO: And you like doing that?

KENRICK: Yeah.

INSOO: [*noticing affection in his voice*] He likes that apparently?

KENRICK: Yeah. He does.

INSOO: You must love him very much.

KENRICK: Yeah, I love all my kids very much.

In this dialogue, Insoo invited Kenrick to talk about what his life would be like when his problem was solved. Noticing both that he had some ideas about how his life would be different and that he was putting the focus on *what he would be doing differently,* she worked hard to have him amplify these differences. She was not content with his statement that his life would be different because he would not be doing drugs. She asked for more information: What would he do when he had cravings? Kenrick answered in more detail and more concretely: He would "play basketball," "run," "talk to somebody," and "make jokes." Insoo asked how doing these things, in particular making jokes, would be helpful; that is, what the meaning or significance of jokes were to him. Kenrick amplified more by offering an interactional meaning. He explained that when others laugh at his jokes, he can feel good without using drugs. Insoo also asked, "What else helps you to cope with the cravings?" Kenrick was able to add more information about doing constructive things with his children.

In solution building with clients, you must work hard to amplify any solution talk that your clients offer. Solution talk is very useful to counter the sense of powerlessness that many clients are experiencing when they first come for services. At first, clients focus on their problems and how these problems make their lives difficult. Once the practitioner invites clients to talk in detail about what they want to have different in their lives and how that might happen, they become more hopeful and even confident about their possibilities. To a certain degree, empowerment is a matter of perception. It is a state of mind that is heightened by clients' solution talk.

Reread the dialogue between Kenrick and Insoo and look for examples of the basic skills discussed in this chapter. There are examples of careful listening, echoing, open questions, paraphrases, noticing the client's nonverbals, compliments, affirming the client's perceptions, natural empathy, keeping the focus on the client, noticing hints of possibility, and exploring client meanings. In this brief segment of dialogue, Insoo integrates practically all of the basic skills into her work. The same is true of the DVD produced to accompany this book. Each DVD clip integrates the basic skills and identifies them periodically through titles on the bottom of the screen.

DVD (See DVD Clips 2 and 3.)

LEADING FROM ONE STEP BEHIND

We try to work in ways that allow clients to be the experts about their own experiences and what these mean. However, this does not mean being passive with clients and waiting patiently for them to express themselves. You can be most useful to clients when you are active and, in a certain sense, lead them. However, we believe that you will lead best when you *lead from one step behind*

(Cantwell & Holmes, 1994). You must adopt a posture of not knowing and develop interviewing skills that allow clients to provide information about themselves and their situation. In our experience, practicing these skills promotes client trust, confidence, and hopefulness about the future.

NOTES

1. In the dialogues in this book, italicized words or phrases within brackets usually identify the skills or procedures being used by the practitioner. On occasion, they indicate what the practitioner noticed or was thinking at that point in the interview.

2. What the client brings to the interaction also influences how the client perceives the practitioner's responses. Practitioners who have integrated the listening and responding skills into their way of being with clients will listen for and attempt to respond appropriately to these differences among clients.

4

Getting Started:
How to Pay Attention
to What the Client Wants

Tell me, and I'll forget. Show me, and I may not remember. Involve
me, and I will understand.
(NATIVE AMERICAN SAYING)

Chapter 2 identified several stages of the solution-building process: describing
the problem, developing well-formed goals, exploring for exceptions, formulating and delivering useful feedback to clients, and measuring and amplifying client
progress. In Chapters 4 through 10, we proceed through these stages and discuss the
skills appropriate to each and their application in different practice situations. We
will demonstrate the skills with dialogues from cases we have encountered.

This chapter focuses on how to get started with clients. We limit our
discussion to the conversation between practitioner and client. We have chosen
not to discuss here how the intake information forms that many agencies ask new
clients to complete can be designed along solution-building lines. We delay that
topic until Chapter 13, where we address how agency forms and documentation
become transformed when practice with clients shifts to solution building.

WHEN YOU FIRST MEET YOUR CLIENT

Names and Small Talk

You would rarely meet a client for the first time without having at least some
information about the client and his or her concerns. Typically, you would get a
completed intake form or some referral information before seeing a client. That

information minimally would include the client's name and some data about the client's family, school, and work contexts. Different practitioners use that information in different ways. We think it is important to use it in ways that set a tone of respect and empowerment right from the beginning.

When introducing ourselves to clients, we ask them how they would like to be addressed. We also tell them that we would be comfortable being called Insoo or Peter. We think it is a good idea in the beginning to ask some questions about how clients spend most of their workday time. While some practitioners view such questions mainly as icebreakers that make it easier for the client and practitioner to get started together, we have found that they begin to uncover useful solution-building information. Often, in answering these questions, clients begin to reveal what and who are important to them, as well as some areas of strength. Here is an example of how Peter began with a client we will call Christine.

PETER: Hello. Welcome. [motioning toward one of the empty chairs] Please take a seat over here.

CHRISTINE: Thanks.

PETER: [looking at the intake form in his hand] I see from what you wrote down here that your name is Christine Williams. To start out with, what would you like me to call you? Christine? Ms. Williams? Something else?

CHRISTINE: Well, my friends call me Christi. I like that.

PETER: OK. And I'd be comfortable if you would call me Peter. Is that OK with you?

CHRISTI: Yeah, I think I could do that.

PETER: OK, that's settled for now anyway. We can make changes on it later if we decide we want to. So, Christi, tell me, how do you like to spend your time?

CHRISTI: Ah, well, a lot of my time goes to my college classes, but right now that is not what I enjoy doing. I like to travel, going to different places. I like to socialize. I like to read. [an embarrassed laugh] I like pleasure reading, not the reading for my courses right now. And I like the outdoors, biking, and playing tennis. Mostly, right now, I like to socialize.

PETER: Socialize? You mean with friends?

CHRISTI: Yeah, both with friends and my family. Right now, I'm spending a lot of time with my friends, maybe too much.

PETER: So you like to talk with people. Is that something you are good at?

CHRISTI: [laughs] Yeah, people like to talk to me, both about fun things and their problems. They seem to want to come to me and discuss what's bothering them. I try to help them.

PETER: Is that right?

CHRISTI: Yeah, I don't put them down for their problems, and I think I'm a pretty good problem solver.

PETER: Is that right? Do they tell you that?

CHRISTI: [smiling] Yeah, they do. They thank me too. I guess that's a main reason that I want to be a social worker.

PETER: Yeah. Already I can begin to understand what you say. You seem to have a real cheerful and easy way about you. I can see that you would be easy to talk to.

CHRISTI: Thanks, but that's part of the reason I'm here. I'm spending too much time with other people and not enough with my school work. That's what I really want to talk about.

Peter's interview with Christi occurred in a professional setting. Sometimes, however, you might find yourself interviewing clients in their homes. Insoo has written about how to get started with clients in this setting (Berg, 1994, pp. 22–23). She suggests that, once invited inside a client's home, the practitioner can notice something nice or attractive or something into which the client has clearly put a lot of effort. The practitioner can also ask questions about family pictures that he or she sees. Such observations and questions put the client into the role of expert and, at the same time, demonstrate respect for the client and uncover interests and strengths. Often, meeting clients where they live makes it easier to begin work because the items on display reflect what interests the clients, and the practitioner can immediately begin to ask questions about those items. Usually, clients are also more relaxed because they are in a familiar place.

Clarifying How You Work

Before going too deeply into the client's concerns, it is a good idea to clarify how you prefer to organize your work sessions with clients and check to see whether that organization is acceptable. Adopting the approach developed at BFTC (de Shazer et al., 1986), we have found it useful to organize sessions by first interviewing clients about their concerns, goals, exceptions, and strengths.

Once this information has been gathered, we like to take a 10-minute break to formulate some end-of-session feedback based on the information obtained. Sometimes we work with a team (with the prior permission of the clients). The team observes the interview through a one-way mirror and can help in developing the feedback. More often we work alone, and the break time allows us to collect our thoughts and decide what feedback would be most useful to the clients in building a solution. In either case, we regularly inform the clients how we prefer to work.

PETER: Before we get into your concern, let me tell you how I like to work and see if that is OK with you. What I'd like to do today is talk with you for about 30 to 40 minutes and then take a 10-minute break to think about what you told me. During the break, if you want, you can get something to drink from the waiting area or you can stay here if you prefer. After 10 minutes or so, I'll be back with some feedback and possibly a suggestion or two for you. Is that OK?

CHRISTI: Sure, that's fine.

Clients are very accepting of how we wish to proceed. We will discuss the advantages of this approach in a later chapter.

DVD **(See DVD Clip 1.)**

PROBLEM DESCRIPTION

Asking for Client Perceptions and Respecting Client Language

To work within the client's frame of reference, you must assume a posture of not knowing. You must ask for, listen to, and affirm the client's perceptions. As you do so, take note of the words the client uses.

At this stage, it is especially tempting for practitioners to listen to clients with the ears of an expert. The helping professions, with their emphasis on problem solving, have all generated elaborate categorizations of possible client problems. Once educated in these, we can apply them and easily lose our focus on exploring the client's frame of reference. In the following dialogue, Peter works at taking a posture of not knowing in exploring Christi's concern.

PETER: So, how were you hoping I could help you? You said earlier that you came here today because you are spending too much time with other people and not enough with your school work.

CHRISTI: Well, ah, I have this disease that a lot of people tend to get in their fourth year of college—senioritis. That's what I have.

PETER: What tells you that you have senioritis?

CHRISTI: Um, I can see the change from my past three years. In this year, I'm just not motivated. I'm interested in my classes this year because they are my major classes, but it's like I'm tired and bored with the whole study process. So that's how it is. I'm just tired of it.

PETER: Mm hmm.

CHRISTI: Like, last year when I had a test or a paper, like, I would get really, really stressed out and devote all of my time to studying, or reading, or being on top of things. This year I don't get stressed out. It's not like I don't study but ... but I don't study as much.... I guess I just don't care as much.

PETER: Uh, does that pretty much say it, or is there more? Is it senioritis—your getting bored, not being motivated, not studying as much—or is there more?

CHRISTI: [slowly] I guess that's about it.

What Is the Client's Understanding of How the Problem Affects the Client?

It is tempting to assume you know what the client's perceptions and experiences mean to the client. In the dialogue with Christi, it would be easy for Peter to assume that senioritis is a problem for her because she is studying less and getting poorer results and so she wishes that she were working as hard as she did last year. However, it is important to always take the next step and make sure the client tells you how this problem is a problem for him or her. Peter got some unexpected and important information when, instead of making assumptions, he asked further questions.

PETER: So, how is your senioritis a problem for you? [*checking out his assumption that Christi is probably doing worse*] By the way, are you doing worse in school this year, or better?

CHRISTI: [laughing] That's what's weird. I'm doing the same. I can't figure it out. But it's not like I don't study at all. It's more like I'm not as into it as I used to be.

PETER: Yeah, that confuses me too. In what sense, then, is this a problem for you?

CHRISTI: Well, just because I feel guilty that I'm not stressed out about this—because, like, I'm getting this expensive education and I should be putting in as much time and getting as much out of this as I can. And I think last year I really did, and this year I'm just trying to get by or whatever.

PETER: So, part of what you would like to have different as a result of our talking is for you to get more out of this education?

CHRISTI: [hesitating] Well, yeah. Well, maybe I'd just like to maybe make the guilt go away.

PETER: Well, ah, what's more important? Is it more important to make the guilt go away, or is it more important to get more out of the education?

CHRISTI: I think they are combined because if I get more out of the education, then I think I won't be feeling guilty feelings.

PETER: Is there anything else that you can tell me that you would like to get out of coming here, besides what you already told me?

CHRISTI: Um, no.

In addition to checking his assumptions, Peter's questions served a second purpose. They gave Christi a chance to reflect carefully on her perceptions—at this point, perceptions about just how her problem affects her.

Client perceptions about anything are more or less fluid and shifting. Given time and not-knowing questions, clients regularly reflect, explore, rethink, struggle to put their thoughts into words, and sometimes shift their perceptions.

For example, Christi seems to have shifted or expanded her sense of her problem from lowered motivation for her studies to guilt. She feels guilty because she is not "getting as much out of this as I can" and because of the cost of college. (Later in the interview, she reported that her parents are paying for much of her tuition.)

Peter did not cause Christi's shift in the perception and definition of her problem by the interviewing techniques he used. Rather, we believe, her perception shifted as a result of the interaction between the two of them. Many clients seek help with problems or concerns that are poorly articulated. It is useful to them and clarifying for us to interact around the meaning of their problems. Peter's part in the interaction with Christi was to engage her in a conversation about how senioritis was a problem for her; his questions were an invitation to interact around the meaning of her problem. Her part was to accept the invitation and work to put her sense of senioritis into words. Their interaction led her to expand or reshape her definition of senioritis.

What Has the Client Tried?

It is a good idea to ask clients what they have tried so far to solve their problems. Clients usually have taken some steps to redress their problems, and these attempts generally have been more or less successful. Asking the question sends the message that we think clients are competent—that is, they have the capacity to make good things happen in their lives. Clients sometimes can tell us in concrete terms what they have done to try to make a difference. By adopting the posture of not knowing, we can learn about their successes and the strengths they used to make the successes happen. Sometimes, clients describe a few things they have tried but indicate that nothing has worked very well. At other times, they say nothing has worked, and they are at the end of their rope. Christi fell somewhere between the extremes.

PETER: Have you tried anything to cure yourself of this disease?

CHRISTI: Yeah, yeah. I don't really go to the library a lot anymore. Like, last year I used to go to the library every night, and this year I go maybe once a week. But I try to study in different places.

PETER: Is that helpful—to study in different places?

CHRISTI: Yeah, yeah, it is. I don't, like, try and say that I'm going to study, like, six hours tonight. Instead, if I feel like reading, I'll read, but if I don't, I don't make myself.

PETER: And if you don't make yourself, what's different?

CHRISTI: Well, I don't study.

PETER: Mm hmm, and does that help with the disease?

CHRISTI: Yeah, because before, when I didn't feel like studying, I would make myself, even though I didn't like it. But now, I just don't.

PETER: Hmm, and you're doing about as well as you did last year. [she nods her head] So, I'm wondering again, how is this a problem for you?

CHRISTI: I guess because of the guilt. I'd like the guilt to go away.... I guess I really haven't done anything to make the guilt go away.... Maybe I could study more, but I don't feel like it.

PETER: Is there anything else you've tried?

CHRISTI: Uh, I can't think of anything else. I really should do something about this.

The dialogue had come full circle. Although Christi said that she had tried studying in different places, she was unable to identify how this was helpful. If she had, Peter would have spent time exploring this as a success and asking where she got the idea to do this and how she went about making it happen. Instead, having come back to the guilt and having heard there was nothing else that she had tried, Peter chose to move on.

What Is Most Important for the Client to Work on First?

We sometimes encounter clients who, when asked, lay out problem after problem, until our heads are spinning. Usually this problem description is mixed with theories about where the problems come from and how they are interconnected. Clients can feel overwhelmed. With such clients, there are several things a practitioner can do. We usually acknowledge how difficult things seem to the client and then simply ask, "Which of these is the most important to work on first?" When the client gives an answer—and practically all do—we follow up by asking, "What is happening in your life that tells you it is important to work on that first?" These questions illustrate again how solution building both works with client perceptions and respects client self-determination.

DVD (See DVD Clip 1.)

HOW TO WORK WITH CLIENTS
ON WHAT THEY MIGHT WANT

If practitioners ask how they can help, most clients respond by giving a description of their concerns or problems. In solution building, we are more interested in exploring what clients want to be different in their lives.

Sometimes, clients begin to specify what they want to be different as they talk about their problems. For example, Christi said she wanted to make the guilt go away and to get more out of her education. These statements are not well-formed goals yet, but they begin to articulate what differences she would like to see in her life.

Often clients talk about their problems in ways that give little or no hint of how they would like their lives to look when their problems are solved or partly solved. Instead, they seem intent on giving a detailed description of how these problems are horrible or difficult. They may also talk at length about what others are doing to make their lives difficult. Many clients are unable to specify strategies they have tried to remedy their situation. When asked about what they have tried, they quickly return to problem description and the fallout in their lives. As noted in Chapter 3, de Shazer (1994) calls this *problem talk*. By contrast, talk about what clients want to have happen differently in their lives is one aspect of *solution talk*. As a practitioner, you will first encounter the challenge of inviting your clients to shift from problem talk to solution talk at the point at which they have had enough time to describe their problems to feel heard. That point is usually 10 to 15 minutes into the first session.

In practice, opening and sustaining a dialogue around what the client might want may sometimes seems simple and easy to do, and at other times, more difficult. Practitioners often say that the most difficult situations in which to talk to clients about what they want is when clients have been pressured or coerced by someone else, such as a parent or the court, to meet with them. Regardless of the circumstances under which a client comes to you, your task as a practitioner at this point in the solution-building process remains the same—building a cooperative, working relationship with the client around a developing definition of what the client might want different in life and is motivated to make happen by doing something different. In the following sections, we examine different interviewing situations you may encounter in working with clients on what they might want, and what we have found useful to do in these situations to stay on a solution-building track.

When Clients Want Something and See Themselves as Part of a Solution

Here, the client and practitioner jointly identify a client concern and begin to build a picture of what the client wants different. In addition, it quickly becomes evident in the client's responses that the client sees herself as contributing to any eventual solution. Often, this interviewing situation occurs when clients have chosen of their own accord to come to us for services, because they have thought about what they want from their work with us and realize that getting what they want will require effort on their part.

The interaction between Christi and Peter is a good example of this situation. In their dialogue, Christi and Peter were successfully engaged in jointly identifying a concern: senioritis. They also jointly identified an initial statement of a goal: making the guilt go away. However, we cannot yet tell from this dialogue whether Christi sees herself as a part of the solution—that is, whether she perceives what she might do differently to build a solution to her senioritis. Nevertheless, Christi and Peter have made a good beginning. They have started a transition into solution talk by identifying, in general terms, what Christi wants. Christi does not view others as the source of her senioritis. Instead, she seems to view herself as part of any solution when she says, "I really should do something about this."

Interviewing Tips   Peter did nothing out of the ordinary to invite Christi to begin solution talking. He first asked Christi for descriptions of her concerns and what she had already tried. While she was giving information, he listened carefully to ascertain whether Christi was identifying a concern and whether she might want something different. When he heard that senioritis was her concern, he turned the dialogue toward her current perceptions of the meaning of senioritis in order to get her understandings of her concern. As she described these, he kept wondering to himself what the implications of these perceptions were for what she might want different in her life. He did not begin a detailed problem assessment. Together, they built an awareness that she did not necessarily want to study more or get higher grades, but rather was more interested in working on making the guilt go away. Having determined that Christi wanted something from their relationship, Peter knew they were now at a point at which they could begin to develop well-formed goals. This is the next stage of solution building, which is considered in detail in Chapter 5.

DVD (See DVD Clip 1.)

A Word of Caution

We want to emphasize that we are writing here about a process of building understandings or meanings between a practitioner and client, in this case between Peter and Christi. We have not labeled Christi as a particular type of client; for example, we have not described or diagnosed Christi as a cooperative or voluntary client. Thinking about clients as voluntary or involuntary or as cooperative or uncooperative can set up inaccurate expectations in practitioners' minds about the relative abilities of different clients to build solutions. We remain more hopeful about the possibilities for our clients when we resist thinking about them in such categories. It is more useful for our clients, and more empowering to us as practitioners, to think about what sort of understandings or meanings are being built between us and our clients.

When Clients Say Someone Else Needs to Change

Here, early on in their interaction, the practitioner and client are able to jointly identify a concern or problem but are not able to identify a role for the client in building a solution. Their dialogue reveals that often the client can describe a problem, and the importance of finding a solution, in detail. However, the client does not yet perceive that he or she is part of the solution. Instead, the client believes that the solution will require change on the part of someone else—perhaps a spouse, child, employer, friend, or coworker. Following is an example of this type of interviewing situation.

INSOO: How can I help you?

ALICE: I sure hope there is hope for my son. He has never been what you would call a motivated child, but he has been worse lately. He is a smart kid, but does he study? No. He has always been on the lazy side. His father was like that—no ambition in life. Only thing he cared about was to hang out with his buddies and being wild. I'm afraid that my son is turning out to be just like his father. He won't come home on time, won't do anything to help out around the house. Now skipping school is all he does.

INSOO: So, how can I be of help to you?

ALICE: I don't know what to do with him anymore. Whenever he doesn't come home, I'm a wreck worrying about him. There is lots of violence out there on the street. Mothers worry about stuff like that. Of course, his father is another story. When he ran off with that woman, all he saw was the woman. His kids didn't matter to him. I begged him to think about the kids, but does it matter? Hell, no. Now I'm stuck with working to keep the family together, but he doesn't appreciate anything I do.

In the preceding example, Insoo and Alice are developing a joint understanding of a problem—the low motivation of Alice's son, and his negative behavior. However, there is nothing there to suggest that Alice sees what she can do differently to begin building a solution. She seems to feel powerless in the situation and problem talks about her son and his father. Initially, conversations between us and our clients often resemble the Insoo-Alice dialogue. People who already perceive themselves as a major part of any solution are more able and likely to take steps on their own. As a practitioner, this means you have to be able to work with clients who, at first, do not see themselves as part of any eventual solution.

Interviewing Tips   In the situation described here, the client often wants the practitioner to change the person (or persons) to whom the client attributes the problem—whether a spouse, child, or coworker. If the problematic person is not already present, the client may ask whether the practitioner thinks it would be a good idea to meet that person. In other words, the client wants the practitioner to fix the other person.

In many situations, it is not realistic or possible for the troublesome party to come in for services. In that case, the client may want instruction from the practitioner on how to change the problematic person. Last, it is possible that the client only wants to express frustration and disappointment with the important people in his or her life and is not really looking to see anyone or anything changed. The client only wants the practitioner to listen.

It is a common belief that clients who do not take responsibility for creating change in their lives need to be educated that blaming others is not going to solve their problems. Egan (2002, pp. 185–190) writes that practitioners must learn "to challenge" clients' "outmoded, self-limiting mind-sets," "self-limiting and self-defeating internal behavior," and "self-defeating external behaviors," all of which can lead to blaming others for problems and block taking steps to solve one's own problems. We disagree. In our experience, challenging or confronting clients' current perceptions is not the most useful approach. We prefer to employ the skills outlined in Chapter 3. With these skills, we attempt to respect the client's current perceptions but at the same time shift the focus from the problematic others to the client and any role he or she might feel able to play in any positive change. Through our questions, we invite the client to shift from problem talk to solution talk. Insoo began this process with Alice.

INSOO: I can see that you have a very serious problem on your hands, and I wonder what do you suppose needs to happen so that your son will be a little bit easier to live with?

ALICE: He has to go to school first. I keep telling him that he won't get anywhere in life without an education.

INSOO: That's a big one. I don't know how he is going to do that, but suppose, just suppose, that somehow he goes to school and stays in school. If that were to happen, what would your son be saying about how you are different with him now?

ALICE: He wants me to not nag him so much. That's what he probably would say—not nagging him and maybe even talking to him nice. Actually, once he starts going to school and doing what I tell him to do, there is no reason why I should nag him. He has no idea how much I worry about him.

INSOO: I'm sure you do. You seem to care about him very much.

Notice that Insoo did not challenge Alice's perception of the problem or who needed to do the changing. She accepted Alice's perception that it would be helpful to Alice if her son would do things differently. She then attempted to bring the focus of the conversation from what is wrong with the son (problem talk) to Alice herself by asking Alice to suppose that her son were indeed different in the ways that she wanted. As Alice began thinking about this possibility, Insoo asked what differences Alice's son might see in her behavior toward him in that situation. Alice accepted the invitation to change the focus and begin solution talking by saying she would probably "not nag him so much." In accepting the invitation, she opened up the possibility that she, in conversation with Insoo, could build new perceptions about what she might do differently with her son as steps toward a solution—things like nagging him less and "talking to him nice." In addition, she opened up the possibility of changing her perception of what she wanted to work on with Insoo. The next task for Insoo would be to pick up on the solution talk and ask Alice to say more about precisely what it means to her to nag less and talk nicely more often and how she might conceivably go about doing this. This is a matter of developing well-formed goals, which will be addressed in Chapter 5.

What If the Client Refuses the Invitation to Solution Talk?   Students and workshop participants often ask us, "What do I do if the client does not accept my invitation to solution talk and continues to criticize and blame others for his or her problems?" This is an important concern, because many clients do just that.

There are several things you can do. One is to bring the focus back to the client periodically by asking, "What is happening that tells you this problem might be solved?" You can also ask, "How were you hoping I might be useful to you?" Another possibility is to ask the client what the chances are of finding a solution, on a scale from 0 (no chance) to 10 (every chance), and then to ask the client to explain the scale value chosen. If the client seems overwhelmed by his or her problems, you can turn to coping questions. These ways of responding are considered in later chapters, especially Chapters 8 through 10.

DVD (See DVD Clip 13.)

When Clients Seem Uninterested or Resistant to Changing

Expect that in practice there will be times when clients start out by talking as though they have no interest in working on something with you. They may tell you they do not have a problem or it is someone else who has the real problem. Clients who have been pressured into services—for example, by courts, children's protective services, schools, or parents—often start out talking this way. They may be confused, frustrated, or even very angry about having to see a practitioner.

Practitioners frequently tell us that this is the most difficult situation in which to get started with clients. The best way to describe how we think and work in this situation is to look at a characteristic case in detail.

Beth: Background Information   Recently, Insoo was asked to consult on the case of a 15-year-old, whom we will call Beth Visser. Even before Insoo met the client or was given any background information about the case, she was told that both social services and Beth's parents had "had it" with Beth. The social worker told Insoo that Beth had "burned all her bridges," that she would most likely "end up in a treatment center for a long time," and that she certainly needed it. Clearly, the social worker was very frustrated with Beth and unsatisfied with how the case was turning out, despite the countless hours she had devoted to problem solving with Beth.

The social worker described Beth as having a core problem—being "uncontrollable, impulsive, and manipulative." The social worker also described the many things she had tried, with considerable expertise, from her problem-solving perspective to change Beth's core problem. She had "tried to talk some sense into" Beth by pointing out her mistakes, reasoned with her, pointed out inconsistencies between Beth's claims and the facts, threatened to send her into residential treatment, cajoled her, recommended probation and seen her placed on probation for a year, arranged for individual therapy with a psychologist, arranged for in-home treatment with another therapist who worked with the whole family, and placed her in a treatment foster home. These increasingly restrictive and costly measures brought no real success in helping Beth stop her destructive behavior. The social worker was understandably frustrated and discouraged.

The social worker and others involved in Beth's case believed that all these attempts failed because of Beth's lack of cooperation. They agreed that her destructive behavior was caused by an underlying depressive tendency. Consequently, they believed that the only remaining treatment option was long-term, intensive individual therapy in a residential setting.

When Insoo encountered the case, the social worker was seeking approval and funding from the court to pay for this expensive, long-term service. She was hoping to place Beth in an out-of-state institution known to treat difficult adolescent cases. The worker favored an institution that was far away and relied on restrictive measures, because Beth had a history of running away and threatening suicide.

The latest crisis in Beth's case had occurred the previous evening, when police called at the Visser home after Beth reported child abuse at the hands of her father. Mr. Visser was handcuffed, taken into police custody, fingerprinted, and finally released on bond. In the meantime, Beth was taken to the hospital emergency room, examined, and released. She showed no evidence of physical abuse, such as broken skin or bruises. The social worker decided Beth would stay with a friend overnight until something more permanent could be worked out. The next day, Mr. and Mrs. Visser requested out-of-home placement for Beth immediately.

Insoo was invited to accompany the social worker to Beth's school, where the social worker planned to interview Beth about the previous evening's events. The interview took place in the principal's office. The social worker took the lead.

SOCIAL WORKER: So I understand there was another big fight with your parents last night. Your parents are pretty upset with you. What happened?

BETH: It's not my fault. My father pushed me against the wall for no reason. He always pushes me around. My friend was there, and she saw it, too. You can ask her. My mom always sides with my dad, but I'm telling you the truth. My dad pushed me against the wall for no reason at all. All I said was I wanted to go out and wanted some money. That's no reason to push me so hard that my head is busted open. I think it's child abuse.

SOCIAL WORKER: I saw the police report, and that's not what it says. Now, why do you think your dad hit you?

BETH: See, nobody believes me. Everybody says it's my fault.

SOCIAL WORKER: You know, Beth, you said there was blood on your head, but the police and the hospital reports say there is no medical evidence that your skin was broken.

BETH: [starting to cry and burying her head in her hands] Everybody is against me, and nobody believes me. Even my grandma says it's my fault, but I'm telling you that my dad pushed me. Ask my friend, Melodie. She was there and saw the whole thing. My dad pushed her, too.

SOCIAL WORKER: Well, it's hard to believe you. You don't always tell the truth, and this time, the hospital report says there is no evidence of blood anywhere. Well, you can't go home now, and we will have to find a temporary place for you to stay.

BETH: [continuing to cry] Everybody is against me. Now I have no place to go, and I am not going to a foster home again. They treated me like I was a pet or something.

SOCIAL WORKER: Don't you think you should be more honest about what happened? Remember how much trouble you got yourself into when you lied about the rape? Wouldn't it be better to be honest about what happened? So, what did really happen?

BETH: Nobody believes me. I am telling you the truth. This time my dad pushed me so hard my head cracked open, and I had a towel against my head, and I saw the blood on the towel. He hit me with a closed fist on this side of my head [pointing to the right side of her head].

SOCIAL WORKER: That's not what the report says. The police report says your dad admitted hitting you with an open hand.

BETH: That's a lie. You've got to believe me. I had to have a towel on my head [putting her right hand on the right side of her head], and when I took it off, there was blood on it.

SOCIAL WORKER: Beth, you have to be honest about these things.

BETH: [starting to cry again] See, everybody is against me. Nobody believes me, but I'm telling you the truth. You've got to believe me because I'm telling you the truth.

SOCIAL WORKER: I don't know what to believe anymore. Besides, I will have to find you a place to stay temporarily until we figure out what's best for you.

BETH: I want to go home, but I know my parents won't take me back. They are mad at me just because I stood up for my rights. I had to call the police, but my grandma says I shouldn't have done that. She won't even talk to me now. Everybody blames me now. Nobody cares about me.

SOCIAL WORKER: I'm trying to do what is best for you, Beth. And your parents say they don't want you home anymore. It means we have to find a place for you.

BETH: I don't want to go to no foster home. If I end up in a foster home again, I will run away or kill myself.

As the exchange continued, Beth became increasingly defensive and stuck with her original story. The more defensive she became, the more the social worker pointed out the facts from the police and hospital reports. Soon the exchange felt more like a tug-of-war than a useful conversation. Clearly, neither Beth nor the social worker felt understood, and both became increasingly frustrated as they remembered that their talks had ended in the same way before.

Interviewing Tip: Be Respectful and Curious about the Client's Perceptions
Cases such as Beth's—long-term cases that practitioners traditionally label as chronic, multiproblem, or difficult cases—present an enormous challenge. Despite the most careful assessments and the best practitioner intentions, such clients often seem uncooperative. They do not follow through on the interventions that practitioners have carefully designed. Consequently, most practitioners have come to expect resistance from many clients, and it has become standard practice in the field to write textbooks that teach beginning practitioners how to recognize and deal with client resistance. Beth's social worker was following one of the accepted procedures for handling client resistance by challenging or confronting (Egan, 2002; Hepworth, Rooney, & Larsen, 2002) Beth's claims of child abuse, which ran contrary to the facts of the police and hospital reports.

We approach such clients in another way. As stated in Chapter 3, we work from the posture of not knowing. When we begin to work with a client, we assume that the client's self-perceptions and perceptions about his or her circumstances make sense within the client's frame of reference at that point in time. Our job is to respectfully ask questions about the client perceptions that do not yet make sense to us. We assume the client is competent even when he or she reports information or observations that seem implausible to us.

Tip: Hold Clients Accountable for Their Perceptions   While respecting the client's perceptions as meaningful, we also hold the client accountable for those perceptions. For example, if a teenage client were to say, "I do better in school when I study less," we would begin to ask exploratory questions: "What is happening that tells you that you do better when you study less?" "How does studying less help you?" While such questions give the client responsibility for explaining his or her perceptions to the practitioner, they do so in a respectful fashion. They imply that the client is competent to perceive accurately and make meaningful statements about those perceptions. Paradoxically, even though such responsibility amounts to pressure on the client, we have found that, as de Shazer (1985) wrote, client resistance fades away.

When we begin a case, there are at least two matters we are genuinely curious about: first, clients' perceptions or understandings about themselves and their circumstances; and second, clients' perceptions about what they might want. We are equally concerned about both, whether clients come to us by their own choice or are required to meet with us. In cases like Beth's, however, in which clients are pressured or coerced to meet with practitioners, the clients' perceptions of their circumstances and what they might want from the professional relationship are profoundly influenced by how the clients got to the practitioner.

Tip: Pay Attention to How the Client Got to You   The manner in which a client enters the system of professional services affects the way in which client and practitioner begin their work together. So, from the outset, we pay careful attention to when and under what circumstances the client entered the system and how it is that the client comes to us for services at this particular time. This information tells us much about how to proceed with the client. In Beth's case, we see that Beth is not the only client. The social worker, Beth's parents, the court, and the school all want certain things to happen. When Insoo first encountered Beth's case, she had a better idea about what these collaterals in Beth's case wanted than about what Beth might want. Initially at least, the collaterals were the real clients. By paying attention to how Beth got to her, Insoo saw that Beth might be very unmotivated to follow through on what the collaterals wanted, and she recognized that she knew very little, if anything, about what Beth might want.

Paying attention to how the client gets into services is crucial because it can play such an important role in how the client views what the problem is and what and who need to change. It may be that, in Beth's view, the problem is not her charges of child abuse, her strained relationships with the courts and school, or her threats of running away and suicide. To Beth, the problem may be that her father is abusive and the system is intrusive. Her definition of the problem will affect her demeanor, what she might want to work on, and how she starts out responding to a practitioner.

Clients who are required to meet with practitioners by some collateral usually have been given some sort of mandate for what they are to accomplish from meeting with a professional—to stop drinking, get a job, be a good parent, go to school and stay off the street, stop being abusive, and so forth. These clients usually feel they have not been given a choice about the goal or the methods used to achieve it. They frequently see this mandate as punishment for no good reason, unfair, or evidence that "someone is out to get me." In these contexts, as Haley (1987) points out, collaterals expect practitioners to perform a social control function. Most coerced clients are aware of this and, therefore, expect their practitioners to listen more carefully to what collaterals want than to what they want.

The natural response to being coerced is defiance, resistance, and a desire to subvert others' attempts at control. Human beings somehow sense that they are being robbed of their dignity when they permit themselves to be controlled. Perhaps this is why, across history and cultures, resistance movements are a common response to oppression. This perspective allows us to make some sense of Beth's reaction to her social worker. Return to the exchange between Beth and the social worker and notice that the two were unable to jointly identify a problem: Beth perceived child abuse, whereas the social worker perceived Beth as stretching the truth and lying about the previous evening's events. In addition, they were not able to jointly settle on a goal: Beth said she wanted to go home, while the social worker did not think this possible and said she would have to find a place for Beth.

It is our observation that without a joint view of the problem and what the client wants, a client is unlikely to be invested in making changes, at least not the changes that others want for him or her. As noted earlier, many in the field believe that social workers should challenge or confront a client's denial and help the client to correctly perceive the problem and the need for change. For example, Ivey and Ivey (2007, p. 261) state: "Although all counseling skills are concerned with facilitating change, it is the confrontation of discrepancies that acts as a lever for *the activation of human potential*." It is the view of these authors that when the facts seem not to support the client's perceptions, the practitioner should try to get the client to change his or her view of the problem or goal through confrontation. However, changing another person's perceptions by confrontation is very difficult. The Iveys, like other writers, call confrontation a complex and advanced skill.

Tip: Listen to and Build on What the Client Wants   Let us return to Beth's case and see how Insoo went about paying attention to the client's perceptions and to how the client got to her, as they jointly worked on defining what Beth might want. The social worker, recognizing that she and Beth were repeating the same frustrating pattern of interaction, turned to Insoo and inquired whether she had any ideas about how to proceed. Insoo asked Beth whether she would be willing to answer a few questions about some matters that were not clear to Insoo.

INSOO: I have been sitting here and listening to how frustrated you are, Beth. How do you want your life to be different, if you could have your way?

BETH: [irritated] I told you, I want to go home. Nobody will let me go home.

By simply asking Beth what she wanted to have different in her life, Insoo established that what Beth really wanted was "to go home." Beth, like many clients in similar circumstances, having already said so much about what she did not believe and did not want, readily responded with what she did want when respectfully asked. It quickly occurred to Insoo that she and Beth might be able to develop a productive working relationship around Beth's going home, whereas Beth had no interest in a working relationship around the social worker's wish that she "tell the truth" or "be honest about what happened." Consequently, Insoo proceeded to ask for more details about what Beth said she wanted.

INSOO: I am confused, Beth. What about going home is so important to you?

BETH: Because I want to live with my parents, not in a foster home. I already have a home.

INSOO: I can see that it is important to you that you go home. Do you think your parents know that? I mean, do you think they know how important it is for you to live with them?

BETH: I love my parents, and they should know that.

INSOO: Do you think they do? I'm not sure they do. What would it take for them to know how much you love them and how much you want to live with them?

BETH: Well, I want to go home.

INSOO: OK, I can see that you really want to go home. So, what would it take for you to go home? I mean, what has to happen first so that you can go home, do you think?

BETH: My parents will have to say I can come home. But they won't say that because they are mad at me because of last night.

Insoo has invited Beth to expand on her wish to go home and live with her parents. As the conversation developed, Insoo became more convinced that this was what Beth really wanted. Consequently, she invited Beth to begin a dialogue on what it would take for that to happen. Notice how Insoo stayed with Beth's perceptions throughout. She asked for more information from a genuine posture of not knowing. She did not give Beth suggestions or advice because she realized that Beth would reject these just as Beth rejected the social worker's advice. Instead, Insoo asked Beth to expand on her perceptions to gain the clearest possible understanding of Beth's point of view. Even though this represented a lot of work for Beth because she might not have thought it through this way before, she seemed motivated to do it. We think this is because it was work around what she wanted to have happen.

INSOO: Well, I guess I can understand how angry they are at you today. So what would your parents say has to happen so that you can go home?

BETH: They think it's all my fault. But my dad really hit me.

It would be a mistake here to become distracted by Beth's apparent attempt to return to the previous night's events and who was to blame. The social worker had already been through that, and as usual, it led to an impasse. Like many clients who have no choice about seeing another practitioner, Beth has probably had many years of experience in debating the facts with adults, social workers, foster parents, psychologists, counselors, and many others who have tried to help her. Such debates about what really happened, why it happened that way, and whose fault it really was rarely lead to solutions. Instead, they usually lead to frustration and feelings of misunderstanding and hurt. It is more useful to circumvent such problem talk by acknowledging the client's perception of the facts and refocusing the conversation on what clients want and what they think it might take for that to happen. That is what Insoo chose to do with Beth.

INSOO: I can see that you believe that your dad really hit you. [with genuine curiosity] So, what has to happen so that you can go home?

BETH: My parents will say I have to apologize and promise that I will listen to them.

INSOO: How likely are they to believe you, if you were to apologize and promise to listen to them?

BETH: I know my dad is really mad at me.

INSOO: So, what would they say it will take for them to let you come home?

BETH: I will have to wait for a few days until he calms down, and then I will have to apologize to them.

Compare the results of the conversation between Beth and her social worker to those of the conversation between Beth and Insoo. Beth and her social worker reached an impasse. By contrast, Beth and Insoo together identified what Beth wanted and began to work on what it would take on Beth's part to make that happen. Insoo did her part by asking questions about Beth's perceptions from a posture of not knowing, and accepting Beth's perceptions as valid and under-standable. Insoo kept the focus on Beth and invited Beth to return to solution talk when she drifted back toward problem talk. Despite the perceptions of those who were thoroughly frustrated with Beth, Insoo assumed Beth was competent—competent to think and talk about what she wanted in tense and difficult circum-stances and competent to figure out and draw on the strengths and resources available to her.

In summary, here are some guidelines on how to get started when clients seem uninterested or resistant to changing:

- Assume the client has good reason to think and act as he or she does.
- Suspend your judgment and agree with the client's perceptions that stand behind his or her cautious, protective posture.
- Be sure to ask for the client's perception of what is in his or her best interest; that is, ask what the client might want. Accept the client's answer. (Implicit in asking someone a question is your willingness to accept that person's opinion.)
- Listen for and reflect the client's use of language, instead of trying to paraphrase the client's words into your way of speaking.

DVD **(See DVD Clips 8 and 9.)**

What if Clients Want What Is Not Good for Them?

This question usually arises when we talk to our workshop participants and students about accepting clients' perceptions regarding what they want. We rarely encounter clients who insist on wanting what we believe is not good for them. However, it could happen.

Let us suppose a client, Bill, tells us he thinks that continuing to use alcohol is good for him and for his family, and that is what he wants. What should we do? It is difficult to answer this question in the abstract because what a client says at one point in a conversation is tied to what has gone on before. Broadly speaking, however, our response would be the same as in the other situations we have discussed: We would respond from the posture of not knowing. We would assume the client is competent and ask him to amplify his perceptions: "What is happening in your life that tells you continuing to use alcohol is good for you? What tells you it is helpful to your family?" We might also invite Bill to think about what he wants from the perspective of his significant others by asking relationship questions: "Suppose I were to ask your wife about how continuing to use alcohol is helpful to your family? What do you think she would say? What would your children say?"

We believe it is possible to maintain a respectful posture even when clients seem to be saying they want something that, at first, seems unhealthy or even dangerous. If taken seriously and dealt with respectfully, a large majority of our clients are remarkably sensible about what they want, even in extreme circumstances. There is always the possibility that the practitioner, however reluctantly, may have to take away client self-determination in certain situations, but we recommend this only after several solution-building procedures have been used. We return to this topic when we discuss solution building in crisis situations (for example, cases that involve abuse and risk of suicide) in Chapter 10.

What if Clients Do Not Want Anything at All?

In a small minority of cases, the client may not seem to want anything at all from the professional relationship with you, even after you have employed several solution-building procedures over the course of a whole session. If this happens, it affects the feedback you give the client at the conclusion of the session. You would not, for example, suggest that the client do anything different at this time because the client has already told you several times by that point he or she does not want anything different. There are, however, useful things you can say to a client in this situation. We will discuss them when we consider end-of-session feedback in Chapter 7.

INFLUENCING CLIENT COOPERATION
AND MOTIVATION

Nearly every textbook on working with clients—whether in counseling, family therapy, medicine, nursing, psychology, social work, substance abuse treatment, vocational counseling, or other helping professions—discusses methods of managing client resistance, ambivalence, or noncompliance and enhancing client cooperation and motivation. Such discussions, while softening somewhat with the development of competency-based models in the field, continue to reflect themes traceable to a Freudian-influenced, medical model of helping people. Implicit in classifying clients as cooperative or resistant is the notion that the experts know what is best for their clients. When the client disregards the expert's learned opinion about the nature of the problem and fails to follow through on the professional's suggested course of treatment, such noncompliance often is attributed to deficiencies in the client involving distortion of reality or even some deep-seated personal pathology. In the medical model, the professional is rarely, if ever, held responsible for the mismanagement of the professional relationship.

The belief in client resistance is longstanding. As noted earlier in this chapter, practice textbooks consistently teach beginning practitioners to expect client resistance and, therefore, to listen for it when they work with clients. Once they think they perceive resistance, especially patterns of resistance, they are taught to challenge or confront it because clients are assumed to be incapable of change unless they own their problems.

Our more skeptical side prompts us to point out that this ideology of resistance and confrontation is self-serving for the field, which has a longstanding commitment to the medical model. The medical model assumes a subject-object relationship between practitioner and client; that is, the practitioner (as subject) is expected to change the client (as object) through the application of expert assessments and interventions. Consequently, if the client shows progress, the practitioner can take credit and feel competent. However, if the client does not show progress, the practitioner obviously cannot take credit. Practitioner and client may feel doubts about the effectiveness of the practitioner's services. However, the notion of client resistance lays most of the blame for lack of progress on the client and allows practitioners to distance themselves from responsibility.

In an article with a dramatic title, "The Death of Resistance," de Shazer (1984) claimed that the field's dominant conceptualization of client resistance more accurately represents the point of view, or construction of reality, of practitioners than it does any aspect of objective reality. Thinking along very different lines, he proposed that what practitioners took to be signs of resistance were instead the unique ways in which clients chose to cooperate. For example, clients who do not follow through on the therapeutic or problem-solving tasks assigned by their practitioners are not resisting but simply cooperating by telling their practitioners that the tasks do not fit their way of doing things (de Shazer, 1985, p. 21; 1991, p. 126).

Just as the notion of resistance flows from the assumptions of the medical model, de Shazer's reconceptualization of resistance as a form of cooperation is also bound to his assumptions. De Shazer assumes that clients are competent to figure out what they want (and need) and how to go about getting it. The practitioner's responsibility is to assist clients in uncovering these competencies and marshaling them to create more satisfying and productive lives for themselves, if that is what they choose to do.

Once we accept the notion of client competence, we are left with a humbling and challenging conclusion: What we once thought of as client resistance is more accurately regarded as practitioner resistance. Impasses and apparent failures in our work do not result from clients' resistance to our best professional efforts to make them well. Rather, they result from our failure to listen to clients and take seriously what they tell us.

In solution building, we do not seek to enhance client motivation by overcoming client resistance but by quieting our own frames of reference, so that we listen with solution-building ears and invite clients to participate in solution-building conversations. The Native American saying with which this chapter begins captures this view of motivation well.

> Tell me, and I'll forget. Show me, and I may not remember. Involve
> me, and I will understand.

We believe this saying could have been written by our clients.

As the case examples in this chapter have illustrated, client cooperation and motivation can change rapidly, depending on what clients see as useful or helpful to them. If the goal of the professional relationship is to be useful to clients, it is only respectful to ask clients for their definitions of problems, what they might want, and possibilities for solutions. For example, it would have been easy to dismiss as unrealistic Beth's wish to live with her family. Instead, Insoo noticed this hint of possibility and proceeded with her respectful questions. Insoo quieted her own frame of reference and opened a dialogue with Beth around what it would take for Beth to go home.

In solution building, the invitation for client participation begins at the first meeting and ends when the client indicates to us that the work is completed. Even someone with Beth's reputation may cooperate with her parents if her voice is heard and she is asked to help shape her own future. Beth might eventually decide that she needs to stay in a residential treatment facility for a time. If she comes to that conclusion through a respectful dialogue with her practitioner, she will be much more likely to cooperate with the program and much less likely to run away or make suicidal gestures. She will be a stakeholder in thinking through what is best for her and her own treatment. We believe such participation represents true empowerment.

We return to Insoo's conversation with Beth to show you how the two of them further developed a workable plan for the short term.

INSOO: It seems like a good idea that you need to wait for a few days until your parents calm down and apologize to them. So, what do you have to do during the next few days while you are waiting for the right time?

BETH: I guess I will have to keep coming to school every day, follow rules, and talk nice to my parents and not demand things from them. I know how to get along with Peggy's mother. I do my chores when I stay with them. Peggy's mom said I can stay there as long as I have to.

INSOO: Wow, you know lots of stuff. I guess they are right about you being smart. So tell me, how is it that Peggy's mom will let you come and stay with her family? Not everybody would want another 15-year-old in their home. [both laugh]

BETH: She is very nice. I like her a lot. I usually help out with the dishes, set the table, and all that stuff. I'm very neat when I stay at Peggy's. Her mom says I can come and stay with her as long as I need to because she says I help her a lot.

INSOO: Really, I can't believe this. Teenagers are supposed to be messy and all that stuff.

BETH: [laughing] Well, I am! But when I stay at my friends' house, I know how to behave.

This dialogue opens up and affirms a side of Beth that likely never would have emerged had Insoo not asked what Beth wanted, and pursued what it would take for that to happen. The conversation clearly reveals that Beth has strengths and past successes that she can draw on in moving toward what she wants. In addition, the longer the conversation continues along these solution-building lines, the more Beth will convince herself that she can be a helpful, neat, organized person. Insoo's task is to keep the solution talk going.

INSOO: Where did you learn this, Beth?

BETH: My mom and grandma.

INSOO: Do your mom and grandma know how much they taught you?

BETH: Yeah, but I don't think they know because I never told them that.

INSOO: What would it take for your mom to know how much she taught you?

BETH: I guess I will have to tell her?

INSOO: How will you do that? I mean, tell your mom how much you learned from her?

BETH: She is mad at me now, but I will tell her in a few days.

Even though at the beginning of the initial meeting, the social worker and Beth were unable to build a working relationship around Beth "telling the truth" and Beth remained defensive and noncooperative toward services, she gradually changed in the dialogue with Insoo and came to see herself as wanting something and having the beginnings of a plan to get what she wanted. Clearly, there is much more work to be done with both the collaterals and Beth, but Beth has moved into a cooperative working relationship with Insoo around building a way for her to go home.

DVD **(See DVD Clips 10 and 11.)**

In this chapter, we have examined the different kinds of interviewing situations you will encounter as you get started with clients. Our goal has been to explain our view of how to build a cooperative working relationship with clients in each situation. While the situations may seem quite different to you in many respects, in each the solution-building practitioner attempts to do the same thing: listen for and get details about what the client might want different. In our experience, respecting and beginning to build solutions around what clients want naturally enhances client motivation and cooperation.

5

❖

How to Amplify What Clients Want: The Miracle Question

There are those who look at things the way they are, and ask why.
I dream of things that never were, and ask why not?
(ROBERT F. KENNEDY PARAPHRASING
GEORGE BERNARD SHAW)

Only when people start creating scenarios of possibility do they move
in directions more satisfying to them, and [their] problems
become lost or much less influential.
(SALEEBEY, 1994, P. 357)

In illustrating his conviction about clients' potential, Saleebey (1994) points to the work of his colleagues (Modcrin, Rapp, & Poertner, 1988) with clients diagnosed as chronically mentally ill, many of whom had a history of previous hospitalizations. These colleagues, who assumed clients' competence and affirmed their goal definitions, witnessed amazing results in their clients.

> These individuals, almost without exception, began to construct a life—
> collaboratively—that no one could have predicted. The interesting thing
> is that they did this "in spite of their illness." In fact, their symptoms may
> have occurred at the same level, but the other parts of them became part
> of their unfolding story: "me as employee," "me as piano player," "me as
> driver," "me as spouse and parent." The symptoms move into the
> background of a much richer symbolic ecology.

(SALEEBEY, 1994, P. 357)

Our experience with clients has been similar. As de Shazer (1991, 1994) and many others (Berg, 1994; Berg & de Shazer, 1997; Berg & Kelly, 2000; Berg &

Miller, 1992; Berg & Steiner, 2003; de Shazer et al., in press; Furman & Ahola, 1992; George, Iveson, & Ratner, 1999; Lee, Sebold, & Uken, 2003; S. D. Miller, Hubble, & Duncan, 1996; O'Hanlon & Weiner-Davis, 1989; Talmon, 1990; Walter & Peller, 1992, 2000) have found, clients often can make impressive moves toward building more satisfying and productive lives.

To illustrate the process of solution building, consider the analogy of a person who plans a vacation. Let us call her Annie. First, caught up in the repetitiveness and pressures of everyday life, Annie thinks she might like to have something different in her life. She muses: "A trip somewhere might be nice." If the thought stays with her, Annie starts to reflect in general terms about where she might like to go: "I'd like to get far away from here; maybe someplace out of the country; maybe even someplace warm, away from all this snow." After recognizing that a trip costs time and money, if she remains intrigued by the possibility, she will begin to define more clearly where she wants to go and what she wants to do when she gets there. She may talk to friends who have gone to faraway places. She may talk to a travel agent. She may go to the library or bookstore and browse through the travel books. As she reads about the Bahamas, Mexico, Greece, Brazil, and Hawaii, Annie develops a richer sense of what lies in store for her if she decides to go to one of these destinations. The Bahamas have picturesque beaches and snorkeling right off the shore. Greece and Mexico offer monuments of past civilizations. Rio de Janeiro in Brazil seems to have exciting nightlife. As she works to develop a clearer sense of what there is at each of several possible destinations, she becomes attracted to some more than others. In addition, as she thinks about the possibilities, she also has thoughts of how she will get there. The costs of the different options start to occur to her: "I could go by plane; it's faster and cheaper. I could go by boat; it's more expensive but relaxing." Thoughts about how to get there could even influence her destination. Annie may decide that the options for getting there are too expensive and change her destination from someplace out of the country to a warmer place within her own country. She may compromise: "At least that way I can drive there and save money."

We offer several observations about this process. First, note that Annie worked her way from a general idea of where she might like to go to a more precise vision of what is in store for her once she gets there. As her vision became more and more developed, she found herself more powerfully attracted to the possibility. Second, considerations of how to get there influenced the choice of destination. Depending on how much time, cost, and work it would take to get there, Annie shifted her perceptions and definitions about the relative attractiveness of different destinations. Third, as a consequence, she discovered that planning a trip can be a lot of work. Fourth, the process was not so much a matter of finding the perfect destination as of finding a destination that would be sufficiently satisfying to motivate her to make the trip a reality.

In terms of the trip metaphor, we find in our work with clients that thinking about destination should take precedence over mode of transportation. When clients first start to think about what they want to have different in their lives, it seems to be most useful to have them begin by conceptualizing what will be different and then move to how they might make that happen. Although these two aspects are often discussed together, with some problem talk thrown into the mix, the "what" still has logical priority over the "how." Thus, building on Chapter 4, we focus on additional interviewing questions that you can use to open and sustain conversations with clients around what they want different in their lives. In Chapter 6, we turn to skills that address the question of how clients can make those things happen.

As seen in Chapter 4, client motivation often increases dramatically when the conversation between client and practitioner turns to what the client might want to be different. Most clients must then struggle to define in more detail what they want. Usually, their initial efforts are abstract and vague. They may say, "I'll know things are better when I feel more motivated to study," "My problem will be solved when I don't feel so depressed about my life," "I'll be getting along better with my parents," "I'll have my children back with me and Protective Services will be out of my life." Consequently, once a client has made an initial statement about what differences he or she would like to see, the next task for the practitioner is to open a conversation that transforms abstract and vague definitions into a concrete, vivid vision of what life will be like when the problem is solved. Berg and Miller (1992) call this the process of developing *well-formed goals* with clients. This process, which is a collaborative one in solution-focused interviewing, involves a lot of work by both clients and practitioners.

Well-formed goals have several characteristics (Berg & Miller, 1992; de Shazer, 1991), as established inductively by solution-focused practitioners. After defining and briefly illustrating each characteristic, we introduce the miracle question, which is a way to open and develop a dialogue with clients around well-formed goals. This chapter introduces two new case studies: Ah Yan and the Williams family. We return to these cases in subsequent chapters to follow them through all the stages of the solution–building process.

CHARACTERISTICS OF WELL-FORMED GOALS

Importance to the Client

Foremost, goals must be important to the client. Whether the goals that the client chooses are those that you as a practitioner believe would be most important for the client is irrelevant. This characteristic reflects the themes in Chapter 4. Unless you make the effort to work with clients so as to identify what they might want, your efforts to be useful to your clients might be defeated before they begin. The case of Beth in Chapter 4 illustrates this truism. When practitioners work hard to understand what clients want for their lives, clients feel respected, are more likely to grow in self-respect, and are more motivated to work on changing their lives (Hepworth, Rooney, & Larsen, 2002; Saleebey, 2007).

Interactional Terms

In the metaphor of planning a trip, the would-be traveler often begins with very vague conceptions of the final destination. The same will be true of clients as they begin to develop goals. Suppose you ask a client what will be different in her life when her problem is solved. She will most likely answer in broad terms: "I'll feel better about myself " or "I'll have a better attitude about my job." You can invite the client to begin to clarify this statement by asking, "When you feel better about yourself, what difference will others notice about you?" You can prompt more detail by asking, "What else will they notice that's different about you?"

As indicated in Chapter 3, Mead (1934) taught that the way in which people perceive themselves—their wishes, strengths, limitations, and possibilities—is greatly influenced by their understanding of how significant others in their social contexts view them. Mead's insight can be put to use in helping clients develop well-formed goals by asking relationship questions. For example, suppose a client is totally at a loss about what might be different in his life when his problem is solved. You decide to ask, "If your mother were here and I asked her what would be different when your problem is solved, what would she say?" The client may then come up with an answer: "Oh, I think she would say that I'd be watching less TV, and I'd be out looking for a job, that sort of thing." Sometimes, when clients shift from looking at themselves through their own eyes to looking at themselves through the eyes of their significant others, they can generate some possibilities where before there were none.

On occasion, practitioners and students have asked us how to question clients about their interactional context when the clients are socially isolated. Our experience is that it is very rare for a client to be completely isolated. For example, a single mother with young children can be asked how the children would describe any changes in her if they had the vocabulary and ability to describe what they saw.

Insoo once had a client who took care of her aged father for years and complained of becoming very depressed after he died. She reported that she was not depressed at work, where she was surrounded by friendly coworkers, but that when she came home, she "put on a different side of me." The woman revealed that she lived with her dog, who was very sensitive to her mood changes. Insoo asked, "If your dog could speak, what would he say would be different about you when your problem is solved?" The woman replied: "He would say I will be bouncy, eager to take him for a morning walk, and I would talk to him in a cheerful voice."

Situational Features

When clients are discouraged and exhausted from having battled their problems for days, weeks, months, or even years, they commonly describe their difficulties as if they are happening all the time and everywhere. Therefore, we try to help them to narrow down what they might want to be different to a certain place and setting. Doing so makes developing goals seem more possible. For example, suppose a client complains to you that she is always late for everything and this is causing problems for her in all parts of her life. Instead of inviting the client to develop a goal around never being late for any important activities and events in her life, it would be more useful to ask, "Right now, at this time in your life, for what do you least want to be late?" She might tell you that it is most important to focus on getting to work on time because she believes that she can be late with family and friends, who are more forgiving. Her employer, in contrast, might fire her.

The Presence of Some Desirable Behaviors Rather than the Absence of Problems

Clients usually begin to describe what they want by describing what they do not want. For example, if you were to ask a woman who has come to see you about family problems what she would like to have different in her family life, she might respond with a lengthy statement.

> I fight with my children way too much. I want to stop yelling and screaming at them because it's no good for them and it's no good for me. Also, I want my son to quit fighting with his sister and to stop stealing money from my purse and lying to me, I want my daughter to stop running away, and I want my husband to get off the bottle so that he can help me more.

A goal description like this is rarely, if ever, useful to a client. Because it is a negative statement, it feeds discouragement, low energy, and a sense of being stuck or trapped. In addition, it focuses what little energy the client may have left on trying to keep this negative something away. It is usually much easier for people to do something they perceive as positive. For example, it is easier for clients to lose weight by getting up and taking a walk than by continually reminding themselves not to head off to the kitchen for a bag of potato chips and a soda. Consequently, well-formed goals are described as the presence of something positive rather than the absence of some perceived problem.

De Shazer (1985) has pointed out that there is a straightforward way to respond to a client's negative goal descriptions and begin working toward a description of the presence of something different. The interviewer has to ask the client what will be there instead when the problem is solved.

JOANNE: I hate it when my son lies to me. I'll know that things are getting better when he stops lying to me. It scares me when he can lie to me with a straight face like that.

INSOO: Of course, I can see that you have good reason to be worried. So, when things are getting better, what will he be doing instead?

JOANNE: He'll be more honest, of course.

INSOO: And what will that look like? What will he be doing differently that will tell you he is being more honest?

JOANNE: Well, he'll admit once in a while that he is lying and apologize for it.

INSOO: And what else will he do?

JOANNE: I don't know. I haven't thought about that.... Maybe his voice will be firm and straight, not evasive and mumbling like he does sometimes.... And he'll look me straight into my eyes, and he will stand straight and tall, instead of all hunched over. He'll be more open with me.

INSOO: I can tell that you know your son quite well. So, he will look you straight in your eyes, his voice will be firm, and he will stand straight and tall. All these make sense. You do know your son quite well, don't you?

JOANNE: Of course, I'm his mother. [laughing] Mothers have eyes in the back of their heads. That's what I tell my Robby all the time.

A Beginning Step Rather than the Final Result

Contacting a professional is generally a last resort, rather than the first option clients seek in solving their problems. They may have tried several remedies that are not working satisfactorily, and so they come to an expert for some answers. At that point, clients often want immediate relief.

This hope is wishful thinking on the part of the client. However, that does not stop them from asking for advice, nor does it lift the pressure you will feel when clients plead for you to relieve their pain. Nonetheless, professionals must not make promises to clients they cannot keep. In most cases, it is simply not realistic for clients to reach an immediate solution. More often than not, solutions are final results reached only after clients have taken some beginning and intermediate steps to do things differently in their lives. What we have to offer our clients is assistance in finding new ways to begin building more successful solutions.

When you ask clients how they will know when their problems are solved, expect them to describe the finish line, rather than the first signs of something different. For example, when Insoo asked the mother in the preceding example what she would like to have different, she stated the final result—for Robby to be more honest. Insoo then asked what that would look like, and she responded, "His voice will be firm.... He'll look me straight into my eyes, and he will stand straight and tall.... He'll be more open with me." This developing definition still sounded more like a final result than a beginning step, so Insoo continued the dialogue.

INSOO: You sure know Robby well. Obviously it is going to take more time for him to be honest with you all the time. So what will be the first small sign that will tell you that, "Hmm, he is beginning to be more honest with me"?

JOANNE: Yeah, I guess it will take some time. [smiling] Of course, I want him to change yesterday. I guess it will be his looking at me when we talk so that I can see his eyes.

INSOO: So, what will you see in his eyes that you don't see now that will let you know that Robby is beginning to be more honest with you?

In this exchange, Insoo invited Joanne to scale down her wish. Joanne was able to narrow her definition to a beginning: "his looking at me when we talk so that I can see his eyes." By concentrating on a single aspect of her son's change, Joanne will be more likely to notice her son's eye contact when it does occur, and that will increase the chances of a changed interactional pattern with him.

Clients' Recognition of a Role for Themselves

When clients begin their work with practitioners, they often feel discouraged about their prospects for something better because they believe their problems have been brought on by the actions of others and they feel powerless to do anything about those problems. Consequently, when practitioners ask such clients what will be different when the problem is solved, the clients respond that certain people they know will be different. As described in Chapter 4, we have found it useful to go with such clients' perceptions and ask for more description of what these significant others in a client's life will be doing differently.

INSOO: So, tell me, supposing Robby were to look at you more when the two of you talk, how would that be helpful to you?

JOANNE: If that could happen, that would be wonderful! It would make my life so much easier. I wouldn't be so scared—scared that he is doing the same thing to other people, like his teacher, for example. I wouldn't have to worry so much about how he might turn out. . . . I could spend more time at the other things I have to worry about—like doing something about my daughter and my husband.

INSOO: And if he were to do that, look at you more, what would he see you doing differently?

JOANNE: Oh, I don't know. . . . I suppose I wouldn't yell at him as much . . . you know, stay more calm.

With Insoo's guidance, Joanne was able to begin thinking about what she might do differently in the relationship with her son. A lot of work remains to be done about what staying more calm and yelling less might mean, but the solution-focused questions that Insoo asked helped Joanne to begin shifting the focus onto herself. Often, when clients are able to make this shift, they brighten and become more hopeful.

Concrete, Behavioral, Measurable Terms

Helping your clients to articulate concrete, behavioral, and measurable goals enables both them and you to ascertain when they are making progress toward satisfactory solutions. When clients sense they are making progress, their success fuels continuing efforts to create more satisfying lives. Consequently, instead of accepting vague and sweeping goal statements—such as "I will feel better when the problem is solved," "I will be happier," or "I will be more productive"—you work with clients to articulate their goals in behavioral terms. For example, when Joanne stated that she wanted her son to be more honest, Insoo's follow-up questions encouraged her to make that goal more concrete, behavioral, and measurable.

Realistic Terms

When asked what differences they would like to see, some clients respond in unrealistic ways. For example: "My heart condition will disappear," "My son will obey me every time I ask him to help around the house," or "I'll win the lottery." These outcomes might be wonderful, but the practitioner thinks, "That does not sound like a realistic goal. Certainly this client cannot become more hopeful and create a better future by focusing on unrealistic goals."

Realistic goals are achievable, given the client's capacities and the context in which he or she lives. Since at first you do not know much about the client's capacities and circumstances, you need to ask about them to get a better sense of whether the client's developing goals are realistic. This can be done in several ways. For example, suppose a client tells you he wants to get along better with his son. Under your questioning, the client defines that goal more concretely as spending more time with his son, asking his son more often what he would like to do on Saturdays, and taking his son's answers more seriously. You could then invite the client to build from there by asking, "Is that something that could happen?" or "Is that something you think you could do?" If the client answers yes, you could follow up with other questions: "How do you know you could do that? Are there times already when you have been able to do at least some of these things?" Very quickly, both you and the client get a clearer sense of the client's strengths and past successes and what the client believes can happen in his context.

Another way of encouraging clients to think in realistic terms is to ask them to consider the interactional consequences of any change on their part. For example, suppose that a father tells you that he wants to talk more calmly to his daughter, instead of yelling at her when she does something wrong. You ask him, "Suppose you were able to do that; what would she do differently?" By doing so, you are implicitly asking him if this change on his part is a realistic possibility, given what he knows about his daughter and her ways of reacting.

A Challenge to the Client

At the outset of services, clients often feel discouraged about themselves and their lives. They may feel disappointed or ashamed that they need assistance. Many clients would rather have physical problems that can be traced to a biological condition and given a medical diagnosis than personal or family problems. Personal or family problems imply there are flaws in the clients and those close to them for which the clients bear responsibility. Biological conditions are usually regarded as beyond personal control and responsibility.

By suggesting that the client's problems will take hard work to resolve, practitioners strengthen the client's sense of dignity and self-respect in several ways. First, the client is reassured that coming for professional services makes good sense. If a problem requires hard work to solve, it must be a difficult problem, and so the client is worthy of professional assistance. Second, in cases where the client makes little or no progress, the client does not need to feel a sense of failure. Instead, the practitioner's statement focuses the client on the need for continuing hard work. Finally, where the client makes rapid progress, awareness of having solved a difficult problem in a short period of time greatly enhances client self-esteem.

By reminding clients about the necessity of hard work, the practitioner is able to place responsibility for change and solutions on the client, without directly saying so. In the beginning, clients often talk as though they want to give their problems over to the professional. The reminder that hard work will be required respectfully conveys that the client will have to participate if change is to occur. Most clients accept these reminders. Though they may wish there were an easier way, they know from experience that some sort of hard work on their part has played an important role in their past successes.

Conclusion

Consider the following additional observations about well-formed goals. First, such goals are developed with clients within their own frames of reference. In solution-focused interviewing, the practitioner refrains from making suggestions to clients about what they need or what they should strive to achieve. Instead, the practitioner persists in inviting clients to conceptualize the goals for themselves and to state the goals in their own words. Second, when they begin their work with practitioners, clients rarely possess well-formed goals. These goals develop over time and in interaction with the practitioner. Like the solution-building process, goal formulation is hard work for clients and requires patience, persistence, and skill on the part of the practitioner.

The practitioner can introduce and sustain a conversation about goals with clients by means of the miracle question. It draws on the client's frame of reference and encourages goal formulation in terms consistent with the characteristics we have discussed.

THE MIRACLE QUESTION

Insoo and her colleagues discovered the miracle question serendipitously. Insoo was interviewing a woman who seemed burdened with the weight of the world: Her children were out of control; the school was calling about their unruly behavior; and her husband of 17 years had been drinking more heavily, with the result that he seemed about to lose his job and, with it, the family's livelihood. The woman was discouraged and talked as if she could not cope with another day. Insoo asked the woman, "What do you suppose needs to happen so you could say the time we are spending together has been useful to you?" The client said, "I'm not sure. I have so many problems. Maybe only a miracle will help, but I suppose that's too much to expect." Committed to picking up on her clients' words and ideas, Insoo asked, "OK, suppose a miracle happened, and the problem that brought you here is solved. What would be different about your life?"

To Insoo's amazement, this woman, who had seemed so overwhelmed and unable to go on, began describing a vision of a different life. She said that her husband would be "more responsible, keeping his job and managing the money better." She said her children would "follow rules at school and at home, doing their chores without putting up such a fuss." Most of all, she said that she would be different: "I will have more energy, smile more, and be calmer with the children and, instead of snapping at them, talk to them in a normal tone of voice. I might even start having normal conversations with my husband, like we used to when we first were married."

Insoo and her colleagues thought about what had happened in the session with this woman. It occurred to them that, even though we do not normally think of miracles as realistic, this client's description of her life after the miracle had happened was certainly a reasonable and realistic picture of a well-functioning family. Her description of her miracle turned out to be a worthwhile set of goals from her point of view. Thus, the miracle question was born. Insoo and her colleagues began asking it regularly.

The miracle question is useful for at least a couple of reasons. First, by asking about a miracle, it gives clients permission to think about an unlimited range of possibilities. They are asked to think big as a way to get started on identifying what changes they want to see. Second, the question has a future focus. It evokes a picture of a time in their lives when their problems are no longer problems. It begins to move the focus away from their current and past problems and toward a more satisfying life.

The miracle question has been asked thousands of times throughout the world. It has been refined as practitioners have experimented with different ways of asking it. The question is best asked deliberately and dramatically.

> Now, I want to ask you a strange question. *Suppose* that while you are sleeping tonight and the entire house is quiet, a *miracle* happens. The miracle is that *the problem which brought you here is solved*. However, because you are sleeping, you don't know that *the miracle has happened*. So, when you wake up tomorrow morning, *what will be different* that will tell you that a miracle has happened and the problem which brought you here is solved?

(DE SHAZER, 1988, P. 5)

Asked this way, the miracle question requests clients to make a leap of faith and imagine how their life will be changed when the problem is solved. This is not easy for clients. It requires them to make a dramatic shift from problem–saturated thinking to a focus on solutions. Most clients need time and assistance to make that shift. As a practitioner, you can be very helpful to clients in this process. We recommend the following guidelines when you ask your clients the miracle question:

- Speak slowly and gently, in a soft voice, to give your client time to shift from a problem focus to a solution focus.

- Mark the beginning of the solution-building process clearly and dramatically by introducing the miracle question as unusual or strange.

- Use frequent pauses, allowing the client time to absorb the question and process his or her experiences through its different parts.

- Because the question asks for a description of the future, use future-directed words: What *would* be different? What *will* be signs of the miracle?

- When probing and asking follow-up questions, frequently repeat the phrase "a miracle happens and the problem that brought you here is solved," in order to reinforce the transition to solution talk.

- When clients lapse back into problem talk, gently refocus their attention on what will be different in their lives when the miracle happens.

Remember that the miracle question is an opening gambit. Clients usually give an answer that does not fit the characteristics of well-formed goals. The practitioner's task is to pose a series of related questions to invite clients to express their vision of a more satisfying future in a manner that reflects these characteristics. For example, let us look at Peter's work with a client whom we will call Ah Yan.

Ah Yan's Miracle Picture

Ah Yan is a 30-year-old Asian-American woman. She is married and has two young children. Peter met her at a public agency where she was seeking assistance.

PETER: How can I help you?

AH YAN: [very anxiously] I've been feeling... I've been having problems. I get nervous—panicky. I just have to sit down and calm down. I'm scared somethin' is gonna go wrong all the time.

PETER: Ah Yan, what's been happening that tells you that you're panicky?

AH YAN: I, I don't know.... I just feel all, like, real nervous inside, and my whole body starts shaking. I feel scared, and I get all short of breath.

PETER: Hmm. That sounds very frightening. [Ah Yan nods in agreement] Is there anything else that's a part of being panicky for you?

AH YAN: Yeah, last year for a while I thought I was crazy or something. I was gonna get up and get out of bed, and my hair is falling out and, like, when I took a shower, there's a bunch of hair in my hand. And I went to the doctor and said: "Doctor, why? Why is this?" And they did tests, lots of tests.

PETER: So you went to the doctor and took tests. Was that helpful?

AH YAN: Yeah. Well, the tests didn't show anything, but they tell you how to cure yourself. The doctors said take walks, ride a bike, maybe rest more.

PETER: And has that helped?

AH YAN: I'm not sure. I tried those things.... Maybe they helped a little, but I still panic. I hyperventilate.

Ah Yan was able to describe her problem, but she was not aware of any pattern to it, nor had she found anything that consistently helped. The doctors, too, were puzzled because they had found nothing physically wrong with her. That is why she came for services.

About 10 minutes into their first interview, Peter chose to begin goal-formulation work by asking the miracle question.

PETER: Now, let me ask you an unusual question. Suppose [pause] that while you are sleeping tonight [pause] a miracle happens. [pause] The miracle is that the problem that brought you here today is solved.
[pause] But because you are asleep, you don't know that the miracle has happened. [pause] When you wake up, what would be the first sign to you that things are *different,* [pause] that a miracle has happened?

AH YAN: I don't know. I guess, I guess I would just be more myself. You know, smile. I smile, but that's on the outside. On the inside, I'm constantly feeling fear—like I'm going to collapse, even that I might die.... My fear is of dying.

PETER: You said that you would be more yourself. What's different when you are yourself?

AH YAN: Nothing. I feel... I want to go out and walk and just smile. I'm smiling, but inside I can feel scared, like I'm gonna collapse.

PETER: So when the miracle happens, what would be there instead of the fear?

AH YAN: Oh, I don't know. I always feel so trapped. That's too hard a question; I don't know.

PETER: Yes, it is. It's a very hard question, and I can see that you are really struggling with your fear. It makes your life difficult and miserable at times. I think it makes good sense for you to be here—to see if anything else can be done. [Ah Yan nods] I'm wondering—the morning after the miracle—what would your husband notice that would tell him that—wow!—things are different, things are much better, something must have happened?

AH YAN: When I talk to him, he tells me that I'm all right and everything is OK. When I'm happy, he's happy.

PETER: So when the miracle happens, you'd be happier? [she nods] So, what would he notice about you that would tell him that you were happier—on the inside as well as the outside?

AH YAN: I'd talk to him . . . . He'd see I was happier. I wouldn't be crying. I'd have something to eat. I'd do more around the house.

PETER: When he sees those things, what would he do?

AH YAN: [becoming less anxious and brightening] He'd be happier because he always worries when I'm scared. He'd hug and kiss me more. He'd ask me if he could help, and we'd make things look better around the house together.

PETER: What else might he do?

AH YAN: That's all. I don't know . . . maybe go out together, look around or something . . . . That's all.

PETER: You said you had two children. How old are they?

AH YAN: Di Jia, he's 6. He's the oldest. Then there is Ah Lan, who's 3.

PETER: Wow, two small children; you must be a very busy person. [Ah Yan nods; pause] So, getting back to this miracle, what would your kids notice that's different?

AH YAN: Di Jia—I don't know. He pays attention when I'm sick, like when I'm trembling. He'll tell me, "Mom, tomorrow morning I'll make you soup." You know, he tries to help out.

PETER: So what would be different when the miracle happens?

AH YAN: He'd go outside, play on the swing set, go around on his bike, running in and out.

PETER: And how would that be for you?

AH YAN: I like it. I like it because it's him. I know then he's not thinking of me, but running and playing.

PETER: And Ah Lan, what would she notice?

AH YAN: She's, like, starting to notice things. I think she would . . . She's a huggable person. She likes to be hugging and kissing and saying "I love you." She'd be happy. She'd notice us playing games and doing things together and enjoying it.

PETER: Who else might notice?

AH YAN: I don't know, maybe my sister-in-law—'cause she knows what I'm going through.

PETER: So what would she notice? What would be the first small thing that would catch her attention, the first thing when she sees you on the miracle morning?

AH YAN: She'd see my smile. She'd say, "Ah Yan, you're smiling!" She'd be surprised.

PETER: And what else would be different around your house when the miracle happens?

AH YAN: I don't know. I don't know any more.

PETER: Well, that's OK. You've already mentioned several things that might be different. Let me ask you this: If you were to decide to do just one part of this miracle tomorrow morning, which part would be the easiest to do?

AH YAN: Oh, I'm not sure. Maybe I could talk to my husband more.

PETER: What might you say to him?

AH YAN: Oh, you know, nothing special. Just say: "Good morning, it's a beautiful day. What are you going to do today?" Things like that. That's all.

PETER: So you can do that? [she nods] What would it take for that to happen?

AH YAN: Just doing it, I guess.

PETER: Really, is that true? If you decide to do something, you can make it happen, just by putting your mind to it?

AH YAN: [nodding] Yes, but it's hard because I can still feel really scared inside and . . .

PETER: Yes, I know. From what you have told me, it's going to take a lot of hard work for you to do that.

In asking the miracle question, Peter invited Ah Yan to enter a conversation with him in which she could work at constructing a hypothetical solution. In terms of the vacation metaphor, he invited her to talk about some possible destinations that, if she eventually chose to work toward them, would make her problem largely a thing of the past. As expected, she started with a very vague concept of what would be different when her problem was solved: "I guess I would just be more myself." Using follow-up questions reflecting the character-istics of well-formed goals, Peter gave her an opportunity to begin shaping a more vivid, more attainable picture. He asked her what would be there instead of her fear (thereby inviting her to describe the presence of something positive). He asked what she would notice that is different when she became more herself (thereby encouraging a concrete, specific, behavioral description and a descrip-tion of something in which she plays a role). He asked what her husband and children would notice that was different about her (thereby encouraging her to describe possibilities in interactional terms). He asked what other family members would do when they noticed those things that she might do differently (thereby inviting her to think in situational, interactional, and realistic terms). He asked what would be the first thing others would notice (thereby probing for a possible beginning step). He asked what part of her miracle would be easiest for her to do the next morning (thereby inviting her to think about which possibilities were most realistic). Finally, Peter acknowledged that turning parts of the miracle into reality would be hard work.

Ah Yan often responded to Peter's questions initially by saying, "I don't know." As discussed in Chapter 3, Peter was not surprised by this. He remained silent, giving her time to think and put her thoughts into words. His patience and use of silence proved helpful because during the silence Ah Yan was able to formulate answers that were meaningful to her.

Most clients find these goal-formulation questions challenging and demanding, but as they work to formulate answers, they brighten and become more hopeful. These questions hold clients' attention. Clients work very hard to answer them.

Occasionally, we encounter clients who refuse to work with the miracle question. They might say, "Miracles don't happen" or "Things have been so bad in my life for so long that I know there is not going to be any miracle for me." If you find yourself in this situation, you could say, "Well, suppose there were a miracle, even a small one." If the client still insists on returning to how painful the problem is, you might also use the phrase "when the problem is solved or less severe," rather than "when the miracle happens." For example, you could start the shift from problem talk to goal formulation by asking, "What will you notice that's happening differently in your life when your problem is solved or less severe?" You can adapt the other questions to develop well-formed goals in the same way.

If you are not experienced in solution-focused interviewing, it will take time and practice before you feel comfortable opening and sustaining a conversation with clients around the miracle question. In an effort to help those who are new to this type of interviewing, we have developed a goal-formulation protocol and a crib sheet of questions for developing well-formed goals (see the Appendix). These tools are used by students in role-playing sessions until they become more familiar with the interviewing questions; practitioners new to solution-focused interviewing also have told us the tools are useful as they shift more toward this way of working.

The Williams Family

In practice, you will often be required to meet with and interview several people at once. Although the basic components of solution-focused interviewing do not change under these circumstances, you must get the perceptions of all present. When these perceptions conflict, as they often do, you must work toward a joint definition of goals and a joint solution. To illustrate how this is done, we will consider a family who came to Insoo for help. Let us call them the Williams family.

When developing well-formed goals in a family case, you are working with two or more persons, all of whom may have different definitions of what is wrong and what life will look like when the family's problems are solved. With their different perceptions, individual family members may carry off the conversation in different directions—frequently in the direction of more problem talk from their particular points of view. You must think of such developments as family members' attempts to be helpful by giving more information about the family's situation, and find ways to return them to the task at hand: developing well-formed goals. Sometimes, you will notice rising tension and conflict among the participants. When this happens, remember to respectfully explore the perceptions of those family members who are stirred up, asking them what they think will be different when the problem is solved. This encourages them to return the focus to the work of developing goals. Finally, as with individual cases, notice what clients are already doing that is useful to them and helpful to their significant others, and compliment them for those actions.

Insoo does each of these things in the lengthy dialogue that follows, reflecting the many starts and stops of goal-formulation work. In the dialogue, we indicate periodically the procedures that Insoo used, along with the motivations for her questions.

The members of the Williams family who came for services are 32-year-old Gladys, her four children, and her 28-year-old brother, Albert. Her four children are Marcus (aged 12), Offion (10), Olayinka (8), and Ayesh (7). Having been "kicked out" by his mother, Albert is currently living with Gladys and her children. When he does not live with Gladys, he lives with other family members or friends. Gladys stated that he is unemployed and "bums off people." She also reported that her husband has been in prison for five years. After going over this information about Gladys's household, Insoo began to explore what the family hoped to gain from seeing her.

INSOO: Now, what do you suppose has to happen for you to say, by coming here, that "it was a good idea that we all came to see that lady"?

GLADYS: That my chest pains I'm having now—that they [the doctors] say is stress related—that it goes away. That I can help . . . that you can somehow help me to deal with these problems that I'm having.

INSOO: So when you can deal with these problems, the chest pains will go away?

GLADYS: I hope they do.

INSOO: OK. What else? What else will happen?

GLADYS: My children will start doing things they know they supposed to do, and I won't have to shout and holler at 'em and put 'em on punishments.

INSOO: Un huh. So they will listen to you more?

GLADYS: Yeah.

INSOO: [*beginning to work toward something different that is realistic*] Well, they're not gonna always listen. Right?

GLADYS: Right, not always.

INSOO: Not always. Kids at that age.

GLADYS: But sometimes you think they would.

INSOO: OK. You want them to listen to you sometimes.

GLADYS: Yeah, and I could learn or get some help on how to control my actions by saying yes or no to my mom and my relatives, and they would hear me when I say it. It's like, when I say it, they do it anyway.

INSOO: So they would hear you when you say no?

GLADYS: Right.

INSOO: OK. What else?

GLADYS: I don't know. At this time, I can't think of nothing else.

MARCUS: We'd all get along.

INSOO: [*respecting the client's words and frame of reference*] "Get along"? What do you mean "get along"? What will you do when you all get along?

MARCUS: Learn to share.

INSOO: OK. Learn to share and get along. What else?

MARCUS: Nothing.

INSOO: Nothing?

GLADYS: But what he says here—he just talking about sharing your things, not his.

INSOO: [to Gladys] So you also agree with that?

GLADYS: Yeah, but he has to learn to share his as well as yours.

INSOO: Right. [to Marcus] I guess you're saying you want to share too. I mean you want to learn to share? Yeah? [Marcus agrees] OK. All right. How about for you, Offion?

OFFION: Make the family come more together. Like at family meetings.

INSOO: So when you have a family meeting, you will all come together?

OFFION: We'll have more time together.

INSOO: More time together? Uh huh. More good time together?

OFFION: Yeah. Mostly we're out all day and never get to do anything.

GLADYS: [laughs] He wants to drive me crazy more than what he's doing. It's not enough. He needs to be there more, see.

INSOO: That's not what you're talking about. I mean you're not talking about driving [your] mother crazy. You're talking about getting along.

OFFION: Somewhat.

INSOO: Somewhat?

GLADYS: Hmm. Lord have mercy!

INSOO: [*inviting concrete, behavioral goal description*] So when your family is together and you have a family meeting and the family comes together, what would your family be doing?

OFFION: Playing.

INSOO: Playing together. What else?

OFFION: Having fun . . . and [pointing to Albert, Gladys' brother] not having him around. [Albert laughs]

AYESH: Having him around.

INSOO: You like having him around, and you don't like having him around. [all laugh; *continuing to explore each person's perceptions*] OK. Let me ask you, Albert. Let's say Gladys somehow handles this stress. She has no more chest pain, and she feels calmer with the kids, and she feels that the kids are listening to her and the family is listening to her, and let's suppose all that happens. What will you see different about her that will tell you, "Wow, she is doing better"?

ALBERT: I don't think I'd be able to [laughing] because it's like, well, I might as well tell you. I got a mind that's out of this world, OK? And I don't think I would be able to tell you—ah, to know the difference.

INSOO: Wait a minute. You have a mind that is out of this world?

ALBERT: Yeah. I sit up, and I just get to thinking, and I talks out loud sometime, and she always laughing, so it like every time I come around, I always have her laughing. So it wouldn't be nothing different to me.

INSOO: [*focusing on something to build on*] I see. But she likes having you around?

GLADYS: Sometime. Sometime he get on your nerves 'cause he do aggravating things that you tell him not to do, and then he gets the kids to do the same things he do, and they follow.

INSOO: OK. So sometimes it's helpful having Albert around. Sometimes it's not.

GLADYS: Yeah. Like tomorrow he got to help move the stuff out the basement, so he can put the furnace and our water heater in. And sometimes I give him money and he buys cigarettes and [pointing to Albert's pants] he bought these pants with the money I gave him.

INSOO: [*complimenting*] So Albert, it seems like your sister's pretty helpful to you, too. You are helpful to her, and she helps you.

ALBERT: You could say that.

INSOO: Yeah, right. So somehow you learned to help each other?

GLADYS: 'Cause when you be raised up in a family where don't nobody help each other then you be like—why don't you never help each other? Then you say, "Well, I ain't gonna be like that." And then you try not to be like this, so you go out and help somebody else. Not only do I help, I help other peoples too. I guess that the heart that I have . . .

INSOO: And you didn't learn that from your mother.

GLADYS: No. Oh no, because mom was never there. She was an alcoholic, and then she would play cards all the time like gambling . . .

INSOO: [*returning to goal formulation*] Suppose that, after you stop coming here, you say, "We got help from that lady." [to Gladys] What will be going on different with your family so you can say, "We don't have to go see that lady anymore"?

GLADYS: They won't be doing the things that they do now, like . . .

INSOO: [*asking for the presence of something*] What will they do instead of that?

GLADYS: They will learn how to control their hands and mouths and keep them to themselves, and I could let them go over to other people's houses and spend the night and don't worry about, like, is they off over there sassing, and fighting, and showing somebody's else child bad habits. That I would be able to trust them to go away and stay by themselves at somebody else's house.

INSOO: [*asking for concrete, behavioral, measurable description*] And what would they do at somebody else's house that you can trust them?

GLADYS: The same thing that they will show me that they would do at my house. Like, if Marcus go to his friend's house, he might fight with the little boy and sass his mama. He'll go over there and be sassing and fighting. Where, instead of him doing that, he'll go over there just so he could play with the little boy and have a good time and come home.

INSOO: OK. So he will not be doing things that he's not supposed to be doing. He will be perfectly well behaved. OK. Like a gentleman.

GLADYS: Right.

INSOO: Good. All right. What about Offion? What would Offion be doing different that it would tell you that "we don't have to go see that lady anymore"?

GLADYS: Offion got this attitude where, if he tell you to do something he want, he expect for you to do it. Or, like, if you're talking and you're not listening to him and he trying to tell you something, he gets real upset, and sometime he'll hit you, and sometime he do violent things to you.

INSOO: [*searching for the presence of desirable, positive behaviors*] So he will stop that. So what would he be like instead of being violent?

GLADYS: If he was talking to you and you didn't want to listen to him, he'd say forget it. You know, go on about his business. Maybe come back to you later and talk to you about what he wanted to talk to you about. He see you busy. It's not like he gonna get upset and wanna hit you 'cause . . .

INSOO: OK. So he can come back and talk to you calmer.

GLADYS: Right.

INSOO: Yeah. That's what he'll be doing. OK. So when he does, both Marcus and Offion can do all this, OK? [*turning to the boys; inviting goal description in interactional terms*] Let's suppose you can do all this. You learn to do all this. How would mom be different?

OFFION: There'd be less things that she had to do.

MARCUS: She won't have they heart pains.

INSOO: She won't have a heart pain. What will she be like when she doesn't have a heart pain?

MARCUS: We can go on picnics and, like, go different places without being all stressed out.

INSOO: Uh huh. I guess you would like to see mom do that. No stress and able to go on picnics and stuff like that. And you too. Uh huh. [*complimenting client strengths*] You must care about your mom very much? Huh? Yeah? Does mom know that?

MARCUS: I don't know.

INSOO: You don't know? Does mom know how much you care about her? What do you think, Marcus?

MARCUS: No, she don't know.

INSOO: She don't know? She don't know how much you care? How about for you, Offion? What do you think? Mom knows?

OFFION: I don't know.

INSOO: You don't know.

GLADYS: Do you know how much I love you?

OLAYINKA: Yes, mama.

GLADYS: I don't even think you know. [her voice rising] I don't think you know 'cause if you did you wouldn't so do the things you did.

INSOO: [*refocusing on possible strengths in the mother-child relationship*] Wait a minute. What do you think, Offion? Do you know?

GLADYS: Do you know?

OFFION: Yes.

INSOO: Yeah? How can you tell that mom cares about you?

MARCUS: Because if she didn't care about us—she's a single parent; if she didn't care about us, we would know.

INSOO: Right. She's a single parent, and she takes care of you. That's how you know she cares about you. How about for you, Offion?

OFFION: 'Cause we have things that other kids don't have.

INSOO: Like what?

OFFION: Everything a kid would want.

INSOO: Yeah, really? You mean, like a Nintendo and that kind of stuff?

OFFION: Yeah.

INSOO: Yeah. Wow. [*complimenting client strengths*] You must be trying very hard with these kids.

GLADYS: I'm trying. I try my best. That's all I can do, and pray that they grow up the right way.

INSOO: Well, it sounds like they know that you're trying very hard.

GLADYS: I would hope they do.

INSOO: Well, it sounds like they know it.

ALBERT: They know, but that ain't doing it.

INSOO: [*inviting the family to think even more broadly about an alternative future*] Now let me ask you some strange questions that I'm gonna ask all of you. OK? Let's say I have a special wand. You know about magic wands? [to the children, who have taken on skeptical expressions] You don't believe it. That's OK. Let's say I have a secret magic wand, and I'm going to sort of wave my magic wand. OK? Today. And, uh, after we talk like this, you guys are all gonna go home, and obviously you're gonna go home and go to bed tonight.

GLADYS: OK.

INSOO: And everybody's sleeping. The whole household is sleeping and, with this magic wand, I just wave a magic wand, and just gold dust comes down, and the problem that brought you here today is all gone, just like that, through this magic. But you don't know. Nobody knows because everybody's sleeping.

GLADYS: OK.

INSOO: OK. Everybody. Every one of you will be sleeping. Except when you wake up the next morning, how will you know that there was magic overnight while you were sleeping?

For many young children, the word *miracle* is too abstract and may not stir their imagination. However, the Williams children, like many others, were able to work with ideas like magic wand, gold dust, and magic.

OLAYINKA: There will be a change.

INSOO: [*emphasizing that a miracle future is a different future*] There will be a change? How can you tell there is a change? What would be different?

OLAYINKA: We ... would do what mama wants, clean the house ...

INSOO: [*asking for amplification to clients' interactional context*] So you automatically start to clean the house and do what you're supposed to do. Every one of you. Uh huh. OK. All right. So when you do that, what will mom do when mom sees all of you doing things that you're automatically supposed to do?

MARCUS: She'll think and scratch her head and wonder what happened. [laughter]

INSOO: What about for you? How will you know that there's been magic overnight?

OFFION: Because when all my brothers and sisters are helping clean house and everything, it's gonna be like, "Why are you guys being so nice? What do you want?"

INSOO: That's what mom would say?

OFFION: That's what I would say.

INSOO: [to Albert] How will you be able to tell? How could you tell that there's been a miracle overnight? That magic happened?

ALBERT: I wouldn't know a heck of a lot.

INSOO: How come? How come you wouldn't know?

ALBERT: Because I told you already, that's the type of mind I got. It just ain't ... Sometimes it function right, and sometimes it don't.

INSOO: [*giving Albert another chance to participate in developing a joint miracle picture*] OK. Suppose it did function right [laughter among family] and there's been magic, and the problem is solved.

ALBERT: Well see, even if I was in the problem and you put your wand over me, I'll probably wake up and probably be like, well, maybe I just changed. I mean I don't know.

INSOO: [*persisting*] OK. Suppose you changed.

ALBERT: But for 23 years, I mean, I ain't changed. I don't think it's gonna change that quick.

INSOO: Well, that's why it takes magic to do that.

ALBERT: Yeah.

INSOO: [*inviting him to think about the possibilities one more time*] That's why it takes magic to do that. So suppose it does. How will you be different?

ALBERT: If it does, I don't know. I'll probably stop drinking. Stop having sex with so many different women. Stop doing drugs.

INSOO: Yeah?

ALBERT: And have my own place and get a nice woman and settle down and have kids, I guess.

GLADYS: That sounds nice.

ALBERT: But, see, that's 23 years I still been trying to stop and make it happen, and it ain't happened yet. So I guess it gonna take a magic wand. So where's it at?

INSOO: [*encouraging Albert to think about what would be different before worrying about how to make it happen*] Wait a minute. So that's what you will do?

ALBERT: Yeah.

INSOO: So you will settle down with a nice woman and you will ...

ALBERT: Get a job, have kids, get married.

INSOO: Like everybody else.

ALBERT: Right.

INSOO: [*inviting him to expand the possibilities by viewing himself through the eyes of a significant other*] Uh huh. So when you do that, what do you suppose your sister will notice different about you that will tell her something happened with Albert?

ALBERT: Well, she probably be like, "Well, he must have got his own and started back selling drugs" or something. I don't know.

INSOO: That's what she would think?

ALBERT: Yeah.

INSOO: But she will know that you were having a normal life, have a job?

ALBERT: [to Gladys] How would you know I changed?

INSOO: [*creating an opportunity for Albert to look at himself through the eyes of a significant other*] Yeah, how could you tell that he changed?

GLADYS: I'd be saying, "God musta came while I was sleep and cleaned that man life up, and he left me."

INSOO: [*persisting, inviting future possibilities by picking up on the client's words*] So suppose he does that. Suppose God comes during the night while you're sleeping. How would Albert be different?

GLADYS: How would he be different?

INSOO: Yeah.

GLADYS: He wouldn't play Nintendo no more.

INSOO: [*continuing to work toward a joint miracle picture with the family*] How would he be different with you?

GLADYS: With me? If I said, if I told him to let the kids go to bed at a certain time, he wouldn't say, "Let 'em stay up five more minutes or ten more minutes." When I say, "Let 'em go to bed at a certain time," he'll say OK. That's what your mom wants you to do, so he'll let 'em do it.

INSOO: So he will help you out with the kids?

GLADYS: Yeah.

INSOO: What about you? [*attempting to focus her on a small beginning step*] So when you wake up tomorrow morning and God's been there overnight and somehow God performed a very small miracle, how will you know? What will be a sign to you that, wow, God must be here?

GLADYS: When I tell my children . . . like, if I tell Offion, I said, "Offion go in there and wash our tub," he won't say, "I didn't do it" or "I washed it out yesterday." I didn't ask you that; I said go wash the tub. Or if I say, "Go downstairs and . . ."

INSOO: [*asking for the presence of something, not the absence*] So when you say, "Go wash the tub," what will he do?

GLADYS: He go do it.

INSOO: He'd go do it. OK.

GLADYS: He won't tell me whose turn it is or who's supposed to do it.

INSOO: So what about Marcus? What will Marcus do different?

GLADYS: He quit thinking he more than everybody. He thinks he more than the other childrens. He, like, think of himself as godlike and, to me, he don't know half as much as they do, but then he go around and talk about them and down them. Like, Offion got a friend . . .

INSOO: How would he change? What would he do instead of that?

GLADYS: He would try to be his brother's best friend. He would try to let his little brother look up to him and not say, "I don't want you around me" and treat him like dirt.

INSOO: So he would act like an older brother?

GLADYS: Right.

INSOO: OK. What about Olayinka? How would she be different?

GLADYS: She'll quit lying. When she stop—if God can perform a miracle, she would never lie again. You do not believe nothing she says.

INSOO: [*asking for a small sign of the presence of truthfulness*] So how will you know that she stopped lying tomorrow?

GLADYS: God would have to come to me himself and say, "Gladys, Yinka is not gonna lie to you no more for the rest of her life." I'm serious. 'Cause just, just looking at her and listening to her, it ain't gonna happen.

INSOO: [*encouraging her toward something more realistic*] Well, God's not likely to do that.

GLADYS: That's right, so I won't believe it.

INSOO: OK. So what would be the first sign to you then that, hmm, I think Yinka is starting to tell the truth?

GLADYS: Then she'll come to me and sit around me, and she'll want to be around me.

INSOO: She'll want to be around you?

GLADYS: Yeah.

INSOO: How will she show you this? She wants to be around you.

GLADYS: Like she, she'll come in. Like when we all in a room watching a video, she'll come. She won't say, "I don't wanna come. I wanna go in my room and play" or "I want to go in the basement and play." That's where all the toys are at. Or if she, uh, like, don't wet the bed no more. Ever. Ever. I'd say, "Wow, God really touched that child. And maybe he touched her for lying. Let me check her out." But that would be a hard one.

INSOO: So she would not wet the bed any more, and she would start to be honest. How could you tell that she started to be honest with you?

GLADYS: I don't know. I ain't figured that one out yet.

Insoo went on to ask more questions about how various family members would be different after the miracle happened and about the consequences of these differences for family interactions. Gladys revealed more about her strengths and how much she wanted things to be different in her family.

GLADYS: They think they get away with things 'cause they smart. They go to private school.

INSOO: [*focusing on a possible success*] They do?

GLADYS: Yeah. Nonsectarian. No religion. Just private.

INSOO: [*exploring a possible success*] How did you manage to get them into a private school?

GLADYS: 'Cause when I called [sigh] . . . I called, like, three schools before I called Crestview, and these people was real rude to me on the phone and it's like, "Well, if you want to come in and fill out an application, I guess you can, but I can't give you any more information." They would hang up. And I called Crestview, and the secretary answered the phone, and I, you know, I hesitated for a while, and she took they names, asked me they names, and then she told me some days that they can come in and we can look at the school, and she said we could come in and talk to the principal and that she would try to do everything that she could to help me, and she told me about some of the programs—they take up speech; they know French. And then she was nice to me. It wasn't like the other two peoples I had talked to before. They hung up in my face, so I didn't want them. I wouldn't want to treat nobody the way they treated me, and I wouldn't want to go to they school.

INSOO: [*affirming client perceptions*] Absolutely. Wow. You care about your children very much, huh?

GLADYS: Yeah, I try to. Didn't nobody care about me when I was little like them. So I told my mom, I said, "I'm not gonna do my childrens the way that I was done when I was little coming up." And she look at me now, and you know I ain't lying. The things I do for my kids, she do not like it. She look at me . . . something like—if I gave them $100 for Christmas, which I did one year. It took me a long, it took me like the whole year to save $400, 'cause I'm just on one income, but I struggled and I saved $100 apiece for them and put it in they stocking, and she got very upset and told them to give her $50 apiece. She demanded $50. And I told 'em no. It took me a long time to save $50, $100 apiece for them.

INSOO: [*recognizing, complimenting, and exploring client strength*] Wow. So where did you learn to be such a good mother?

GLADYS: By being abused.

INSOO: Yeah?

GLADYS: If somebody keep treating you like a dog all your life, you'll say, "I don't wanna do that. I don't wanna treat nobody like that." At least that was my mind. I thought peoples, like, would think that way, but everybody don't. My husband, he was abused, but he didn't think like that. He wanted to go and abuse other people.

INSOO: Right. So how did you learn to be such a good mother?

GLADYS: By being abused. I was sexually molested when I was little. And then my mother was never there to listen to me. Then when she was, it was like, "So what? Get out of my face." And I got to the point where I said, "Naw, that ain't right. If I had kids, I wouldn't wanna treat my kids like that."

INSOO: [*complimenting*] How did you know that ain't right?

GLADYS: 'Cause the things they did to me wasn't right.

INSOO: Oh, you knew that already.

GLADYS: Yeah.

INSOO: When you were a child.

GLADYS: Yeah.

The Art of Interviewing for Well-Formed Goals

The preceding dialogue includes examples of all the solution-focused interviewing procedures discussed so far in this book. Insoo made use of everything from complimenting and affirming the clients' perceptions to the miracle question and its follow-up questions. All this work centered on helping the clients to develop well-formed goals, within their respective frames of reference. Insoo's task was to explore an alternative future, affirm those helpful things the clients were already doing, and invite them to amplify their successes. The clients' part was to struggle to concep-tualize answers to her questions from their points of view and past experiences.

If you are new to solution-focused interviewing, one aspect of Insoo's goal-formulation work with the Williams family might be especially useful to you. Begin-ners often have difficulty in sustaining a conversation around well-formed goals and feel awkward asking the miracle question, even though clients may find it intriguing. Insoo's work with the Williams family offers a way to address both concerns.

Let us return to the dialogue and study its development. Insoo chose not to begin the goal-formulation work by asking the miracle question. Instead, she opted to shift the Williamses' focus from problem description to goal-formulation work less abruptly, by asking some other questions. She started by asking what would have to happen for the clients to feel that it had been a good idea to see Insoo. Using the Williamses' answers as a starting point, she asked follow-up questions to elicit the characteristics of well-formed goals. Thereafter, she asked variations of her first question: What would be different when the family's problem was solved? What would be different when the family was doing better? What would be different when the family did not have to visit Insoo any more? She gave the family members many opportunities to expand and clarify their answers with appropriate follow-up questions. Only then, after the family mem-bers had spent several minutes describing various future possibilities, did she ask the miracle question and its follow-ups. Thus, by using other goal-formulation questions to build up to the miracle question, Insoo sustained the conversation for much of the first session and, at the same time, eased the conversation from less unusual questions to the more intriguing miracle question.

Avoiding Premature Closure

This lengthy dialogue, which represents considerable effort for both practitioner and clients, is only the beginning of a process in which the Williams family thinks about and settles on a more attractive future. The Williams family, individually and together, will most likely continue to ponder Insoo's questions after they leave the office. You should not expect to reach closure with clients when amplifying the miracle picture. In fact, it is preferable to leave the dialogue open-ended, so that clients have the freedom to explore further possibilities.

Nevertheless, we know how difficult it can be to let clients explore for themselves the possibilities that might exist for them. We, too, have been tempted to push clients toward closure and offer them suggestions from our points of view in an attempt to relieve their confusion and frustration. Over time, we have found it increasingly easy to persist in our questioning and to avoid pushing for immedi-ate closure on goals. Experience has taught us that clients are competent. Given the chance, not only are they able to formulate and aspire to more satisfying futures, but also, in the process, they reveal many of their strengths and past successes. Insoo certainly found this to be the case with the Williams family.

DVD [DVD](See DVD Clip 2.)

Exploring for Exceptions: Building on Client Strengths and Successes

> When I focus on what's good today, I have a good day, and when I
> focus on what is bad, I have a bad day. If I focus on a problem, the
> problem increases; if I focus on the answer, the answer increases.
> (ALCOHOLICS ANONYMOUS, 1976, P. 451)

Chapter 5 began by discussing the process of planning a trip as a metaphor for the solution-building process. Both processes involve two main steps. First, both the would-be traveler and the client must decide on a destination. To do so, the traveler gathers more information about what there is at each of several possible destinations, whereas the client generates ever more concrete and detailed descriptions of what will be different in his or her life when the miracle happens. Second, once a sense of destination begins to develop, both traveler and client must think about how best to get there. The traveler considers the pros and cons of different modes of transportation, whereas the solution-building client explores exceptions, the subject of this chapter.

EXCEPTIONS

Definition

As noted in Chapter 3, when we first meet with our clients, they tend to be very problem-focused. They have done a lot of thinking about those things in their lives they wish were not happening and can usually describe them in great detail.

For example, suppose you have a client named Joy, whose problem is her disobedient children. Joy can describe what her children do when they are disobedient ("they sass me and refuse to do what I ask"); can indicate the times this happens ("whenever I ask them to do their chores"); is able to state who is involved ("all three of them do it, but my oldest, Ken, is the worst"); can describe where the problem happens ("anyplace we happen to be together"); and is able to indicate when the problem is most severe ("it's worst when they want to watch TV or a friend is over"). Such problem descriptions can be helpful because they allow clients to vent their frustrations and unhappiness, thereby offering some relief. They can also provide a preliminary idea of how dangerous a situation might be for the participants involved. However, we have not found that problem descriptions are a useful resource for building solutions. Descriptions of exceptions are more useful for that purpose.

Exceptions are those past experiences in a client's life when the problem might reasonably have been expected to occur but somehow did not (de Shazer, 1985). For example, returning to Joy, an exception would be anytime Ken obeyed her order and did the dishes without sassing.

Exceptions may be a matter of lesser degree. Ken may never have done all the dishes without any sassing, but there might have been a time in the recent past when, after five minutes of talking back to his mother, he did some of them.

Interviewing for Exceptions

As a solution-focused interviewer, you will quickly learn that there are several identifiable parts to the exploration of exceptions. The first is to find out from your client whether he or she is aware of any exceptions. You might ask, "Have there been times in the last couple of weeks when the problem did not happen or, at least, was less severe?" If the client cannot answer that question, you could ask: "Suppose I asked your best friend whether you had any better days recently. What would your best friend say?"

Notice that these questions ask for exceptions in the recent past. Recent exceptions are most useful to clients because clients can remember recent experiences in greater detail, and because the experiences just happened, it is all the more plausible they could happen again.

Once the client has identified an exception, you should ask for details. In doing so, pay special attention to the ways in which this exception time was different from the problem times. Whereas a problem-focused interviewer would explore the who, what, when, and where of client problems, you should be interested in exploring the who, what, when, and where of exception times.

As with questions designed to elicit well-formed goals, clients may struggle to answer exception questions but will find them intriguing and do their best to answer them.

In listening to a client's answers to exception questions, notice what is different between the exception and problem times. It is a good idea to paraphrase and summarize such differences for clients because those differences are part of the raw material for solution building.

Deliberate and Random Exceptions   When clients have done what they can to describe their exceptions, you can proceed to explore how the exceptions may have happened. To find out about the "how" of an exception, you inquire about who did what to make the exception happen. Sometimes a client is able to describe how an exception happened. For instance, Joy, when asked how it happened that Ken did the dishes once last week without sassing her, might tell you that she had decided to wait until after he had eaten supper and was in a better mood before reminding him it was his turn to do the dishes. If she agrees that this shift in her behavior may have made the difference, you will have uncovered what de Shazer (1985) calls a *deliberate exception*. If, on the other hand, Joy responded to your questions about Ken's behavior by shrugging her shoulders and saying, "I don't know. Lightning must have struck him," you would regard Ken's doing the dishes as a *random exception* from Joy's point of view.

It is important to develop a keen awareness of whether a client is describing deliberate or random exceptions. This distinction plays a key role in determining what feedback is given to the client at the end of a solution-building session, as presented in Chapter 7.

Ah Yan's Exceptions

Let us return to the case of Ah Yan to see how Peter explored exceptions with her. Ah Yan wanted help with her panicky feelings. When Peter asked the miracle question, she was able to begin describing some things that she, her husband, and her children might be doing differently after her problem had been solved. At that point, Peter turned to some exception exploration.

PETER: Ah Yan, are there times, in the last month or so, which are something like the miracle picture you just described?

AH YAN: Yeah, there are times when I feel real good. I'm OK, like everything is gone.

PETER: When was the last time you felt real good?

AH YAN: I don't know, maybe one day three weeks ago.

PETER: What was different about that day?

AH YAN: I felt real good. It's like—I can breathe better, no shakes, no worry. . . . I'm happy.

PETER: Really, you were happy, no shakes! That must have felt great! How did that happen?

AH YAN: [pause] I don't know.

PETER: If your husband were here and I were to ask him what he noticed you doing different that day, what would he say?

AH YAN: He tells me to sit down, stop doing housework, to eat right.

PETER: Is he right? Do those things help?

AH YAN: I can't just sit there and watch my kids make a mess. I have to . . . people come and the house is a mess.

PETER: What about eating right?

AH YAN: Yeah, I have to do that—fruit instead of cookies and candy. My sister-in-law says the same.

PETER: What else does she say?

AH YAN: To eat right every morning. Mostly I don't, and my stomach is upset. She says to walk and exercise and take a deep breath when it's bad.

PETER: And do those things help? Do you do more of those things on a real good day?

AH YAN: Ah, maybe ... I don't know. I can't figure it out—what's wrong with me. I don't know what to do. I got all these feelings. ... I gotta figure out what's wrong with me.

This dialogue gives some useful information about how far Ah Yan has come with her solution building. She is clear that there are exception times in her life. She says these are days when she feels real good. She can also give some description about how they are different from her problem days: "I can breathe better, no shakes, no worry. ... I'm happier." However, when Peter followed up, she could not give a more detailed description of these exception days, nor was she able to answer when he asked about how they happened. At this point in their conversation, she was experiencing random exceptions rather than deliberate exceptions. Because she was unable to describe step by step how her real good days happened—much less what she might have done to make them happen—she did not have a sense of control over her panicky feelings. In her frustration, at the end of this interchange, she returned to her original frame of having to "figure out what's wrong with me."

In this first session with Ah Yan, Peter chose to explore exceptions after he had asked the miracle question and its follow-up questions. You do not have to do it this way, but there are some good reasons for following his example. First, clients beginning work with practitioners are rarely aware of exceptions because they are focused on describing their problems. Asking exception-finding questions at that point can seem jarring. However, once a client has been able to give a concrete description of what life will be like when the miracle happens, as Ah Yan did, it is very natural for the practitioner to move on to exception exploration. Second, this sequence makes it more probable that the client will give exceptions directly related to the miracle—that is, to the amplified version of what the client might like to have different in his or her life. These are the most useful exceptions for solution building because they are most closely related to what the client wants.

Client Successes and Strengths

By exploring exceptions you can help clients become more aware of their current and past successes in relation to their goals (De Jong & Miller, 1995). Whenever you and a client bring an exception to light, both of you become aware that some good things are happening in the client's life, and consequently, you can both feel more hopeful about the client's future. For example, when Peter and Ah Yan became aware that Ah Yan recently had a day during which she felt real good— that is, something of a successful day—they sensed that she might have possibilities for a more satisfying future. Correspondingly, we have noticed that clients' interest in solution building often picks up when they are able to identify exceptions. They frequently sit up straighter, smile more, and seem more willing to work hard.

Specific client strengths are also often uncovered during exception exploration. If a client is able to describe what he or she did to help make an exception happen, the practitioner can readily paraphrase that description and compliment some strength of the client. Let us return to the example of Joy and the night Ken did the dishes. When Joy relates that her contribution to that exception was that she decided to wait until after he had eaten supper and was in a better mood before reminding him to do them, you could point out and compliment some of her strengths in a variety of ways. You might ask, "Was that new for you— waiting until after he had eaten and was in a better mood?" or "How did you know that waiting might be helpful?" You might comment, "You seem to know your son very well" or "You must be a mother who cares. You realize how important it is for a son to do his chores."

Respecting the Client's Words and Frame of Reference

Exception exploration is similar to other aspects of solution-focused interviewing in that it respects the client's frame of reference. In exploring exceptions, an interviewer listens for a client's words and then demonstrates respect for these words by asking the client to clarify them. When Ah Yan told Peter that she had had a real good day, he asked her what was different about that day that made it real good. Ah Yan's words were used as the doorway to her experiences and frame of reference. Ah Yan was treated as the expert about these words and their meaning, while Peter's role was to ask the questions that would allow him to learn more about Ah Yan's view of her world.

DVD **(See DVD Clip 3.)**

SCALING QUESTIONS

By means of scaling questions, a practitioner can help clients to express complex, intuitive observations about their past experiences and estimates of future possibilities (Berg, 1994; Berg & de Shazer, 1993; Berg & Miller, 1992; de Shazer, 1988). Scaling questions invite clients to put their observations, impressions, and predictions on a scale from 0 to 10. For example, you might ask Joy, "On a scale of 0 to 10, where 0 means no chance and 10 means every chance, what do you think the chances are that sometime in the next week Ken will do the dishes again?" When asking scaling questions, the practitioner cites a specific time in the client's life, such as "today," "the day you made the appointment to see me," or "sometime in the next week." Scaling is a useful technique for making complex aspects of the client's life more concrete and accessible to both practitioner and client. Like the miracle question, scaling questions were first introduced into solution-focused conversations by clients. Steve de Shazer (personal communication, January 23, 2001) tells the story that early in the 1970s he was interviewing a client who claimed to be feeling better. He says he asked the client, "How much better?" The client responded, "On a scale from 1 to 10, I've gone from 1 to 7." De Shazer reports this happened spontaneously several times before he started regularly using scaling. Now scaling is a trademark question of solution-focused work used in virtually every session.

Scaling questions have great versatility. They can be used to access the client's perception of almost anything, including "self-esteem, presession change, self-confidence, investment in change, willingness to work hard to bring about desired changes, prioritizing of problems to be solved, perception of hopefulness, and evaluation of progress" (Berg, 1994, pp. 102–103).

What follows are scaling questions that are often used during the first meeting with clients. The first of these questions represents another way to uncover exceptions in clients' lives.

Presession-Change Scaling

In the past, it was a common assumption that clients begin to change when the practitioner starts to help them with their problems. Practitioners would talk about clients as "stuck" or "overwhelmed" before they came for services. To the contrary, change is regularly happening in most clients' lives. When asked, two thirds of clients report positive change between the time they made the appointment for services and their first meeting with practitioners. This is called *presession change* (Weiner-Davis, de Shazer, & Gingerich, 1987).

In solution-focused interviewing, you can call your client's attention to the existence of presession change by using a scaling question. By exploring any change you discover, you can further sharpen the client's awareness of exceptions. Some clients who were not able to identify exceptions when asked exception-finding questions do acknowledge presession change if the practitioner employs scaling questions. With follow-up questioning, these clients usually are able to begin identifying exceptions.

In his first meeting with Ah Yan, Peter asked her to scale any presession change.

> PETER: Here is a different kind of question, Ah Yan, one which puts things on a scale from 0 to 10. Let's say that 0 equals how bad the panicky feelings were at the time you made the appointment to see me and 10 is the miracle you described to me earlier. Where are you on that scale today?

AH YAN: Umm, about a 6.

PETER: A 6, no kidding. That's pretty high. What's different about being at 6 than at 0?

AH YAN: I can't just sit. I have to do somethin'. . . . Try and do things, like come here and figure out what's wrong with me.

PETER: Besides coming here, what else makes you a 6?

AH YAN: Talking to my sister-in-law. She says, "If there's something you want to talk about, let's talk." And try to talk and go out more.

PETER: So you've been going out more lately?

AH YAN: Yeah, with my husband and the kids on weekends, like to the lake.

PETER: And anything else?

AH YAN: Yeah, pray. I've been praying more.

You might notice three things about this sequence. First, Ah Yan paused after Peter asked her the presession scaling question. It was as though she had an intuitive sense that things were better today than when she made the appointment, but she had to think for a moment before she could put a number to her intuitive sense.

Second, by asking the scaling question, Peter offered Ah Yan an efficient and even satisfyingly accurate way to express that sense. Instead, suppose that Peter had asked, "How are things today compared to the day you made the appointment to see me?" This question might have been more difficult for Ah Yan. She might have found herself struggling to decide what parts of her experience to report, and in what words. The scaling question gave her a way to represent her perception in a straightforward and accurate manner.

Third, when Ah Yan surprised Peter by choosing a 6, he had a meaningful way to explore for exceptions that may have happened just before their first meeting: He asked Ah Yan what was different about being at 6 rather than 0. He expected her to say something about feeling better and more fully describe some exceptions, but she skipped over that. Instead, she started identifying some of the things that might account for her being at a 6. Peter found this very interesting because she had seemed perplexed earlier in the session when he had asked how her exceptions were happening. Asking the presession-change question not only confirmed the existence of Ah Yan's exceptions for both of them, but also began to build their awareness of who might be doing what to make the exceptions happen.

It is not surprising that presession-change exploration can reveal new information. Solution-focused interviewing tends to build on itself in the direction of a solution. It does not work by hitting on the only possible solution to some complex puzzle. This is another reason why we prefer the language of solution building to that of problem solving.

Scaling Motivation and Confidence

It is useful for both you and your clients to know how motivated they are to work on building solutions. Clients' answers to a scaling question about how hard they are willing to work will help you in formulating end-of-session feedback. Clients who indicate a high motivation to work are generally more likely to continue what has worked for them in the past and to try new strategies they suggest might be useful.

Scaling motivation to work hard is a simple matter. This is how Peter did it with Ah Yan.

PETER: I want to ask another scaling question, this time about how hard you are willing to work on the problem which brought you in. Let's say that 10 means you are willing to do anything to find a solution, and 0 means that you are willing to do nothing—just sit and wait for something better to happen. How hard, from 0 to 10, are you willing to work?

AH YAN: Ten. I've gotta.

PETER: A 10—that's top of the scale. Where does all that willingness to work come from?

AH YAN: I gotta, for me and my family.

Peter did not stop when Ah Yan indicated a 10 on willingness to work. By asking where her motivation came from, he gave Ah Yan an opportunity to say that her willingness to work was "for me and my family." As most clients do, Ah Yan tied her motivation to her values. This observation confirms the critical importance of finding out what is important to the client and what the client might want.

Early in your relationships with clients, you will also find it useful to regularly scale the clients' perceived confidence that they will find a solution to their problems. Peter almost always does this in first sessions with clients, after goal formulation and exception exploration. By that stage of the session, clients have had many opportunities for solution talk, and their confidence usually has increased.

PETER: If 0 means you have no confidence that you will find a solution and 10 means you have every confidence, how confident would you say you are right now that you will find a solution to the panicky feelings?

AH YAN: Ten. I'm not gonna stop until I'm all the way.

PETER: Are you that kind of person—once you decide to do something, you're confident that you can make it happen?

AH YAN: I have to, I want to, I can't sit there the rest of my life. I want the answers.

PETER: OK, so where does all your confidence come from that you'll find a solution?

AH YAN: Well, my mom, she told me to finish school, and I didn't. She was right, and I learned my lesson. I want it, and I have to.

PETER: You seem very determined.

AH YAN: Yeah.

Scaling questions offer clients opportunities to define themselves in particular ways. Each time Peter offers Ah Yan a chance to state her determination or her confidence, she has an additional opportunity to convince herself that she is a determined and confident person.

Similarly, by scaling motivation and confidence, you can explore and reinforce client strengths. Peter learned that Ah Yan is a determined person who cares about her family, can learn from past experiences, has long-range personal goals, and can prioritize her goals. He was especially impressed by Ah Yan's self-description as a very determined person who learned from her mistake of not listening to her mother.

Finally, when responding to scaling questions about their levels of motivation and confidence, clients frequently identify more exceptions, which the interviewer can then pursue.

DVD (See DVD Clip 7.)

EXCEPTIONS: THE WILLIAMS FAMILY

In her first meeting with the Williams family, Insoo worked mainly on developing well-formed goals. In the rest of that interview, she focused on exceptions. She did not ask any scaling questions.

The Williams family consisted of Gladys, her four children, and her brother Albert, who came to live with her from time to time. Gladys had been struggling with stress-related chest pains, which her doctors could not tie to physiological causes. Insoo helped the family begin to develop a joint picture of what they wanted. In the goal-formulation work, family members were able to suggest several things that might be different in their family life when the problem that brought them in was solved: the children would be better behaved when they visited their friends' homes; the children would be more obedient and helpful to Gladys and one another; Albert would have his own place and get a nice woman and settle down and have kids; Olayinka would want to be around her mother more because Olayinka was telling the truth; and so on. Once several possibilities had been identified, Insoo began to explore exceptions.

> INSOO: [*asking for the perception of exceptions*] Now, let me ask you. Are there times when little bits of these miracle pictures, little bits—not all of it, little bits of it—happen? Even now?
>
> GLADYS: Yeah. Like Yesh stopped peeing in the bed for two weeks.
>
> INSOO: [*acknowledging an important exception, Insoo responds with excitement in her voice*] She did?
>
> GLADYS: And last night she peed in the bed. So I didn't say nothing 'cause she stopped for two weeks.
>
> INSOO: [*very interested and asking about how the exception happened*] Two weeks? How'd you do that?
>
> AYESH: I didn't drink as much and . . .

INSOO: Yeah? So when you don't drink as much you have a dry bed? Wow. So, two weeks. OK. [*asking for more exceptions*] What else happened? Other little pieces.

GLADYS: Offion got a friend.

INSOO: Got a friend? A good friend?

GLADYS: Yeah.

INSOO: [to Offion] Do you have a good friend? [he indicates two] Yeah? Two friends?

GLADYS: Who, Antowan? And Brian.

INSOO: And they are good kids?

GLADYS: They are. They are good kids. I don't mind them coming around me. They can even spend the night.

INSOO: [*asking about how the exception happened and indirectly complimenting*] How'd you do that? How'd you get two good friends?

OFFION: Going to summer school and going to Crestview.

INSOO: Yeah? Huh. [*complimenting*] They must think that you're a pretty good kid, too, then. Is that right?

OFFION: I don't know.

INSOO: They must. Right? Uh huh. [Offion agrees] That's great. That's fantastic. What else?

GLADYS: I forgot now. I don't know what else.

INSOO: Little bits of the miracle picture that we were talking about . . .

GLADYS: Sometime, sometime, like, I don't have to tell Marcus to clean up. I don't have to tell Offion to pick his clothes up from over behind the bed. See, Marcus's side of the room stay clean.

INSOO: [*complimenting an apparent strength*] He's very neat.

GLADYS: Yeah. But then you look at Offion's side, you say, "Is this the same room?" He like . . .

INSOO: But sometimes he picks it up?

GLADYS: Every blue moon I hear Marcus in there saying, "Offion, you have to pick up them clothes. You know mama gonna come in here." The majority of the time he says, "So what?" and he won't pick 'em up.

INSOO: [*focusing on the exception times*] But sometimes he listens to Marcus?

GLADYS: Yeah. And sometimes he'll say, "Yeah, I better go and pick 'em up," and he'll do it.

INSOO: [*complimenting*] Is that right? So sometimes you're being a big brother? Wow, it's a good start. What else? Little pieces.

GLADYS: [indicating Ayesh] When she take and, uh, don't bring food in the room and leave it for the roaches. See, they go to private school so I have to fix lunch. She bring the lunch home 'cause she don't eat, and then she say, "Forget it" and hide it in the room. Why hide it in the room? If you don't want it, throw it in the garbage. Not her.

INSOO: OK. Now I'm wondering about the little pieces—pieces like the miracle?

GLADYS: I mean I see her pick her clothes up, her new clothes, and hang 'em up. Yeah. I don't have to tell her to do it. She'll pick 'em up and hang 'em up.

INSOO: Really? She knows how to do that?

GLADYS: Yeah. She knows how to clean up her bed, she know how to sweep the floor, she wash dishes. She 7 years old. She do all that stuff.

INSOO: [*indirectly complimenting and asking how the exception happens*] Where did you learn that?

AYESH: Offion, Yinka, and Marcus.

INSOO: Oh. They taught you? They taught you how to do that? Oh. Fantastic.

GLADYS: [*proudly*] And she match her own clothes. She put this on. She went and got that and put it on. Everybody get they own clothes. So they wear what they wanna wear.

INSOO: [*complimenting by pointing to how the children are dressed*] They did a very good job!

GLADYS: If they put on something that's for winter, I say, "You gotta take that off. That's for winter." Then they go get something else. They say, "How 'bout this?"

INSOO: [*acknowledging exceptions and a strength in the children*] So they do listen to you sometimes?

GLADYS: Sometimes. On some things. Not all the time, though.

Several aspects of exploring for exceptions are demonstrated here. Insoo asked about the perception of exceptions. She also asked questions to clarify how the exception times are different from the problem times. She highlighted and indirectly complimented client strengths by paraphrasing the implications of exceptions for what the various family members can do. For example, the fact that sometimes Offion listens to Marcus's appeals to pick up his own clothes indicates that, even though he is inconsistent, Offion does know how to pick up his side of the bedroom. When an exception emerged, Insoo asked about how it happened, thereby beginning to gather information about whether the exceptions are random or deliberate.

In working with exceptions, as in goal formulation, clients tend to minimize or dismiss the importance of their perceptions. In minimizing their exceptions, they return to problem talk and indicate how frustrating and serious the problem seems. This is to be expected because, at first, client exceptions may not appear to be of much value to either the client or the practitioner in the face of seemingly overwhelming problems. Even so, clients can start to build some momentum by gaining an increased awareness of moves in the right direction. Success tends to feed on itself—even when successes are small. Consequently, when family members left exception description for more problem talk, Insoo listened for a short while and then returned her clients to solution talk by paraphrasing the hopeful signs and small beginnings that had already emerged.

In summary, as a practitioner, you should follow these guidelines:

- Get accustomed to regularly asking your clients exception-finding questions.
- Tune your ears so as to hear exceptions even when the client minimizes their importance.
- Ask about how exception times are different from (or better than) problem times.
- Find out who is doing what to make the exception happen.
- Paraphrase and affirm client strengths and successes embodied in the exceptions.

BUILDING TOWARD A DIFFERENCE
THAT MAKES A DIFFERENCE

In exception exploration, as in goal formulation, practitioners new to solution-focused work tend to push for closure too quickly. As soon as a client mentions an exception, they want to turn this difference into the solution. For example, a couple seeking help to reduce the conflict in their relationship may say, "We fight less when we go out together for dinner." At this point, the novice is often tempted to say, "Well, do you think it would help if you started going out to dinner more often, say, once a week?"

For most clients, such a move for closure is premature. Exception-finding questions are new for most of them. They are more accustomed to problem-focused questions. When asked about exceptions, they may be noticing them for the first time. They may doubt whether those they notice are indeed exceptions. They are not yet ready to decide whether an identified exception represents a solution to their problem. Rather than pushing for closure, the practitioner should give clients opportunity for dialogue about the meaning and significance of their exceptions on the basis of our guidelines.

Another of de Shazer's (1988, 1991) observations is helpful in this context. Influenced by Bateson (1972), de Shazer characterizes what occurs in exception dialogues as working toward a difference that makes a difference. He emphasizes that solutions are often built from formerly unrecognized differences; that is, exceptions (de Shazer, 1988, p. 10). Having heard and explored these exceptions, the practitioner needs to incorporate information about them, together with information about client goals and strengths, into session-ending feedback for clients. This feedback is designed to give clients every chance of both repeating past exceptions and producing new exceptions that come ever closer to solutions—closer, that is, to differences that make a difference. Chapter 7 looks at how to formulate feedback.

7

Formulating Feedback
for Clients

*Each of you pick two days over the next week, secretly, and on
those days, we want you to pretend that that miracle we talked
about has already happened.*
(DE SHAZER, 1991, P. 144)

Previous chapters have discussed several components of a solution-focused way
of interviewing clients: how to form productive working relationships with
clients, how to respect what clients want, how to interview for well-formed
goals, and how to explore for exceptions. This chapter examines how you can
take the information you gather in interviews and organize it into feedback that
will be useful to clients in their solution building.

End-of-session feedback in solution building is not the same thing as intervention in the problem-solving approach. In the latter case, the practitioner uses
assessment information about the nature and severity of client problems to decide
what actions would best benefit the client. The practitioner takes those actions, or
encourages the client to do so. These actions or interventions are thought to
produce the positive changes for the client. Because interventions are designed
by practitioners on the basis of expert assessment information and professional
theory, the practitioner is the primary change agent in the problem-solving
approach (Pincus & Minahan, 1973).

Solution building, by contrast, does not regard session-ending feedback as any
more important than any other component of the process. Instead, solutions are
built by clients through the hard work of applying their strengths in the direction of
goals they value. Clients, not practitioners, are the primary agents of change. In the
interview, clients disclose information about themselves and their circumstances.
Session-ending feedback merely organizes and highlights the aspects of information
that likely will be most useful to clients as they strive to build solutions.

In this chapter, first, we indicate at what point of the session to formulate feedback. Second, we discuss the structure of feedback messages to clients. Third, we explain how to formulate feedback on the basis of interview information. We illustrate this process by returning to the cases of Ah Yan and the Williams family. Fourth, we present several common messages used in feedback by solution-focused interviewers. Finally, we offer a protocol for a complete first meeting with clients that identifies and sequences several interviewing activities.

TAKING A THINKING BREAK

When interviewing clients in a solution-focused manner, practitioners generally take a break of 5 to 10 minutes before giving clients feedback. This will have definite benefits for you and your clients.

At the beginning of your first meeting with new clients, as stated in Chapter 4, you can clarify how you like to organize work sessions. Mention your wish to take a break and explain the purpose of the break: It gives you time to think about all they have told you and formulate some feedback you hope will be useful to them. We have noticed that clients readily accept this rationale for a break. The break increases clients ' anticipation about what we have to say when we return. They listen very carefully.

Sometimes we work with a team. Team members monitor our sessions from behind a one-way mirror. We meet with the team during the break, and they offer their suggestions for feedback. However, mostly we work alone and use the break for quiet reflection.

When we take a break, we leave. The client remains in the interviewing room or, if it is a home visit, in the living room or kitchen. Usually, the client reflects on what we have been talking about, or sometimes the client reads a magazine or goes outside for a cigarette. If you interview clients in your office, you might want to ask your clients to return to a waiting room. After you have formulated your feedback, you can invite them back into your office.

Some practitioners give clients an assignment during the break. For example, when working with a team, Andersen (1987, 1991) has clients listen in on the team's ideas. Another example is asking clients to think of a suggestion for themselves during the break that they think might be useful in their situation (Sharry, Madden, Darmody, & Miller, 2001). When the clients do come up with a suggestion, the practitioner blends it in with his or her own feedback. These examples represent efforts to make work with clients as collaborative as possible.

THE STRUCTURE OF FEEDBACK

In formulating feedback for clients, we recommend you adopt the structure developed by de Shazer and his colleagues (de Shazer et al., 1986). There are three basic parts to this structure: compliments, a bridge, and usually a task or suggestion. All are designed to convey to clients that you have been listening carefully and agree with their views about their problems, what they want to have different in their lives, and the steps they might take to make their lives more satisfying.

Compliments

Compliments are affirmations of the client. First, compliments affirm what is important to the client. For example, it is clear that Ah Yan cares very much about the well-being of her husband and children. She said she wanted to figure out what was wrong with her for the good of her family, as well as herself. She can be complimented as a real family person who wants to be the best she can for the good of her husband and children.

Second, compliments affirm client successes and the strengths these successes suggest. In Ah Yan's case, when she and Peter were exploring exceptions and presession changes, she stated that there were times when the panicky feelings were not as bad, that she was doing better at the time of the first session with Peter than she had been several days earlier, and that she had tried several strategies to control her panic. Ah Yan could rightly be complimented for her persistence, hard work, and creativity in trying several different ways to build a solution.

Beginning the feedback with a list of compliments can have a surprising and dramatic effect on clients. Most clients, struggling under the weight of their problems, are not expecting to hear a series of affirmations about what they want and what they are already doing that is useful to them. More often, they are feeling discouraged about their past choices and prospects for the future. When the practitioner returns from the break, many clients are thinking negatively and nervously ask, "Well, how bad is it?" or "Do you think there is hope for us?" Beginning feedback with compliments not only creates hope, but also implicitly communicates to clients that solutions are built around client goals by drawing mainly on client successes (exceptions) and strengths.

If you offer compliments to clients, watch their reactions to the affirmations. Their reactions will give you important clues about whether the compliments make sense to them. If your observations connect, clients usually will shake their heads in agreement or smile or say "Thank you." If they do not, you can reevaluate your thinking about the information you have gathered before you see them again. At minimum, clients tend to be intrigued by the compliments we give. More often, they seem demonstrably pleased with them.

The Bridge

The bridge is the part of the feedback that links the initial compliments to the concluding suggestions. Any suggestions the practitioner might offer must make sense to clients, or they will be ignored. The bridge provides the rationale for the suggestions.

The content of the bridge is usually drawn from client goals, exceptions, strengths, or perceptions. Commonly, the practitioner begins the bridging statement by saying, "I agree with you that . . ." When possible, it is also a good idea to incorporate client words and phrases. For example, in feedback to Ah Yan, Peter might offer the following bridging statement: "I agree with you, Ah Yan, that trying to figure out your panicky feelings is an important goal. It would not be good for you or your family for you to sit there with those feelings for the rest of your life. Therefore, I suggest that . . ."

Suggestions

The third component of feedback is to give suggestions to clients. Although there are important exceptions to this rule, suggestions are usually given in solution-focused work. These suggestions fall into two main categories: observational suggestions and behavioral suggestions (de Shazer, 1988). In an observational suggestion, based on information gathered in the interview, the practitioner suggests the client pay attention to a particular aspect of his or her life that is likely to prove useful in solution building. For example, Peter might instruct Ah Yan to pay attention to those days when she is feeling less panicky, especially to the ways in which they differ from her bad days. He would also suggest she keep track of those differences—when the better days happen, what she was doing then, who she was with, and so on—and report them to him the next time they met.

Behavioral suggestions require the client to actually do something, to take certain actions the practitioner believes will be useful to the client in constructing a solution. As with observational suggestions, behavioral suggestions are based on information gathered during the interview and should make sense to the client within his or her frame of reference. Because Ah Yan has implied that talking to her sister-in-law is somehow helpful to her, Peter can assign her the behavioral suggestion of continuing to do so.

In formulating solution-focused feedback for clients, you will discover that deciding whether to give a suggestion and what type of suggestion to give will be the most difficult part of feedback. Workshop participants and students consistently tell us that summarizing client successes and strengths in a list of compliments is easy and enjoyable and that figuring out a bridging statement is feasible once they have settled on a suggestion. However, coming up with a suggestion often leaves them feeling confused and ambivalent. Formulating suggestions requires you to review the content of each of the dialogues you had with the client—dialogues about problems, what clients might want, well-formed goals, exceptions, motivation, and confidence.

DECIDING ON A SUGGESTION

Does the Client Want Something?

Chapter 4 discussed possible interviewing situations that you will face when starting solution-focused conversations with clients about what they might want to have different in their lives. Sometimes clients will tell you there is a problem for which they want a solution, and they see themselves as a part of any eventual solution. At other times, they say there definitely is a difficulty that needs a solution, and the only solution will be for someone else to do the changing. There also are situations in which clients tell you they are only meeting because it was someone else's idea for them to be there. They say they really do not see a problem that needs work and make it clear that, consequently, they do not want to work on anything with you.

Chapter 4 gave several ideas about how to respond in each of these situations. All of these interviewing tips involved taking a not-knowing approach to clients' perceptions and listening carefully for any hints about what clients might want different in their lives. Almost always, by the end of a first session, practitioner and client have moved on and together have built a clearer understanding of something the client wants, even in those cases when the client at first did not seem to want anything at all. For the purposes of deciding on a suggestion, this is the first and most important thing to notice; whether a client wants something different or not, you can always make some sort of suggestion. In those situations where, at the end of the session, clients want something and see themselves as part of any solution, it often makes sense to make a behavioral suggestion. In situations in which clients see a problem but cannot yet see themselves as part of the solution, it does not make sense to suggest they take any behavioral steps; often, however, there are useful observational suggestions that you can give. In those much more rare cases in which, at the end of the session, clients still do not want anything at all, making a suggestion of either type only runs the risk of clients believing you were not listening to what they said during the session. In these cases, we think it only makes sense to compliment clients on what they are doing in their current circumstances that is useful for them.

Are There Well-Formed Goals?

Chapter 5 described the characteristics of well-formed goals and the interviewing questions you can use to sustain a dialogue with clients around goals. Developing well-formed goals is a demanding process for most clients, and you can be most useful to clients by not pushing for closure too soon.

When you formulate feedback, it is important to reflect on how far along your clients are in developing well-formed goals. Have the clients specified what differences they might want in their lives? Can the clients define those differences in concrete, behavioral terms? Can the clients define them as the presence of something desirable rather than the absence of problems, and as a beginning step rather than the final result? Can the clients describe them in interactional and situational terms? Clients vary in their capacities to describe precisely what they want. As their descriptions correspond more closely to the characteristics of well-formed goals, you can be more confident that a behavioral suggestion based on their goal descriptions will make sense to them and will aid them in solution building. Therefore, when formulating feedback, also ask yourself, "To what extent has my client developed well-formed goals?" When you are working simultaneously with more than one client, as in the example of the Williams family, you must ask yourself the same question about well-formed goals for each of the clients present at the interview. If one client has well-formed goals and the others do not, you probably will not give the same suggestions to all the clients.

Are There Exceptions?

The final step when formulating feedback is to review exceptions. Was the client able to identify exceptions related to what he or she wanted to be different? If so, assign the client an observational suggestion focused on the exception. If the client could not identify any exceptions but the two of you had jointly defined a problem on which to work, you might still assign an observational suggestion, but it would be more general. Ask the client to pay attention to what is happening in his or her life that indicates the problem is solvable.

If you and the client identified an exception related to what the client wants to be different, ask yourself whether the exception is random or deliberate. If random, suggest an observational suggestion, such as paying attention to similar exception times that occur in the future, and especially to how they happen. If the exception is deliberate and the client is able to specify his or her contribution to making the exception happen, the client has already defined the appropriate behavioral suggestion—to do more of the same (de Shazer, 1988).

FEEDBACK FOR AH YAN

After Peter had spent 30 to 40 minutes interviewing Ah Yan, he announced he would like to take a break to think about what she had told him. His thoughts first turned to what suggestions the interview information indicated, because suggestions are the bottom line in formulating feedback. Once an interviewer has settled on the suggestion, it is relatively easy to formulate the compliments and a bridge.

Peter first thought about what Ah Yan wanted. They had been able to jointly identify a problem (the panicky feelings) and a beginning definition of what she wanted (to reduce her fear and sense of being trapped and to do what is good "for me and my family"). In addition, Ah Yan indicated that she saw herself as part of any eventual solution. (When asked about how motivated she was to work hard for a solution, she scaled her motivation as a 10 and said, "I gotta, for me and my family.")

Next, Peter thought about how well-formed Ah Yan's goals seemed to be. He decided that their conversation around the miracle question indicated that Ah Yan was developing well-formed goals. She had said that when the miracle happened, several things would be different: She would smile more. Her husband would see her doing more around the house. She and her husband would make things look better around the house together and hug and kiss more and maybe go out together. Noticing that she was doing better, her 6-year-old son, Di Jia, would feel more free to go outside, play on the swing set, and ride his bike.

Third, Peter reflected on the exceptions Ah Yan had identified. He remembered that Ah Yan had said she did have some real good days. On exploration, these days proved to be random exceptions, because she could not describe who did what to make them happen. Later in the interview, however, Ah Yan indicated there had been presession change. When he had asked her how she was feeling, on a scale from 0 to 10, where 0 described the panicky feelings at the time she made the appointment and 10 described the miracle, she responded that she was a 6. She was doing considerably better than 10 days earlier. She was able to identify some things she was doing to move toward her miracle picture: talking to a professional and her sister-in-law, going out more with her family, and praying.

In summary, Peter concluded that (1) Ah Yan clearly wanted a solution and had a fairly well-developed miracle picture, (2) Ah Yan's real good days were random exceptions, and (3) her improvement since making the appointment could be traced to deliberate exceptions. On the basis of the interview information, he developed three suggestions that reflected these conclusions. Drawing again on the information from the interview, he formulated compliments and a bridge. He wrote down the feedback, so that he could deliver it to Ah Yan accurately and with confidence. He felt he could deliver it with conviction because he believed in its truthfulness and usefulness.

PETER: Ah Yan, I have thought about the many things you have told me about yourself and your situation. I have some thoughts and suggestions for you. I have written them down because I did not want to forget any of them. [Ah Yan nods, to indicate that she is listening and understands] [*compliments*] First, I want to tell you that there are several things about you which impress me. For one thing, I can see that you care very much about your family. You want to talk more with your husband and see him happier. You want your kids, like Di Jia, to go out and play on the swing set without worrying about you. You are a person whose family is important to her, so you want to figure out about your panicky times. I'm also impressed by how clear your miracle picture is. You can tell me specifically about what will be different around your house and about how you will be different when you figure things out. I'm struck, too, by how hard you are willing to work and how confident you are of finding solutions. And, finally, I can see you are already doing things which make a difference—things like coming here, praying, and trying to talk to others and go out more. And when others, like your sister-in-law, make a good suggestion, you have the good sense to give it a try and see if it works for you. Sometimes you come up with a good idea, like praying, and you have the courage and strength to try it. I am really impressed with all you have tried and how hard you've worked. With all this, I am not surprised that you are a 6 today.

[*bridge*] Ah Yan, at this time, I'm like you: I haven't figured out yet either what's wrong. But, while we both continue to think about it, I suggest the following: [*suggestions*] First, continue to do the things that got you to 6.

Next, pay attention for when you have a good day and what's different about it—all kinds of information about when it happens, what's different around your house that tells you it's happening, who is doing what, and so forth. Then, come back and tell me about it.

And, the last thing, pick one day between now and the next time we meet and pretend the miracle, that is, just live that day like the miracle has happened. But don't tell anyone. Just do it and come back and tell me what's better.

Peter delivered this feedback deliberately and carefully watched Ah Yan's reactions to each point. He felt he was connecting because she was consistently nodding her head in agreement. At times, she smiled and said "Yeah" or "Uh huh."

FEEDBACK FOR THE WILLIAMS FAMILY

Following the same solution-focused format for her session with the Williams family, Insoo took a thinking break after she had interviewed the family about their concerns, goals, and exceptions. Insoo was working with a team on the Williams case. When she took her break, she went behind the one-way mirror to the viewing room to confer with her team members. Because several members of the family were present at the interview, the team discussed each family member separately before settling on the final content of the feedback. They began with Gladys. (Review the Williams's interview information from Chapters 5 and 6.)

The team quickly concluded it was Gladys's idea to seek assistance. Not only had she set up the appointment; she also was the one who identified the problem when Insoo asked how she could be helpful to the family. Together, she and Insoo identified a problem (Gladys's stress and chest pains and the need to shout at the children and "put 'em on punishments" to control them) and a beginning definition of what she wanted (to get the children to listen more, and to learn ways to say yes and no to her relatives so they would hear her). However, the interview information also suggested Gladys tended not to see herself as part of the problem. She viewed it more as children who would not listen and a brother who did aggravating things. Nor did the information suggest that she viewed herself as part of the solution. Her answers to the miracle question and its follow-up questions were mainly in terms of what others would do differently when the miracle happened. (Albert would not be playing Nintendo and would leave, her husband would not want to do the things that put him in jail, Marcus would be a friend to his brother, Olayinka would quit lying, and so on.) Finally, Gladys did acknowledge the existence of exceptions. She mentioned times when she did not have to tell Marcus to clean up, Ayesh picked up her clothes, and Offion played with friends who were good kids. The team noted these were random exceptions, because there was no information yet about what Gladys and the other family members might be doing to make the exceptions happen.

The team concluded that, although Gladys seemed motivated and had general goals, her goals were not yet well formed, nor did she clearly perceive a role for herself in any solution. Consequently, the team decided it would be most helpful to make an observational suggestion around the random exceptions she had identified.

Regarding the children, the team concluded they all acknowledged the stress on their mother and generally wanted to share and get along better. When Insoo asked, they made some contributions to the family miracle picture, but their answers were consistently in terms of what the other children would be doing differently. For example, Offion stated that when the miracle is happening, "all my brothers and sisters are helping clean house." Further, the children did not identify exceptions or say anything to indicate they were motivated to work hard for a solution. Consequently, the team decided to give them compliments but no suggestions.

The team's thoughts about Albert were similar to those about the children. Albert's responses to Insoo's questions only tacitly acknowledged a problem for the family, if one existed at all. He did not define himself as part of the problem, as did Gladys and the children. When asked to contribute to the family's goal formulation, he had little to offer. (He could not answer the miracle question, he said, "because . . . that's the type of mind I got. . . . Sometimes it function right, and sometimes it don't.") Albert did describe an individual miracle picture for himself ("have my own place and get a nice woman and settle down and have kids, I guess"), but he expressed no hopefulness or motivation about making any parts of it a reality. In addition, he did not identify any exceptions, whether random or deliberate. The team thought he, like the children, should be given compliments but no suggestions.

The team's response to Albert and the four Williams children illustrates another guideline for preparing feedback: Be conservative. During a break, when thinking back over what clients told you during an interview, you often will find yourself undecided about whether to give a behavioral or observational suggestion, or whether to make a suggestion at all. In such situations, base your feedback on the conservative estimate of how far along in their solution building clients have come. Thus, while both Albert and the children did say some things in the interview that suggested they might want something different regarding the problem Gladys defined, none contributed to a joint miracle picture by identifying themselves as doing anything different, expressed motivation to make that picture a reality, or identified related exceptions. So, the team decided on compliments but no suggestions at this time. By being conservative, you reduce the risk that you might misinterpret the interview data and make a suggestion that makes little sense to the clients. Being conservative also protects clients from later having to save face for not carrying out a suggestion you made. Finally, we regularly find that clients stretch themselves far beyond the suggestions in the feedback. By remaining conservative, you will be in a position to authentically compliment clients for the often insightful, dramatic, and unforeseen steps they have taken to build solutions.

The team developed the following feedback for the Williams family. Notice how simple and straightforward it is, despite the thoroughness of the thought on which it rests. Observe that family members chose to interject comments and offer more information as Insoo delivered the feedback. These comments demonstrate that the feedback fit the family's current frame of reference.

INSOO: OK, I have something to tell you. I have lots of things to tell you.

ALBERT: OK.

INSOO: [*compliments*] To all of you. First of all, Gladys, we want to tell you how impressed we are that, considering what you've been through, and considering that your life has not been easy . . .

GLADYS: I know.

INSOO: No, it has not been easy. And, in spite of that, you have a very good idea of what kind of a good mother you want to be for your children. You have done a very good job.

GLADYS: I take parenting class, too.

INSOO: [*indirectly complimenting a possible success and an indication of strength and motivation*] You do?

GLADYS: Yeah, over at the center. I got a certificate—well, I can go pick it up. You go once a week, every week.

INSOO: So it's very important to you to be a good mother.

GLADYS: Yeah.

INSOO: You've done a good job with these kids.

GLADYS: [*identifying another exception*] Yeah, like, this lady down from me—I don't know her that good, but she, like, beat her kids all the time. And I told her, I said, well, when I want something from my kids and I done called 'em like five times and they don't wanna come, then I start counting 1, 2, 3, 4, up to 10. When I get to 10, then they in trouble, but they always come before I get to 10.

INSOO: You figured that out, too. Great. It's like, even with your very difficult circumstances, you have real nice kids. [*directly complimenting Gladys and indirectly complimenting the children*] The team noticed they have been very well behaved here.

GLADYS: Yeah. [*identifying more exception times*] They like that anywhere.

INSOO: Is that right?

GLADYS: All except when I'm not around. When I'm not around, they do anything. If I'm there, then they be halfway civilized.

INSOO: Wow! They're very well behaved here. They are very attractive, very well mannered, you know; nice kids you have. And obviously, it's because you work so hard being a single parent. It sounds like you raised them properly by yourself.

GLADYS: [*beaming*] Yep.

INSOO: So we just have to give you a lot of credit for that.

GLADYS: [smiling] Thanks.

INSOO: [*beginning to build a bridge*] And I guess what's amazing to us is that, because of what you've been through, you want to give your children a better life than you had.

GLADYS: Yeah.

INSOO: You want them to have a good life.

GLADYS: Yeah, like him. [points to Marcus] He don't want to go to private school no more 'cause a boy told him that public school is better. But, to me, he can go to private school 'cause I never went, and he can get something that I never had and that little boy, the same little boy that told him that public school was better, now he want to go to the same school that he go to.

INSOO: I'm just really impressed by how you kept at it and made sure that you got them into private school.

GLADYS: Yeah. It took a lots of work.

INSOO: [*complimenting Gladys's strengths*] You want them to get a good education. I mean you went through a lot of trouble to find a school that would be good for them. You figured it out that, if the school people are not so friendly with you, they're not gonna be friendly with the kids. You figured out what's good for the kids, what kind of education you want for them.

GLADYS: Yeah.

INSOO: Yeah. And sometimes they even do things . . . on their own, trying to help out.

GLADYS: Sometimes.

INSOO: It's a good start, right?

GLADYS: Yeah.

INSOO: The fact that they know how to do that sometimes?

GLADYS: Yeah. I know they know how. It's just getting 'em to do it.

INSOO: Right. Absolutely. Absolutely. So you taught them all the right things.

GLADYS: Yeah, I try to.

INSOO: You're doing a good job. We can see that.

GLADYS: Yeah, and two weeks and I'll be in the nut house.

INSOO: Now, Albert. We really like your miracle picture.

ALBERT: My who?

INSOO: Your picture of a miracle. When [quoting Gladys] "God comes" and takes care of all your problems, how you like things to be. And, I guess the good thing is that sometimes you are very helpful to your sister, and you come over, and she can count on you to help out.

[*more compliments*] And we are also very impressed that all of you, all of you, all six of you, want a better life for everybody. That you want to get along better, you want to be a good family, and you want to have fun together.

　　[*turning to Gladys*] Little kids like this, they all know that's what they want. So I guess we have to give you a lot of credit for that.

GLADYS: Thanks.

INSOO: [*making a bridging statement*] So you've done a very good job. OK, so we know that you want your kids to have a good life and to be good kids who listen. And we know that, at times, they can be well behaved and very well mannered, and that you are working hard, doing a lot. What we don't know much about is how you are doing all this. So, we want to meet with you again.

GLADYS: OK.

INSOO: [*giving an observational suggestion to Gladys*] OK. And we want you to pay attention—between now and when we meet again—so that you can tell us how it is that you manage to do all this good work for this family.

GLADYS: OK.

INSOO: OK. So let's go set up another time for us to get together.

ALBERT: Me too?

INSOO: Sure, you are welcome to come back.

GLADYS: No. He can't come back again.

INSOO: He can't come back?

GLADYS: No. He got to go home.

Gladys's assertion at the end of the feedback that Albert cannot come back again is striking in that, at the very beginning of the session, Gladys had said that one of the things she wanted to be different was to learn how to say yes or no to her relatives so they would hear her. This is an example of the wisdom of being conservative when formulating feedback. Given the information from the interview, Insoo and the team chose to give Gladys an observational and not a behavioral suggestion. Yet, before she left the first session, Gladys seemed to be moving her solution building beyond the limits of the feedback, to be taking action rather than simply observing. In doing less, the team paradoxically may have been doing more.

FEEDBACK GUIDELINES

In solution building, the feedback you give to clients at the end of a session is intended to aid them in their development of well-formed goals, focus them on those exceptions in their lives that are related to their goals, and encourage them to notice who is doing what to make these exceptions happen, especially what they themselves might be doing. The following guidelines are useful for formulating and delivering feedback to clients:

- Find the bottom line first: What suggestions do the interview data indicate?
- When unsure about the bottom line, favor the more conservative option.
- Develop suggestions by assessing whether clients want something, the extent to which well-formed goals exist, and the existence and type of exceptions.
- Agree with what is important to the client and what the client wants.
- Compliment the client for what the client is doing that is useful for solution building.
- Provide a bridging statement so that any suggestions seem reasonable.
- Use the client's words to stay within the client's frame of reference.
- Keep the feedback simple and straightforward.
- Deliver feedback deliberately and authentically, and observe the client's reactions.

COMMON MESSAGES

As you gain experience in formulating feedback for clients, you will discover that certain situations arise repeatedly. There are some basic statements, called *common messages,* around which you can build your feedback in these recurring situations. Originally developed by de Shazer (1985, 1988) and his colleagues, they have spread throughout the solution-focused literature (Berg, 1994; Berg & de Shazer, 1997; Dolan, 1991; Durrant, 1995; Furman & Ahola, 1992; George, Iveson, & Ratner, 1999, 2006; Metcalf, 1995, 1998; S. D. Miller & Berg, 1995; S. D. Miller, Hubble, & Duncan, 1996; O'Hanlon & Weiner-Davis, 1989; Selekman, 1993, 1997; Turnell & Edwards, 1999; Walter & Peller, 1992; Weiner-Davis, 1993). We present the most widely applicable common messages in their simplest forms. With experience and practice, you can adapt one of these messages to most feedback situations you encounter.

These common messages are intended to focus clients on those aspects of their experiences and contexts that will be most useful in building solutions. As noted in the guidelines, where you decide to point a client depends on your assessment of (a) whether the client perceives a problem and wants something different, (b) the degree to which the client has developed well-formed goals, and (c) the presence or absence of random and deliberate exceptions related to what your client wants.

When Clients Do Not Perceive a Problem
and Do Not Want Anything

If, after meeting with a client, you judge that you and the client did not develop a joint understanding of a problem, nor of something the client wants different, then, from the client's point of view, there is nothing for the two of you to work on. In such situations, the bottom line is to give the client compliments and say you would be happy to meet with him or her again. For example, Insoo gave the following feedback to such a client, who had been sent to her for substance abuse services (Berg & Miller, 1992, p. 99).

INSOO: Curtis, we are very impressed that you are here today even though this is not your idea. You certainly had the option of taking the easy way out by not coming. . . . It has not been easy for you to be here today; having to give up your personal time, talking about things you really don't want to talk about, having to take the bus, and so on. . . .

    I realize that you are an independent-minded person who does not want to be told what to do, and I agree with you that you should be left alone. But you also realize that doing what you are told will help you get these people out of your life and you will be left alone sooner. Therefore, I would like to meet with you again to figure out further what will be good for you to do. So let's meet next week at the same time.

If Insoo had given this client an observational or behavioral suggestion, it would have made no sense. It would have indicated she was not listening carefully. By giving only compliments at the end of the session, she ensured that, when he left, the client knew that his perceptions had been heard and respected. This approach increases the chance that the client might decide there is something he wants to work on and will return.

When Clients Perceive a Problem But Not a Role
for Themselves in a Solution

No Exceptions and No Goal   In this situation, your interview information at the time of the break indicates that you and your client have jointly defined a problem, but the client cannot identify exceptions or so minimizes them that you believe the client doubts their existence. Such clients tend to focus on detailed descriptions of the severity of their problems, which they believe to be caused by sources outside of themselves, such as other persons or organizations. With no sense of any role in the problem, they also do not see anything they might do to solve the problem. They tend to feel powerless. Generally, they have little sense of what they might want to be different, except that they want others to be somehow different. As seen in Chapter 4, it is easy to become impatient with such clients and start offering them advice about what they could do differently to solve their problems.

    There are two common messages you can choose from in this situation. The first simply repeats, as an observational suggestion, an interviewing question that we frequently use in interviews with such clients. In this case, you first set a positive, respectful tone by authentically complimenting the client for carefully observing this problem and its effects on his or her life and for thinking so hard about it. You then create a bridge by agreeing that this is a serious and stubborn problem and then make this suggestion.

Between now and the next time we meet, pay attention to what's
happening in your life that tells you this problem can be solved.

Such clients have little sense of what they might want. Consequently, the
second option in such cases is to offer a suggestion that directs the client toward
those parts of his or her experience and context from which some sense of
direction might emerge. This suggestion, called the *formula-first-session task*
because it was originally given in the first session to all clients to assist them in
goal development (de Shazer, 1985), focuses the client on that part of his or her
life where the problem is located but suggests the client look for anything
attractive there, instead of the aspects that are painful and problematic. In this
case, begin by complimenting the client for whatever useful work and thought he
or she has invested and for expending the effort and time that meeting with you
may have required. Then, after agreeing with the severity of the problem, offer
this suggestion (de Shazer, 1985, p. 137).

Between now and the next time we meet, I would like you to observe,
so that you can describe to me next time, what happens in your (pick
one: family, life, marriage, relationship) that you want to continue to
have happen.

Exceptions but No Well-Formed Goals   In this situation, you and the client
have developed a joint definition of the problem, and the client can identify
exceptions. However, the client views the problem as existing in the outside
world and does not yet perceive anything he or she might do differently to create
a solution. (Insoo and her team faced this situation when formulating feedback
for Gladys.) The bottom line should be an observational suggestion around the
identified exceptions.

Between now and the next time we meet, pay attention to those times
that are better, so that you can describe them to me in detail. Notice
what is different about them and how they happen. Who does what to
make them happen?

This sort of observational suggestion does two things. First, it implies to the
client that exception times will happen again—in a sense, that better times are
inevitable—and thus creates hope. Second, it suggests that the useful information
lies, in large part, in the client's own experience.

A slight variation on the suggestion may be useful when a client has been
able to tell you something about how the exceptions happened, but the client's
description is framed completely in terms of someone else (often a significant
other) somehow having decided to do something differently. Though the exceptions may have resulted from deliberate actions, the client implies they were
someone else's actions. For example, Peter once had a client, Alice, who was very
discouraged about her relationship with her boss. She described him as "over-
bearing, demanding, and uncommunicative." However, she described some
occasions when her boss was more polite, reasonable, and open toward her—
"when he acted like a real human being." Peter asked how those times happened,

but Alice could not identify anything she might have done differently. Instead, she said the exceptions "happen because of him; sometimes he tries harder." Not perceiving a role for herself in the exception, she seemed to feel powerless and clueless about possibilities for a solution. Peter offered her an observational suggestion that respected her perception of the exceptions but, at the same time, suggested a possible place to begin looking for clues to a solution.

> Alice, pay attention for those times when your boss is more reasonable and open, the times when he acts like more of a human being. Besides paying attention to what's different about those times, pay attention to— so you can describe to me next time—what he might notice you doing that helps him to be more polite, reasonable, and open toward you. Keep track of those things and come back and tell me what's better.

When clients view the problem as existing outside of themselves but are able to identify random exceptions, modify the basic observational suggestion by adding an element of prediction (de Shazer, 1988). For example, Peter could have described the suggestion to Alice in these terms.

> Alice, I agree with you. There clearly seem to be days when your boss is more reasonable and open and acts like more of a human being and days when he doesn't. So, between now and the next time we meet, I suggest the following: Each night before you go to bed, predict whether or not tomorrow will be a day when he acts more reasonable, open, and polite to you. Then, at the end of the day, before you make your prediction for the next day, think about whether or not your prediction came true. Account for any differences between your prediction and the way the day went and keep track of your observations so you can come back and tell me about them.

De Shazer (1988, pp. 183–184) notes that adding an element of prediction might be useful in this situation. He admits that he really does not know why these suggestions work and that "at first glance having someone predict anything about the next day prior to going to bed seems rather absurd." On the other hand, experience suggests that prediction suggestions are useful. Why?

According to de Shazer, their usefulness probably lies in the power of suggestion they contain. The client has already admitted that exceptions do occur. By giving the prediction suggestion, the practitioner suggests the exceptions will occur again, probably within the next week. Moreover, having accepted this suggestion and predicted a better day, the client is likely to have higher expectations for a better day and thus, unknowingly, set in motion the processes involved in having a better day. Expecting a better day, the client may also be more inclined to look for signs of it and therefore be more likely to perceive such signs. According to de Shazer, a prediction suggestion includes several elements that increase the probability of setting a self-fulfilling prophecy in motion.

When contemplating whether to frame an observational suggestion in a prediction format, you should be guided by how confident the client seemed that the random exception did in fact happen. Sometimes, clients suggest that exceptions may be happening but minimize their significance or vacillate on their existence. Gladys is such an example. At other times, clients are more definite. "Yes," they say, "there are times that are better." When you ask, "When was the last time a better time happened?" they describe the time and place of the exception. When you ask, "What was different about that time?" they give concrete details.

Recognizing these differences among clients' descriptions of random exceptions allows you to word your suggestion effectively. For example, when the random exceptions seem more clearly defined, it makes good sense to frame the observational suggestion in the prediction format. The wording of this suggestion implies a fairly distinct demarcation in the client's mind between good and bad days. When the client's random exceptions seem less clearly defined, we suggest you use the other wording of the suggestion, as Peter actually used with Alice and Insoo used in her message to Gladys. That wording only requires the client to look for any exceptions between the current session and the next, no matter how vague they might seem.

When Clients Want Something and See Themselves as Part of a Solution

A Clear Miracle Picture but No Exceptions   You and your client have developed a joint definition of the problem, the client accepts that he or she will have some role in the solution and seems motivated to work, and the client has been able to describe a concrete miracle picture including changes made by the client. However, the client cannot identify exceptions—certainly not deliberate exceptions. In such situations, compliment the client for the clarity of the miracle picture and suggest the client pretend the miracle has happened (de Shazer, 1991). For example, Peter said the following to a client named Ann.

> Ann, I can see that you have been through a lot. Things are very tense at home, what with Al [her husband] and Tina [her teenage daughter] always yelling at each other. I think it makes good sense for you to be here. It shows that you care a lot about your family and about yourself. Like you said, it's getting to where you just can't take it anymore.
>
> Ann, what also stands out for me from what we talked about is what a clear miracle picture you have. You described several things that will be different around your house when the miracle happens and several things you would be doing differently with Al and Tina. [she nods in agreement]
>
> I agree with you that something has to be done. But I'm like you. I'm not sure yet what the solution is going to be. So, for now, what I suggest is this.
>
> Pick one day over the next week and without telling anyone, including Al and Tina, pretend the miracle has happened. As you live that day, pay attention to what's different around your house, so that you can tell me about it when we meet next time.

By asking clients to pretend the miracle has happened, the practitioner gives these clients permission to try the various possibilities they have been able to generate. Asking them to do it once (or perhaps twice) rather than every day is recommended because it is a smaller step toward a solution and, thus, requires less effort. In addition, doing it once sets off the miracle day from other days and makes it more likely clients will notice any difference that might occur.

Remember, pretending the miracle has happened is a behavioral suggestion. It requires the client to *do* something different. It is more demanding than an observational suggestion, and the stakes are higher: Success may be sweeter, but failure can be more bitter. Before offering this suggestion, you should be convinced the client is motivated to carry it out.

High Motivation but No Well-Formed Goals   In this situation, you are faced with finding the bottom line for a client who says, "Something has got to change" and "I'd do anything to find a solution." You may be strongly impressed with such clients. Your heart will go out to them because, almost always, they have tried several things to find a solution, but without success. They can describe to you in detail what they have tried. Their high motivation to work hard is obvious. However, they are unable to identify exceptions, particularly deliberate exceptions. As you formulate feedback, you may find it difficult to come up with something that will offer hope of improvement.

In such situations, it is a mistake to think that, from your frame of reference, you could ever come up with anything specific that will be the difference that makes a difference for the client. We have learned from our clients that, as a rule, it is wiser to trust their perceptions of their resources and their intuitive understandings of what might be helpful.[1] De Shazer (1985) and his colleagues have designed a suggestion to allow you, when formulating feedback in this situation, to put the focus squarely on the client and his or her resources. It is called the do-something-different suggestion. Here is an example that incorporates the wording of the suggestion that de Shazer recommends:

> I am so impressed with how hard you have worked on your problem and how clearly you can describe to me the things you have tried so far to make things better. I can understand why you would be discouraged and frustrated right now.
>
> I also agree with you that this is a very stubborn problem.
>
> Because this is such a stubborn problem, I suggest that, between now and the next time we meet, when the problem happens, you "do something different, ... no matter how strange or weird or off-the-wall what you do might seem. The only important thing is that whatever you decide to do, you need to do something different."
>
> (DE SHAZER, 1985, P. 123)

This suggestion gives the client permission to be spontaneous and creative at those times when it is most needed.

Clients who successfully use this suggestion come up with solution-building strategies that surprise even themselves—strategies their practitioners could never have foreseen or designed for them ahead of time. For example, Peter once gave this suggestion to a couple who complained of deteriorating marital and family relationships. Their problems had begun several years earlier, when the husband suffered a severe back injury. The husband had been forced to go on disability. With a significant reduction in family income, it was almost impossible to make ends meet in their family of five. The couple had grown isolated and estranged from each other and from their children. Family members did not talk to each other except to criticize, and no one smiled anymore. They had tried several things, such as making sure to have one meal per day together and setting aside one evening per week for a family activity, such as going to a game or a movie. Nothing seemed to help. Peter, convinced they were motivated to work toward a solution, gave them the do-something-different suggestion.

When the couple returned, Peter asked them what was going better. The two shrugged their shoulders and said they were not sure, but both were smiling about something. With further questioning, they related a really "bizarre evening." Earlier in the week, when the family was beginning supper, with dad and the children around the table and mom getting the spaghetti sauce from the stove, one of the children made a cynical comment to his father. Feeling "angry and down," the father stuck his fork in the noodles and "flicked them at my son across the table. I hit him right in the face." The other kids laughed cautiously and looked up to their mother, who was carrying the sauce to the table. Thinking back, she recalled, "I was so mad. I was so ready to start in on my husband about 'that's no way to handle a child.' But all I could remember to do . . . was that you had said whatever I did, I should do something different. . . . So I stuck the spoon in the sauce and flipped it at my husband, and we got into this 5-minute food fight with noodles and sauce flying all over the kitchen." The couple knew something unforeseen but important had happened, and further discussion revealed the family had spent "two hours cleaning up the mess we made in five minutes, but talking and laughing like we hadn't done in three years." Peter spent the rest of the session exploring with them what they had done during the cleanup to make such family communication happen, and what they thought they would have to do to keep it going.

Well-Formed Goals and Deliberate Exceptions   In this situation, the client has described times that are better and told you step by step about the sorts of things he or she has done to make them happen. In addition, the client has implied that these deliberate exceptions, although not yet a complete solution, are moves in the right direction. That is, they represent satisfactory strategies for bringing about what the client wants. Often, such clients seem more hopeful and confident at the time of the break than at the beginning of the interview. In this situation, which Peter encountered with Ah Yan, formulating feedback for clients is easy to do. The following is an example of such feedback.

Ralph, I am impressed with you in several ways. First, how much you want to make things go better between you and your children. Second, that there are already several better times happening like [give examples]. And third, that you can describe to me so clearly and in such detail what you do to do your part in making those times happen, things like [give examples]. With all you are doing, I can see why you say things are at a 5 already.

I agree these are the things you have to do to have the kind of relationships with the children you want.

So, between now and when we meet again, I suggest you continue to do what works. Also, pay attention to what else you might be doing, but haven't noticed yet, that makes things better, and come back and tell me about it.

The suggestion here is to do more of the same, with an added observational suggestion that implies the client is probably doing more than he or she realizes and should pay attention to those extra strategies. It is a concrete and meaningful way to compliment a client for successes and encourage the client to build on them.

When you encounter clients who identify deliberate exceptions, it is important to make sure that what they do to make those exceptions happen represents aspects of potential solutions that are acceptable to them. Even when they are related to the difference the clients want to bring about, deliberate exceptions do not always represent solutions for clients. For example, Peter once interviewed a young mother who was discouraged about how early-morning piano practices were going with her 8-year-old daughter. The practice sessions were tense. At the end of the sessions, both she and her daughter were in tears "80 percent of the time." The mother described two deliberate exceptions: There were no problems whenever she paid her daughter to practice, and whenever she permitted her daughter to practice after the daughter's normal bedtime. Although Peter was impressed with the exceptions, the mother was not: "Somehow doing it that way just doesn't sit right with me." As things stood at that point, Peter knew that payment and delayed bedtimes did not represent solutions.

OTHER USEFUL MESSAGES

Solution-focused practitioners have developed several other useful messages (Berg, 1994; Berg & Miller, 1992; de Shazer, 1985, 1991; Weiner-Davis, 1993), but since most of them are either more specialized than those already presented or variations on those messages, they are not discussed here. We will, however, examine two more suggestions that are widely applicable in basic practice.

The Overcoming-the-Urge Suggestion

This suggestion, developed by de Shazer (1985) and his colleagues, is useful when clients define their problem as an inner tendency to feel or act in some way they want to see changed (for example, a tendency to feel scared, angry, or discouraged or to engage in certain behaviors such as yelling at others, hitting them, or using alcohol or drugs). When interviewing such persons, you will find they vary in whether or not they see a role for themselves in a solution, the clarity of their miracle picture, and the existence of exceptions. Regardless of whether an observational or behavioral suggestion is indicated, you will usually be able to give some variation of the overcoming-the-urge suggestion as the bottom line. Here it is stated as an observational suggestion for clients who have been able to describe random exceptions. For example, let us say the client tends to get panicky.

> Pay attention for those times when you overcome the urge to get panicky. Pay attention to what's different about those times, especially to what you are doing to overcome the urge.

This suggestion, like the others described, encourages solution building by pointing clients toward episodes of success in their lives and the strengths they are using to make them happen.

Addressing Competing Views of the Solution

During interviews about their concerns, couples or families often argue with each other about what is the best solution to their problem. It is a mistake to take sides. By doing so, you lose credibility with the person whose view you are ignoring or rejecting. To handle this often tense and difficult feedback situation, you need to formulate a suggestion that affirms the different participants and their multiple perspectives. The following is an example of how Insoo, working with a team, used this approach with two parents who were arguing about how to solve a serious problem with their son. The parents had said they could see their different family backgrounds at work in their conflicting views.

> We are impressed by how much both of you want to help your son stop stealing. The team is also impressed by what different ideas the two of you have about how to help your child through this difficult time. We can see you were brought up in different families and have learned different ways to do things.
>   The team is split on which way to go. One half feels like you ought to pursue John's ideas, and the other half feels like Mary's ideas might work best. Therefore, we suggest that each morning, right after you get up, you flip a coin. Heads means that Mary is in charge, and you do things her way with Billy, while John stays in the background. Tails means John is in charge that day. And also, on those days when each of you is not busy being in charge, pay careful attention to what the other

does with Billy that is useful or makes a difference, so that you can report it to us when we meet again.

This suggestion is noteworthy in three ways. First, it affirms the views of both parents and encourages each, to a degree, to do what he or she thinks is best for Billy. Second, it undermines the categorical either/or thinking of two people who are caught up, as many clients are, in the idea that there must be a right answer to their problem (de Shazer, 1985). Such thinking leads to win/lose impasses, where each person is privately thinking, "Either I'm right and my spouse is wrong, or it's the other way around." The suggestion offers them a face-saving replacement for the impasse by implying that both of their approaches are likely to have elements of value, and a way to build a solution is to discover and use the best of both. Third, the coin flip is a clever way to remove the opportunity for yet another argument between two seemingly independent, determined people.

When assigned this suggestion, most clients build a solution by combining elements from both possibilities. You can then explore the contributions of each client and compliment them for these. However, emerging solutions do not necessarily have to be combination constructions. Sometimes clients build a solution incorporating only one of the two original possibilities. Theoretically, when John and Mary return to see Insoo, they may both be convinced that Mary's way worked best. In that case, Insoo, respecting client expertise and maintaining the stance of not knowing, would explore with them how they had concluded that Mary's way was the most helpful for Billy. Once the exploration was completed, Insoo might compliment Mary for having a mother's deep understanding of a son and the ability to act on it and compliment John for having the wisdom and flexibility to see the value of Mary's way of handling their child.

The same sort of suggestion can be used with individual clients who cannot decide among options. In such situations, it is important to compliment your client for moving deliberately and carefully, because clients struggling among clearly defined possibilities often feel very anxious or discouraged about not yet having made a choice. For example, Peter said the following to a client who was trying to decide whether to break up with a verbally abusive boyfriend.

> Nadia, I first want to say that I think taking your time to decide what to do about your relationship with Bill is the right thing to do. A lot of people would not have the strength to think it through the way you are doing. Bill is important to you. At times he is wonderful, and the two of you like to do a lot of the same things. On the other hand, he does put you down and that really hurts, and you don't know if he can change.
>
> Second, I'm impressed by what you have already done to get him to understand. You've talked to him straight out and told him things have to change or you can't stay in the relationship. I can see that telling him those things was difficult for you. It took a lot of courage. [she agrees] I'm like you. I'm not sure about whether it would be best for you to stay in the relationship with Bill or leave him and begin a new life. I agree

this is a tough decision, and figuring it out is going to take more hard work. And, as you continue to work on it, I have a suggestion for you.

I suggest that each night before you go to bed, you flip a coin. If it comes up heads, live the next day as much as possible as though Bill is no longer a part of your life. Don't contact him. Start to take the first steps toward the things you said you would do differently if you were on your own, like spending more time with your friends and family and so forth.

If it comes up tails, live the next day as though he is still a part of your life—all those things you described to me about what that means for you. Then, as you do these things, pay attention to what's happening that tells you that you are becoming more clear about whether to leave him or stay in the relationship, realizing, of course, that usually a person cannot be 100 percent sure. And come back and tell me what's better.

An alternative approach to individual clients who are confused about different options is to suggest an observational suggestion. Ask them to pay attention to what is happening that tells them it is a good thing to be confused about their problem at this time. Suggest that the client keep a ledger sheet and record both the good things and the bad things for him or her about being confused. Unlike the previous suggestion, this one does not suggest that a solution probably lies in becoming more clear about a particular option. Like the previous one, however, it does suggest that it is acceptable and even an asset to be confused sometimes.

DECISIONS ABOUT THE NEXT SESSION

Notice the messages in this chapter consistently end with a statement that assumes the client will come back and describe progress that has occurred between sessions. It is important to understand that these messages, although easily adaptable for use in later sessions, are formulated for use at the end of the initial meeting. Unless clients have made it quite clear they do not need to return, end the feedback in first sessions with a suggestion that they come back. If they balk at the suggestion, explore their concern. In second meetings and beyond, ask clients whether they think it useful to continue meeting and, if so, what interval should elapse before they return. Later chapters present suggestions on how to get client perceptions on this matter.

During first sessions, clients are taking measure of us and the context in which services are offered. That is, they are beginning to build a sense of whether they can trust us and whether they want to work seriously on anything with us. In addition, most clients who come for services expect that it will take more than one session to solve their problems. In that case, if clients are asked at the end of the first session whether they think it makes sense to come back, their perception may be that we do not want to work with them, we lack confidence in our abilities to be useful, or we lack confidence in their capacities to build solutions. Consequently, at the end of the first meeting, we suggest you tell clients you want to see them again and that, when they come back, you would like to hear about what is going better. This approach best fosters client trust and confidence in the practitioner and, at the same time, has the added benefit of fostering an expectation of positive change in the client. At the end of the feedback in the first session, ask the client, "So, when do you think it would be most useful for you to return?" This question begins to send a message to clients that they are competent to decide what is best for themselves, while at the same time letting the clients know you think it would be useful for them to see you again. In later sessions, after clients have become more confident in both your capacities and their own, begin asking whether they think they need to meet with you again.

CRIBSHEETS, PROTOCOLS, AND NOTETAKING

Formulating feedback for clients can be difficult and confusing. During the session, clients give a great deal of information, which must be organized in a short period according to the criteria summarized earlier. If you are new to solution-focused interviewing and developing feedback, it is easy to get lost or overwhelmed during the break and end up responding to the client according to a paradigm with which you are more familiar. Doing so may leave you disappointed and wondering whether you will ever be able to stay consistent in offering clients feedback that is focused on solutions of their own making.

Many of our workshop participants and students find that cribsheets and protocols help them to stay on track. They are especially helpful for those who are just beginning to learn the procedures. Once students are more familiar with the techniques, the cribsheets and protocols may be used periodically as refreshers. Chapter 5 directs you to a cribsheet in the Appendix consisting of questions for developing well-formed goals. The cribsheet summarizes the interviewing questions discussed in Chapter 5 and provides several examples. Two more items in the Appendix relate to material covered in this chapter. The first is a protocol for formulating feedback to clients. Use this form during the break. If, with the client's permission, other practitioners or students are observing the session, they can use the protocol to record ideas for the bottom line and compliments that occur to them during the interview. Second, there is a summary of the common messages presented in this chapter.

All of the basic interviewing and feedback procedures necessary for you to conduct a first solution-building meeting with your clients have been presented. These have been described in a sequence to follow during your first meeting with clients. This sequence began in Chapter 4, in which we suggested that, after some preliminaries, you begin by asking your clients, "How can I be helpful?" It ended with your giving feedback and scheduling a next meeting (if you and your clients so decide). The protocol in the Appendix, which lists the various parts of this sequence, can be used as a map in your first meeting with clients.

When this protocol is offered to workshop participants and students, they often ask how to use it. In particular, they wonder whether it is advisable to take session notes on this protocol. Although both of us take notes during sessions, Insoo does not use the protocol, whereas Peter often does. Insoo prefers to trust her sense of which solution-focused procedures to pursue and in what order, while Peter appreciates having the structure of a protocol on which to fall back. We both take notes on the clients' words for their problems, miracle pictures, exceptions, scaling responses, and so forth. Insoo writes these on a blank piece of paper. Peter records them on a copy of the appropriate protocol form. Writing down clients' words sensitizes us to clients' shifting perceptions in the solution-building process and gives us the information needed to formulate end-of-session feedback. We both include these notes in the clients' files and use them as the basic resource for completing any other necessary client paperwork. Like Benjamin (1987), we notice that clients consistently accept our notetaking after we explain that we are doing it to better remember what they tell us about themselves and their circumstances.

DVD (See DVD Clips 4 and 5.)

NOTE

1.   We realize there are circumstances in which we would move to connect certain clients with community resources. We address such circumstances in later chapters.

8

Later Sessions: Finding, Amplifying, and Measuring Client Progress

No man ever steps in the same river twice, for it's not the same river and
he's not the same man.
(HERACLITES, GREEK PHILOSOPHER)

Always there and listening to me. Always made time for me.
Encouraged me to get on with what I have to do; he had confidence in
me and that helped me get on with what I knew I had to do.
(BRIEF FAMILY THERAPY CENTER CLIENT, DESCRIBING HER
PRACTITIONER)

Throughout this book, we have been emphasizing that clients build solutions
more by drawing on their successes and strengths than by analyzing their
problems. All of the interviewing procedures presented reflect this emphasis. This
chapter describes how to interview clients in later sessions in ways that will
continue to encourage them to build on their strengths.

The purpose of all later meetings is the same—to open and sustain a dialogue
around what's better for the client. The purpose is for the interviewer to engage
the client in a search for exceptions that have occurred since the last time they
met. These exceptions are the building blocks for a solution.

The structure of later sessions reflects their purpose. As the exceptions
emerge from the interaction between practitioner and client, the practitioner,
using solution-focused interviewing procedures, invites the client to amplify the
exceptions. This work takes up most of the later sessions. Thereafter, the practitioner uses scaling procedures to get the client's estimate of progress to date and to

do some additional goal-formulation work. The goal-formulation work includes determining what the next steps are for the client and thinking more about what will have to be different in the client's life for the client to feel ready to terminate services. Then, as in first sessions, the practitioner takes a break, develops feedback, and returns to deliver the feedback.

This chapter reviews each of the components of a later session. These components are summarized in the protocol for later sessions included in the Appendix. The discussion is organized to correspond broadly to that protocol. Segments of dialogue with Ah Yan and the Williams family are presented as illustrations.

"WHAT'S BETTER?"

We begin later sessions with clients by asking, "What's better?" Many workshop participants and students have told us that, at first, this seems strange. "Wouldn't it be more logical," they ask, "to begin by asking whether the client followed through on the suggestion made at the last session?" Or they ask, "Why not be more cautious and inquire, 'Is anything better since we last met?'" There are reasons for doing neither.

We do not explicitly ask if clients have followed through on suggestions for the following reasons. First, as indicated in Chapter 7, we do not view our suggestions as the solutions to clients' problems. Instead, they are offered to clients as an extension of the information that emerges from the interaction between us and our clients. It is important to maintain the view of the client as the expert with regard to the suggestions given. Clients, not practitioners, can best decide whether following through on a particular suggestion would be useful to them in building solutions. Second, by not explicitly asking about the suggestion, we avoid putting both our clients and ourselves into an awkward position. If clients have not followed through on the suggestion, they might feel obliged to explain why they did not do so, and we might have to explain why we now imply the client should have done what was offered only as a suggestion at the previous meeting. Third, as mentioned at the end of Chapter 7, clients often go beyond the limits of our suggestions. Alternatively, something may have happened in the client's life soon after the previous session to make the suggestion less relevant. In that case, the client would understandably take solution building in another direction. (In such cases, the client may even forget the suggestion.) Therefore, begin later sessions with a question that is sufficiently broad to cover a range of possibilities.

Do not begin later sessions by asking, "Is anything better since we last met?" As Insoo has written elsewhere (Berg, 1994, p. 150), to ask this question implies we are somewhat doubtful about improvements, and we thereby feed any client ambivalence about progress. Consequently, following the advice of de Shazer and his colleagues (de Shazer et al., 1986), begin later sessions by simply asking, "What's better?" This question reflects our confidence that clients are competent to have taken steps, no matter how small, in the direction of what they have said they want.

The most fundamental reason for beginning later sessions by asking this question is it once again reflects the conviction that solutions are primarily built from the perception of exceptions. Given that both problem times and exception times will most likely have happened in any client's life since the previous session, begin later sessions by asking about what is most useful to the client—any perceived exceptions that have occurred.

You should expect different responses when you ask clients, "What's better?" Berg (1994) identifies three different groups of clients on the basis of their responses. The first group, easily the majority, is able to identify experiences that are better since the last session. Some are able to identify these exceptions right away. Others need encouragement and probing from the interviewer. A second group will say, "I'm really not sure" or "I think things are about the same." A third group, a small minority, will say things are worse.

When you encounter clients who fall into the second or third group, pursue the same line of questioning for a while. With probing and encouragement, many clients who are at first unsure about any improvement are able to identify exceptions that later turn out to be valuable. A useful technique is to ask the client to think about whether particular days went better than others. For example, if a client is unsure whether anything was better, you can ask, "OK, let me see. The last time I saw you was last Thursday morning. So, was last Friday any better than Thursday afternoon?" Then you might ask, "Was the weekend any better than Friday?" Ask about the past week one day at a time. Usually, with more specific questioning, ambivalent clients and those who start out by saying things are worse are able to identify some exceptions.

Thus, with some persistence on the interviewer's part, the majority of clients will be able to identify exceptions. The interviewer's task is to open and sustain a conversation with clients around their exceptions and move in the direction of solutions. Because the majority of interviewing work in later sessions involves such conversations, this chapter describes solution-focused procedures you can use in these sessions. Chapter 10 will address the much less common situation in which, despite the interviewer's best efforts, the client cannot identify exceptions and may be feeling deeply discouraged.

EARS

Once a client identifies an exception, however vaguely or unconvincingly, it is your role to explore it in detail. Practitioners at the Brief Family Therapy Center (BFTC) have spent many years working out new and more effective ways to do this (Berg, 1994). They have developed the acronym EARS to capture the interviewer's activities in this work. *E* stands for *eliciting* the exception. *A* refers to *amplifying* it, first by asking the client to describe what is different between this exception time and problem times, and second, by exploring how the exception happened, especially the role that the client might have played in making it happen. *R* involves *reinforcing* the successes and strengths the exception represents, largely by noticing exceptions, taking the time to explore them carefully, and complimenting wherever appropriate. Last, *S* reminds interviewers to *start again* by asking, "What else is better?"[1]

Ah Yan

As you develop a solution-focused way of interviewing, you can expect to devote an increasing share of later sessions to EARS activities. To illustrate this process, let us look at Peter's second session with Ah Yan.

PETER: What's happening that's better, Ah Yan?

AH YAN: Umm. Well, umm . . .

PETER: Well, what have you noticed that tells you that things are better?

AH YAN: I'm back to work. I didn't go to work all week last week.

PETER: [*wondering if returning to work might somehow represent an exception*] Oh, you went back to work this week?

AH YAN: Yeah, this week I went back to work.

PETER: [*noticing that she seemed pleased with herself and complimenting her apparent success*] Well, good for you!

AH YAN: Thanks.

PETER: So did you work today?

AH YAN: We worked till seven. I just got out.

PETER: Oh, wow! You must be very busy?

AH YAN: Uh, yeah, this week we are working 12 hours.

PETER: Twelve hours a day?

AH YAN: Yeah. And I work Saturday, too.

PETER: Saturday?

AH YAN: Yeah.

PETER: Are you working 12 hours each day, six days a week?

AH YAN: Yeah.

PETER: You're working 72 hours a week?

AH YAN: Yeah. Well, I didn't work last week, so it's kind of OK.

PETER: It's OK this week. Are you going to work that much next week, too?

AH YAN: No, I don't think so. I think it's just this week because he [her employer] got a big order in, and so he wants to try to get it all in.

PETER: So, sometimes you have a lot of work, and then it falls off.

AH YAN: Yeah.

PETER: How did it happen that you went back to work?

AH YAN: I felt better. Like, um, I told him I was ready to work.

PETER: [*now more convinced an exception has been elicited and beginning to explore it*] And, ah, when did you wake up feeling better, knowing that you could go back to work?

AH YAN: Monday.

PETER: Monday morning?

AH YAN: Yesterday. Sunday it was like, um, I don't know. All weekend it was like ... bad, like I was going to get the shakes. It would make me feel, you know, ... that way, and I just get these feelings that I just can't really fight. And I just want to lay down, just ... I don't know. It puts me down.

PETER: [*affirming her perception and asking Ah Yan to begin amplifying the exception*] Yeah, it sounds very difficult. But sometime during the weekend, you said, you felt better?

AH YAN: Yeah, and this weekend, I fought it. Me and my husband went to a dance. We went to a wedding dance Saturday, and I got kind of sick there in the middle of the dance. And he, my husband, asked me, "Are you OK?" And I says, "No, I don't think so. I want to get out." You know. And he says, "Well, let's go outside." And we went outside for a walk, you know. We went walking like 10 minutes. And he says, "Are you OK? Do you want to go home?" And I says, "*No!* We're not going to go home."

PETER: [*exploring for what was different about the exception and indirectly complimenting*] Really? Was that different for you—saying no to leaving like you did?

AH YAN: Yeah, it was, and I said, you know, "We're not going to stop." You know, I just—I have to keep going.

PETER: [*reinforcing with an indirect compliment and asking for more description*] How did you know that what you needed at that time was to listen to your husband and leave the dance and go for a walk with him?

AH YAN: [*amplifying her description of both the exception and how it happened*] I don't know. I feel like, 'cause we were—well, there was a lot of people, OK? I don't know if it's me or, I don't know, I can't say, because I feel like it's too stuffy. It's too ... you know, and I felt like I couldn't breathe. I don't know. I just—I don't know if I was nervous or what. I don't know. I just told him I was going to have to get out. "I want to be alone right now." You know. "Let's get out." You know, so we just went outside for a while, you know, and then we were just talking and, you know, and he said, "Are you OK?" And I said, "Yeah, let's go back in."

Clients usually have to struggle to conceptualize their exceptions, their roles in bringing them about, and the significance of these exceptions for their lives. Ah Yan's work is a good example of that process. Peter's task was to keep her focused on solution talk. To do so, he identified successes and strengths that could be reinforced through compliments and asked for more amplification. In the following segment, pay special attention to how Ah Yan developed a clearer and more complete sense of her role in building a solution to her problem.

PETER: That's amazing! [*indirectly complimenting*] Did you know that would work?

AH YAN: Huh? No, but I just walked out, you know, just not going to let it stop me. There were too many people in there, and it was real crowded, and I had to get out. You know, I just walked outside, you know, to cool off. It was better for me.

PETER: Yeah. And then you went back to the dance, and did it come back?

AH YAN: Like it wanted to, but I'd just ignore it, and it wanted, you know—I just kept talking, and, you know, just ignored it. Something like . . .

PETER: [amplifying by explicitly asking for her role in making the exception happen] How do you do that—ignore it?

AH YAN: Because it's like, when it starts, and my mind goes to what's happening to me, it gets worse. It gets worse. And if I just, like, brush it off, you know, like they say, brush it off, just forget it, I, like, start talking, you know, paying attention to the people that are talking to me and just . . . I forget about it. You know.

PETER: And when you brush it off, what do you do differently? You said, talking to other people?

AH YAN: Just talking to them, yeah, or laughing, and dancing.

PETER: You like to dance?

AH YAN: Yeah.

PETER: Is dancing something you are good at?

AH YAN: Yeah, real good.

PETER: Yeah? Great, not everyone is, that's for sure. OK. And I know that you like to talk with people. You were telling me last time that you liked to talk to your sister-in-law. [asking for more amplification of how she makes the exception happen] So, what else do you do when you brush it off?

AH YAN: I don't know. Pay attention to something else, you know, 'cause, I don't know, I'm trying to figure it out myself, too.

PETER: I can tell you're working pretty hard at figuring yourself out.

When Ah Yan talked about figuring it out, Peter recalled she had used the same phrase several times in the first session. It occurred to him that these words seemed to be taking on a different meaning for her. In their first session, she spoke of figuring out what was causing her shakes, shortness of breath, and hair falling out, as though she had to uncover some underlying cause in order to stop these symptoms and get better. (She wondered aloud whether her heart or personality might be the cause.) Now, figuring it out seems to mean discovering strategies she can use to keep it (presumably, the shakes) under control. As she develops a clearer sense of her exception times and what she has been doing to make them happen, any concern she had about underlying causes seems to have been set aside or forgotten.

Ah Yan's changing use of this phrase is an instance of something witnessed regularly in solution-building work: Client perceptions and meanings shift over time, sometimes dramatically. As those of us working with a solution focus have become more aware of this, interviewing procedures have evolved toward ever greater openness and flexibility, tracking the client's shifting perceptions and meanings.

Notice the continuing shift in Ah Yan's sense of what it will take to solve her problem and even of the problem itself.

AH YAN: I guess, too, after I left from here last week, I went to the library, and I found a book of, what was that, anxiety panic or anxiety attacks?

PETER: Anxiety attacks.

AH YAN: And I was reading through it, and a lot of the symptoms is what I'm going through. I feel like those are the symptoms, you know, and it says, "The less you worry, the healthier you are," and it says, "Who's in charge: you or your brain?" or something like that. You know, I'm trying to read, and maybe that's what it is, just worry too much, you know, and what really got me was, "The less you worry, the healthier you are." I don't know, those words meant a lot to me.

PETER: That was in the book?

AH YAN: Yeah. I'm still reading it.

PETER: And those words are: "The less you worry, the healthier you are." And those words are real meaningful to you?

AH YAN: Yeah, they are. And it says, "Who is in charge?"

PETER: [*echoing*] "Who is in charge?"

AH YAN: "You or your mind" or "your brain." I don't remember which it said: mind or brain. It's like, you got to control your thought. Your brain controls you, or you control it. You know. Seems like maybe that's what's wrong with me. 'Cause it's—I don't know, I'm reading all these symptoms they have on it, and it's what I'm going through. And it's like, I couldn't explain it to nobody, but I don't know—when there's so many feelings I'm going through, all these symptoms I go through, and all these thoughts I have, and you know, it's hard to explain. It's hard to explain to somebody, so I got the book, and I'm reading it. I'm not done with it, but I just started it.

PETER: Wow, you're learning a lot. So, you have the book at home.

AH YAN: Yeah.

PETER: OK, and it's really helpful.

AH YAN: Yeah. And I'm trying to learn it.

PETER: [*asking once again for amplification*] I can see that you are. Seems like you've already learned a lot. OK. Is there anything else you do differently to put yourself in charge?

Although Ah Yan had already indicated several things she had done to account for feeling better and had clarified for both Peter and herself how she was doing them, Peter kept asking for more details about how she made the exception happen. It is clear that she identified herself as having the major role in making the exception happen, and it seemed to Peter that her confidence about her own capabilities was building. Consequently, he wanted to get as much detail as possible about her deliberate exceptions around feeling better.

AH YAN: Faith. I got to have faith in myself before I do anything. And deep breathe, saying, "OK, you know, stop thinking about what's wrong," you know, 'cause I'm that type. I get a little panicky, "Oh no, what's wrong with me?" You know. Now I says, "No, that's the way I was before," and then, you know, I think back to the way I used to get, really bad. I'm thinking, "At the time that was happening, what was I thinking then?" I was thinking to myself, I would think more things wrong—you know, "This is going to happen to me, what if this, or what if . . . ?" It just—my mind was going and going and going, you know, and it's like . . .

PETER: So instead of that, now you're doing what?

AH YAN: I'm trying to, you know—how do you say this? [she takes an exaggerated breath]

PETER: You take a deep breath?

AH YAN: Yeah, and say: "OK, do what you have to do, or keep doing what you're doing. Don't stop." You know, 'cause I used to stop and just, like, start thinking, "Oh no, what's wrong with me?" You know. Now it's like I say: "No, just keep going," you know, do what I have to do, you know. Or it's like, I'm going to take control.

PETER: Yeah, yeah. Is this new for you—what you're doing differently?

AH YAN: Yeah! Yeah, it's new . . .

PETER: Does that surprise you that you're able to do that?

AH YAN: Yeah. It's just like every day that's going by, I'm trying to figure, you know, something, you know, and I feel like, any stuff that I can take, I'll take it. I can, and, like, I read that book. "Who's in charge: you or your mind?" Or—well, you know. Like, *I am!* I am going to do it, you know, and if you really think about it, I don't know. I am really—if I really put my head to it, you know, I will.

PETER: Ah Yan, that's amazing. Congratulations!

AH YAN: Yeah, thanks. And I see it does help. You know, it's not all on you, but I have to learn how to control myself too, you know. That's what I think, you know. It takes time.

PETER: Yes, it takes time. It takes practice.

AH YAN: Yeah, practice, yeah.

PETER: [*continuing to reinforce and compliment her success and strengths, focusing especially on the role she played in the exceptions*] Yeah, and you're working. Seems like you're working very hard at this. Very hard. So, you told me that the way you've been putting yourself in charge is by deep breathing, by keeping going with whatever it was you were doing at that time, and sometimes, um, you take charge by leaving the situation—like leaving the dance for a while when you knew that it was too crowded.

AH YAN: It was too many people. People were smoking, and it's like, "No, I just have to walk out," you know.

PETER: Is that different for you, to figure out what's a good situation for you, what you need in a situation?

AH YAN: I guess it depends where I'm at. Like Sunday, I was kind of, you know, kind of getting like the way I get when we were in the car. You know, and it was like, you know—I try, I guess. When it's happening to me, I figure, "OK, I'm here. What am I going to do here?" You know, there's no way I'm going to get out of the car, you know; it's going, you know. So I just roll the window down ...

PETER: So, you had that to work with—the window.

AH YAN: Yeah, I roll the window down. Anything where I feel comfortable, that's what I do. We were at my Grandma's Sunday, till—no Saturday—and all my relatives were there. We were talking, and I guess I started getting these symptoms again, and I just got out the paper. It's like, you know, we're all laughing, and just gradually, you know, I calm down. It's like, I'm trying to do it where people don't realize, you know, and I don't think that they realize that anything is even wrong with me, you know.

PETER: So, usually you don't even tell the other people around you.

AH YAN: No, I don't. No.

Ah Yan continued to describe exceptions, times when she felt better during the previous week and what she was doing to take control. Peter went on to the fourth letter of the EARS acronym, the *S* for starting over. He asked: "What else is better?" In the resulting conversation, Ah Yan was able to describe that she was learning to distinguish between times when it was good for her to tell others that her anxiety was coming on and times when it was not. Besides the exception with her husband at the dance, she described another involving her sister-in-law, in which she discovered that her sister-in-law had her own fears. Ah Yan found opening up to her sister-in-law helpful. She concluded, "I'm not the only one who gets panicky" and "It's OK to show that you're human."

As Peter continued to ask her what was better, Ah Yan began to say, "I don't know." Then Peter turned to relationship questions as a way of sustaining Ah Yan's solution talk. He asked, "So when you're feeling better, what do you suppose your husband notices different about you that tells him you're feeling that way?" He asked similar questions about Ah Yan's mother and her children. Sometimes new exceptions emerge through relationship questioning; sometimes they do not. In either case, such questions help clients view the consequences of any progress they might be making from a contextual or systemic perspective. What follows is a brief illustration.

PETER: How about the kids? What do you imagine the kids might notice that's different about you that would tell them that their mom is feeling better?

AH YAN: I don't know. They're always all over me. They're all over me. I don't know, um. I don't know. They still play. I don't know, I guess they're

just themselves—the way they're supposed to be. They don't even
have to look at mommy, you know. I'm OK, you know; they're
playing. But when I don't feel good they're like . . .

PETER: You mean they're worried, too?

AH YAN: Yeah, you know, they're playing, but they're kind of quiet . . .
watching me . . .

PETER: Now they don't need to watch as much?

AH YAN: Yeah, when I'm better, they don't even remember mommy when she's OK.

PETER: When they remember mommy but go ahead and are little children,
how is that for you? What's different for you?

AH YAN: It's good. It's real good. It's what I want. [tearfully] You know, they
have to not worry about me. Let them be them. They're kids. They're
not supposed to worry.

PETER: "Real good." Yes, I can see, "real good." [pause] So, is there anything
else that's better that we haven't talked about yet?

AH YAN: No, we took care of everything.

DOING MORE OF THE SAME

When clients can identify exceptions, it is useful to inquire about what it would
take for the exceptions to happen again. This is especially helpful when clients
seem unclear about how the exception happened, but it is important even when
clients can state what they have been doing to make the exceptions happen. For
example, Peter might ask, "What will it take for you to keep on with what you
have been doing to make yourself feel better?" Perhaps he could ask, "What's
most important for you to do to keep all this going?" He did not ask either of
these questions. Instead, he asked for similar information by scaling confidence.

DVD (See DVD Clip 6.)

SCALING

Peter and Ah Yan talked about what was better. It seemed to Peter that she was
developing a clear sense of both the several exceptions to her anxiety and the
steps she was taking to make these happen. Judging that she was ready to move
on to something else, Peter turned to scaling, in accordance with the protocol for
later sessions. After scaling Ah Yan's perception of her current level of progress
and her level of confidence, he used her scaling responses for further goal
formulation. Notice how scaling helps Ah Yan and Peter get a sharper awareness
of Ah Yan's progress and what she needs to do next.

Scaling Progress

When Ah Yan told Peter they had covered everything that was better since their last session, he began scaling.

> PETER: OK, great. So, let me ask you a question using my numbers again, OK? Let's say that 10 equals the miracle and 0 was where you were at when you decided that you were going to come in and talk with me about this. Where would you say you are at this week?
>
> AH YAN: Now?
>
> PETER: Yeah, now.
>
> AH YAN: Seven, maybe 8.
>
> PETER: Oh, wow, 7 or 8! OK. Sure, that makes sense. You've been telling me about feeling better and all the things you do to make that happen: Like you're back to work, and you're smiling more, and even when it comes on, you come up with ways in which to handle it . . .
>
> AH YAN: Yeah, yeah, that's right. I'm doing that.

The number that Ah Yan chose made sense to Peter. Because she had so many deliberate exceptions, Peter expected her to select a high number. Had she chosen a low number, he would have explored the apparent discrepancy. Such exploration often uncovers important new information.

Scaling Confidence

Peter went on to scale Ah Yan's level of confidence that she could maintain her gains.

> PETER: OK. So you're at a 7 or an 8 . . . umm, and I've been asking you about all the things that you do to keep them at a 7 or an 8. Now, if I were to ask you, "On a scale from 1 to 10, where 1 means that you have no confidence and 10 means you have every confidence, how confident are you that you can keep them at a 7 or an 8?" What would you say?
>
> AH YAN: I think a 9.
>
> PETER: Is that right?
>
> AH YAN: Yeah, and I can tell because some things just, I don't know . . .
>
> PETER: Where does that confidence come from? What tells you that you can be that confident, that sure?
>
> AH YAN: I want to be that way . . . to repeat it.
>
> PETER: [*complimenting an apparent strength*] So you're determined.
>
> AH YAN: Yeah, I am. I want to be . . .
>
> PETER: So where does that determination come from?
>
> AH YAN: I don't know. You know, it's just the way I feel right now. It just feels good to feel like this. I just want to keep quiet, so it doesn't come back

anymore. I just want to keep going. I know how positive it feels, you know. It's very good.

Ah Yan seemed to have an intuitive sense that she could continue her recent gains but could not articulate its source beyond saying emphatically that this was how she felt. Other clients will more fully describe the source of their confidence. They will describe past experiences that reveal their strengths. Ah Yan did not. To follow up, Peter could have asked her whether there were times in the past when she had similar feelings and, if so, whether they had been similarly helpful.

NEXT STEPS

To this point in the second session, everything had centered on Ah Yan's exceptions and their implications for building a solution. It is important in every later session to also address goals, mainly because clients' perceptions of their goals may shift, just as their perceptions of problems and possible solutions do. For example, after considering what's better since the last session and finding little, clients may decide their original goals are unrealistic and revise them so they seem more achievable. On the other hand, clients who have made more gains in the solution-building process than they had expected may develop additional goals.

Goal formulation in later sessions does not involve repeating the miracle question. As a solution-focused interviewer, you can shift easily and effectively into goal formulation on the basis of the client's answer to the scaling question about progress. For example, when Ah Yan said she was at 7 or 8, Peter could have asked her, "What will be different when you're a 9?" Asking her to think about what will be happening in her life when she moves up the scale is an invitation to explore her present perceptions of what she wants next, given her awareness of what's better since the previous session. By moving up the scale in small gradations, Peter encourages her to work toward smaller, more realistic goals.

In later sessions, goal formulation begins later than in the first session because it depends on thorough exploration of what has been better. Approximately 30 minutes into their second session, Peter initiated a dialogue on goals with Ah Yan.

PETER: Let's talk just a little bit about the next step. When you move up to say, an 8, what will be different that will tell you that you're at an 8, instead of a 7 or an 8?

AH YAN: I think I wouldn't be so scared to even think like . . . wherever I'm going to go—I mean, I get these symptoms and—and, you know, I don't think I would even—it's like forgetting about it. I think I would beat the level of training.

PETER: So when you forget about it, what would you be thinking about instead?

AH YAN: Healthier and happier and . . . I don't know.

PETER: How about when you move all the way up to a 9?

AH YAN: Nine? More healthier and happier thoughts like now, I guess. I don't know.

PETER: So it sounds like it'll be more of the same thing of what's happening right now.

AH YAN: Yeah.

Aside from the miracle question, all of the goal-formulation questions in Chapter 5 may be used in later sessions. How far you want to go with the goal-formulation dialogue depends on the interviewing situation. You will do more goal formulation with clients who have unclear or seemingly unrealistic goals and with clients for whom little has gone better over the past week. When you work with clients like Ah Yan, who spend approximately 30 minutes describing progress and how they produced it, you will have less time and, sensing their confidence, less need to work on goal development because such clients have a greater sense of direction.

When Peter asked Ah Yan about possible next steps, she gave a fairly vague answer: She would be having happy and healthy thoughts more of the time. Peter could have followed up by seeking greater clarification and specificity. Instead, he chose to invite Ah Yan to work at goals by asking relationship questions involving her husband, mother, and children. The following dialogue stemmed from the relationship question he asked with regard to her children. Notice how, in working on goals here, Ah Yan mentioned a new exception. This illustrates how asking relationship questions can clarify, and perhaps enhance, what is happening in the client's solution building.

PETER: So, when you move up to 8, what will your children notice that will tell them that you are doing just that much better?

AH YAN: With my kids, I have to be more—I have to let them go a little bit. I see other kids, and I have to like ... My little boy, I never wanted him far from me. I was scared something's going to happen to him or hurt my girls. And it's like, "You stay in front of the house. *Don't leave the front of the house. Don't.*" All these kids his age are on their bikes, going around the blocks, you know. And it's like—let him go, let him go, just give him a certain length, you know. And I tell him, "Now, OK, five houses this way and three houses this way; you cross the street just make sure you watch for cars." And I don't know, I saw him Saturday, I let him go. I saw him.

PETER: [*noticing an elicited exception*] Was that different for you?

AH YAN: And it felt like, like, ah, relief. OK, it's a big step, you know. I'm still kind of like, "Don't cross the street."

PETER: [*exploring the exception*] You did that on Saturday.

AH YAN: Yeah.

PETER: [*echoing her words*] Really? You let him go?

AH YAN: Yeah. He crossed the street.

PETER: So that's another thing that you did differently?

AH YAN: Yeah, he crossed the street. I don't know, it's still scary, but he has to grow up, too.

PETER: How old is he?

AH YAN: Di Jia, he's 6.

PETER: He's 6? Is this the first time you let him go across the street like that?

AH YAN: Yeah, yeah.

PETER: [*indirect compliment, a single word to punctuate the exception*] Wow!

AH YAN: And it's like, I kind of—I wanted to cry, and I wanted to laugh. I don't know. It's something that I did let him go, you know, but it's hard, 'cause I'm scared something's going to happen.

PETER: Yeah, it really is something.

AH YAN: I just can't . . . I hear all these things that kids get hit, you know. I just think that's what bothers me. I'm scared to lose somebody.

PETER: Yeah. Sure, of course.

AH YAN: When I saw him, I kind of laughed, you know, and I wanted to cry, you know, at the same time. He's so big, and it's like, I want him by me. It's like, I can't do that. I just can't.

PETER: It's not easy, is it?

AH YAN: My little girl got stitches. She was running, of course, like kids do. And she got a stick, and it went in her hip. And I see at times that I can be happy, and then something goes wrong. It makes me think wrong, you know, or think bad, like what happened to my little girl. OK, but my little boy, he was playing OK, and it made me feel good because I let him go, you know—kind of like he's got to have confidence . . .

PETER: Wow, I'm impressed. That was so tough for you to do. How did you get yourself to do that?

AH YAN: People tell me, "You don't let your kids do anything. Let them go, you know. Let them go. You're too close to your kids," they tell me.

PETER: [*refocusing on Ah Yan's success*] What told you on Saturday that these people were right, that what you needed to do was to let him go?

AH YAN: Because I see all these little kids. They're playing, and he's looking at them.

PETER: Sure, of course.

AH YAN: He feels left out. I don't know. I think I would feel left out if I was in his place, so I have to. I have to. He's got a bike, the kids got a bike, and they're his age. Why can they go, and he can't? He's going to be left out.

PETER: So you're paying attention to him and figuring out what's right and good for him?

AH YAN: Yeah, and I says, "OK, you're going to go this many houses, and that's your part, and that's how far mom is going to let you go. And you can't go around the block because I can't see you." And I think he still kind of answers to that. And I said, "You can cross the street. Be careful. Please. You know, and this part, you can't go too close because there's more traffic out this way, you know." I saw him, and it felt good 'cause he looked happy. He looked like, "I'm on the street," you know, and it's like—I don't know, it feels good. My little girl got hurt, you know. She was running and running. There was sticks, and she got it, and she got stitches. And it's like, why, why did I let her do that? You know, but I can't think that way. My sister-in-law says, "My little girl's had a broken leg, a da-da-da, a finger's broken, arm broken, you know, all of it." And it's like she goes, "Things happen. It don't matter if they're in the same place. Things happen." And like . . .

PETER: Things happen.

AH YAN: It's hard to, I don't know—just kind of scared any—something else is going to happen. You know, I have to because, if I don't, they're not going to grow up, you know. They're not going to learn how to do things by themselves. They're going to want me there 'cause I'm going to show them that way. But I want them to have confidence in themselves. I'm trying. I'm trying.

PETER: [*amplifying and complimenting her determination to do what is best for her children*] Yes, I can see that. I can see that you want to let them go more, so that they can have confidence. You care very much about them.

AH YAN: Yeah, I love them.

Peter made it possible for Ah Yan to arrive at her own conclusion: "I love them." Rather than praising Ah Yan for loving her children, Peter asked questions that helped Ah Yan make her own assessment of her strengths. This is true empowerment. In this process, clients make their own claims about what kind of good and competent people they are.

DVD (See DVD Clip 7.)

TERMINATION

In solution-building interviews, you think about, and work at, termination with clients from the first session. The initial goal-formulation question asked of clients in the first session reflects that attitude: "What needs to be different in your life as a result of coming here for you to say that meeting with me was worthwhile?" The same attitude continues in later meetings.

You can address termination efficiently and naturally in later sessions by working from clients' responses to the scaling question about progress. After working on additional goals, you can begin a conversation about termination by asking, "What number do you need to be in order not to come and talk to me anymore?" The following is what happened when Peter asked this of Ah Yan.

PETER: OK, let me ask you this. Right now, you're at a 7 or 8. What do you need to be in order not to come back here and see me anymore?

AH YAN: To learn not to worry and, I don't know, to just stop thinking wrong, you know, like the opposite of good. And I just want to feel good about myself.

PETER: What does that mean in terms of a number? You're at a 7 or an 8 now. Is that good enough for you? Can you live with a 7 or an 8?

AH YAN: Yeah, yeah, 'cause I have confidence right now. I don't know, when I'm lower, it's just like I'm not sure. I'm kind of scared, more scared than positive. I'm trying to fight the scared away. The book, you know, it helps, and the talking about it, the talking and opening up . . .

PETER: That helps, too.

AH YAN: I think, when I talk to people, I don't know, I don't feel so like—like, when I didn't talk to anybody, it was like nobody's listening to me, nobody.

PETER: You felt alone.

AH YAN: Yeah, I felt alone. I felt trapped. I don't know. I just felt so lonely. And now that I'm talking—like, my sister goes, "I heard that you didn't feel good," and she says, "I told mom you worry too much. You think too much." You know, now that I talk to people, it's like I can talk to anybody, you know. Someone can be there. It's not—I guess it's me that wouldn't talk so no one would be there. And now I talk, and it's like, we both share each other's problems or . . .

PETER: Is that different for you that sometimes now you're the one that's taking the first step?

AH YAN: [*seemingly broadening her concept of her problem*] Yeah, it's different. I'm always listening and never talking. Maybe that's my problem too: I never talk, always keeping everything inside. And, now, I'm starting . . . and it kind of makes me, "Oh, someone's listening to me." It makes me feel better.

PETER: That makes a lot of sense. That makes a lot of sense. You've been doing a lot of thinking about this, haven't you?

AH YAN: I just want to get better. I just want everything better.

PETER: Yeah, I can see that you're working very hard to do that. OK, so right now, I was asking you what number you needed to be in order not to come back again. I'm still not clear on that.

AH YAN: The symptoms, I just want them to go away. They're like, I don't know. I go to my husband—I feel like they're little attacks, like seizures or something, but I mean, like, I have a brother that has epilepsy—you know, he gets attacks. He doesn't remember anything. He blacks out, and I don't. I know what's going on, and it feels like a dream to me. It feels like a dream to me, and the more I put my head to what's going on with me, that now it's worse, and when I feel like that, I just forget about it, and it just goes away. You know, it's like I'm trying to figure out if I can control it, if it's just me. It's me that's letting myself be like this, you know, and—I don't know. It's so weird ...

PETER: And now you're doing some of the things you need to do to control it.

AH YAN: Yeah, and now I'm noticing I can control it if I want.

PETER: What's the most important thing that you need to, ah, to do to make sure that you keep things at a 7 or an 8, to keep your confidence?

AH YAN: What I feel like—I don't know. I'm trying, you know, I'm trying to get everything together. I feel like it's really me that's making myself feel like this. I feel it's me. I'm trying to figure out things, and—I don't know. People can tell you, OK, they tell you you get exhausted, you know, you're tired, and you just want to bum around. They tell you that, but, I don't know, I realize that I think I do put too much on myself. I think that's my problem, and I think—I'm not positive about it, but I think I need help for them to show me, I don't know, like how to ... I don't know. I don't know; I can't explain it.

PETER: OK. Listen, I'm going to take a break and think about what you told me. OK? [she nods] Is there anything else we should talk about first?

AH YAN: No, I said it all.

Although Ah Yan never gave Peter a number, she did begin to ponder what would have to be different for her to feel comfortable and confident about terminating services. She said she would like the symptoms to disappear, but she also seemed to be developing the idea that the severity of the symptoms had a lot to do with her ("it's really me that's making myself feel like this") and that she had some control over them ("now I'm noticing I can control it if I want"). Realizing Ah Yan was not ready yet to define a scale score for termination, Peter decided to take a break and formulate feedback, instead of pushing her to come up with a number. His decision illustrates an important point: When clients have done their best to put words to their perceptions and cannot for the moment, the interviewer must accept that situation and respond respectfully. As always, the question plants the seed, and the client may do more thinking later.

THE BREAK

At this point, turn to the Appendix and review the protocol for formulating feedback. Complete this protocol for Ah Yan, on the basis of information from the second session. Write down a bottom line, compliments, and a bridge for Ah Yan. Read it aloud, as if you were delivering it to her. As you follow the account of Peter's reflections during the break, compare your conclusions with his.

The second session with Ah Yan reminded Peter how much clients' perceptions can shift during solution building. In their first session, Ah Yan talked as though the problem troubling her life was some unknown cause that was producing frightening symptoms like hair loss, shakiness, and hyperventilation. By the end of the second session, she seemed to be shifting toward a different definition, in which the problem was Ah Yan herself and the way she made certain choices ("I think I do put too much on myself"). Her perceptions, definitions, and meanings seemed to be changing over time and through interaction with others—her husband, mother, sister-in-law, children, and Peter.

During the break, Peter did not need very long to figure out a bottom line. He realized the problem (feeling panicky) and what she wanted (to reduce her fear) still stood. Near the end of their second meeting, Ah Yan seemed even more aware of herself as part of the problem and any eventual solution. Peter also noted that several exceptions had occurred since the first session. Ah Yan's description of them indicated they were deliberate exceptions. Finally, she seemed to have well-formed goals: She perceived that her deliberate exceptions had been successful ("I'm noticing that I can control it [the panic] if I want"), and she seemed to have every intention of repeating just what she had been doing to make the exceptions happen. Therefore, Peter decided the obvious bottom line was to suggest she do more of the same. He formulated compliments and a bridge, and he decided to give Ah Yan more responsibility for deciding about a next session. Then he was ready to deliver his feedback.

FEEDBACK

Compliments

PETER: OK, Ah Yan, I thought about all that you told me and, as I'm sure you can imagine, I am very impressed with what's been happening and what those things suggest about your strengths. First, you seem to be a very *creative* person. Just in this last week there have been so many different ways in which you have been able to brush it off and things you have done to put yourself in charge, things like leaving the dance when it came on, to take a break and get some air; like rolling down the window and breathing deep; like talking more and opening up with your sister-in-law; and so forth.

AH YAN: [smiling and nodding] Yeah, thanks.

PETER: And, uh, I'm also impressed that you want to educate yourself about these panicky feelings, that you took the time and made the effort to get that book, and that's another way in which you're taking charge. You know, you're getting more knowledge about it, and you found some real meaningful ideas in that book—like "who's in charge here?" And "the less you worry, the healthier you are."

AH YAN: Yeah, OK.

PETER: You also are a person with *courage*. After being away from work, you got your courage back up, and you went back to work. That's really something because, even though you felt better, you didn't know how it would turn out when you went back to work. Umm, I also think that it takes a lot of courage to decide that you're going to put yourself in charge. And it takes courage to then take the risks to try new things, such as talking more to get out of the trap of loneliness, or deciding that you have to do things differently with Di Jia and then taking the risk of letting him cross the street. That was a big step for you to take; that took courage and strength.

AH YAN: Yeah, it did.

PETER: Right, no wonder that you're at a 7 or an 8! [pause] And it's also impressive that you not only are doing things, but that you are paying such careful attention to exactly how you do it. That makes it two times impressive.

Bridge

PETER: Ah Yan, I agree with you when you say the words, "it's me that makes me feel this way," and I agree that a big part of the solution for you lies in your taking charge.

Suggestion

PETER: So what I suggest you do is that you continue to do those things that you've figured out for yourself that have been working, and as you continue to get better, I suggest that you pay attention to what else you might be doing that's helpful, things that you haven't noticed yet.

AH YAN: [nodding] Yeah, yeah.

PETER: OK. And now I'm thinking about, what next? Do you think it's a good idea to come back and talk more?

AH YAN: Yeah, I want to try not coming, but I don't know yet.... I want to have confidence. You know, what if it happens again?

PETER: Right. OK, I thought so from what you said. So, when? One, two, three weeks, or what?

AH YAN: I think two weeks.

PETER: OK, that sounds good. Let's set it up.

AH YAN: Thanks, I think that's good.

THE SECOND SESSION WITH THE WILLIAMS FAMILY

The second meeting with the Williams family provides an example of working simultaneously with several family members in a later session. Insoo works with the perceptions of individual family members but, at the same time, uncovers and works with the strengths of the family as a unit.

"What's Better?"

Gladys returned with her four children for the second session. As she had indicated she would at the end of the first session, Gladys sent her brother Albert away and did not invite him to the second session. Insoo began the session by asking, "What's been better since the last time we met?" Gladys answered that she had sent her mother home, too, and she and her children had spent a week at the Salvation Army Family Camp, where they went swimming and fishing and enjoyed other recreational activities. Gladys and the children indicated they had a good time there and got along well. Insoo then shifted the focus to family interactions at home.

INSOO: [*exploring for exceptions*] Yeah. So when the kids are getting along better, what are they like?

GLADYS: To me they like sisters and brothers should be. They play together, and they're not fighting each other. It's not like I gotta sit there and constantly watch 'em. But that's only when they outside. If they in the house, then I still have to watch 'em.

INSOO: [*asking about exceptions again, by refocusing on the original question*] OK. So tell me about—what are they like when they get along?

GLADYS: It's peaceful.

INSOO: You said they're like brothers and sisters. What's that mean?

GLADYS: They're not fighting. They not fussing and arguing at each other. Like Marcus, he argues all the time.

INSOO: What's he like when he doesn't argue with them?

GLADYS: I don't know yet because it's, like, he got this Nintendo, and he feel like he's the only one that should play it. And he always arguing with them because they're in his room and they want to play it, too. I could put it in the living room and use his TV, but he wouldn't like that. So I said, "Well, I'll put it in your room and you can play," 'cause the kids, they don't be there in the daytime, so he have all day to play it. Then, when they get home, they can play it, but he don't want them to play it.

INSOO: Uh huh. So you want him to share. [*to Marcus, asking for an exception*] What are you like? You must get along with somebody sometime, right?

MARCUS: Yeah.

INSOO: Yeah. Who do you get along well with?

MARCUS: I get along with my friends, and sometimes I get along with Offion.

INSOO: How do you do that?

MARCUS: When, like . . . me and my friends, we, like, well like, we go to birthday parties and everything. We go bowling and basketball games and baseball games. And, like, over at the center, that's, like, a place where I can go, like, and Offion and them, they're not allowed. It's just for teenagers. I can just go and have fun.

INSOO: [*indirectly complimenting*] Is that right? And you don't hear complaints from where he goes?

GLADYS: No. I get complaints in my house around the clock. I don't understand how he can go and play with somebody else, but he have to live with us, and he can't play with the ones that in the house. I don't understand that.

INSOO: [*affirming her perception*] Yeah. This must be baffling for you.

GLADYS: [*returning to problem talk*] Yeah. It's like these are your brothers and sisters. You got to stay with these people. You got to live with these people. Then when you get grown, you might need them one day. And then he say he don't want to be around them. He said they—uh, he always say he wants to go somewheres where peoples are his age, but Offion is 10 an' he's 12. That's his age.

INSOO: Now, so you're concerned that they may be—what? Fighting too much? You want them to love each other?

GLADYS: Yeah, that's a big concern.

INSOO: Uh. OK. Now do you think that these two fight more than most 12-year-old and 10-year-old brothers?

GLADYS: I don't know. . . . I'm not gonna say the two of 'em; I'm gonna say Marcus. He be fighting too much and don't listen.

INSOO: What do you make of this? How come he listens to other people and he doesn't listen to you?

GLADYS: Rebellion. Yeah. It's like, "Hey, let me test her. Let me see how far I can get with her." To me, that's what I see in him.

INSOO: That's what you think. OK. [*continuing to explore for exceptions;* asking about Offion] Now, are there times when he is nice to his sisters?

GLADYS: It's a lots of times when he's nice to them.

INSOO: Yeah? Tell me about this. Tell me about the times you're nice to your sisters.

OFFION: When they want me to play with them, I'll play with them.

INSOO: You do? Really? Huh. Is that right? He plays with you? [to Olayinka and Ayesh] Do you like to play with him? [they nod]

OFFION: And it's like more funner 'cause Marcus, he's always in the room playing Nintendo, not bugging us.

INSOO: [*exploring for an exception around Marcus's behavior*] OK. Now, what happens when you and Marcus are home alone? Without these three?

GLADYS: Then I go to sleep, and he stay in his room, or he go where he wanna go in the house, because no one's there but me and him.

INSOO: So, then he's no trouble.

GLADYS: No. He'll go outside and ride his bike, or he goes to the Center, but I would have to tell him sometimes to turn the TV down.

INSOO: [*asking for what is different about the exception times*] How come you're no trouble then?

MARCUS: Because it's like I have the whole house to myself. Mom's usually not really telling me to do anything and, like, if I know it's my turn to do dishes or something, I probably will do dishes, and then I'll ask her, "Can I go ride my bike?" because I can't just leave out the house, 'cause she'll wonder where I'm at. But I ask her, and then I go.

INSOO: [*complimenting*] Is that right? You do dishes sometimes?

MARCUS: Well, we all have to do dishes. We take turns.

INSOO: Oh, you all have to do dishes. Not you. Not you. You do, too? My goodness. Honest?

OFFION: All of us do dishes.

OLAYINKA: We take turns.

INSOO: [*complimenting Gladys*] You trained them well.

GLADYS: They hate dishes—to wash dishes.

INSOO: [*persisting in her complimenting*] But they do it, though.

GLADYS: Yeah.

INSOO: [*emphasizing Gladys's success with her children*] Even though they hate it, they still do them.

GLADYS: Yeah, but they don't always get 'em clean.

INSOO: Of course. Wow. You did a very good job of training them.

GLADYS: Wow. Thanks.

INSOO: Not many kids this age can do that.

GLADYS: Really?

INSOO: [*asking for exceptions around what the family had identified as the toughest problem; to Marcus and Offion*] So tell me about what you two are like when you get along?

MARCUS: Well, like, sometimes, this, like, really never happens. But sometimes we're outside playing, and then I—me and Tony, we're, like, playing a game, and then we go, "Well, I'm tired of this game. Why don't we play another game." And then we toss the football back and forth.

INSOO: No kidding. You do that?

MARCUS: Sometimes we can play Nintendo together. Sometimes.

At this point, well into the session, it was clear to Insoo the Williams family perceived that it had successes and strengths. They described that they had been to family camp together; three of the children had enjoyed each other's company; Gladys indicated she had set more boundaries on extended family members whom she felt to be unsupportive of her; and Gladys demonstrated she cared very much about rearing responsible and caring children who could participate in family chores and get along with her and with one another. It was also clear to

Insoo that Gladys was the leader of this family and the person primarily responsible for holding the family together. Consequently, although the most worri-
some difficulty to Gladys at the moment was Marcus's rebellion, Insoo decided to
set that matter aside for the present and focus on Gladys's strengths and successes.

INSOO: [*complimenting and asking about how she makes good things happen in her
family*] Now Mrs. Williams, how did you get this idea that you wanted
to be such a good mother?

GLADYS: I didn't. It was ... like, after I started having kids, I knew I didn't want
to treat my kids like I was treated. So I had to do something about that.
I chose not to abuse them. That's where it came from, I guess. But it
wasn't, like, planned that way, 'cause I didn't want any kids.

INSOO: So somehow you turned out to be real conscientious about you being
a good mother.

GLADYS: Yeah.

INSOO: You try very hard to be a good mother.

GLADYS: I guess after what happened to 'em too, with the abuse from their father,
that, like, made me more aware of watching 'em closer and taking 'em
with me everywhere I go now. 'Cause I used to leave 'em with him, by
him being the father, and felt I didn't have to take and drag them everywhere I went. Even in the wintertime, I would go and cash my check and
pay my bills and come back home, and I felt like why take the childrens out
and it really wasn't necessary. He could stay at home and keep 'em, and I
didn't have a car. They had to go on the bus and go everywhere I walked.
And he was doing these cruel things to 'em, and I just wasn't aware that he
was doing these things to 'em, or they would have been with me then.

INSOO: [*quickly recognizing the need for confidentiality*] Umm, let me ask the four
of you to go out in the waiting room and wait, because I want to talk
with your mom. OK?

GLADYS: Good-bye. Au revoir.

MARCUS: Bonjour.

GLADYS: Bonjour, bonjour.

MARCUS: Bonjour.

INSOO: "Bonjour"? My goodness.

GLADYS: Oh yeah, they learning French.

INSOO: Great. [*returning focus to Marcus*] Marcus is a pretty bright kid, isn't he?

GLADYS: Yeah. To me, he is. A's, that's the highest he can go. He do get B's,
but the top grade is A's and he got more A's than B's.

INSOO: Wow. You must be very proud of him.

GLADYS: [*indicating another success and more strengths*] Yeah. I like the work.
He just keep doing the work. I help him with his work if I can.
I went back to school and they put me on a level that he's on

now and I was able to teach him some of the things that they was teaching me.

INSOO: And he talks very nice. Did you notice that? He can explain himself very well.

GLADYS: Hopefully, because going to that school, you know, because they teach him the correct way to talk, and I do too at home. If they say, like, he keep saying "can't" and "ain't," [giggle] I told him, I say it's not a word, and he get mad. He goes get the dictionary. He say it's a word. But at least I don't feel he should use it.

INSOO: He goes to get the dictionary and show you that it's a word?

GLADYS: Yeah, to show me it's a word.

INSOO: Is that right? You have very bright kids.

GLADYS: Yeah. Tell me!

INSOO: Yeah. And that's hard to raise bright kids. Don't you know that?

GLADYS: Well, thank God, I can do it.

INSOO: Yeah, really. Thank God, you can do it, and it seems like you're wanting to keep up with that.

GLADYS: Yeah. 'Cause I want them to go to college, too. Umm, Marcus, he's, like, into art. He really don't want to go to college if he can avoid it. He wants to go to art school.

INSOO: Oh, he does?

GLADYS: Yeah. Offion is fascinated with limousines and Cadillacs. He'd be more reluctant to go to college.

INSOO: At this age, he is. He would be.

GLADYS: I said, "In order to get those things, you have to go to college," and he's like, "Yeah, OK. If that's what I have to do." But Olayinka and Ayesh, I don't know yet.

INSOO: Yeah, well they're too young yet. You have to wait awhile. [*complimenting*] Wow. So you have a lot of ambition for your children.

GLADYS: Yeah.

INSOO: [*indirectly complimenting and asking about the source of her strength*] Where did you learn to do that?

GLADYS: I don't think it's—it was like learning. It was the things that I went through, if I had learned anything. It was the things that I went through that taught me. Like, when I had Marcus, I was 15 and I wanted to go to school. I continued to go. And then I got afraid that when Offion and my mom ... I was paying her $100 a month for rent and $50 a month to see to Marcus while I went to school. And she got my food stamps, all of my stamps. And when I got pregnant with Offion, she didn't want to see to him anymore. Even though I hadn't had the baby, I was just pregnant with 'im, wasn't even showing. I was about a month, if she even knew. And I said, you know, I found out I was pregnant, and I was gonna continue to go to school, and she said, no, she's not gonna keep him anymore. So . . .

INSOO: So, even then you were pretty ambitious.

GLADYS: Yeah. If I could've went to school, I would have continued going, but she didn't want to help me out. So I say forget it, and then she started, like, you have to find your own place and get out. So.

INSOO: So, you've been independent ever since.

GLADYS: Well, I couldn't leave. When I did leave, she called the police on me and came and got me, so I didn't leave anymore until I made 18. And when I made 18, I had three. So, I had moved out. I had two and was on my way with my third one.

INSOO: So life has been pretty tough for you. You've been through a lot.

GLADYS: Yeah. And I don't want to see my kids have to go through nothing that I had went through. And if I can keep them from going through it, I will.

INSOO: Yeah.

GLADYS: My mom. I sit down and try and talk to her like I'm talking to you, and she tell me she don't want to hear it.

INSOO: [*exploring for how Gladys makes her successes happen*] So, you know it seems like, in spite of all those things that happened with your mother, somehow you decided not to listen to all that. How come?

GLADYS: Yeah. Because I know what I went through with her, and it's like, if I sit and listen to her, my life would be like hers.

INSOO: [*emphasizing her determination to break the cycle and assert her independence*] And you want your life to be different than your mother's.

GLADYS: Yeah.

INSOO: How successful are you, that your life is different already from hers?

GLADYS: I have my own home. I don't have a man over me, controlling me. I have my childrens to myself. If I tell one of them to do something, more than likely they will do it. Sometimes I have to threaten them to do it, but more than likely when I tell them to do something, they'll do it. Umm, I don't have—I have a small savings account. Forty dollars, I found out today, but it's mine. I can—I have clothes that I can wear. I don't have to borrow other people's clothes. When I get ready to take a bath, I have deodorant, and soap, and shampoo.

INSOO: So you already, at your age, you have done better than your mother has done. [*inviting Gladys to amplify her perception of her strengths*] Where'd you get this kind of ambition?

GLADYS: I—to me, I wanted to get out the house so bad. I had been molested by my father. My mother wouldn't believe it, and he would beat me, because he didn't want me to tell her. She would beat me, because she said I was lying on him by him being her husband, and I wanted to get away from that. And

I kept saying, "If I can get out, I know I will make it." And after I got here in this city, me and my husband, he didn't get paid for three weeks, and I started to going around, and peoples started telling me where food pantries were and how I could get my kids some clothes and, you know, how to do volunteer work and get things. And if you tell me how to do something—I might can't read that good or spell that good, but if you can show me or tell me, then I can help me and my family out from there. And that's what happened here. And my mother, she came to me when she was here last week, before she left, and she wanted to move in with me, and I said no.

INSOO: [*indirectly complimenting and asking about the how of the exception*] So how did you know that you don't want to do that? How were you able to say no to your mother when she wanted to move in with you?

GLADYS: [Sigh] My husband is in a halfway house right now, and he's . . .

INSOO: Yeah? Oh, he's in a halfway house.

GLADYS: Yeah. He's—he went. He turned himself in, for what he did to the kids. To me, that was a start. Better than my father, you know. And I said, well, maybe it help him after all. Who knows? But if I did want to wait until my childrens get grown and go back to my husband or somewhere down the line before they get grown—get to be big enough where they can really handle themselves, and I want to go back to my husband, I don't want her staying in my house telling me that I couldn't. And right now, that's what she's telling me, and she's not in my house. But she's still with my father, and he hasn't served a day of sentence. He done abused me, her sister, and my little sister, and you still with this guy? And you gonna tell me that I can't be with my husband, and he the one that served time for what he did? I don't understand that. So I told her, I told her, I said, "Well, my husband might come back," and I know she don't like him and, to keep down confusion, I am still his wife. And I said, "To keep down confusion, you get your own house, then you won't have to see him."

INSOO: Good. Good. So I guess this is something you will talk about, your husband coming back.

GLADYS: Yeah.

INSOO: OK. We could do that next time then.

GLADYS: OK.

INSOO: OK. All right. So I want to take some time and talk to my team, and I'll come back in about 5 minutes. OK?

GLADYS: OK.

Break

Insoo chose not to scale progress and do additional goal formulation using the results in this session with Gladys. However, Insoo's questions about exceptions and the strengths Gladys was using to make them happen had provided clear evidence that, despite difficult circumstances, Gladys was making impressive things happen, both with her children and in her extended family. Further complicating Gladys's life was the prospect of her husband's release. He had abused the children, and now was in a halfway house awaiting release.

At this point, take some time to write out what you would say if the Williams family were your clients. On the basis of the guidelines in Chapter 7, organize your feedback into compliments, a bridge, and a suggestion (if warranted). Let us look at how Insoo presented the feedback that she and the team developed.

Feedback

Compliments

INSOO: OK. The team wanted me to tell you kids that we're absolutely astounded about how well you behaved here. All four of you. It's sort of boring to sit here and talk about things, right? When adults sit around and talk, it's boring, but you really handled it very well. And also, they said they could tell that there's a lot of love and affection going on underneath. Under there, underneath it all. And this is what especially they wanted me to mention about Marcus, about how well he speaks and how smart he is. [turning to Gladys] And we think that what's important is that you know that each child has its own good points.

GLADYS: Mm hmm.

INSOO: You can see that. Each one of them. And they are different, and you can see that.

GLADYS: Yep.

INSOO: So we again wanted to tell you what a wonderful job you have done all by yourself.

GLADYS: Thanks.

INSOO: And it has not been easy.

GLADYS: No, it hasn't. It's still not easy.

INSOO: Still is not easy. You have a long way to go.

GLADYS: Yeah.

INSOO: But, so far, you have done a very good job.

GLADYS: Thanks.

INSOO: And uh, they are just nice kids. Just nice kids. And uh, it's because, I think, that you raise them with love, and you want them to be successful.

GLADYS: Thanks.

INSOO: OK. So. Well, you guys, we want you to keep it up, OK? And if you want to go wait outside again, I want to talk with your mom a couple more minutes. OK?

GLADYS: Au revoir. Bonjour.

AYESH: Bonjour.

OLAYINKA: Bonjour, turkey.

GLADYS: [laughing] I'm getting you for that one. Did you hear? She called me a turkey! I'll get her.

INSOO: [laughs] Umm, again, I can tell, you've been through so much. Yet in spite of that, here you are. You have a very good idea what you want to do with your children—how you want to raise your children. You want them to do better than what you have done. And you want them to not go through what you have gone through, and already you are a good mother. Already. You have a long way to go, but you're amazing because, in spite of the fact that your mother didn't praise you, still you can see that each child has good points.

GLADYS: Yeah.

INSOO: And you're trying to figure out . . . "How can I help each child bring out his good points?"

GLADYS: [*pointing to still another success*] Yeah. I can do that when I sit down and look at each one of them. Like Offion, he need lots of help in reading and math, and when he's learning, it make him feel better. And I ordered some books for him.

INSOO: Yeah. And you're doing that. And it's amazing, because your mother has never done that with you. And still you figured it out how to do that.

GLADYS: Yeah.

INSOO: Yeah. Umm, the other thing is that you are using your life experience to not only help yourself, but also help your children.

GLADYS: Yeah.

INSOO: You are learning from yourself.

GLADYS: I didn't understand with my husband why he did what he did, because he said that it was done to him. But it was done to me too, and it didn't make me want to do it.

INSOO: And you didn't. That's right.

GLADYS: And I didn't understand that, but that's his reason.

INSOO: That's right. Yeah. We can talk about that next time. [pause] You are very resourceful, you know, coming here at a young age to a strange city. You figured it out—what you had to do. And you figured out how to get food, and how to get clothes for your kids, and how to take care of your children. You did it all by yourself. There was nobody helping you.

GLADYS: Yeah.

INSOO: And so I think that you are a real good role model for your children.

GLADYS: I keep telling—you know, I don't know how to read and spell that good, but it don't—if you want to do something, then you'll find a way.

INSOO: Yeah, and you were doing it. And again I think that you figured it out—what you need to do with your mother—and, you know, you want to be different. So you have figured out what is best for you and best for your children. That's a lot you've figured out.

GLADYS: Yeah. I'm trying to leave the church I'm at, because the childrens, they, like, go because I make 'em go. [*indicating her thoughtful use of another community resource*] But I took 'em to other churches, and they—they want to go back. They have children programs.

INSOO: And you said you've done the same thing about figuring out about school.

GLADYS: Yeah.

INSOO: So you're using the same ideas.

GLADYS: Yeah. They like the school they at.

Bridge

INSOO: Good. Good. Right. So the team—we are all amazed at what you are doing for yourself and your children, and we agree that it's important and worthwhile for you to do it.

GLADYS: Yeah. Thanks.

Suggestion

INSOO: So we think you should keep right on doing what you're doing, continuing to figure out what's best for you and for your children.

GLADYS: OK.

INSOO: And also, about all this stuff about what to do with your husband. Do you know when he's going to be released?

GLADYS: No. I don't know when, but he just moved where he is, and I do go see him and the kids can too. And they seem to be comfortable with him.

INSOO: OK. So he came out of prison, and he's in a halfway house now.

GLADYS: It's not—to me, it's not like a halfway house. It's still a correctional facility, because a halfway house he can get out and go back at a certain time. He can't go on the streets.

INSOO: So he can't come out. He can't come home for now?

GLADYS: No. Not this place. He can't come out for weeks.

INSOO: OK. So, let's go set up a time for us to get together. OK?

GLADYS: OK.

Insoo's work with Gladys toward the end of their second session demonstrates how keeping the focus on successes and strengths helps clients to sharpen their sense of what they are doing that is useful for solution building. By directing and redirecting the dialogue toward solution talk, Insoo kept giving Gladys opportunities to remember and verbalize her past successes. Gladys did just that. As she related those successes, she increased her confidence that she could respond successfully to the challenges facing her family.

SETBACKS, RELAPSES, AND TIMES WHEN NOTHING IS BETTER

Life is full of ups and downs. Sometimes, when you ask "what's better," you must expect your clients to respond with a description of how things have taken a turn for the worse. They may tell you that their teenager who was making such good progress was caught breaking and entering last week, they have started drinking again, or they are more depressed than ever. You may find these reports discouraging, especially when you and your clients have already worked hard at solution building. Clients, too, will be discouraged. They may feel embarrassed or ashamed at having to report setbacks and relapses. In these situations, it is easy for the practitioner to feel like nothing seems to work and for clients to wonder what use it is to try so hard.

We view setbacks and relapses differently. Without change, how would we recognize stability? Without stability, how would we recognize change? Similarly, we cannot know successes without failures. They are two sides of the same coin. Most people tend to focus on one side of the coin. They forget its opposite. For example, most people tell you how the fight started and how it continued but forget that the fight stopped somehow. Perhaps they tell you they fell back into drinking last week for three days but fail to mention that somehow they have not had a drink in the last two days.

When clients are intent on relating their failures and do not respond to your attempts to explore what is better, it is important to respectfully listen to these accounts and accept and normalize their disappointment. After they feel heard, you can move on to ask them about how the fight stopped or how they managed not to take the next drink. We believe that clients have the capacity to control their own behavior. Therefore, it is logical, for example, to ask a client who drank 12 beers, how the client knew not to take a 13th. Similarly, if a young mother was tempted to hit her sassing child, ask how she managed to walk out of the room instead. When clients become more aware of their ability to stop themselves instead of following their usual patterns, the instances in which they stop themselves become perceived exceptions and something on which to build.

In rare instances, a client will respond consistently to your questions about what's better by saying, "Nothing, nothing is better. In fact, things are horrible and getting worse." The client's manner may suggest that he or she is deeply discouraged and is having trouble in completing simple daily activities. In such circumstances, turn to coping questions, which are discussed in Chapter 10.

CONCLUSION

All the skills and procedures normally used in first and later sessions of solution building, with both individual clients and families, have been presented. Perhaps you have lost sight of the big picture—the flow of the whole process. Therefore, go back to Chapter 5 and find the point where the case of Ah Yan begins. Follow her case from start to finish by reading the dialogues between her and Peter in Chapters 5 through 8. Once you have finished, go back and do the same for the Williams family. As you read, note how consistently Peter and Insoo maintain the posture of not knowing and, thus, invite their clients to be experts about their own lives. Notice how solution-focused interviewing keeps the focus on clients' perceptions of their own successes and strengths. As a result of this focus, practitioners can conclude sessions by giving feedback that draws attention to client competencies.

NOTE

1. By now you can see that asking "what's better" is another way of finding exceptions. For a summary of different ways to ask clients about exceptions and the various points at which to do so, see the cribsheet of exception-finding questions in the Appendix.

9

Interviewing Clients in Involuntary Situations: Children, Dyads, and the Mandated

> The Achilles' heel of social workers and other clinicians
> is the resistant client.
> (HARTMAN & REYNOLDS, 1987, P. 205)

> [B]ehavior that is commonly labeled as "resistance" can be usefully
> redescribed ... in terms of "cooperating." ...
> (DE SHAZER, 1984, P. 13)

"Resistant," "hostile," "disrespectful," "angry," "intimidating," "full of attitude," "unmotivated," "defensive," "afraid," "difficult," "negative," "untrusting," "often overwhelmed," "evasive," and "unmotivated" are the words practitioners used when asked to describe the clients with whom they have worked in involuntary situations. You might find this description unnerving when you learn that most practitioners see many, if not mostly, such clients (Ivanoff, Blythe, & Tripodi, 1994; Rooney, 1992).

Clients who feel forced or pressured into meeting with a professional are in an involuntary situation. They include children whose parents send them to counseling because of problems such as bedwetting or uncontrollable temper tantrums and adolescents whose parents are at a loss about what to do with them because they break curfew, do not do their school assignments, or use drugs. They also can be one member of a dyad (i.e., a two-person relationship such as two roommates, a couple, or a parent and child) when the other member of the dyad insists that the two of them see a counselor "or else." Last, they include clients who are mandated into services by an agent who has the legal authority to do so, for example, when a judge mandates therapy for someone convicted of driving while under the influence of alcohol.

The professional literature has not been helpful in offering effective practice procedures for work with clients in involuntary situations. This is the conclusion of many experienced practitioners as well as those new to the field with whom we have spoken during our workshops and internship seminars. Their view is not surprising, because practice procedures in the helping professions originally were developed for work with clients in voluntary situations (Ivanoff, Blythe, & Tripodi, 1994). These procedures involve first engaging clients through active listening and empathy and, once trust and cooperation are building, moving on to problem solving. This approach assumes clients have chosen to get help and, although frequently unsure about making changes, still are motivated to figure out and solve their problems.

The assumptions of this traditional approach do not apply to clients in involuntary situations. By definition, these clients have not chosen to see their practitioners. They frequently view these contacts as unwanted and intrusive and the solutions recommended to them as meaningless or even harmful (G. Miller, 1991). In addition, research shows that clients in involuntary situations often do not respond to warmth, genuineness, and empathy, nor are they likely to admit their problems. Consequently, work with these clients often breaks down before it gets started. Practitioners often are confused about how to work productively with clients who have been pressured to see them.

More recently, books are being published that maintain the field must pay more attention to how to develop a fit between client motivation and the services practitioners have to offer (Ivanoff, Blythe, & Tripodi, 1994; Rooney, 1992; Trotter, 1999). These authors write about influencing strategies that can enhance this fit and increase client motivation and compliance. Trotter, for instance, instructs practitioners to pay attention for "positive or prosocial comments or behaviours" of clients and openly praise these. He also emphasizes challenging or confronting antisocial comments or behaviors, but doing so cautiously and in the context of providing a balance of positive comments. Rooney writes that past research supports the following strategies: (1) emphasizing client choice wherever possible, (2) informing clients about what to expect during treatment and their part in it, (3) making contracts around goals and treatment procedures, and (4) fostering client participation throughout the treatment.

We have written elsewhere that we think these strategies and the assumptions that stand behind them are definitely a step in the right direction (De Jong & Berg, 2001). They are noteworthy because the strategies attempt to maximize clients' sense of choice and control while at the same time being clear with clients about any nonnegotiable matters such as parental (in the case of children and adolescents), agency, or court requirements. While appreciating these contributions, we also recognize that solution building, through its paradigm shift, has thrown a different light on the topics of clients' goals, client choice, motivation to change, and how to interview those involuntarily seeing a practitioner.

TAKING A SOLUTION FOCUS

We hope it is clear from the previous chapters that solution building does not focus on client goals and choice as a *strategy* to increase client compliance or motivation. Early in the development of solution-focused interviewing, observers at the Brief Family Therapy Center (BFTC) came to the conclusion that practitioners do not directly influence or change clients. Instead, clients change themselves, most often by choosing to do something different. Practitioners can most efficiently and effectively facilitate this process by assuming clients are competent to change if they decide to do so and respectfully asking about and amplifying what clients want different and how to make that happen.

Observers at BFTC learned that progress occurred more quickly and authentically when practitioners had no investment in client outcomes. At first glance, this may seem to be a startling and even unacceptable conclusion. You might ask, "Ought not practitioners care about whether a compulsive drinker stops using alcohol or a parent who neglects his children starts to pay more attention to meeting their needs?" We would answer: Of course, in an ethical sense and from the point of view of the quality of life of clients, we care deeply about client outcomes. However, the professional practice issue that must not be lost is how to be most useful to clients. Paradoxical as it may seem, BFTC observers soon noticed that the more invested practitioners became in client outcomes, the more their agendas for client change motivated their interviewing questions. Clients, intuitively sensing that practitioner agendas reduced their freedom to explore and freely choose possibilities for their lives, became less invested in making changes. These observations led to the conclusion that practitioners work most effectively when they do not think of themselves as change agents but as respectful, not-knowing questioners who always attempt to put clients in the position of informing practitioners of what they (clients) might want, what could happen in their lives, and how to go about making those things happen. Interestingly, this conclusion applies equally to clients in involuntary and voluntary situations, so that the procedures you can use to build solutions with clients in both types of situations are the same.

KEY IDEAS FOR SOLUTION BUILDING
WITH CLIENTS IN INVOLUNTARY SITUATIONS

Taking a solution focus with a client involuntarily meeting with a practitioner was illustrated in Chapter 4 in Insoo's interview of Beth. The following discussion is the basis for the guidelines, useful-question list, and protocol offered in the next section.

Recall that Beth was the teenager who claimed she was physically abused by her father. When the abuse was not substantiated, the social worker attempted to work with Beth by pointing out her mistakes, reasoning with her, confronting her with the inconsistencies between her claims and the facts contained in the police report, threatening her with residential treatment, and so forth. The social worker's approach was not useful. On the other hand, Insoo began the process of solution building with Beth. She asked for Beth's perceptions of the situation, paid attention for clues to who and what were important to Beth, learned how Beth had gotten into services, and began to solution build around what Beth wanted and how that might happen from Beth's point of view.

Begin by Assuming the Client Probably Does Not Want Anything from You

Reread the pages in Chapter 4 about Beth's case. Note that the first thing to keep in mind is that clients involuntarily seeing a practitioner likely believe the practitioner has little of value to offer them. Many, like Beth, have had past experiences in which practitioners did not listen to what the clients might want but were more interested in getting them to own problems as the practitioners themselves viewed them and to comply with interventions that their practitioners thought might be useful. When you begin with the assumption that the client probably does not want anything you have to offer, it puts you in the proper frame of mind to go slowly and be prepared to hear clients complain of frustrating past experiences with professionals like you.

Responding to Anger and Negativity

When you begin to interview, you must be prepared to hear things like:

- "I don't need to be here."
- "It wasn't my idea to come."
- "You help me? I don't think so."
- "I've seen lots of counselors, and it never did me any good."
- "I'm not the one with a problem. It's my mom. She should be here, not me."
- "I've known lots of social workers, and they just ruin people's lives."

The client also may simply sit silently in front of you with arms folded, which seems to communicate "I don't have anything to say to you."

Our workshop participants and students say these moments in an interview are among the toughest. Remember, in all of these situations, you must think of the client as simply not wanting anything from you yet. Also, do not take the comments or standoff attitude personally. There is a story behind every client response, and that is a good place to go next. Accept these client perceptions and ask more about them. Following the principle of basing your next question on the client's latest response, you might respectfully respond to the comments in the preceding list by saying:

- "Oh, you don't. What tells you that you don't need to be here?"
- "So whose idea was it that you come here? What do you suppose they want different as a result of your seeing me?"

- "You must have a very good reason for saying I can't help you. Can you tell me what it is?"
- "Oh, so you've seen counselors. What happened?"
- "What tells you that your mom is the one with the problem?"
- "You must have had some bad experiences with social workers for you to say that. What happened? What could they have done differently that would have been useful for you?"

To the client who remains silent after you introduce yourself and ask how it was that he or she came to be in your office, you might continue with, "You must have a very good reason for not wanting to talk. Can you tell me your good reason?" This question reflects an assumption of client competency by focusing on the client's presumed good reason for not talking instead of implying client resistance by focusing on the client not talking.

Listen for Who and What Are Important

Once a client begins to give you his or her understandings of the situation, you can begin listening for who and what are important to the client. With clients who have not chosen to see you, you often have to tune your ears to listen for what is important that stands behind clients' angry comments. For example, a teenager might say, "My parents make me so mad. They are always asking me if I'm doing drugs again." Rather than asking for details about what the teenager's parents say to her or about her drug history, you could begin solution building by saying, "Oh, so you want things to be different between you and your parents." This paraphrase highlights what seems to be important to this teenager, and assuming she agrees with your statement, the door is open to ask for more details about what she might want and what it would take for that to happen. Even though strong negative or angry comments might naturally intimidate us as interviewers, especially when we are new to the field, there is a silver lining. The silver lining is that if we listen, these comments are quite clear about who and what are important to the client and provide beginning ideas about what the client might want. Once you have that information and accept it, the feel of the interview begins to shift. As Peter's students tell him, "involuntary clients quickly start to feel like voluntary ones."

Use Relationship Questions to Address Context

Clients, whether seeing a practitioner voluntarily or involuntarily, must make choices about whether and what to do differently in the context in which they are currently living. With those receiving services involuntarily, the persons and agencies that make up that context are often clearly identified from clients' early comments or information given to the practitioner through the referral process. For example, Beth's context included her parents, the social worker, previous counselors and service providers, the police, and the court. In solution building, instead of challenging or confronting clients with "the facts" and "demands" of important persons and agencies in their contexts, you can invite them to build their solutions in context by asking relationship questions. In Beth's case, Insoo quickly learned that Beth wanted to go home. Insoo invited Beth to contextualize her goal by asking relationship questions formed around Beth's parents.

- "I can see it is important to you that you go home. Do you think your parents know that?"

- "What would it take for them to know how much you love them and how much you want to live with them?"

- "So, what would they say it would take for them to let you come home?"

Clients' answers to such relationship questions inform clients and their practitioners whether emerging goals and solutions are useful and realistic.

Incorporating Nonnegotiable Requirements

You may be wondering whether involuntary situations bring with them requirements with which the practitioner must confront the clients because a referring or mandating agent insists on them. For example, parents of a teenage daughter might tell you, as the teenager's counselor, that their daughter "must stop seeing her druggie friends or get thrown out of the house." Perhaps you may be seeing a mother whose children have been placed in foster care because the mother continues to live with the man who abused her children, and you know there is no chance that the court will reunite her children with her as long as he remains in the home. In these examples, as well as many others, we believe it is not necessary to confront, but only to respectfully give clear information and proceed with related not-knowing questions. For example, you could say the following to the teenager: "I understand from your parents that they are insisting you stop seeing your friends—the ones who use drugs. Is that your understanding too?" If the client says yes, you can proceed with, "So, are they serious about this?" or "What have you thought about doing about this?" or "Knowing your parents the way you do, do you think they would really throw you out? What would it take to change their minds?"

Giving Control to Clients

The bottom line is that solution building works as well and in the same way for clients seeing a practitioner involuntarily or voluntarily when the clients are approached using the guidelines given in the next section. After thinking about this and conducting and observing countless interviews, we have concluded that this is probably the case because in using solution-focused questions, the interviewer is always giving control and responsibility back to clients. Clients are given control of how to talk about their situations (for example, "What is your understanding of your situation?"), how to talk about themselves ("Do you agree with your parents when they say you are _____ ?"), what to talk about ("What do you want different?"), and what possibilities might be useful ("Knowing yourself and your parents the way you do, what are the chances that talking to them about _____ will be useful?"). In solution–building interviews, clients soon sense that they are safe and free to explore what they want and how to make it happen. As discussed in Chapter 4, there is no need for clients to protect themselves or for practitioners to get into a tug-of-war with them.

GUIDELINES, USEFUL QUESTIONS, AND A PROTOCOL FOR INTERVIEWING INVOLUNTARY CLIENTS

Now that some additional, general clarification about how to solution build with clients in involuntary situations has been added, that clarification can be transformed into guidelines and added to the list started in Chapter 4 based on Insoo's interview of Beth.

- Assume you will be interviewing someone who probably will start out not wanting anything you might have to offer.
- Assume the client has good reason to think and act as he or she does.
- Suspend your judgment and agree with the client's perceptions that stand behind his or her cautious, protective posture.
- Listen for who and what are important to the client, including when the client is angry and critical.
- When clients are openly angry or critical, ask what the offending person or agency could have done differently to be more useful to them.
- Be sure to ask for the client's perception of what is in his or her best interest; that is, ask for what the client might want.
- Listen for and reflect the client's use of language.
- Bring the client's context into the interview by asking relationship questions.
- Respectfully provide information about any nonnegotiable requirements and immediately ask for the client's perceptions regarding these.
- Always stay not knowing.

In addition to these guidelines, we have written a list of useful questions and a protocol for interviewing clients in involuntary situations. These tools are in the Appendix.

BUILDING SOLUTIONS WITH CHILDREN

We are often asked about how solution-building thinking applies to working with children, because most practitioners believe that working with children requires additional techniques and skills that are not dependent on language skills.

Most also believe that one can do an enormous amount of damage to children because they are thought to be more fragile. If you share these beliefs, the prospect of working with children may seem like a specialized, delicate process that leads to responses we cannot fully comprehend because children have limited vocabularies and abilities to express themselves. However, you probably already have learned a great deal about how to be effective with children by observing good parents, teachers, pediatricians, and child care workers who themselves have developed a rich, intuitive sense of what children require to grow and develop, and how to be helpful to them.

Children as Involuntary Participants

In our years in the field, we have never heard of a situation in which a child called a professional person and said, "I have a behavior problem, and I need help." Children who see a practitioner are essentially in an involuntary situation. That is, their problems and successes are defined by important and influential adults in their lives who constantly monitor, evaluate, reinforce, compare, support, and reprimand children as they see fit. By the time children are sent to professionals, many concerned and caring adults in their lives, including parents, teachers, relatives, neighbors, baby-sitters, clergy, and even the police, have tried many things to help them. If you become a practitioner to whom children are sent for services, it usually means you will face situations in which the remedies that several adults have tried so far have not worked, and the adults therefore are frustrated and anxious to have the child change (Berg & Steiner, 2003).

You can imagine from the perspective of the children how many times they may have been told what is wrong with them. By the time they reach your office, they are probably worn out and fed up with all the "good advice," reprimands, scoldings, and adult attempts to help. You also can imagine how discouraged and frustrated they must feel because of so many negative messages and their apparent failures. You may ask yourself, are children already seriously damaged by all these messages by the time they see me? You can assume you will be facing youngsters who likely start out perceiving they have no interest in anything you might have to offer.

Getting Prepared to Meet a Child

Depending on the age of the child you are about to meet, it is a good idea to have small chairs the child can sit on, a low table where the child can write or draw pictures, puppets, storybooks, and other age-appropriate toys. Also, have artwork supplies, such as crayons and paper or a white board, available so the child can draw pictures while talking. Make sure your office is childproofed so you can remain calm and collected. It should also be large and uncluttered so children can spread out and move around.

Think in terms of short sessions, depending on the child's age. A good rule of thumb is "the shorter the better," especially for those children who become easily distracted. Consider going for a walk with the child, since children of all ages have more energy than adults and like to move around.

Getting Started with Positives

Always begin the session by getting to know the child. Get to know who his best friends are, her teddy bear's name, his pet's name, or her favorite book or television show. Notice something positive about the child: the ribbon in her hair, his cool new shoes, the Pokémon card the child is so proud of—anything that stands out about the child. Ask about his or her family, parents, how many brothers and sisters, who lives where, and so forth. Also ask who is helpful to the child (including relatives, cousins, neighbors, and favorite teachers) and what they do that is helpful. This positive beginning readily engages most children and may be a welcome contrast to what they may have expected from you as a practitioner.

In addition, be sure to use simple, everyday language and avoid large words that seem to talk down to the child. Notice and use the child's words without correction, because children with limited language skills are often eager to please adults and tend to imitate adults' language. It is also a good idea to get down on the floor and sit with the child at eye level so that he can see you without looking up.

The following beginning of a session between Insoo and Sam illustrates getting started with a child. Sam is a 5-year-old boy brought by his mother for a consultation regarding the work he had been doing with the school social worker so that Sam can better control his temper at school. The session between Insoo and Sam was taped, and DVD clips are included on the DVD produced to accompany this edition of the book. Insoo began with the first thing she noticed about Sam.

INSOO: Now, you still have your jelly beans in your mouth?

SAM: [giggling] Yeah.

INSOO: How is that jelly bean?

SAM: Yummy.

INSOO: Yummy? Good, good. Now, let's see. I understand you are six years old? Six.

SAM: Five and a half.

INSOO: Five and a half. I'm sorry. So when will you be six?

SAM: Uh, August 10th.

INSOO: August 10th. Ah ha, okay. That's pretty big, isn't it? Five and a half? Yeah. Right. And you have brothers? Sisters?

SAM: Sister.

INSOO: Sister. One sister? Uh-huh. Younger or older?

SAM: Younger.

INSOO: Younger, uh-huh.

SAM: One and a half.

INSOO: One and a half. That's a baby, isn't it.

SAM: Mm-hmm.

INSOO: Yeah. Right. So do you take care of her?

SAM: Mmm.

INSOO: Do you help her?

SAM: Only help her.

INSOO: Only help her. You help your mom take care of her.

SAM: Mm-hmm.

INSOO: Right, good. So you must be going to school? Yeah? What grade are you in?

SAM: Kindergarten.

INSOO: Kindergarten. Right. How do you like school? What do you like about kindergarten?

SAM: I like playing and I like going outside and I like playing games.

You can also use relationship questions early in a session to bring out the positive side of a child and more quickly engage and get to know the child. For example, Insoo could have gotten more details about Sam's strengths by asking, "Suppose I asked your mom about what you do to take care of your little sister, what would she say you do that is so helpful to her?" Similar relationship questions include:

- What would your best friend say about what you are like when the two of you get along?

- What would your mom say you are good at that you are too shy to tell me about?

- What about your teacher? What would she say you are best at in school?

These questions can be adapted to the child's situation to help the child to figure out what he is currently doing that other people appreciate about him. By asking these questions, you are communicating to the child that you are confident the child is already successful and others have acknowledged it to the child in some ways. Thereafter, you can gradually move on to other more troublesome areas, such as his or her temper, tardiness, or disobedience to parents.

DVD (See DVD Clip 15.)

Enlisting Adults as Allies

When working with children, from the very young to teenagers, it is important to build alliances with the significant adults around any child because at the end of the session the child will return to interaction with these parents, teachers, and others. Because it is adults who have defined the child's behavior as problematic, only the same adults can change or revise their definition about the child's problems. Children's problems get resolved in two different ways: (1) when the troublesome behavior no longer occurs, and (2) when the adults decide the problematic behavior is not a problem anymore. The second resolution happens more frequently than you might suppose. For example, two parents may decide that their children's "problem" of sibling rivalry is normal for their children's ages and that, given the strong-willed tendency of both children, they will face similar rivalry later in life as adults; therefore, it is better to learn how to face such rivalry now in the confines of a loving and caring home. Interestingly, as the parents discuss the matter, they may also change the way they talk about it, from "solving the problem of sibling rivalry" to "learning how to live together in a competitive world." Whether change occurs one way or the other, what is important is the shift in the adults' perception that the children have changed or are changing. The shift is likely to lead to a changed attitude toward the children, thus creating different interactional patterns between the adults and the children, hopefully more loving and positive ones toward each other.

Because adults have more ability, capacity, know-how, and other resources to change than do children, we prefer to work with adults around the presenting problems of children, especially when the children are very young. This can be done by working with the parents alone or through conjoint work where parents and a child are seen together (see the next section, on interviewing dyads). It is more expedient to empower the parents or other adults, especially when they feel besieged by a child's so-called "uncontrollable behavior problems." As parents or other adults feel empowered by developing different ways to interact with their children, they are also empowering their children through these more useful interactions.

However, there are situations in which it is not realistic or possible to have access to parents or the other adults involved. Sometimes parenting figures are not available because of incarceration, frequent professional travel, or children in placement out of home. Perhaps, when available, the significant adults may be worn out by the behaviors of the child and demand the child must change first before they invest any effort to make changes. In these cases, it is necessary and possible to begin the work with the child first.

Getting the Child's Perceptions

Because so many adults are interested in helping a child, it can be difficult for you, as a practitioner, to be clear about what you and the child are working toward. Most children you will see have had multiple helpers. Each helper has his or her own ideas about a child's problems and will share with you, or demand that you do, what he or she thinks would be helpful. It can be overwhelming and confusing. Whatever the situation, be sure you ask the child what his or her perceptions of the situation are and what might be helpful. It is entirely possible that no one has yet seriously asked the child what his or her ideas are about how not to get into further trouble.

Soon after she began her interview with Sam, Insoo started to get his perceptions of his situation by using scaling.

INSOO: You're learning your math. Oooh. So you know all the numbers there is, right? Uh-huh. Great, good. And you're learning all the alphabets. Uh-huh. And you learned all the colors, right? Good, great, uh-huh.

Now I understand you have been talking to Mrs. B? Uh-huh. And so I'm going to ask you just a few questions about your talking to Mrs. B. Is that okay?

SAM: V.

INSOO: V. Oh, Mrs. V, okay. Good, I thought it was B. So that's okay with you if we talk about that a little bit. Good. Wonderful. So I'm going to ask you, since you know all the—you do the math already. I'm going to say, I'm going to draw a line, and this is 1. This is a line here. And the bottom here is 1, and the top here is 10. All right?

SAM: Mm-hmm.

INSOO: Okay. And this means, 1 means um, the problem that teacher thought you had with your temper and things like that...

SAM: Mm-hmm.

INSOO: Yeah? That was the baddest, that was the baddest, okay?

SAM: Mm-hmm.

INSOO: That's 1. And 10 means that Mrs. V says, "Ah, Sam's temper problem is all under control. I don't have to see Sam anymore." That's 10. And your kindergarten teacher also agrees with Mrs. V, and your mom agrees with Mrs. V. Right, okay? All that, that means 10. Where do you think you are at right now? What number would you say you are at between 1 and 10 today?

SAM: Mm, 10.

INSOO: Ten? Okay. That's good, good. So you think you're at 10. All right. Suppose I ask Mrs. V same question, say to Mrs. V, "Well, Mrs. V, 10 means Sam doesn't have to come and see you anymore. And 1 means his temper problem was the baddest when he first came to see you." What would Mrs. V say where you are at between 1 and 10?

SAM: Nine.

INSOO: Nine. She would say you're at 9. Wonderful. Good. I'm going to ask one more kinda question, okay? Now, I ask your mom same question. I ask you and Mrs. V and your mom. So this is Mom. I ask the same question. What would Mom say?

SAM: Mmm. Mmm, 9.

INSOO: Nine. Mom would say you're a 9 also. Wow. So you have come this far and this far, right? That's a lot of numbers you have come. Wow. How do you suppose you have done that? Nine and 9 and 10.

This segment is interesting because it shows that even with a young child, once the child has a concept of higher and lower numbers, scaling can be used to elicit the child's perceptions. Sam clearly believes he has made lots of progress on controlling his temper. Insoo next wanted some details about Sam's perceptions of how far he had come. Instead of asking him to describe 1 and 10 verbally, she did the following.

INSOO: Uh–huh, okay. So what do you do now instead of having a temper?

SAM: I be good.

INSOO: You are good. Aah. Good. So you know, Sam, you could draw some pictures if you want. Can you tell me, can you draw me a picture here when things, when your temper was very bad? And now, now that you are at 10, how things are different? Can you draw a picture for me? Great.

SAM: Use red for the bad one.

INSOO: You want to use a red one, great. That's for the bad one. Yeah, right.

SAM: That be also good.

INSOO: [*relationship question*] Yeah? And so now that you are doing better, you are doing really good, what does Mom do? How is Mom different with you?

SAM: Uh . . . well she's buying me things.

INSOO: She buys you things. Like jelly beans. Ah ha, right. I see. . . . This is who?

SAM: Boom.

INSOO: Boom. Oh, this was when your temper was really bad.

SAM: Mm–hmm.

INSOO: Okay. Now, can you draw a picture of now?

SAM: [selecting a different colored pen] Mmm . . .

INSOO: Oh, can you explain that a little bit?

SAM: It's me giving somebody something.

INSOO: Who's this? Which is you?

SAM: Mm.

INSOO: I see. There's a smile there. Yeah, you're right. Uh–huh. I see. That's very nice.

Drawing a picture representing their perceptions makes it easier for many children to talk about their perceptions. Drawing slows down the discussion, gives the child time to think, is calming, and gives the child something more concrete to talk about once the picture is drawn. It also makes it easier for the practitioner to stay not knowing as Insoo did by asking for details about what it was Sam was drawing. Sam, like most children, was creative. He picked red to draw a picture of the times when his temper flared and a softer color for a picture of the other, more positive end of the scale.

Sometimes asking for and respecting a child's perceptions of what will improve things will break your heart, especially because you are likely to be introduced to a child with lots of information about what the child is doing wrong. Insoo once interviewed a child who was described by both his mother and his teachers as a severely troublesome and disruptive child. She asked the boy how he could tell the next morning that a fairy godmother had come to his house during the night and waved her magic wand so that all these problems his mother and teachers were describing were solved, just like that. He replied that he would

FIGURE 9.1 Sam's drawing.

know the fairy godmother had been there because he would wake up and hear his mother singing, he would see her smiling, and he would have enough money to give her anything she wanted. Besides bringing a tear to your eye, this sort of answer tells you the child likely will be motivated if only you keep asking about what would be helpful to make parts of this miracle happen and about related exceptions.

DVD (See DVD Clip 16.)

Other Tips for Interviewing Children

Once you make the adjustments described previously to respect the developmental levels of children and adolescents, the solution-building process is essentially the same with them as with adults (Berg & Steiner, 2003). A good example is Insoo's interview with Beth, described in Chapter 4 and again earlier in this chapter. Regardless of the age of the person interviewed, change occurs through paying attention to who and what are important to the client, what the client wants, and related exceptions. However, there are a few "do's and don'ts" that stand out when interviewing children and adolescents.

Use Many Relationship Questions   By nature, all children and especially adolescents are sensitive to others' assessment and evaluation of them. They have learned a great deal about how to cope with the many adults who assume they know how the children they parent or otherwise supervise think and feel, even to the point of frequently speaking for them. After repeated attempts at correcting adults, many children just give up and let the adults assume what they will. This is particularly so with children who are thought to be troublesome, difficult, obstinate, and hard to control and have had numerous brushes with disciplinary actions at home, at school, and in the community.

Most children seen for services also are confused about how they feel and think because their attempts to voice their opinions have often been rebuffed, ridiculed, or dismissed. Therefore, they are more likely to respond to questions that allow them to distance from themselves. That is, they are much more willing to respond about other people's ideas. Relationship questions are a perfect tool for working with children and adolescents, as they are for working with all clients seeing a practitioner involuntarily. This way of questioning sets up a safe distance between the responder and the answers.

Some examples of relationship questions that can be used with children and adolescents follow. They reflect the importance of focusing on positives, especially when you begin engaging a child or adolescent. Pay special attention to how the questions allow the distancing element and increase the likelihood you will get an answer from someone who at first may not want to talk to you.

- What would your mother tell me is your best subject in school? What about the teachers?
- What else does your mother like about your talent that you are too shy to tell me about?
- What would she say she likes the best about having you around the house?
- Where did your mother get the idea that you need to come and talk to people like me?
- What would she need to see from you that will tell her you do not need to come to see me anymore? What else?
- Suppose you were to decide to do those things. What would be different between you and her?

Relationship questions also have the added benefit of teaching children and adolescents about how others' perceptions of them determines others' interactions with them without the practitioner giving them another lecture. For children and adolescents, "others" are the adults in authority over them, to whom they must adapt. The child's significant adults are the context in which he or she must develop solutions. Consequently, in the earlier dialogue, Insoo not only asked Sam to scale where he thought he was on controlling his temper at school; she also asked him for his perceptions of where his mother and his teacher would scale him. Relationship questions can help to balance what the child wants and is willing to do with the wishes and demands of the adults around the child. Most of the time what the adults want and what the child wants are similar; that is, that the child behave better, be calmer, be able to follow the rules more closely, get along with others, and so forth.

Avoid "Why" Questions   Asking for the "why" behind someone's behavior can seem reasonable enough and even demonstrate genuine concern. For example, if a person who walked normally now begins to limp, someone will ask, "Why is he limping?" However, adults have asked this question so many times of children as a form of scolding or reprimand that they usually receive one of several responses: a shrug of the shoulders, a grunt, silence, an "I don't know," or a defensive response. Many children associate a "why" question with a harsh voice and forefinger pointed at them, which immediately conjures up uneasy, guilty, and shameful feelings. Consequently, you should substitute "how come" for "why." The information you get by asking "how come" is the same as the information you would hope to obtain by asking "why," and you are more likely to get the useful information you wanted.

Responding to "I don't know"   Whether practitioners are new to the field or have years of experience, their most frequently asked question about how to work with children and adolescents probably is how to respond to "I don't know." Adolescents in particular seem to have a monopoly on that phrase. If you are inexperienced, this response will seem especially difficult and perplexing because it puts so much pressure on you to make the next move which, if it is asking another question, will probably elicit another "I don't know."

Our first suggestion is to stay calm, don't overreact, and instead of assuming some dark motive or resistance, take the adolescent's words literally. It is very possible that he or she really does not have the answer. You can respond by saying sincerely, "I realize that I'm asking you some tough questions. [pause] So, suppose you did know, what would you say?" Asking clients to pretend they know the answer is so unusual that it catches them off guard, and they start to respond, often in ways that are new to them as well as you. Another suggestion is to bring in the perspective of significant others by asking, "What would your best friend say. . .?" "Best friend" is very useful with children and adolescents because, by definition, best friend means someone who is on your side and accepts you without making undue demands.

When nothing else works, which is rare, try to think of the "I don't know" or silence as a positive trait. Perhaps the child has learned not to speak too soon or is a deep thinker and not likely to answer before he knows for sure. Sometimes the child can be looked on as "a strong, silent type," and you can wonder with her if that is the case, and give compliments based on that. It certainly takes a strong will and determination to remain silent when adults are expecting an answer. If you decide to say something like this to a teenager, it is important to allow him or her a long time to be silent. This requires you to develop the capacity to seem like you have all the time in the world. Sometimes children need this sort of demonstration of unconditional acceptance before they are able to answer your questions.

Another rare but difficult situation in which children may respond with "I don't know" or remain silent is when they are so depressed and hopeless about their situation that they have given up entirely on their future. As discussed in Chapter 10, coping questions are very useful in such situations. These questions are easier to answer because they ask for small, undeniable successes such as how a person managed to get out of bed this morning or get to the practitioner's office. Combining coping and relationship questions offers the best chance of bringing out the client's own description of strengths and summoning the will to keep trying under extreme circumstances.

Assume Competence   Recently Insoo was consulting with a residential treatment center and was presented with a case of a teenage boy, Adam, who had repeatedly failed to keep his promise of finding a job as a transition to moving to independent living. Adam had several ideas for the job he might want and could easily get, such as one at a fast-food restaurant or the more demanding but higher paying job of kitchen worker. At first the social worker was very hopeful about Adam's prospects, but that soon changed when he failed to follow up on his ideas. The social worker found herself "nagging Adam," knowing that nagging was what everybody else had been doing with him and was not helpful.

At these times you can become frustrated with clients and act as though you are skeptical about their abilities and motivation. After consulting together, Insoo and the social worker decided to try another approach with Adam, one that assumed he was competent and could make changes if he so decided. At the next opportunity, the social worker approached Adam casually and, during their conversation, said, "You know, Adam, I've been thinking about how I've been nagging you about getting a job, and I realized you must have very good reasons for not getting a job. Can you tell me about your good reasons?" Adam immediately replied that he really did not have a good reason. He had been "just plain lazy" and was not taking life seriously. It was time he "got it together" and moved on. The social worker politely listened, not really expecting Adam to do anything spectacular but thinking about the very different conversation she was having with Adam. However, the next time Insoo and the social worker talked, the social worker reported that Adam was hired at a fast-food restaurant and had been working for two weeks without missing a day.

Listen for Hints of Exceptions Once children or adolescents are becoming engaged and talking to you about what has brought them to you, be alert for exceptions. Exceptions often are your first opportunity to get into solution talk. One of our colleagues, a psychologist (Cynthia), relates the following case of a boy named Justin, who had a record of shoplifting. Justin was on the verge of being sent away to a correctional institution because the probation officer and judge were weary of his habitual shoplifting. Because of his youth, the nonviolent nature of his crime, and Cynthia's reputation for working effectively with youngsters, Justin was referred to her as a last resort. With no mention of shoplifting, Cynthia asked Justin about how he got into liking shopping so much, how much time and money he spent at malls, his favorite kind of shopping, how much money he guessed he spent on buying things, and similar matters. Justin casually volunteered that he never paid for any of the things he owned: CDs, shoes, shirts, clothes, or anything he had wanted and gotten. In the course of their conversation, he mentioned that once he paid for a CD. Recognizing an exception, Cynthia asked in detail about how he decided to pay for that CD. Justin became very involved in relating his experience of standing in line at the counter, how he was given a colorful envelope with the store's logo and a receipt that the clerk put in the envelope. He went on to describe how he walked out the door waving the shop's envelope, got on a bus and sat with the envelope on his lap, and kept handling the CD and pulling the receipt out of the envelope so others around him could see he had bought it.

Cynthia reported that Justin looked proud, as if he had made a great accomplishment. She asked for more details about how he decided to buy that particular CD and what was different about him now that he had done it. At the end of the interview, she complimented him on his accomplishment, his strengthening conscience, and how proud his mother must be of his decision to buy the CD. Justin went on to stay away from shoplifting for one year and was eventually released from probation.

Once you and a client are able to identify an exception, follow Cynthia's example and get as many details as you can about the exception, including how the child was able to do it. Insoo did that with Sam in the following exchange.

INSOO: Ah ha. That's wonderful. How did you learn not to punch somebody?

  SAM: I, I . . .

INSOO: What do you do when you feel like punching somebody now?

  SAM: Count to ten.

INSOO: Count to ten.

  SAM: Ten, nine, eight, seven . . .

INSOO: Show me how you do that.

  SAM: Six, five, four, three . . .

INSOO: Show me how you count to ten.

  SAM: Ten, nine, eight, seven, six, five, four, three, two, one.

INSOO: Great.

SAM: Backwards.

INSOO: It goes backwards, too. Uh-huh, okay. That's good. So counting to ten, that helps.

DVD **(See DVD Clip 17.)**

Conclusion   When working with children, you need to remember that children and adolescents usually come to you involuntarily or even having been mandated to do so. Because they are dependent on the support, approval, and continued goodwill of adults around them, it is always important to give credit for any change to those adults who are important to the child. If a child is doing better in his or her work with you, instead of taking credit for the child's successes, you can be most helpful to the child and empower the child's significant adults by emphasizing how the adults have laid the foundations for the child's successes and continue to care about and support the child.

Because children are creative and have good imaginations, you should keep thinking of ways to allow them to use these strengths. It is most important that you remain genuinely interested in listening to children's ideas of what will be helpful, and respect and build solutions with them from these. All children are sensitive enough to realize when you are sincere and honest with them. Sincerity and respect also mean not promising something you cannot deliver and not trying to use the latest, hip language of children or adolescents unless this is natural to you. By all means, enjoy working with them, and be willing to learn from them, for they, like other clients, have much to teach us about themselves and how we can be useful to them.

INTERVIEWING DYADS

A dyad is two persons who are in a close relationship. Examples are a parent and child, husband and wife, student and teacher, coworkers, roommates, and so forth. Practitioners often must interview two persons at the same time when participants in a dyad are unhappy with each other and their relationship. When two people come to see you together, it is almost always one person's idea to do so more than the other's. For example, in a parent-child dyad, it is nearly always the parent's idea, not the child's. While the parent comes voluntarily, the child generally comes involuntarily, and the guidelines discussed in this chapter come into play. This type of interviewing is also called conjoint interviewing.

You, like many practitioners in the field, may be intimidated by the thought of interviewing two or more people at the same time. This is natural because one of the clients is likely to be involuntary, and the person he or she is there with is likely to be the source of frustration and coercion. It is characteristic for participants in a dyad to be angry with each other and ready and willing to fight it out in your presence. In addition, they come to you with a history to their relationship including a private language and way of relating. They tend to be acutely attuned to each other's nonverbal gestures including body movements and positions, grunts, sighs, looking down at the floor or up at the ceiling, rolling eyes, and so forth. If you come into the interview assuming you must quickly decode all of these cues to understand what is going on in their relationship, you will be overwhelmed. It is much better to adopt a not-knowing attitude and assume that, with some well-formulated questions, the clients can serve as your guides to their relationship, just as any individual client does.

Focus on the Relationship

With dyads or any conjoint work, it is important to think at the level of relationships. This may be a challenge for you because most couples and family dyads who come to see you talk at the level of individual personalities. A mother may say about her daughter, "She is so selfish. Her moodiness affects the whole family. She acts like there are no other people living in the house." You can assume that when one person in the dyad has complaints, the relationship is not going well, and the "selfish" daughter also has her own complaints about her mother. She may respond with, "My mom is always criticizing me, like I don't help out enough at home and I hang out with the wrong friends." You can begin a relational focus at the beginning of a first meeting when clients criticize each other this way by the way you paraphrase and summarize. You might say to this mother and daughter, "Okay, so right now, things between the two of you are not going the way either of you want them to." Thinking and responding at a relational level will help you avoid getting into the details of each participant's negative view of the other, with the other then being forced to defend himself or herself to you. Throughout the following solution-building interview with a dyad, while asking each participant for his or her individual perceptions, the interviewer stays focused on their relationship.

Getting Started

It is a good idea to know ahead of time something about how the clients came to you. Usually, there has been a call by the person who wanted the meeting, sometimes with a brief statement of a problem such as, "My son and I are not getting along. We need some help." After introductions, one way to start would be to state to the mother, "I understand you called, and you are concerned about how things are going between you and your son." When you begin this way, expect the mother to begin with her concerns and complaints about the son. You must ask for the son's perceptions of the concerns and then paraphrase and summarize with a relationship focus. As you paraphrase and summarize, listen for what is important in the relationship to each person and also what each might want to be different. Follow the guidelines for interviewing in involuntary situations given earlier in this chapter.

There is another way to begin. It is preferable because it offers a good chance of avoiding or reducing the initial conflict so common in interviews with dyads. Because of the dyad's long history and familiarity with each other, an interview has the potential to get out of control quickly. Family members, couples, or friends can readily pick up on old and familiar cues for disagreement. They know each other's buzzwords and how to push each other's buttons. It is safe to assume they have had numerous discussions and arguments before seeking help and are primed to tell you their own sides of the story. One way to avoid this potential for conflict is to start with the person who is most likely to be there involuntarily, and focus on strengths. That is what Insoo did in the following interview with a 15-year-old boy named Alex and his mother, Nancy, who brought Alex to counseling because of arguments over household chores. (DVD clips from this interview are included on the DVD produced to accompany this book.)

INSOO: Hello.

ALEX: Hi.

INSOO: You mentioned your name was Alex.

ALEX: Yes.

INSOO: Alex, okay. Alex. How old are you, Alex?

ALEX: Fifteen.

INSOO: Fifteen. Ooh, does that make you a junior? Sophomore?

ALEX: Freshman, freshman in high school.

INSOO: [to Alex's mother] Oh, good. Is he a good student?

NANCY: Excellent student.

INSOO: Okay, oh. Wow. Where does he get this brain?

NANCY: From his mom.

INSOO: [laughing] From his mom, of course.

NANCY: Yes, yes.

INSOO: What do you think? Where do you get your brain?

ALEX: [joining the fun] Ha. Not quite sure on that one.

INSOO: You're not quite sure. You're not sure, eh?

ALEX: No.

INSOO: You just got one. Are you born with it? Or did you develop it?

ALEX: I think I developed it.

INSOO: You think you developed it.

ALEX: Yeah.

NANCY: [also joining the fun] Genetics had nothing to do with it?

ALEX: No.

INSOO: Oh no! [everyone laughs] Good, good. What's his best subject? What is your best subject?

ALEX: Probably English and math.

INSOO: English and math. Oh, oooh. That's good.

NANCY: Yeah, very proud of him.

Notice that Insoo focused the conversation on Alex's strengths by asking Alex's mother to participate in engaging Alex, by using her as the expert witness on Alex. Insoo asked Nancy whether Alex was good at school. Once she found out he was, the three of them were on their way to getting some details about this strength and having some fun in the process. You can do the same thing by essentially asking the voluntary member of the dyad what the other person is good at or what he or she appreciates about the other person. Once some strengths of the person most likely to be there involuntarily have been discussed, you can balance things out as Insoo did with Alex and his mother.

INSOO: So, what do you like about Mom? What does Mom do well around the house?

ALEX: Well, she's a good cook. [laugh]

INSOO: She's a good cook. Ah ha. [laugh] I can tell he likes to eat, huh?

NANCY: Uh-huh. Yeah, he hasn't missed any meals. [laugh]

ALEX: Um, she's just fun to be around. She's like, I like the way she interacts with our friends.

INSOO: Your friends?

ALEX: Yeah.

INSOO: [impressed] My goodness.

ALEX: Yeah.

NANCY: I'm also the president of the football booster, so . . .

INSOO: Football booster. Ah yeah.

NANCY: I'm at school a lot and . . .

INSOO: Aah. Right. Great. Wonderful.

ALEX: She's real supportive and . . .

INSOO: She's very supportive.

ALEX: Yeah.

INSOO: Ah, so on top of being very smart and very busy, she's also a very good-hearted mom.

ALEX: Mm-hmm.

INSOO: Ah-ha. Great. Wonderful.

This process of clients complimenting one another by describing each other's strengths in response to solution-focused questions is not uncommon, even when there is potential for serious conflict, as in many dyads. This is not surprising, because participating in a dyad usually means periods of enjoyment for both as well as frustration. This way of beginning is very useful because it generates hopefulness and goodwill, which usually makes the rest of the solution building proceed more quickly and with less conflict.

DVD **(See DVD Clip 13.)**

Work toward a Common Goal

Asking What Clients Want   With dyads, move quickly to asking each client what he or she wants different, because developing a conversation around this topic is another way to minimize the potential for conflict. The future focus of asking about what each might want invites clients to move away from past problems and frustrations in their relationship to something more productive and satisfying. Asking what each wants is also the way to begin the process of working toward a common goal, which is essential to an improved relationship. Consequently, immediately after finding out what Alex and his mother appreciated and admired about each other, Insoo turned to what they wanted different in the relationship.

INSOO: So, what do you suppose needs to come out of this meeting today so that you can say maybe this was helpful?

NANCY: Um, for me I think it would be helpful to know that Alex has a clear understanding, or a better understanding I should say, of how important it is for him to follow the rules at home, participate in household chores, kinda be accountable in that respect. In particular, we take turns on chores like dishes. Stuff like that. So, if he could understand how his participation in that without a lot of obstinance, um, would not only help me, given that I'm wearing all those hats that I'm wearing, but also really to help the family.

INSOO: [*realizing solutions involve doing something different*] Mm-hmm. So were you thinking about his just understanding or his doing something about his understanding?

NANCY: Good question. Um, both. Yeah, I would love to see him be able to understand and then to do something about it.

INSOO: To do something about it. Okay. Right. Uh-huh. How about for you, Alex? What needs to come out of this that will make you say, "Hey, that wasn't so bad!"

ALEX: Well, for her to understand how I feel on that subject.

INSOO: On the subject.

ALEX: Yeah.

INSOO: Oh, okay. So you just want your mom to understand it? Or do you. . .

ALEX: Just understand it.

INSOO: [*relationship question*] Just understand it. Okay, that's interesting. Okay. So suppose she does. Mom understands your feelings about it, your opinions about it, about this issue, is that right?

ALEX: Mm-hmm.

INSOO: Okay. What would change?

ALEX: I think her reactions towards, um, for the future. How she'd react—not now, but how she'd react a week from now or any time later.

INSOO: Okay.

NANCY: React to what?

INSOO: Yeah, say some more about how she would change.

ALEX: Okay. If, for example, I get home and I just been from track practice, and I had school all day, and all these other stuff, if... or if I go over to my dad's, just the other week, and I didn't eat any dishes over there, eat any food over there, then I don't feel I should have to do any dishes. I didn't dirty up the dishes.

INSOO: Ah. Okay. Right. Well, you have a good logic there.

ALEX: Yeah.

INSOO: Uh-huh. Right. Okay. So then once Mom understands that, then what, she will not make you do the dishes on the night that you go visit your dad?

ALEX: Right. Or we could come to an understanding that I should have less dishes or...

INSOO: Ah-ha. You mean less dishes or less dishwashing days?

ALEX: Less dishes.

INSOO: Less dishes.

ALEX: Yeah.

INSOO: On the day that you have to wash.

ALEX: Mmm.

INSOO: [*relationship question*] Yeah, okay. Yeah, well, I can understand that. Okay. What about for you? When Alex understands this, why he must participate in this helping out with the chores, what difference is it gonna make for the two of you?

NANCY: It'll, um, slow down the bickering, you know, back and forth a little bit. "No, it's your turn! No, it's not! It's my turn!" And for him to understand that everybody has a turn whether he's gone to his dad's or not, you know. Home is still home, and he may not have eaten on Thursday 'cause he was at his dad's, but here it is Friday, and there's still dishes that have to be done. That's the rotation. The rotation is what it is. If it's his turn he should just do them, whether he was there or not.

INSOO: So you're interested in less friction in the home.

NANCY: Right.

INSOO: Between him and other children?

NANCY: And myself.

INSOO: And you. Okay. And so, what, that will make things... how would that help?

How to Stay Focused on the Relationship   Although not always the case when interviewing dyads, Alex and Nancy begin right away to state what they want different. As described in earlier chapters, Insoo begins to clarify and amplify each client's developing goals. Notice that she is careful to encourage each of them to keep their emerging goals focused on their relationship so they have the opportunity to work toward a common goal for their relationship. She does this in an identifiable and deliberate way. As each is able to define what he or she wants different, Insoo asks each of them to suppose that what he or she wants were to happen, and to imagine what difference that would make between himself or herself and the other person. For example, after Alex says he wants his mother to understand how he feels on the subject of dishes, Insoo asks him to suppose his mother were to understand what he wants and to describe what changes he might expect to see as a result. Alex, staying with the focus on his relationship to his mother, begins to relate how she might adjust her demands regarding the dishes based on how busy he was on a given day or whether he was away for dinner at his father's home on a day when he was scheduled to do the dishes.

Maintaining Balance   The preceding dialogue illustrates how carefully Insoo maintained an even balance in her interaction with Alex and Nancy. Just as she gave equal time to exploring the strengths of each person early in the session, now she asks each what they want and what difference that will make in the relationship. Once Alex has explained what he thinks the difference that he wants will make in the relationship, Insoo turns to Nancy and asks what difference it will make between herself and Alex if Alex understands he must help out with the chores. In dyads, maintaining this balance is an effective way to demonstrate respect for both persons and communicate that the involvement and ideas of both are necessary to building a more satisfying relationship. Sometimes one member of the dyad comes in almost demanding that the practitioner change the other person, such as when a parent instructs the practitioner to literally "fix" his or her child. Even if the practitioner attempted to do so, it probably would not be helpful because the child soon would recognize that the practitioner was like another parent siding with his mother.

Reinforcing the Invitation to Construct a Common Goal   Besides maintaining a focus on the relationship and giving equal time to each client in the dyad, the preceding line of questioning continually invites clients to work toward a common goal for their relationship. As each is asked to project what he or she wants into the future and hypothesize about its implications for change in the relationship, both persons are being given the opportunity to reflect on the possible usefulness of that idea. Those reflections inform and serve to generate additional possibilities. The practitioner then asks the clients to project those possibilities into the future and consider the implications for possible change in the relationship. In most cases, this process reveals that both clients want the same thing—an improved relationship—and making that happen will require them to work together.

When Clients Problem Talk   In many interviews with dyads, when you ask what each person wants different, you will not get the responses Alex and Nancy gave, in which both began to formulate what they wanted immediately. Instead, no matter how carefully and deliberately you ask your question, clients respond by describing what they do not want. Couples say such things as, "We are so tired of fighting all the time. We cannot keep this up anymore. We act like we hate each other." Perhaps a parent might say, "My son is so disrespectful to me all the time. He just thinks he knows it all." When this happens, remember the guidelines listed earlier in this chapter about turning a complaint into a beginning goal. For example, you could respond to the preceding complaints with "So, you would like to get along better with each other, is that right?" or "So, you'd like to have your son become more respectful of you, is that what you mean?" Once such clients accept the general goal statement implicit in their complaints, you can proceed to the line of questioning described previously. For example, in the case of the parent who wants her son to be more respectful, you can ask the following questions.

- So, when your son becomes more respectful toward you, what will you see him do that will let you know that "Ahh, he is finally being respectful of me now"?

- Suppose he starts to do those things; what will be different between the two of you?

- (looking at the son) Suppose you are respectful of your mother, as she just described. What would you see different with your mother that will let you know that "Ahh, mom is finally recognizing that I'm respectful of her"?

- (focusing back on the relationship) And suppose you see that; what will you do that's different?

DVD (See DVD Clip 13.)

Asking the Miracle Question   Once your clients are answering these beginning questions, which invite them to construct a common goal for their relationship, you can give them further opportunity to develop a well-formed goal by asking the miracle question. With dyads you can use all the follow-up questions you would normally ask after asking the miracle question, just as you would with an individual. Notice that interviewing a dyad naturally encourages you to ask many relationship questions. You can include the other person in the relationship question even though that person is present. For example, suppose you were interviewing two roommates named Ann and Audrey. You might ask Ann, "Suppose I were to ask Audrey what is the first thing she will notice tomorrow morning after the miracle happens, what would she say?" Even if Ann says, "She's right there. Why don't you ask her?" you can respond, "Well, I'd like to hear from your point of view, knowing her the way you do, what do you think she would notice first?" Clients readily answer such questions because they intuitively know that a large part of participating in a relationship means being attuned to the thoughts, feelings, and reactions of the other person.

You may also wish to use the miracle question early in an interview as another way to move beyond conflict to something more productive when two people in the dyad are intensely criticizing each other. Insoo once was interviewing a very outspoken, verbal, and articulate couple. The couple had come to her at the wife's insistence because she (Leslie) was "fed up." Leslie said she was carrying all the burden in the family by balancing a career in a management position with raising two young children without her husband's assistance. Bill, her husband, was at work 60 to 70 hours per week trying to build his own career. The two began the session stating their intense frustration with each other, criticizing each other for no longer being close, and otherwise fighting about who was most at fault for the sorry state of their relationship. Insoo decided to ask the miracle question about what would be different when things were going the way they wanted them to be, and the language quickly changed from angry accusations to wanting something in common.

BILL: [sighing, taking a deep breath, and responding first to Insoo's miracle question] I'll smile first thing in the morning, instead of avoidance.

INSOO: You will smile at Leslie.

LESLIE: He will put his arm around me.

INSOO: He'll put his around you. OK.

LESLIE: That would be a real sign of a miracle at this point.

INSOO: OK. All right, suppose he does. What will you do in response to that?

LESLIE: I won't turn my back to him. [Laugh]

INSOO: All right, is that right? Is that what she would do? Would that be a miracle for you?

BILL: Yeah, that definitely would be.

INSOO: That would be a miracle for you.

BILL: It would be very different.

INSOO: So, when she's facing you, when you smile at her, she'll face you instead of turning her back toward you. What will you do when you see her do that?

BILL: I don't know. I suppose I'll embrace her, probably.

INSOO: What about you, Leslie? What will you do when he gives you a hug?

LESLIE: Well, if he gives me... hugs me, I'll hug him back.

INSOO: OK. What will come after that?

LESLIE: Tomorrow is Saturday, you never can tell! [says with sexy gesture toward Bill and laughs]

INSOO: [laughing] OK.

BILL: A miracle![*]

Using Scaling to Continue Generating Possibilities   Even though the participants in most dyads can agree they want their relationship to improve, the individual participants often continue to hold very different views about who and

---

[*]Transcript from videotape, *Irreconcilable Differences* (1995). Used with permission of the Brief Family Therapy Center, Milwaukee, Wisconsin.

what will have to change for that improvement to happen. There will be times while interviewing a dyad when you will feel that the participants have reached an impasse, that they have thrown down the gauntlet and refuse to give an inch more. At those points, you will be tempted to give advice or confront their apparent stubbornness. Do not do this. Instead, turn to scaling. Scaling is useful to keep the conversation going in the direction of reaching a common goal and developing a way to get there. Even the clients who are the most discouraged about their relationships are rarely at the bottom of the scale. They are at least partway toward the 10 they want. Asking scaling questions helps clients to tap into their successes and strengths and gives them a way to talk about what next steps might be useful. Insoo used scaling with Alex and his mother to invite them to continue building a solution with which they both could live.

INSOO: Okay. So let me ask you this way. Let's say you think that the chances of Mom, or you persuading Mom with your persistence, the chances of that happening. . . . The 10 means that you are very confident that you can somehow hang in there long enough to have your mom change her mind about this, and you're very confident about that. That's 10. One is "Forget this! Mom's never gonna change her mind. I might as well just give up on this. I'm gonna spend my energies on something else." That's 1. Where would you say you are at between 1 and 10 right now?

ALEX: Right now?

INSOO: Yeah.

ALEX: Probably about a 1.

INSOO: About 1.

ALEX: Yeah, but as I keep asking it grows.

INSOO: Yeah?

ALEX: Yeah.

INSOO: But even though it's only at 1, you're not gonna give up on this.

ALEX: No.

INSOO: Ah, okay. What do you know about your mom that tells you there is hope?

ALEX: I don't wanna say, um, she's not weak, but I think I know how to push her buttons.

INSOO: Oh, very smart young man.

ALEX: Yes.

INSOO: Right.

ALEX: But I don't mean it like that.

NANCY: Is it okay if I choke him now?

INSOO: [laugh]

NANCY: [laugh] Can I just choke him now?

INSOO: Um, so you seem very confident that you know about your mom, and you know what to do if you just hang in there long enough.

ALEX: Mm-hmm.

INSOO: I see. Okay. [turning to Nancy] How about for you? Let me ask you this way then. Knowing Alex as well as you do and what kind of child he is, how persistent he is, what would you say you're at and his chances of you persuading him on the same scale?

NANCY: His chances of persuading me . . .

INSOO: Yeah.

NANCY: Um, I could probably easily give him about a 4.

INSOO: About a 4. So you give him higher then?

NANCY: Mm-hmm. Only because I think that, I wanna think that I'm open to listening to his points of view. That doesn't necessarily mean, though, that I'm going to change my mind.

INSOO: Yeah.

NANCY: But at least I wanna be open. He may have a good point. He's still gotta do the dishes, but he may have a good point.

INSOO: I see, okay. Right. That's very difficult isn't it?

NANCY: Mm-hmm.

INSOO: Yeah, right. [turning to Alex] So what do you think about this? How do you understand this? Mom thinks you have about a chance of a 4, going up to 4, and you are at 1 right now. So when Mom, I mean, when you get up to 4, what will change between you and your mom do you think?

ALEX: The way things happen around the house.

INSOO: Okay. Can you explain that a little bit more about what would change then? How things will happen around the house?

ALEX: Um, she'd have a better understanding of where I'm coming from, how I'm feeling.

INSOO: Mom will.

ALEX: Yes. And I'd have the same for her.

INSOO: Okay. Right. So suppose you get up to 4. Somehow both of you get up to 4. What would change, do you think, between the two of you? What would be different?

NANCY: I would expect that the level of tension would decrease. Um . . . I think if we each understand each other and accept that we do understand each other, um, that will eliminate some of the arguing and bickering.

INSOO: Right, okay. So even though you might still have the same rules.

NANCY: Right.

INSOO: The bickering will decrease.

NANCY: Hopefully.

INSOO: Okay. And the tension will decrease.

NANCY: Hopefully. Right.

This scaling conversation reveals to Alex, his mother, and Insoo that Alex's mother is open to listening to Alex's point of view and that doing so may lead to less bickering and tension in the home. Insoo can now turn to asking what each will notice that is different when there is less bickering and tension, what it will take to make those differences happen, and exceptions related to those differences. The focus on a common goal is now well established in the session, and the remainder of the work will proceed as in any other solution-building session.

DVD (See DVD Clip 14.)

Other Tips

More on Handling Conflict and Interruptions   Although asking solution-focused questions tends to reduce conflict between the participants in a dyad, some participants continue to bicker, take verbal shots at one another, or otherwise lapse back into problem talk. There are some additional ways to handle this. One way is to do as Insoo does when a client returns to problem talk. When the client does this, she interrupts and says, "Okay, okay, we'll come back to that." She rarely returns to that topic because once the clients have moved on to a more clearly defined common goal, they have no need or wish to return to the topic. Another way to handle conflict involving ongoing interruptions is to gently but assertively interrupt clients who are interrupting each other and say, "It's very important that I hear what each of you has to say if I am going to be useful to you. It would help me if one person would speak at a time. Can you agree to that, _____ (name of first person)? And you too, _____ (name of second person)?" It is important to get both persons to agree to this ground rule. Once in place, should an argument begin again, you can respectfully remind the clients of the agreement.

Maintaining Neutrality   Implicit in interviewing dyads is that the interviewer must remain neutral. As soon as you lose your neutrality and begin to side with one person or the other, your usefulness to clients diminishes. If you were to lose your neutrality, you would risk harming both persons. The person with whom you sided might unrealistically believe that his or her perceptions count for more or are more correct than the other's, while the other person would likely feel disrespected. Maintaining neutrality is much more difficult than it sounds, especially when the issue is close to one's heart, such as helping children who are mistreated by their caretakers, or women who are treated in mean-spirited or abusive ways by their partners.

How can you recognize that you are losing your neutrality in the face of watching someone being badly or unfairly treated? The most likely sign is a personal negative reaction against one member of the dyad. For example, in the case of Alex and his mother, you might begin to believe that Alex's mother is unfair or unreasonable and begin to be more sympathetic to Alex's position that he should not be required to do the dishes on days when he did not eat at his mother's house. Once you become sympathetic with one person's position on a solution, you narrow, not increase, the options and choices for solutions. The way to avoid taking sides is to refuse to take a position on any possibilities generated by either client, and focus on the relationship. For example, Insoo did not get pulled into a debate about whether Alex should or should not do the dishes under certain conditions. Instead, she focused on what it would take to produce more understanding and less tension and bickering in the home. On other more significant issues such as whether to get married, how to reduce yelling and screaming among family members, and how to reduce fights that escalate into violence, assume the same posture of neutrality. When practitioners maintain neutrality, dyads have the best opportunity of building a solution that both of them contribute to and are motivated to make happen. In regard to working with clients in this and other involuntary situations, practitioners are most useful when they function as though they have no investment in client outcomes.

Always Look for the Goodwill When you first meet with a couple or a parent and child, it is easy to forget that they care about each other, because they seem so angry, hurt, and disappointed with each other. It can help to remember that the other side of anger, hurt, and disappointment with the other person is the wish to be cared about, respected, valued, and loved by that person. It is always helpful to be aware of both sides of emotions, not just the side that is showing. Remember that when people truly do not care about another person, they do not get stirred up about the other but coolly walk away from developing conflict. To illustrate, you generally do not get upset by the disrespect shown you by strangers, more easily brushing it off with thoughts that the stranger is having a bad day, is ignorant and uneducated, or something similar. The reason clients become so upset with one another is because they care deeply about these other persons. Staying aware of both sides makes it easier for you to ask the questions that invite clients to construct something more satisfying.

Our task as practitioners is to foster and highlight the signs of caring and goodwill between the participants in dyads to promote hope for the relationship. You can accomplish this by highlighting the positive side of the complaints. For example, suppose that parents bitterly complain about their child. Rather than reading this complaining as evidence that the parents hate or dislike their child, thus risking disliking the parents yourself, you should read it as an indication that these parents have not given up on the child. You can compliment them for coming in to see you, which indicates they have not given up in spite of all the disappointment the child has caused. You can proceed with questions such as, "You know about your daughter better than anybody, I imagine. What do you know about your daughter that tells you she can learn to behave better?" A similar approach is useful with warring couples. When a couple argues about every aspect of their life together and seeks your help so they can stay together, instead of starting to feel hopeless about the couple, ask, "You have known each other for two years now, right? So, you know each other quite well. What do you know about each other that tells you things could be better between the two of you?" Another way to ask the same question is, "What do you know about this relationship that tells you that you could get along better?"

Clients respond to these questions by describing exceptions. That is, they begin to talk about past times when things were going better in their relationships. Once they do that, you are back on familiar ground and can proceed to gather details about the past successes, how they happened, and what it would take for them to happen again. Seeing the caring and attachment behind the criticisms and using the not-knowing questions are often the key to building goodwill and persuading both you and your clients that there are resources in the dyad for building a more satisfying relationship.

When One Member Refuses to Meet   Students and practitioners frequently ask what to do when one of the participants in a dyad refuses to attend a conjoint interview. For example, the adolescent in a parent/adolescent dyad or the male partner in a couple refuses to see a professional. This is not a major problem. You and the one participant can still work on the relationship. Often the complaints that individual clients bring and the goals they develop involve relationships with the important people in their lives. The key is to use the expertise of the client with whom you are meeting by asking relationship questions to bring the missing person into the room. For instance, if you are meeting with the father of an adolescent son who the father says is "noncommunicative and belligerent even to the point of refusing to see a counselor," you can ask the following.

- Would your son agree that he is noncommunicative and belligerent?
- Suppose he were here, and knowing him the way you do, what do you suppose he would say he would like to see different between the two of you?

Conclusion

The primary difference between working with dyads and individuals is maintaining a focus on the relationship represented by the dyad. This focus begins when the practitioner asks one member what he or she appreciates about the other, and continues through goal formulation and exception exploration related to an emerging common goal. No new solution-focused questions or principles are required for conjoint interviewing, only adaptations of procedures described earlier in this book.

WORKING WITH THOSE MANDATED
INTO SERVICES

These are clients who have been ordered into services by the court and are distinguished from those informally pressured into services by a school, parents, or a spouse. The descriptions of clients in involuntary situations mentioned at the beginning of this chapter are probably most commonly applied to those mandated into services. This section illustrates the application of the guidelines given earlier in this chapter (see page 176) with the case of Tim. Tim is a client mandated into foster care services on the removal of his two sons (2 and 4 years old) by a county protective-service worker for physical abuse of the younger boy. Peter is the interviewer. Several segments from Peter's first interview with Tim are included on the DVD produced to accompany this book.

Getting Started

Getting started in a mandated situation puts some additional demands on you as an interviewer. Because there is a legal mandate involved, you, like the client, are subject to certain nonnegotiable requirements. For example, in Peter's work with Tim, both he and Tim must abide by the expectation that the foster care worker (Peter) and client meet within 30 days to formulate a formal agreement about what changes the parent will make to remove the concerns of the court before the children will be returned to the parent's care. This and several other requirements form part of the context within which any solutions Tim and Peter might develop will have to be built. As an interviewer, it is your responsibility to know what these requirements are and be prepared to communicate them clearly and respectfully to your clients when appropriate. One advantage of certain matters being nonnegotiable is that you do not have to defend them to the client. As long as they are in effect, you as well as the client must work within their limits. In mandated situations, you must be prepared to clarify your role to the client.

It is also important to be clear on what you know about the client's case. What is relevant is what has happened in the recent past that played the biggest role in how the client got to you. Beyond this, follow the guidelines given earlier in this chapter. Peter began with Tim as follows. For your information, Peter had called to set up an appointment, but Tim's phone was disconnected, so Peter showed up unannounced at Tim's door.

PETER: [knocks on door]

  TIM: [opens door] Yeah?

PETER: Hello, Mr. Tim Smith?

  TIM: Yeah.

PETER: Yes, my name's Peter De Jong. [*role clarification*] I'm from Children Services, from foster care services.

  TIM: Right.

PETER: Um, I've got an identification here.

  TIM: Is this about my kids?

PETER: Yes, it is. It's about your children.

  TIM: Oh.

PETER: Um, I tried to call last week, but found out that your phone was disconnected.

TIM: Yeah, something to do with the bill or something like that. I don't know. It's crazy.

PETER: [*stating what he knows about the client's situation*] Yeah, I understand that there was a preliminary hearing last week?

TIM: Right, right.

PETER: And that your children were removed.

TIM: Yeah. Do you know anything about that? Were you in on that or something?

PETER: [*more role clarification*] Well, I'm from the foster care services, and I do know that your children are in foster care now.

TIM: Yeah, that's what they said before. That's what that PS [protective services] woman said before.

PETER: [*role clarification*] Right, right. And so what I'm here to do is uh, I would like to talk to you about what might happen next. And um, was hoping that I would be able to set up an appointment with you.
[*giving control to client*] I called um, actually, um, I could meet with you now for 45 minutes or so or, if that's a possibility.

TIM: Um, yeah, I guess. I guess that'd be okay, but you know, I'm still real irritated about that whole thing at court. I mean, that's still what's wrong, and it sounds like, you know, if you were in on that, I don't think I want you in my house.

Because Tim was not expecting him, Peter was especially careful to state who he was and clarify his role. It soon became evident that, as with many clients in mandated situations, what was most on Tim's mind was his most recent experience with the system. Tim clearly believed he was treated unfairly and disrespectfully. Keeping the guidelines for working with clients in involuntary situations in mind, Peter accepted these perceptions and began to ask for details (see the following dialogue). As he listened to Tim, he tried to notice what was important to Tim and paraphrase it so Tim could clarify and expand Peter's understanding of his point of view. This process is the quickest way to de-escalate a tense and potentially conflictual encounter and foster a cooperative working relationship.

PETER: [*accepting client's perceptions*] Well, yeah, I understand. I talked, uh, heard from the PS worker, that things did not go the way you wanted to in court.

TIM: No, not at all, not at all. I mean, there were just lies upon lies.

PETER: [*asking for details*] Oh, there were?

TIM: Oh yeah. The PS worker was lying, and uh, the courts just took it for that. Um, so are you with her? Or with PS on this thing?

PETER: [*role clarification*] Well, no, no. Well, um, once children are put into foster care, a foster care worker is assigned to work with the parents.

TIM: Yeah, they said that.

PETER: To see what the parents want to do about the situation and um, a protective-service worker is not here with me today.

TIM: Right.

PETER: And protective-service worker is not involved at this point.

TIM: Yeah.

PETER: Um, may come back to court in the future, but um, your case has been assigned to me right now.

TIM: Right.

PETER: [*asking for more details about client's perceptions*] And I understand from what happened in court that you were very upset.

TIM: Oh yeah.

PETER: Were very upset with the abuse being substantiated.

TIM: Right, right, because there wasn't any abuse, but yeah.

PETER: In fact, the PS worker said that um, there was even some shouting in the court.

TIM: Yeah, oh yeah. Oh yeah, yeah. I wanted my point to be heard.

PETER: [*acknowledging what is important to client*] Oh, you did.

TIM: Yeah, absolutely.

PETER: And you didn't feel as though it was.

TIM: No, no.

PETER: [*offering to respect what is important to the client*] Well, I would like to listen very carefully to what you have to say and...

TIM: Okay.

PETER: And would like to try to figure out if we can find a way to work together.

TIM: Yeah.

PETER: Um, to make happen what you want to have happen. See what you care to do about this situation.

TIM: Yeah, okay.

PETER: [*giving control to client*] Would it be possible for us to meet now?

TIM: Yeah, that'd be okay to meet now. I mean, it sounds like, uh, you know, I don't know you, but it sounds like maybe you're being up front with me, like the PS worker wasn't, but you're being up front with me. So maybe, yeah, we could meet now.

PETER: I'll try very hard to be straight with you.

TIM: Yeah, that would be helpful.

PETER: [*promising to keep the client informed about his case*] All the way through so there are no surprises.

TIM: Yeah, 'cause I certainly will be. I certainly will be straight.

PETER: Okay.

TIM: Yeah, yeah. It sounds good. Okay, okay. You can come on in then.

PETER: All right, thank you.

By this time, less than five minutes into their first meeting, Tim was willing to let Peter into his house to talk more. The content of their conversation at the door is very characteristic of what you can expect to face with clients mandated into services. Often suspicious and potentially defensive at the outset, they are concerned about having their perceptions listened to and respected and being kept informed about developments in their cases and how the system works. Unless they realize you might be different from those who did not listen to them, you may not be invited in.

DVD (See DVD Clip 8.)

Getting More Details about the Client's Understandings and What the Client Wants

While Peter now knew what Tim wanted from him as a social worker, he still knew little about Tim's current circumstances and what he might want different. Once inside, he asked for more information about Tim's situation and continued to listen for who and what were important to Tim, and what Tim might want.

PETER: Okay. So let's back up. What's your understanding of um, what's happened here? Of the situation?

TIM: Yeah, I don't know. I never, you know, um, you know, I'm really not sure. I just know that uh, you know, these kids are, you know, my boys are taken from me. You know, all's I know is they, I was told in court that they're in some foster home.

PETER: Mm-hmm. Yes, they are.

TIM: Yeah, and uh, I don't know what the story is. You know, it's upsetting. I don't know when I'm gonna see them.

PETER: Mm-hmm.

TIM: You know, I mean, 'cause I know they wanna see me. Um, I know this is all ridiculous. Just ridiculous. This is crazy. Just crazy. I think the system's just out to make money, and that's what they do, take kids to make money of yeah.

PETER: Oh, okay. So, well, you said a whole lot here already. Um, one thing that's real clear is that you wanna see, that you wanna see your children.

TIM: Yeah, I wanna see them, yeah. They said that at court. They said at court I'll see my kids each week.

PETER: Mm-hmm, mm-hmm. And before we finish up today, we'll talk about that and um, set up that first visit.

TIM: Yeah, that'd be great, you know, 'cause I'll do whatever it takes to see my boys and get them back.

PETER: Okay.

TIM: Yeah, whatever it takes.

PETER: And that's uh, that's very clear, too. You want those boys back.

TIM: Yeah, absolutely. You know, they belong here.

PETER: Okay.

TIM: They belong here.

In mandated situations, it is often soon clear what the client wants. Clearly, Tim's two boys are important to him, and he wants them back home where he believes they belong. Ideally, the court wants the same thing, provided Tim can present evidence that he can provide a home for his sons that is safe and nonneglectful.

DVD (See DVD Clip 9.)

Asking about Context with Relationship Questions

As an interviewer, it is important to note the last sentence of the previous paragraph because it puts the responsibility on Tim, not Peter, of providing evidence of a home environment acceptable to the court. Peter can be most useful to Tim by asking not-knowing questions about the context in which Tim must build a solution. Since it was the protective-service worker who removed the children and persuaded the court they should be placed in foster care, Peter begins there. Notice that by using a relationship question, Peter avoided taking sides with Tim or the protective-service worker and simply gained access to Tim's perceptions, which any eventual solution must respect.

PETER: If the PS worker were here, what do you suppose she would say about um, how come she took the children?

TIM: Uh, you know, she's just talking crazy. If she was here, you know, she'd be saying that I was a terrible father. You know, that I abused my kids. Um, spank them or something like that, which isn't true at all. You know, um, somebody, I know some neighbor, and I think I know who it is, called PS saying that, it's you know, I have people over here late at night, and it's loud and you know, to talk with the kids. I don't know what they told them, but it was just lies upon lies. Um, so I think she would just make it up as she went anyways. You know, and I think that's what she was doing at court. Um, so I think it's really crazy. Just crazy. Um, just about this whole situation. You know, I'm still . . .

PETER: [*clarifying the client's perceptions*] So, so, to you there's no truth in this . . .

TIM: No, not at all.

PETER: That abuse occurred.

TIM: Not at all, not at all.

PETER: [*bringing in client's context*] Now, I did, I did read the report. And the report, uh, the report said that there were um, that there were marks on Sean.

TIM: Yeah, Sean, yeah, Sean. Yeah, he was playing on the couch, and he fell. You know, he was playing. He's two, he's starting, he moves around and crawls, you know. And I wasn't here um, and uh, he fell, you know.

PETER: He fell off the couch.

TIM: Yeah, fell off the couch. You know, he cried a little bit, but you know, he was okay. He's okay. Then the PS worker thinks I did it, or I hit my son or something, which isn't true at all.

PETER: Oh, oh. Okay.

TIM: You know, next thing I know the kids are gone.

PETER: [*clarifying the facts as the client sees them*] Uh-huh. So you were out of the room or whatever when he fell off the couch.

TIM: Yeah, I wasn't, you know, I wasn't even here.

PETER: I see.

TIM: You know, this happened uh, you know, I went to the store real quick, and there's a store around the corner, a party store, and I just went over there real quick uh, you know, just to pick up some cigarettes. And uh, you know, came back, yeah, and he was crying, you know.

PETER: Uh-huh. Okay. So you don't agree at all with the findings about . .

TIM: No, no.

PETER: . . . the findings of that report.

TIM: Mhm-mm, mhm-mm.

PETER: Okay. Okay. Can you tell me anything else about the situation and how it happened that the PS worker took your case to court?

By using relationship questions to get details about the client's view of his or her context, the practitioner can ask about topics that are highly charged without jeopardizing the developing trust between the client and practitioner. In fact, asking about tough topics in this respectful way enhances the development of a cooperative working relationship.

DVD **(See DVD Clip 9.)**

There are several other aspects of Tim's context that can be addressed using relationship questions. Because Tim has already made his general goal clear—reuniting with his children—these other relationship questions should reflect that goal. Doing so demonstrates Peter was listening carefully and working in the direction that Tim wants. It also increases Tim's chance of hopefulness about his situation and his motivation to take steps to get what he wants. Useful relationship questions Peter could turn to include:

- Based on what you heard in court, what is the court expecting you to do before your children will be returned?

- What do you suppose it will take to convince the protective-service worker that it is safe to return your boys home? What else?

- Supposing they could answer, what would your boys say they would like to see happen in this situation?

- What would your boys say they would like to see different before they return home?

Each of these questions about Tim's context should be followed up with others that might be useful to him as he describes in more detail what he wants to do in his situation. Regarding the court's expectations, once Tim indicates what he thinks the court expects, Peter can ask Tim:

- Suppose you decided to do that. What would be different between you and your boys?

- What would be different between you and the court?

- What else would be different for you?

- Knowing yourself the way you do, which of these things would you be able to do?

- How do you know you can do that?

- Would that be enough to persuade the court to return your boys to you?

- What is the minimum, do you think, that you will have to do for the court to return your boys?

Peter asked Tim several of these follow-up questions, and Tim readily gave answers.

DVD (See DVD Clip 11.)

Coconstructing Competence

For clients to generate the courage and willpower they need to take new and demanding steps, they need hope and confidence. This comes from prior successes and an increased awareness of the strengths related to the successes. Clients in mandated situations can feel powerless against the system and less aware of their past successes and strengths. Therefore, as you interview these clients about what they want, be on the lookout for hints of related past successes. What follows is how Peter did that with Tim.

PETER: Heidi, okay. Now Heidi left six or seven months ago?

 TIM: Yeah.

PETER: And uh, she's the mother of your children?

 TIM: Yeah, yeah. We never married, you know, but we'd been together off and on again for six years or something. And, so.

PETER: [*noticing a hint of a success*] Oh, six or seven years...

TIM: We weren't always together, but you know, kinda lived together and then kinda with each other and then not and such, so.

PETER: [*asking for details*] Well, that um, that must've been a big, big change for you.

TIM: Yeah, it was, you know, crazy. You know, she leaves and leaves me with the two boys.

PETER: You had the two boys.

TIM: Yeah, just takes off.

PETER: [*complimenting*] A lot of um, a lot of single parents may not have kept those children, but you kept those children.

TIM: Yeah. I told the court that, too. You know, I said I'm doing the best I can as a single parent, you know.

PETER: [*asking for details*] Has that been difficult for you?

TIM: Yeah, it has. It's been real hard.

PETER: Uh-huh.

TIM: You know, lining up school and being here for them and you know, being both roles, you know. You know, it's stressful. It's stressful, but I'm doing it.

PETER: [*asking for more details and indirectly complimenting*] How've you been able to do that?

TIM: Uh, you know, just a lot of uh, self-will, wanna do it, and you know, being a man about the whole thing 'cause usually it's the women. The men usually leave. It's usually just the woman raising children. And uh, you know, I'm not like that at all. You know, I was raised in foster care myself and getting moved around, different foster homes. I'm not gonna allow that to happen to my boys. That's why I'm so irritated right now is that, you know, um, I'm not gonna let the system raise my boys. You know, that's what happened to me, and it was wrong. So that's part of why I'm you know, here doing this, sticking with my boys. And I'm gonna raise them.

PETER: So you're very determined about that.

TIM: Absolutely, absolutely.

PETER: Very determined about that. So is that where that self-will comes from?

TIM: Yeah, it is, you know...

PETER: Because of the experience you had when you were in foster care?

TIM: Yeah. Getting pushed around from place to place. You know, being blamed for this, blamed for that. And you know, that's, you know, that didn't do me any good, you know? My boys don't need that.

PETER: So what do you want different for your boys?

Tim: You know, I want them raised by their family, by their father. Um, you know, I want that. And that's what I'm doing. You know, I had them in school. I had them in day care when I was working at times, you know, I'd have them in day care. You know, and I'd spend time with them and stuff. You know, like that. You know, so that's what I want different is that that continues, that they come back with me.

DVD **(See DVD Clips 10 and 12.)**

Back on Familiar Ground

With clients mandated into services, once you have clarified your role, worked through any initial suspiciousness and anger about the system by noticing and exploring what you might do differently to be most useful, and begun co-constructing what the client wants by formulating questions that incorporate the client's context, you are back on familiar ground. Because these procedures are focused on what is important to the client and what the client wants, they regularly lead to a cooperative working relationship. From this point on, your interviews with clients in mandated situations will be much like other interviews. You will continue with goal formulation work including the miracle question, scale the client's confidence and progress so far, and formulate a session-ending message. In later sessions, you follow the protocol for any later session.

What about Making Recommendations
that the Client Opposes?

If you are like other practitioners and students, you might be asking the following at this point: "Okay, I can see where this is a good approach to getting started with mandated clients and getting on track with what they want and how that fits with court expectations, but what happens when a practitioner, after doing all of this, still has to make a recommendation to the court to which the client is adamantly opposed?"

Working with clients this way leads to far fewer situations in which the client and practitioner end up far apart on an issue. Consider also whether the practitioner, in such cases, has not inadvertently stopped solution building with the client. For example, Peter was once asked by a foster care case manager what she might do about a client who formerly was in a cooperative working relationship with her but later became angry and distancing because she had told the client that at the next court hearing (a three-month review hearing) the practitioner would be recommending that the one child still in foster care ought not to be returned home at this time. The reason for her recommendation was that there had been documented, recent instances where the mother's supervision of her four younger children had lapsed for several 30-minute periods. This was a major concern because the mother had a history of inconsistent supervision, and especially because the child still in foster care, the oldest, had been abused sexually and was known to sexually act out with his younger siblings. Both the mother and the social worker had previously agreed that the return of this son was contingent on the mother being able to provide consistent, close supervision.

Although you can understand how the practitioner could believe she has important evidence that the mother cannot maintain the close supervision required to protect the younger children and, therefore, ought to recommend that the child not be returned home at this time, there is more solution building that the practitioner and client could do together. In this case, it is clear that both the mother and the social worker agree that the son should be returned home as soon as the safety of all the children living together can be ensured. Rather than stopping the solution-building process by telling the mother that she was recommending against returning the son, the social worker can invite the client to continue solution building by asking the following questions:

- I can imagine that the children's attorney and the judge will be concerned about these lapses in supervision. What do you think their response will be?

- Now that we know how tough it is to supervise the children that closely, what do you think it will take to convince the court that it is safe to reunite your son with his sisters and brother? Could those things happen?

The social worker can use scaling questions to get the mother's perception of safety issues.

- Suppose I ask Teddy (older brother) how confident he is that he will behave appropriately with his younger sisters and brother if he is returned home right now, where would he put himself on a scale of 0 (no confidence) to 10 (100 percent confident)? What do you suppose he would say about what it is that puts him at that number right now? What would he say would be different if he were one number higher? What would it take for that to happen? What do you suppose the court would say about his level of confidence? Is that enough for the court to return Teddy at this time?

- Suppose I ask your younger children how safe they feel around their brother, where would they put themselves between 0 and 10? What would they say it is that puts them at that number? What do you suppose they would like to see different before their brother is returned home, so that they could feel as safe as possible?

- Knowing everything you know about your situation, on a scale from 0 to 10 where 0 is "the younger children are not at all safe" and 10 equals "they are 100 percent safe," how safe do you think the younger children would be if your son were to come home right now? What tells you it's that number?

After asking the preceding questions, if the client and social worker have not reached an understanding about the recommendation, the worker can state the following and ask:

- Knowing that I have to make a recommendation to the court about whether to return Teddy home at this time or leave him in foster care for the next three months and reevaluate at that time, if you were in my position, and knowing all we know about your situation, what recommendation would you make to the court? What's happening that tells you that it is the right recommendation to make at this time? What else? Would the younger children agree? What would they say? What would Teddy say?

- Suppose I were to make the recommendation you suggest. What do you suppose the response of the younger children's attorney will be? How will the judge respond?

- Suppose it turns out that the court decides not to return Teddy at this time. What do you suggest I look for during the next three months that would tell me you are making more progress in the way you supervise the children? What would the younger children notice that would tell them they could be even more sure they will be safe?

Respectfully opening up a solution-building conversation about what is at issue between practitioner and client is the most likely way to create possibilities when there seems to be nothing but disagreement and hard feelings. In the case illustration, more conversation in the areas suggested often leads to a more detailed safety plan for the return of the client's son with the result that the worker, court, and client are all more clear and confident about how to proceed in the case. A client may choose to pull out of conversation with a practitioner, but as long as the practitioner has not closed the door to additional possibilities by saying "this is what we are recommending to the court at the next hearing and that is final," the practitioner knows it was the client's choice to cease conversation, and the client will have to live with the natural consequences of that choice. However, clients usually remain in conversation as long as they believe there is the possibility of being heard.

FINAL WORD

In solution building, there is no final word. In the preceding case, even if the court takes an action of which the client disapproves, there are ways to continue solution building.

Chapter 4 ended with a discussion of influencing client cooperation and motivation in which we stated that we have found de Shazer's (1984) reconceptualization of client resistance as a form of cooperation to be persuasive. It is persuasive not so much because it is true in any theoretical or moral sense, but because it is the most useful posture from which to approach clients. When clients are angry, resistant, or otherwise unmotivated with regard to the particular topic of conversation at the moment, it is most useful to remind ourselves that our clients are competent and we have not yet found a way to cooperate with them. Perceived resistance becomes a signal to us to struggle to formulate a not-knowing question about what the perceived resistance suggests is important to the client rather than conclude the client is resistant or unmotivated. This posture applies equally to solution building with all clients, whether we are meeting with clients who come to us voluntarily or involuntarily.

10

⬦

Interviewing in Crisis Situations

Great emergencies and crises show us how much greater our vital
resources are than we had supposed.
(H. JAMES, 1920, P. 254)

At the very least, the strengths perspective obligates workers to
understand that, however downtrodden or sick, individuals have
survived (and in some cases even thrived). They have taken steps,
summoned up resources, and coped. We need to know what they have
done, how they have done it, what they have learned from doing it,
what resources (inner and outer) were available in their struggle to
surmount their troubles.
(SALEEBEY, 1992, PP. 171-172)

In the helping professions, a crisis may be various events or circumstances that
provoke strong reactions in people. Roberts (1990, p. 4) lists the following
examples: "The aftermath of a violent crime, a suicide attempt, a drug overdose, a
natural disaster, a divorce, a broken romance, sexual impotence, or an automobile
crash." Others include reactions to sexual assault, military combat, a diagnosis of
terminal illness, and the death of a family member or cherished friend. Such
events disrupt people's lives and often leave them feeling disorganized, disorien-
ted, vulnerable, frightened, and alone. Victims may also experience flashbacks to
the traumatic event, have nightmares, or lose their ability to concentrate on daily
activities.

After a crisis, people need immediate support to stabilize their reactions and
begin the process of adapting to the disruption in their lives. The recognition of
this need has spawned crisis services in hospitals, as well as the rapid growth of
crisis hotlines, rape crisis programs, shelters for abused women and children, crisis
centers for youths, and home-based crisis intervention programs. In addition,
support groups and individual counseling services have expanded to provide
ongoing support and therapy for victims.

R. K. James and Gilliland (2005) have reviewed several different definitions of a crisis. Like earlier theorists in the field (Carkhuff & Berenson, 1977; Parad, 1971), they share the view that a crisis is characterized not so much by any particular situation as by the individual's perception and response to that situation. They write that a "crisis is a perception or experiencing of an event or situation as an intolerable difficulty that exceeds the person's current resources and coping mechanisms." (R. K. James & Gilliland, 2005, p. 3). This approach acknowledges differences in individual reactions to the same traumatic event and different rates at which people adapt. Our experience with clients confirms that a crisis is a matter of perception. We would add that clients' perceptions of crisis events can and do shift. These shifts are further evidence of clients' strengths. Solution-focused interviewing fosters these positive shifts.

SOLUTION FOCUS VERSUS PROBLEM FOCUS

When you meet with a client who has just experienced a traumatic event or is contemplating suicide or injury to others, your tendency will probably be to dwell on the details of the trauma. You will be tempted to make a problem assessment of just how deeply in crisis the client really is. Once you have gathered that information, you will feel more confident about what services to recommend. This problem-focused response represents a return to a problem-solving approach. Its appeal in this situation is obvious. Clients who have just experienced a trauma will most likely have been caught off guard by events and will have lost a sense of control over their lives. They will either be withdrawn and uncommunicative, or else they will say, "I can't handle this. I think I'm going crazy." These responses seem to indicate a client's lack of resources, and so you will find yourself reluctant to begin any solution building.

Students and workshop participants have told us that they find it particularly difficult to be solution-focused when working with clients in crisis. They ask, "Shouldn't I just supportively and empathically explore the client's crisis symptoms and then suggest ways in which the client can become more stable? Shouldn't I leave the work of solution building for a later meeting, when the client is more together?"

In our experience, most clients in crisis situations stabilize and make progress as they participate in the solution-building process. Like any other clients, clients in crisis improve by focusing on what they want to see different and drawing on their past successes and strengths. Consequently, solution-focused procedures are as useful to them as to anyone else. That said, we would also caution that clients in an *acute* state of trauma often at first are able only to make short-term plans and respond best to more frequent meetings. Short-term plans usually revolve around where to stay the night, how to get through the night, who to stay with, what to eat, and so forth. Working with acutely traumatized clients around these concerns at short intervals amounts to taking "one small step at a time," an approach we have found more productive and empowering to them than is making decisions for them.

We now outline an approach to interviewing clients in crisis situations that invites them to draw on strengths and resources masked by their reactions to crisis events. Sometimes the interview develops as in any other first session; sometimes it calls for another set of questions—coping questions (Berg, 1994).

GETTING STARTED: "HOW CAN I HELP?"

Begin as you would in any first session by asking the client how you might be useful. This approach immediately puts you into the posture of not knowing and begins to counter any preconceptions you might have about what clients in crisis situations are like and what they need from you. Like other clients, those who have recently experienced a trauma or disruption in their lives usually begin by describing the traumatic event and their reactions to it. This is problem description, and your task (see Chapter 4) is to listen for the clients' perceptions and the words they use to describe these perceptions, for who and what are important to them, and for hints about what specific differences they want to see.

If clients seem frightened, angry, or tearful, use the skills of naturally empathizing and affirming their perceptions presented in Chapter 3. Empathizing and affirming their perceptions assures them that you genuinely care about their plight and are committed to understanding their experiences from their point of view. Empathic and affirming responses also give them a chance to amplify and examine their own perceptions. This may both ease their sense of personal isolation, which often accompanies trauma, and foster a beginning sense of control as a result of putting their experiences into words.

Sometimes, right after a traumatic event, clients are withdrawn. They are either reluctant or unable to speak. In such situations, pay attention to their nonverbals. It may be useful to ask what they are experiencing at the moment and reassure them of your concern. You might say, "From the expression on your face, you seem very tense. I'm wondering if you're thinking about what just happened to you. I want you to know that I'm willing to listen to whatever you have to say." Some clients, feeling very disorganized, are unable to talk. In such circumstances, it is helpful to simply sit with them without speaking. Just your physical presence and a periodic reassurance of your concern and patience can be comforting. Once a client begins to talk, proceed as you would in any solution-building conversation.

Begin cases involving trauma much as you would any other case. This approach is not only consistent with the belief in client competency and strengths, but it also reflects the belief in the inevitability of change. Trauma in a person's life represents a change. Many problem-focused practitioners tend to view a crisis as a disruption of the person's equilibrium, and crisis intervention as a restoration of that normal balance. We have found it more useful, however, to view traumatic change as an opportunity that calls for an extraordinary marshaling of strengths; it can lead in any of several directions, depending on the client's wishes, motivation, and capacities.

Reports from clients about their experiences with trauma have shaped this approach. For example, clients will sometimes call and insist on an appointment immediately because they are "in a crisis and can't cope without help." By the time they are seen, later the same day, they are often much calmer. When engaged in a solution-building conversation, they are able to describe what they have done to improve their situation and what they need to do next. In fact, some clients do not even show up for their emergency appointments. In those circumstances, some practitioners might wonder whether such clients are personality-disordered persons who thrive on chaos; we prefer to assume that they have found a way to cope.

As a practitioner, you need to recognize that clients are always in the process of adapting to whatever they encounter in their lives. They adapt to traumatic events as part of the same process. Neither you, nor the client for that matter, can know ahead of time what capacities and strengths a client will bring to a particular trauma. You can only proceed as you normally would—by adopting a posture of not knowing and assuming client competency until the client demonstrates otherwise.

DVD (See DVD Clip 18.)

"WHAT HAVE YOU TRIED?"

Clients confronting trauma almost always respond to your initial questions about what might be helpful with problem description. Once you believe your clients have had an opportunity to express themselves about their problems and reactions and you have had an opportunity to affirm those perceptions and demonstrate your understanding and concern, you can proceed to ask what steps the clients have taken to deal with the situation. Many clients in trauma can describe coping strategies. Some clients will say, "I deep-breathe to overcome the images in my head." Others may tell you that they called their best friends or family "to talk to someone I could trust." They might say that they sought out emergency services, such as a hospital crisis unit or a crisis hotline, to talk to someone who knew about "my kind of problem."

When clients have already taken steps on their own behalf, respond as you normally would at this point in a first session. Compliment them directly and indirectly for what they have done. Explore where they got the idea to respond as they did, whether they have surprised themselves in the process, and how effectively they think they are handling themselves and their circumstances. As with any first session, expect to hear problem talk mixed in with a description of successes and strengths.

DVD (See DVD Clip 19.)

"WHAT DO YOU WANT TO HAVE DIFFERENT?"

In some cases, clients experiencing trauma can describe efforts to adapt, and in others, they can do little except describe the trauma and its associated pain and terror. In either situation, it is important to ask the clients what they want to have different as a result of meeting with you. This question is intended to open a conversation about goal formulation. Although at first you may not feel comfortable about putting this question to someone who seems traumatized, we have found it useful for such clients. Asking clients to begin to consider where they want to go in their painful situation sends the message that they have some control over their future, however small it may seem at the moment. In addition, their answers give you an idea of whether they have the capacity to work on goal formulation at that time.

We never cease to be amazed by clients' capacities, even in the toughest of circumstances. We cannot count the times that clients' problem talk suggested that they were overwhelmed and incapable of going to work on their inner emotional turmoil or circumstances, and yet, when we turned to goal-formulation questions, they were able to begin useful work. Neither the depth of their pain nor the apparent severity of their trauma perfectly predict their capacity to start working on goals. Therefore, you must refrain from making assumptions on the basis of the severity of a traumatic event or your clients' symptoms. If clients are able to converse with you about their pain, begin to ask goal-formulation questions sometime in the first meeting and see what develops. Often, your clients' mood and degree of confidence start to improve as they begin to perceive and shape possibilities for themselves.

Insoo adopted this approach with a client named Jolene. Jolene was a walk-in client who said she had a crisis in her life and needed help. She said that three days earlier she caught her husband of four years sneaking out of their house with some of his things. He had not returned, and she had "been doing nothing but crying since." She was unable to eat, sleep, or function as she normally did. Although she seemed dazed, she was able to answer questions about her name, address, daily routine, and with whom she lived. She said she had been married for four years and had a 2-year-old daughter. In the early stages of the interview, she stated repeatedly that her main problems at the moment were her inability to sleep and confusion about what to think.

Insoo was not surprised to hear that Jolene was having difficulty sleeping. This is a common response right after a major upset. After gaining a sense of Jolene's perception of her immediate problems, Insoo opened a dialogue intended to help Jolene start thinking about possible goals.

JOLENE: Sleep. I just have to start getting some sleep.

INSOO: So suppose you got some sleep, how would that be helpful to you?

JOLENE: If I just knew why he left me, but he won't talk to me. I don't know where he lives, and I tried to call him where he works, but he won't take the phone call.

INSOO: So this came as a complete surprise to you—his wanting to leave you?

JOLENE: I never knew he would do this to me. We never fought. He never said he was unhappy. All marriages have their difficult times, so I thought we were pretty normal.

INSOO: If we were to pretend—I know he will not come here to talk to me—but if we were to pretend that he was here and I was to ask him how likely it is that he will come back to live with you, what would he say?

JOLENE: He would say that he will never come back to live with me. I was sleeping and I heard some noise and just woke up and saw him walking out the door with a bag. I begged him not to go, but he just walked out, saying he doesn't want to be married anymore. So, I don't think he will come back. If that's the case, I have to find a way to go on with my life and take care of my baby. But I am so tired all the time. I need some sleep.

In this exchange, though Jolene seemed dazed, she was able to begin some solution talk about what she might want to be different in her life. To invite her to think realistically, Insoo asked about the chances of her husband returning. Even though deeply distressed, Jolene did not break down and return to problem talk. Instead, she thought about Insoo's question and answered that her husband was unlikely to return. There was no way ahead of time for Insoo to know that Jolene had the capacity to begin this goal-formulation work. To learn this about Jolene, Insoo had to open the conversation and see what developed.

Listening to Jolene's answers, Insoo noticed that Jolene, although still confused about the end of her marriage, was able to think about the future and the needs of her baby. Clearly, her baby and parenting were very important to her and would play a big role in how she would eventually choose to organize her future. However, Insoo also listened to Jolene's assessment of her immediate need—the need for sleep. To respect her client's priorities, Insoo followed up on that need.

INSOO: So, what happens when you try to sleep? What gets in the way?

JOLENE: I can't sleep because whenever I try to go to sleep, I get really mad that he is doing this to me and wonder if there is another woman in his life. And then I get even more mad, and I start to cry. And then I have to get myself calmed down again.

INSOO: [*asking Jolene to amplify solution talk*] So how do you get yourself calmed down at times like that?

JOLENE: I try not to think about how mad I am. I read books, watch TV, do deep breathing. If only I could just stop thinking. . . . I am going round and round and get really mad and then start to cry. I've been crying a lot. Oh God, I didn't know I had so many tears in my body.

You can see that the conversation between Jolene and Insoo is already taking on the familiar character of a first session. Jolene is engaging in solution building by starting to converse about her difficulties in getting to sleep and what she is doing to overcome them. She mixes problem talk with solution talk. To focus the dialogue on more solution talk, Insoo has several options: she could compliment Jolene for her efforts; she could ask which of Jolene's ways of calming herself work best; she could explore for any exception times to the sleep problem since Jolene's husband left; or she could ask Jolene to scale how well she is adapting to the problem and then return to goal formulation by asking what will be different when Jolene is doing just a little bit better.

The remainder of the session with Jolene proceeded as would any other first session. Insoo asked solution-focused questions aimed at goal formulation and exception exploration and then took a break to formulate feedback. It seemed to Insoo that while Jolene's efforts at relaxation were useful, she was still struggling to find ways to calm herself when she went to bed. In her feedback, Insoo suggested an additional strategy that might help Jolene to calm herself.

> Jolene, first of all, I want to tell you that you did the right thing by coming here today, which I'm sure took lots of courage for you to do. You have had a big shock just three days ago, and I think the reactions you have been having are quite normal and to be expected. I can see how you would be crying a lot, be mad at him, and have difficulty sleeping. These are normal reactions to a terrible event, and maybe even more understandable in your case because he hurt you even more by the way he left you. And, on top of all that, it is even possible that you may never find out why he did what he did because, as you say, he refuses to talk about it. I want you to know that I am very impressed with how you are handling all this because, despite all your pain and upset, you still have a clear idea about how you want to raise your daughter. . . . I agree that the thing for you to do right now is to figure out how to get some good sleep. [Jolene nods in agreement] So I have some suggestions for you.
>
> First, since you already know the relaxation exercises, I suggest that you continue to use them. When you are in bed in a comfortable position, relax your entire body, using your relaxation techniques and your breathing techniques. And, second, after you have gone through your routine, there is one more thing you can do. As you lie in bed with your light off waiting for sleep to come, keep your tongue away from the roof of your mouth and keep your eyes open at the same time—until you quietly fall asleep. And last, between now and the next time we meet, I would like you to pay attention and keep track of all the things you do to make things just a little bit better.

DVD (See DVD Clip 19.)

Asking the Miracle Question

Workshop participants and students often want to know if it is appropriate to ask the miracle question of clients in crisis. Certainly, it is not the first thing you would do, and thereafter, it depends. If the conversation unfolds as it did with

Jolene, who was able to indicate generally who and what were important to her and what she was doing to overcome her difficulties, you might ask the miracle question. As described in Chapter 5, the miracle question allows clients to dream about their future or, as one client put it, "to paint a more colorful life for myself." If they are to work with the miracle question, clients need energy and at least some glimmer of hope that life can be different. If your client does have energy and a little hope, it can be useful to ask the miracle question.

However, the miracle question should be tailored to the particular client. With clients who have experienced a major disruption in their lives, it is important to scale down the miracle. Perhaps the miracle is that the client wakes up tomorrow morning and is starting to put his or her life together or, in Jolene's case, that she has slept a little better. When you ask what will be different as a result of the miracle, be prepared to hear answers that often do not seem related to the client's current perception of the problem. For example, Jolene might answer, "I'd have more energy and take my daughter out to play." Although not apparently related to Jolene's sleeping difficulty, more focus on her relationship to her child may somehow help Jolene to calm herself.

DVD (See DVD Clip 20.)

In contrast to Jolene, some clients in crisis seem utterly hopeless and helpless. They answer all your questions with problem talk. They describe at length their disorienting and painful reactions to the trauma in their lives. Their manner may indicate that just to make it from one moment to the next is all they can handle. These are a small minority of clients. Usually, it is not helpful to press these clients on goal formulation or ask the miracle question. For the moment, such clients are caught up in their suffering and feel doomed to suffer for a long time to come—perhaps even for the rest of their lives. Following are some ways to interview such clients.

COPING QUESTIONS

Coping questions attempt to draw clients' attention away from the fear, loneliness, and misery of life's ugly and horrific events and refocus it on what the clients are doing to survive their pain and circumstances. Coping questions are a form of solution talk that has been tailored to make sense to clients who are feeling overwhelmed (Berg, 1994). These questions help the client and practitioner to uncover together those times and ways in which the client struggles against his or her plight. As you gain experience, you will find that asking coping questions feels like a special case of exploring for exceptions.

The Case of Jermaine

One day Insoo's office received a call from a man who was very troubled. He said that he was having a "hard time of it lately" and finally agreed with his wife that he "better get some professional help." He reported that he was having "flashbacks and blackouts" and asked the secretary, "Could I please see someone right away?" Insoo was available later the same day.

When Jermaine walked into Insoo's office, he seemed visibly upset. He was hunched over. He looked very tired, with dark areas under his eyes, and he was rubbing his hands nervously. As Insoo began her meeting with him, he focused on his symptoms. He said he was waking up in the middle of the night with flashbacks, had difficulty falling asleep, was experiencing rapid heartbeat and sweaty palms, was fearful of leaving his house, and when he did go out, was constantly looking over his shoulder to see if someone was following him. "Most of all," he said, "it's not getting any sleep that makes me so jumpy. If only I could get rid of these horrible nightmares." When asked, he assured Insoo that these reactions were "not at all like my normal self."

Insoo asked when these symptoms had started. Jermaine said it had been about three weeks ago. One day, he had gone to withdraw some cash from an automated teller machine (ATM) in his neighborhood. After withdrawing the money, he returned to his car and climbed in. To his dismay, two men rose up from the backseat with guns pointed at his head. They demanded Jermaine's cash and told him to drive off to another ATM. In sheer panic, he did as he was told and drove from machine to machine until his withdrawal limit was reached.

To Jermaine's horror, the gunmen decided to hold him and locked him in the basement of a house. They also took his keys and wallet and, therefore, learned his name and address. The next day, under the threat of "blowing my brains out," they put him through the same experience. They drove him from ATM to ATM until his withdrawal limit was reached.

The longer Jermaine was with them, the more his abductors seemed to relax around him. Three nights into his ordeal, while his tormentors were partying upstairs, he banged on the locked basement door and moaned: "I'm sick in my stomach. I'm going to throw up." One of his abductors let him step out of the back door, and he ran, managing to escape. Since then, he said, he had been trying "to pull myself together, but I just can't." He added, "I'm exhausted and not able to go back to work because I'm too scared and tired, and thinking about how much income I'm losing only makes things that much worse."

When Insoo asked him what he had tried so far to deal with this traumatic event and its consequences, Jermaine said he had talked to his wife about some of what had happened to him and some of its aftermath, but he also said that he was "holding a lot back because I do not want to upset her." In the belief that all people who have been abused and assaulted have their individual ways of coping and resisting the abuse (Dolan, 1991; Wade, 1997), Insoo decided to respect and explore what he had done so far by asking coping questions.

Coping Exploration

The way to open a conversation around coping is simply to ask, "What have you found helpful so far?" This question suggests that you think the client has some-how found useful ways to begin adapting to his or her traumatic experiences. It also demonstrates that you respect the value of any client-generated coping strategies and you want to start with these and build any additional strategies around them. Insoo took this approach with Jermaine.

INSOO: I am sure it is quite scary to wake up in the middle of the night sweating and with your heart pounding. So, when you wake up from the nightmares and flashbacks, what have you found to help yourself calm down?

JERMAINE: [after a long pause] I lie in bed very still because I can't tell if the nightmare is real or not. When I lie still—very scared—I can hear my wife's breathing in her sleep.

INSOO: [asking for client meanings] OK, what about that—listening to her breathing is helpful?

JERMAINE: [pauses again] You know, I haven't thought about it before, but it helps to listen to her breathe in her sleep, lying there next to me. [pauses to think] Because when I listen to her breathing next to me, it means I'm home with my family. It means I'm safe.

INSOO: I guess you are right.

JERMAINE: When I lie there for a long time, listening to her breathing, so peaceful—then when my eyes get adjusted to the dark, I can look at her sleeping face.

INSOO: So what about that is helpful, looking at her sleeping face?

JERMAINE: When I can finally see my wife's face, it means I'm really safe, that I'm really home. I don't have to be so scared anymore. Knowing that my family is safe helps, too.

INSOO: What else have you found helpful?

JERMAINE: When I can't go back to sleep, I walk around the house in the dark, listening to classical music with my headphones on. That calms my nerves. I've tried watching TV, but it's terrible with all the commercials. I also tried reading. I've been reading a lot, but you can only read so much.

INSOO: I guess you are right. You can only read so much. So, what else have you found helpful?

JERMAINE: I try to help around the house. It breaks my heart that my wife works so hard. She is really tired when she comes home. She has such a tough job. So, I try to be helpful to her by cleaning the house. [smiling faintly] We have the cleanest house in town because I clean it every day. I try to make sure dinner is ready, too, when she comes home tired.

INSOO: I'm sure she appreciates that.

JERMAINE: She is a good woman. I tell her I'm lucky that I have her. She is good at what she does, and she tells me that I should take my time getting better. I want to keep this marriage.

INSOO: I would imagine that she would say that you are a good husband, too.

JERMAINE: Yeah, she tells me that all the time.

Like other solution-building dialogues, those around coping usually lead to a process of mutual discovery. Insoo did not know how Jermaine was coping before he told her, but neither did he, at least not to the degree he did after working to answer Insoo's questions. By sharpening his awareness of what he is already doing, Jermaine can become more confident that he is not stuck or overwhelmed but is already on the way to recovery. Through the conversation, he comes to realize more fully that he himself is developing these strategies. We have come to think that this awareness, more than anything else, builds hope and motivation in clients to continue to work in the toughest of circumstances.

DVD **(See DVD Clip 19.)**

Connecting with the Larger Picture

To build coping momentum with clients, you need to notice and compliment those connections they make to people and experiences that are important to them. These connections often provide the motivation for them to cope against heavy odds and serve as the access point to many of their most meaningful successes. Thus, when Jermaine mentioned that he copes in part by helping around the house, cleaning and preparing dinner, Insoo indirectly complimented him on this, and their dialogue soon incorporated Jermaine's supportive, successful marriage, which is a source of strength and hope in his life.

DVD **(See DVD Clip 21.)**

Using Coping Questions with Clients Who Talk Suicide

Most practitioners feel doubt and anxiety about interviewing a client who has threatened suicide. This is understandable because of the finality of the act for the client and also the incredible suffering the act can bring to those who survive the client. Anyone who has experienced the suicide of a family member, friend, or client knows how devastating it is for the survivors. It may haunt them for years.

Many beginning practitioners lose their composure when clients talk of suicide. Their initial impulse may be to persuade such clients that suicide is illogical, dangerous, hurtful to others, or an otherwise distorted response to their situation. However, practitioners who give in to this impulse may unwittingly exacerbate the risk of suicide because by contradicting the client's perceptions, they further isolate the client. Other beginning practitioners have been known to take an opposite but no less extreme approach: They minimize or refuse to believe what may be a client's desperate cry for help and, at times, the client's attempt to solve what seems to him or her as an insurmountable problem.

Most beginning practitioners believe that suicide talk by clients probably calls for drastic solutions like medication and hospitalization. That may be the case. However, before resorting to drastic recommendations, you should engage such clients in a coping dialogue.

Shifting into Coping Talk   As with all difficult tasks, the toughest part for you will be getting started. Clients who are thinking about suicide will tell you about lives full of pain, suffering, and traumatic humiliation. They may speak of a profound sense of personal inadequacy and failure. As a compassionate listener, you may feel drawn into their apparent hopelessness.

We have found that the best way not to feel hopeless about a client's prospects is to tell ourselves that there is always another side, and then set about exploring it. It is also reassuring to keep in mind that any client who is talking to you about suicide is still present with you and is still alive and breathing. Somehow the client has managed to survive, despite past traumas and present pain. In this sense, clients who talk suicide are no different from Jermaine, and your best chance of helping them to mobilize their strengths and reestablish a sense of control over their emotions and circumstances is to ask coping questions and encourage them to amplify their answers.

Clients talking about suicide are among the most overwhelmed. Some ways to phrase coping questions that respect clients' immediate perception of life's hopelessness but still invite them to think about how they are surviving follow.

"How did you get out of bed this morning?" It is important to start small and start with something that is undeniably real. This question satisfies both criteria. A client who made it to your office or even got out of bed, dressed, and met you at his or her home has done something requiring a lot of energy for a person who is deeply discouraged.

When you ask this question in a sincere and curious manner, be prepared for your client to be puzzled and even disbelieving. Sometimes, clients give you a look that seems to say, "Here I am telling you about all this suffering in my life, and you ask me how I got out of bed. I can't believe you're asking such a dumb question." At other times, clients take the question seriously and try to answer it. In either case, the question is a good place to engage clients in a description of their smallest levels of success. A client named Ruth responded to the question in the following way.

INSOO: [*after listening to and empathizing with several horrible events in Ruth's life*] With all that has happened to you and as discouraged as you have been lately, I'm amazed that you managed to get out of bed this morning and face another day. How did you do it?

RUTH: What? Getting out of bed? Anybody can do that.

INSOO: [*indirectly complimenting*] Oh, I wouldn't say that. When someone is as discouraged as you have been, some people can't even manage to get out of bed all day.

RUTH: Yes, I know. I've had days like that myself. I forgot about those days.

INSOO: [*quickly recognizing that today was somehow a better day and therefore an exception*] So what did you do different this morning so that you got up and came here today, instead of being in bed like those other, worse days?

RUTH: It started out horrible. I even took my guns out and looked at them, but then I put them away. I also thought about taking a bottle of pills but decided to call here instead because, I don't know, something inside me made me think that it is stupid to check out now.

As Ruth's responses demonstrate, asking the question about getting out of bed can lead to important information that may be useful in the first stages of solution building. Next, Insoo might have asked (1) for more details regarding what was different about this morning, as for any exception, (2) about past worse days and how Ruth coped with these, or (3) about the something inside that helped Ruth decide suicide was stupid for her right now.

In adopting any of these options, Insoo is back on familiar ground as a solution-focused interviewer. She explores (coping) exceptions and, in the process, hears about who and what are important to Ruth.

"How did you survive long enough to get here?" This is a variation on the previous question. It may be appropriate when clients tell you they are surprised to be alive because their pain is so overwhelming that they came very close to suicide "just yesterday" or "a few hours ago." After you respectfully listen to the clients' account of their pain and begin to appreciate its depth, you can start the transition to coping talk with this question.

"How often do you have these thoughts?" It is surprising how often clients who experience suicidal thoughts discover that they are not preoccupied with these thoughts 100 percent of the time. Between periods of crying, clients report they take their children to school, prepare food for their families, go shopping, function at their jobs, and go about other daily activities. We have often been impressed by how well people can function in the midst of being depressed. Thus, potential solution patterns exist side by side with problem patterns. Asking about the frequency of suicidal thoughts conveys to the client that everyone has periods when they are not thinking about suicide. Even with clients who report that they think of suicide 95 percent of the time, you can explore what they are doing the other 5 percent of the time, in the hope of identifying something that might help to reduce the intensity of the suicidal thoughts or even to make the thoughts go away for a while.

"How have you managed to cope for so long?" Some clients have struggled with their painful feelings for years. At times, they feel overwhelmed and hopelessly out of control. At the point of contemplating suicide, many of these clients have a strong tendency to place overly high demands on themselves and others. They become preoccupied with a sense of failure, either their own or that of significant others.

When you encounter a client who talks this way, ask how they have managed to cope. This question, again reality-based, invites clients to recognize that somehow they have coped with seemingly insurmountable difficulties for a long time already. It implies that they have past successes and strengths worth talking about.

"How come things are not worse?" Sometimes, a client describes past horrors—a brutal assault, repeated childhood molestation, a disfiguring degenerative disease—

in such vivid, compelling detail that you feel amazed this person is able to carry on with life at all. When you learn to ask this question with curiosity and a sincere desire to understand, you are likely to hear some inspiring accounts of courage and human dignity.

Peter once met with a client who had been sexually assaulted several times as a teenager by two coworkers. Her tormentors kept control of her for two years through threats to both her and her sister. She described how, more than 10 years later, she still suffered from flashbacks, disorientation, and periods of dissociation. As he listened, Peter realized this woman relived her terror and humiliation almost daily, and regularly had thoughts of ending her life. He was amazed that she was not overwhelmed.

PETER: I cannot imagine living with what you have had to live with all these years. I can see how you might have decided to give up a long time ago. Yet, I know that you hold a job and take care of a family. It seems like you should be overwhelmed, but obviously you are not. How come things are not worse?

LINDA: There are many times each week that I want to give in and end the images I still have in my head. They are so powerful and frightening. [she begins to describe them again and becomes more frightened and tearful]

PETER: Yes, I know, I know. From what you've been describing, they are truly horrible. So, let me ask you, what else is there about you so that these images and memories did not completely take over your life?

LINDA: It hasn't been easy, but I think I got lucky. I met a kind, gentle guy who just wanted to be my friend, and for several years that's all we were. [she describes their relationship] Then he asked me if maybe I would be interested in getting married, and I got terrified. I was so mixed up and so close to losing it almost every minute of every day. But I prayed and prayed, and he stayed nearby, and eventually I did it. I married a man. I never thought I could ever be with a man and love him.

This was the beginning of a coping dialogue in which Linda and Peter explored how Linda drew on other memories and images in her past and the present—those of her husband, child, and job—to struggle against the memories of her abuse.

SCALING QUESTIONS

Clients' perceptions shift as they are encouraged to talk about their successes and strengths, however small these may seem at first. Once you have worked with clients to uncover coping strategies, you can use scaling questions to reinforce their coping successes. Scaling questions also help clients to formulate a next step in their struggle. Some ways you can use scaling questions with clients in crisis situations follow.

Scaling Current Coping Ability

Most clients in crisis become at least a little more hopeful as they talk about their successes. Therefore, it is helpful to ask clients to express their perceptions of success more explicitly (Berg & de Shazer, 1993; de Shazer et al., in press). This is accomplished by asking a scaling question. For example, "On a scale of 0 to 10, where 10 means you are coping with your situation as well as you can imagine anyone could, and 0 means you are not coping at all, how well would you say you are coping right now?" Sometimes the number the client gives makes sense in view of the previous coping dialogue. Sometimes it is a surprise. In either case, follow up with questions that clarify the meaning of the number and thus further help the client to build confidence.

Peter once met with a man named Jim who had made "a serious suicide attempt" one week earlier, when the woman he was living with threw all his belongings on the front porch. She attached a note to say she had found someone new and never wanted to see him again. Jim said he was "destroyed." He went to his parents' home because they were away traveling. That evening, he said, "I got into my truck with the garage door closed, rolled up the windows, started the engine, laid down on the front seat, and closed my eyes." To his astonishment, "the next morning I woke up with my truck in the driveway, and the window was rolled down, and I was still alive."

Jim told Peter that he had asked for an appointment because "my relatives are scared I might try to kill myself again and said I should get checked out." Jim reported that he was doing better. In the last few days, he had begun to eat and sleep more regularly, and three days earlier he had returned to work. When Peter asked him how he was coming to terms with losing his girlfriend, Jim said he had "just made up my mind that I was not going to let it bother me." Peter complimented his determination and asked what was proving helpful in this process. Jim replied that he had returned to remodeling a house he had built and also to his hobby of building guns. After 30 minutes of coping talk, Peter asked Jim to scale how well he was coping.

JIM: [long pause] You know, I feel like I'm an 8. Yeah. Maybe even a 9!

PETER: [surprised] Wow! I was expecting to hear a 4 or 5, but you say maybe even a 9. So what's happening that makes it so high?

JIM: I know, 9 seems so high. That's why I was thinking so hard. [pause] Maybe it has to do with what happened yesterday at work. My boss and I never got along or said much to each other. He's real religious, and he doesn't like the way I live or my jokes or much of anything else about me. . . . Except I do my job, and he can't do anything about that, can he? So yesterday, I thought, "What the hell! I almost did myself in. I'm going to clear the air." And you know, we did. We talked and talked a lot about what was bothering us.

Peter immediately began to examine Jim's new experience with his boss as an exception. Peter asked for a description of what happened, exactly what Jim's part was in the important event, and how the conversation with his boss was helpful to him. As Jim talked, Peter became amazed at how much progress Jim had made in one week—even in their hour together. Despite what his relatives wanted, Jim decided not to return for another visit because, as he said, "I'm OK now. I don't need to come back."[1]

Scaling Presession Coping Changes

No matter how long it has been since the traumatic event, it can be useful to ask clients to think about how well they are coping now as opposed to immediately after the shock. This can be helpful even a few hours after the trauma, provided the client is emotionally organized enough to converse with you. The first step is to establish a caring, understanding contact with someone who has just been traumatized. Once that rapport is starting to develop and you have inquired about the client's efforts at coping, you can ask a presession scaling question, such as the following example.

PETER: Allen, I know it is just hours since you were mugged, and I know from what you said that you are starting to pull yourself together. I'm wondering if you can tell me how successful you are being at this? On a scale of 0 to 10, where 0 was how you were doing immediately after the mugging and 10 is you are coping better than you possibly could have imagined, how well are you coping right now?

After a major shock, almost all clients will begin to reorganize to some degree and will provide a number higher than 0. You can then explore what the client might have done to move from 0 to the present level.

Scaling the Next Step

Having begun a conversation about the scale number that represents how well the client is coping, you and the client have a beginning from which you can pursue goal formulation. You can point the client to the future by asking, "OK, you say you have things at about a 3. What is the most important thing for you to remember to do to keep things at a 3? What's the next most important thing for you to remember to keep doing?" Or you can adapt the procedure for goal formulation in later sessions (see Chapter 8) and start working your way up the scale with your client: "So, when you are coping at a level of 4, what do you suppose you will be doing to handle things that you are not doing now?" "What do you suppose your best friend will notice that you are doing differently when you are coping just a little bit better?" "What will it take for that to happen?" Depending on how engaged and energized your client becomes, you can adapt any of the goal-formulation questions discussed in Chapters 5 and 8. In some cases, a modified form of the miracle question can be used to explore possibilities for future coping.

Scaling Motivation and Confidence

Once you have worked on coping goals, ask your clients to scale how hard they are willing to work on achieving those goals and how confident they are that they will eventually find ways to successfully cope. To review this kind of scaling, see Chapter 6.

FEEDBACK: DOING MORE OF WHAT HELPS

Once you sense that a client is close to being overwhelmed and you start asking coping questions, the interview will closely resemble any other solution-building interview. Coping exploration is a form of exception exploration. You can use scaling questions in the usual ways. The same is true of end-of-session feedback. In coping situations, the feedback is usually organized around the suggestion that the client continue to do more of what the coping dialogue reveals as helpful. Insoo adopted that principle in her feedback to Jolene, considered earlier in this chapter.

Another example of end-of-session feedback is from the case of Jermaine, the client who had been abducted at gunpoint and was experiencing flashbacks, nightmares, and fears of leaving home. The first thing Insoo did in her feedback was to compliment him.

> Jermaine, you have told me an incredible story of horror. You were not only forced at gunpoint to hand over your cash that first day, but you were held for three days and forced to do it again and again, all that time not knowing if you would be killed and never see your family again. I am amazed that you found the strength to endure that horror; certainly not everyone could. And not only did you endure it, but you kept your wits about you and you figured out a clever way to escape. You waited for a time when their guard was down and came up with something believable so they would let you out of the back door. And then you ran—you managed to escape. I want to congratulate you on being very strong and very smart.

Insoo formulated the rest of her feedback around an idea that emerged later in their session. Jermaine's wife had told him that his symptoms had a name— posttraumatic stress syndrome. He said he found that comforting because having a name for his symptoms meant there was an explanation for what he was experiencing and he was not crazy. Recognizing that posttraumatic stress syndrome was now a part of Jermaine's frame of reference and the label was helpful to him, Insoo decided to incorporate it into her feedback.

> Because your reactions are a part of posttraumatic stress syndrome, and because what happened to you was so frightening and lasted for several days, I think that you may continue for a while to have nightmares, blackouts, and fears about leaving your house and who might be following when you are in your car. This kind of hypervigilance to make sure that you are safe is normal and a useful survival instinct. It is a big part of what helped to save your life during the extraordinary and horrible experience that you told me about today. It is as though your mind is still trying to make sense of that horror by going over it again and again in nightmares and in other ways, and it may take some time for your mind to figure out that you are really safe now.
>
> So, in the meantime, while your mind is continuing to figure things out, I suggest that you continue to do what you have found that helps, giving

yourself time to heal. Continue to listen to your music, clean the house, cook, and talk to your wife so both of you can be reassured that you are continuing to get better. [he nods in agreement] And keep paying attention to what else you discover in the coming days that's helpful, and come back and tell me what's better.

GATHERING PROBLEM-ASSESSMENT INFORMATION

When interviewing traumatized and overwhelmed clients, beginning practitioners tend to feel more comfortable asking problem-assessment questions, rather than solution-focused questions. Although solution building through coping dialogues is more helpful than is detailed problem assessment, there is a place for problem assessment.

Client perceptions and frames of reference can change as clients interact with practitioners. Problem assessments, whether administered as standardized paper-and-pencil tests or as a series of questions asked by a practitioner, amount to a snapshot of some aspect of a client's perceptions at one point in time. They give a static view. Only a second testing allows you to evaluate change. In addition, as problem assessments, they do not measure client strengths, past coping successes, what and who are most important to clients, and client capacities for hope and for discerning next steps. In other words, they do not measure the components of solution building. Consequently, even in crisis situations, we recommend that problem assessment take a backseat to solution building.

Nevertheless, it is very important for you to become familiar with the main criteria that are used to assess a person's basic needs for living. Abraham Maslow (1970) has identified and ranked human needs for living. At the most basic level, he identifies physical and life-sustaining requirements, such as the needs for food, water, air, and shelter. At the next level of the hierarchy, he identifies physical-safety requirements, such as the need for protection from attack and disease. These most basic needs are more concrete than others in his formulation, which include the needs for love, self-esteem, and self-actualization. In crisis situations, clients are generally dealing with threats to life-sustaining and physical-safety needs.

Individual clients differ in their perception of what they must have in order to satisfy these basic needs. Various researchers have formulated questions that provide information about clients' perceptions of whether they are having difficulties meeting these needs. Other questions yield information about so-called objective indicators of problems in satisfying these needs. For an introduction to the criteria and measurement questions that can be used to assess clients' life-sustaining and safety needs, you can consult a variety of sources that cover the assessment of, for example, the different aspects of a person's mental status, the type and degree of substance abuse, the likelihood of harm to self or another person, and the presence of child abuse or neglect (R. K. James & Gilliland, 2005;

Lukas, 1993; Martin & Moore, 1995; Sheafor & Horejsi, 2007). If you familiarize yourself with this information, you will more quickly understand and empathize with the fear and inner sense of losing control that clients in crisis experience. You will also sharpen your capacity to attend to the factual aspects of the events and personal reactions clients describe to you. It can be beneficial to read first-hand accounts by those who have experienced different crises. Novels can also be helpful. For example, Peter's students read Judith Guest's novel *Ordinary People* for one intimate view of a family's reaction to the crisis of losing a son and brother.

Once you are familiar with problem-assessment information around basic human needs, you will notice that much of that information spontaneously emerges as you explore the client's frame of reference and begin the solution-building process. As you ask your solution-focused questions, the client moves back and forth between problem talk and solution talk. The problem talk includes data on problem-assessment criteria, but often without the specificity that you or your agency may require. It is simple enough to ask for clarification and then return to solution talk, as in the following dialogue.

PETER: So when the miracle happens, what else will you notice that's different?

EMMA: [pause] I guess another thing is that I won't think about ending my life so often. Right now my life is so miserable, with me having no money and Protective Services after me. They already took my kids and put them in foster care. I'm so sad when my kids aren't with me.

PETER: Yes, I can see you love them very much and wish they were with you right now.

EMMA: I sure do, and I keep thinking that I can't live without them, and I keep thinking about killing myself.

PETER: How long have you been having these thoughts?

EMMA: Ever since my kids were taken away two weeks ago.

PETER: Did you ever have thoughts like that before?

EMMA: I've been discouraged before, but never like this. I never really had thoughts like this, and they keep coming back.

PETER: I'm wondering. . . have you come close to actually doing it? Have you ever made an attempt to take your life?

EMMA: No, I couldn't do that. It hurts so bad not to have them with me, but I couldn't do that—leave my kids without their mom. [tearfully] I just want it to hurt less. It hurts so bad not to be with them.

PETER: Yes, it can feel unbearable to be separated from those you love. [pause] So, thinking about what you just said, it sounds more like you think about killing yourself as a way to stop the hurt than that you really want to be dead? Am I understanding you correctly?

EMMA: Yeah, that's right. I don't want to be dead. I want to be with my kids and for the hurt to stop. I'm so lonely without them.

PETER: I'm also wondering about one other thing. I think I know the answer, but it's our practice here at our agency to ask this question when someone has told us that they are in so much pain that they are having thoughts about taking their life. My question is this: Have you thought about *how* you might go about taking your own life if you were to change your mind and decide to do it?

EMMA: No, I never think about that. I only think about how to make the pain stop. I don't want my kids to have a dead mother.

PETER: You must love your children very much. Even though you're hurting so much, you seem determined to endure your pain so that you can be there for your kids.

EMMA: [nodding in agreement] Yes, they mean everything to me.

PETER: So getting back to this miracle, when it happens, what will be there instead of the pain and the thoughts of killing yourself?

You can also adapt scaling questions to get problem-assessment information. For example, Peter could have asked Emma, "On a scale of 0 to 10, where 0 means that there is no chance that you will take your life and 10 means that there is every chance, what would you say the chances are that you will really do it?" Once Emma gives a number, for example 2, Peter can explore the meaning of 2 for her. This problem assessment dialogue, based on the client's perceptions and descriptions, could be amplified by formulating the scaling question with a relationship focus: "Suppose I were to ask your best friend—on the same scale—what the chances are that you will actually take your life. What would she say?" Obtaining assessment information with scaling questions has the advantage of giving you a ready route back to solution talk. Once the client has explained what is happening that makes things a 2, you can easily shift to questions about why things are not so bad that the number would be a 4, a 6, or even a 10.

The use of coping dialogues with clients in crisis has revealed a paradox: The best assessment information generally is the extent and type of clients' solution talk. By pursuing coping questions and scaling questions focused on formulating the next small steps with clients, you come away from interviews with the best information about whether clients will be able to meet life-sustaining and safety needs in their current circumstances. That is the ultimate purpose of problem assessment. The practitioner gathers details about the nature and depth of clients' current crises or problems in order to evaluate whether clients can cope by drawing on their own resources, or whether additional resources and steps such as hospitalization are indicated.

WHEN THE CLIENT REMAINS OVERWHELMED

After engaging in coping exploration and asking scaling questions, you may come to the conclusion that the client is overwhelmed and does not have the inner or outer resources to cope. In such situations, which are not common in our experience, you would begin to explore with the client and possibly recommend the available community resources to the client. Information on such resources is part of the orientation at the agency or clinic where you work, along with the agency's preferred procedures for making such recommendations to clients. It is a good idea for you to call in your supervisor or a senior staff member when you decide to move to such recommendations, especially if you are new to the field or the agency.

As a rule, clients who feel overwhelmed will be more open to more extreme measures like medication and hospitalization when you have first worked hard with them in coping dialogues. If you have engaged a client in a coping dialogue and the dialogue reveals few if any current coping capacities, the client often comes to realize that he or she needs more intensive care and monitoring. The information gathered from the coping dialogue will allow you to feel more confident and assertive in your recommendations, as well as in your case documentation.

CONCLUSION

Clients in crisis are not that different from other clients. Even though the events that bring these clients to you are more immediate, terrifying, and horrible than those described by other clients, clients in crisis build solutions through the same process used by other clients. In the examples in this chapter, both Insoo and Peter interact with such clients in the same ways as with clients who have not recently experienced trauma in their lives. The major difference in working with clients in crisis is that fewer of them accept the invitation to engage in goal formulation. Instead, they stay focused on problem description. In response, we set aside goal formulation for the moment and turn to coping questions. These questions serve to uncover the small, undeniable successes that a shaken, overwhelmed client is experiencing in day-to-day or moment-by-moment coping. As clients identify their microsuccesses, and their energy and confidence start to build, we return to goal formulation on a more limited basis by using scaling questions to help clients formulate their next steps in coping.

Whenever you set aside goal formulation and turn to coping questions, you are only changing the order and immediate scope of the solution-building process. You are not shifting to a different process. Consequently, when interviewing clients who have recently experienced trauma, first of all think less about whether they are in crisis and more about discovering their immediate capacity to engage in goal-formulation work. These ideas are reflected in the protocol for crisis interviewing and the list of useful coping questions included in the Appendix.

NOTE

1. An additional resource on the use of coping questions and scaling with a person at risk for suicide is a recording of an interview conducted by Insoo Kim Berg with a teenager named Carl on the day after Carl made a suicide attempt. The recording is available from the Brief Family Therapy Center (www.brief-therapy.org).

11

Outcomes

Beginning was useful. I only came one time and made a beginning, but it helped.

The question about the miracle was good. It was good then, and I've kept on thinking about it; it's still helpful.

My husband responded well to concrete goal orientation; he has never done well in therapy, but at BFTC he liked the focus on doing.

(OBSERVATIONS MADE BY BRIEF FAMILY THERAPY CENTER CLIENTS 7 TO 9 MONTHS AFTER THE END OF SERVICES)

How helpful can you expect the procedures described in this book to be for your clients? It is important to know about the overall effectiveness of these procedures if you are to use them with confidence with your clients and to learn about their effectiveness with diverse persons and different types of client problems.

Although some of the solution-building procedures described in this book may resemble procedures used in other approaches, most were developed in the past 25 years and are organized in an innovative fashion. Consequently, outcome data about their effectiveness only began to appear in the past 20 years, with the number of studies increasing significantly in the past 10 years. The first studies are descriptive studies lacking control groups. These studies tend to measure outcome by asking clients whether they believe their problems were solved and whether they are satisfied with the services they received. More recent studies have begun to incorporate comparison and control groups, and better approximate the experimental design believed by most in the profession to yield the most persuasive test of an approach's effectiveness.

This chapter, first of all, introduces you to the early outcome research that we and our colleagues conducted at Brief Family Therapy Center (BFTC). We start here because BFTC is the place where solution-focused procedures were developed, in part guided by this research. We pay special attention to the data from a BFTC 1992–1993 study because it was designed to gather data about the overall effectiveness of the procedures and begin to address whether solution building represents a different paradigm from that of problem solving. (The latter question is addressed in Chapter 15.) Thereafter, we give a summary of more recent research on solution-focused therapy from around the world.

EARLY RESEARCH AT BRIEF FAMILY THERAPY CENTER

The earliest research at BFTC was exploratory and qualitative in character, involving intense observation of which clients made progress (as clients defined progress), and what practitioners might be doing that contributed to that progress. These investigations led to the original development of solution-focused techniques. Studies about the effectiveness of parts of the approach also were conducted (e.g., Gingerich, de Shazer, & Weiner-Davis, 1988; Weiner-Davis, de Shazer, & Gingerich, 1987). The first study of outcomes of the approach as a whole at BFTC was conducted by Kiser (1988; Kiser & Nunally, 1990). The results of this unpublished study have been summarized by de Shazer (1991, p. 162): "We found an 80.4% success rate (65.6% of the clients met their goal while 14.7% made significant improvement) within an average of 4.6 sessions. When contacted at 18 months, the success rate had increased to 86%." These results are impressive and suggest that solution-focused procedures are effective.

1992–1993 Study Design Participants

The participants in this study were the 275 clients who came for services at BFTC from November 1992 through August 1993. Most of these clients were seen by one of the eight practitioners employed by BFTC. A small minority of the interviews were done by trainees learning solution-focused procedures. In all cases, these latter interviews and the end-of-session feedback included the participation of a BFTC practitioner situated behind a one-way mirror.

Clients knew that they might be asked to participate in an outcome study. Printed information given to them when they first came for services indicated that BFTC would probably be contacting them in future months to ask about the usefulness of the services they received. Clients signed a form to grant permission for future contact for research purposes. The same procedure was used to obtain clients' permission for observation of their sessions through the one-way mirror.

BFTC is located in an economically and culturally diverse neighborhood and has chosen to serve a variety of clients. This diversity is represented in the data. Of the 275 clients in the study, 57 percent identified themselves as African

American, 5 percent as Latino, 3 percent as Native American, and 36 percent as white. At the time they first visited BFTC, 43 percent of these clients were employed, while 57 percent were not. (The majority of those not employed were referred to BFTC by public welfare agencies and had their services paid through public funds.) By gender, 60 percent of the clients were female, and 40 percent were male. Children, teenagers, and younger adults are somewhat overrepresented among the 275 cases. In one third of the cases, a child, 12 years of age or younger, was the identified client. In 15 percent of cases, the client was a teenager (13 to 18 years old). Altogether, 93 percent of the clients were 45 years of age or younger.

Outcome Measurement

Outcomes were measured in two ways. The first involved a scaling question. BFTC practitioners asked clients the following question in each session, as a measurement of ongoing client progress: "On a scale of 1 to 10, where 10 means that the problems you came to therapy for are solved and 1 is the worst they've been, where are your problems now?" Practitioners recorded this *progress score* in their session notes, which are included in each client's file. By comparing progress scores from first sessions to final sessions for each client, the first measurement of outcome was obtained. This comparison is a measurement of intermediate outcome. BFTC practitioners recorded client progress scores 80 percent of the time.

Outcome was also measured on the basis of telephone interviews with clients conducted 7 to 9 months after their final sessions at BFTC. Fifty percent of the former clients were reached by telephone. All of those who were reached consented to be interviewed. Following the precedent of earlier studies by Weakland, Fisch, Watzlawick, and Bodin (1974) and Kiser (1988), former clients were asked, "Overall, would you say your treatment goal was met or not met?" Clients who answered "goal not met" were asked the second question: "Would you say there was any progress made toward that goal?" Clients were given the options of answering "progress made toward treatment goal" or "progress not made toward treatment goal." By combining the responses to these two questions, a measurement called "final outcome" was obtained.

RESULTS

Length of Services

Table 11.1 presents data on the number of interviews for the 275 cases studied.

Many clients (26 percent) came for only one session. More than 80 percent came for four or fewer sessions. The average (mean) number of sessions was 2.9.

TABLE 11.1 Number of Interviews*

Frequency of Interviews	Number of Cases	Percent (%)
1	72	26
2	80	29
3	47	17
4	31	11
5	20	7
6	10	4
7	5	2
8	4	2
9	2	1
10	1	0
11	1	0
13	1	0
23	1	0
Total	275	100

*In Tables 11.1 through 11.3, percentages are rounded to the nearest full percent.

Intermediate Outcomes

The measurement of intermediate outcome was calculated by subtracting the progress score for the first session from the progress score recorded for the final session. For example, a client who came to BFTC for four interviews and said that things were at a 2 at the first session and at a 5 by the final session received a score of +3 on intermediate outcome.

Table 11.2 gives the distribution of scores on intermediate outcome.[1] It shows that scores on intermediate outcome range from -3 through 8. For ease of presenting data, intermediate outcome scores are labeled as follows: -3 through 0 as "no progress," 1 through 3 as "moderate progress," and 4 through 8 as "significant progress." Organizing the data this way indicates that 26 percent of the cases showed no progress on intermediate outcome, 49 percent had moderate progress, and 25 percent showed significant progress.

Final Outcomes

Table 11.3 shows that when telephoned 7 to 9 months after their last interview at BFTC, 45 percent of former clients said their goal for treatment was met. An additional 32 percent said that, even though their goal was not met, some progress was made. Twenty-three percent said no progress was made.

TABLE 11.2 Frequency and Percentage Distributions for Intermediate Outcome (I.O.)

I.O. Value	Frequency	Percent (%)
−3	2	1
−2	3	2
−1	8	6
0	24	17
1	24	17
2	18	13
3	27	19
4	8	6
5	15	11
6	7	5
7	4	3
8	1	1
Total	141	100

TABLE 11.3 Frequency and Percentage Distributions for Final Outcome (F.O.)

F.O.	Frequency	Percent (%)
Goal met	61	45
Some progress	44	32
No progress	31	23
Total	136	100

COMPARATIVE DATA

The outcomes of solution-building procedures in the early studies at BFTC compare favorably with those of other approaches at that time. First, with regard to average number of sessions, Garfield (1994) found that the median for all approaches ranges from 3 to 13 interviews, with a clustering around 6. The median found for cases at BFTC in the 1988 study is 3, and for the 1992–1993 study it is 2. Because the research reviewed by Garfield involved problem-solving approaches of one type or another, the BFTC data suggest that clients may be able to make progress more quickly through exposure to solution building.

Regarding the effectiveness of therapy, Lambert and Bergin (1994) reviewed the controlled research across different approaches and concluded there is an average success rate for psychotherapy of 66 percent; that is, 66 percent of clients who receive therapy show improvement, while only 34 percent of those who do not receive therapy improve on their own (1994, p. 147). The success rates for both intermediate and final outcomes presented for BFTC clients (74 and 77 percent respectively) compare favorably with their average figure of 66 percent. In addition, the BFTC success rates were achieved over fewer sessions—a median of six for the studies reviewed by Lambert and Bergin compared to three and two for the two BFTC studies.

OTHER STUDIES OF SOLUTION-FOCUSED THERAPY

Several sources summarize research on solution-focused procedures. McKeel (1996, 1999) summarizes some 35 studies divided into three categories. The first category is outcome studies. These studies indicate success rates of 65 percent or higher for a broad range of client populations and problems, with an average number of sessions from 3 through 5.5. Three of these studies compared solution-focused with other models, showing solution-focused equal to or superior to the other treatments.

The second category is investigations of solution-focused techniques such as solution talk, pretreatment improvement, presuppositional questions, miracle question, and the formula-first-session suggestion. These studies consistently indicate that solution-focused techniques contribute to positive outcomes.

McKeel's third category involves studies of both therapists' and clients' views of solution-focused techniques. Therapists, for example, rate the miracle question as most therapeutic and say they use scaling questions most frequently. Clients say the "focus on strengths, noticing differences, focusing on what works, and the positive atmosphere of their therapy" is useful (McKeel, 1999, p. 5). This research also indicates that clients become critical of solution-focused therapy when the therapist over-focuses on techniques and does not listen carefully to client concerns and express natural empathy for clients' situations.

George, Iveson, and Ratner (2006) is a second source that summarizes the available outcome research. They draw on the compilation of 44 studies gathered by Macdonald (2006), which includes 4 randomized control studies and 13 comparison studies. They conclude: "As can be seen, the results, from different settings and with different populations, are very impressive and give justification to clinical impressions as to the effectiveness and brevity of the [solution focused] approach" (George, Iveson, & Ratner, 2006, p. 30).

Franklin (2006), a third source, summarizes 28 studies on her web page (www.utexas.edu/courses/franklin). She and a colleague observe: "Most of these studies have been completed since 1997, and the majority demonstrated positive findings showing that solution-focused therapy is a promising model that deserves further study" (Franklin & Streeter, 2006, p. 10).

The fourth source is Gingerich and Eisengart (2000, 2001). These authors review the 18 controlled studies of solution-focused brief therapy reported in the literature through summer 2001. Their criteria for inclusion required that a study implement solution-focused therapy, employ a form of experimental control, assess client behavior or functioning as opposed to client impressions of outcome, and measure outcomes at the end of treatment or at follow-up. They also assessed the level of experimental control according to these standards: "1) uses a randomized group design or acceptable single-case design, 2) focuses on a specific, well-defined disorder, 3) compares SFBT [solution-focused brief therapy] with a standard reference treatment, placebo or no treatment, 4) uses treatment manuals and procedures for monitoring treatment adherence, 5) uses outcome measures with demonstrated reliability and validity, and 6) uses a sample large enough to reliably detect group differences." Using these rigorous criteria, Gingerich and Eisengart identified 7 strongly controlled studies meeting five or six of the standards, 5 moderately controlled studies meeting four standards, and 6 weakly controlled studies meeting three or fewer standards. Their summary indicates that 17 of the 18 controlled studies report client improvement using solution-focused therapy, with the improvement being statistically significant in 10 studies. In the 11 studies that compared solution-focused to a standard treatment, 7 indicate that solution-focused treatment was equal to or exceeded the effectiveness of the standard treatment.

The aforementioned sources each identify individual studies and summarize the setting, design, outcome measures, and results of each study. When studies include a comparison of solution-focused to another practice model, the sources also indicate whether solution-focused treatment led to inferior, equal, or superior results. An alternative to this study-by-study approach is to conduct a meta-analytic review of the existing studies. As Kendall, Holmbeck, and Verduin (2004, p. 34) explain, meta-analysis involves the use of statistical techniques that "synthesize results across multiple studies by converting the results of each investigation into a common metric (usually the *effect* size)." The effect size typically indicates the average difference in outcome between the experimental or treatment groups and the control or comparison groups across the studies included in the meta-analysis. So far, one such analysis has been conducted on solution-focused therapy (Kim, 2006).

Kim searched the professional literature and found 63 studies that identified themselves as empirical studies of solution-focused therapy. He decided to include all studies that indicated they used at least one of four commonly identified solution-focused procedures and included the necessary statistics from which to calculate effect sizes. The four procedures are asking the miracle question, scaling, taking a break, and giving postbreak compliments and suggestions. Using these criteria, Kim was able to include 22 of the original 63 studies in his meta-analysis. He divided the studies among three categories and calculated effect sizes for each. The categories are studies of internalizing behavioral

problems (anxiety, depression, low self-esteem), externalizing behavioral problems (hyperactivity and other problems of conduct), and family and relationship
difficulties.

Kim reports that, relative to other meta-analyses, he found overall small
effect sizes, with those for internalizing problems being somewhat larger than
for externalizing or relationship problems. At the same time, he points out that
several individual studies had large effect sizes; effect sizes were similar to other
meta-analyses that also include dissertations as well as published studies;[2] and the
effect sizes for solution-focused treatment were essentially no different from the
other, better-researched psychotherapies in the comparison groups. Kim also
qualifies his findings by noting the analysis is based on a modest number of
studies (22); practitioners in many of the studies received very little training in
solution-focused procedures (only 2–20 hours in several instances); and adherence checks to ensure that practitioners were indeed doing solution-focused
work in their sessions lacked rigor and consistency. So, while Kim's study is
interesting and important as a first meta-analysis of solution-focused therapy and
contains several findings that again suggest solution-focused therapy is a promising new approach, Kim's meta-analysis cannot be considered conclusive because
of the limitations of the individual studies it analyzed.

Next Steps

In 2000, Gingerich and Eisengart came to this general conclusion about the state
of research on solution-focused therapy:

> Although the current studies fall short of what is needed to establish the
> efficacy of SFBT [solution-focused brief therapy], they do provide pre-
> liminary support for the idea that SFBT may be beneficial to clients. The
> wide variety of settings and populations studied and the multiplicity of
> modalities used suggest that SFBT may be useful in a broad range of
> applications, however, this tentative conclusion awaits more careful
> study. (p. 495)

Although there are now more studies of solution-focused therapy in the
literature than when Gingerich and Eisengart made this statement, their conclusion of the need for more careful studies of solution-focused therapy continues to
be accurate. The more careful study they refer to would be more studies that
meet the standards of experimental control given earlier. McKeel (1999), Franklin & Streeter (2006), and Kim (2006) concur, stating that too few studies of the
efficacy of solution-focused therapy so far have used comparison groups, random
assignment to treatment conditions, and strong and varied outcome measures.
For the sake of illustration, one such well-controlled study of the outcomes of
solution-focused therapy would be that of Lindforss and Magnusson (1997).
These researchers were interested in studying the effectiveness of solution-
focused therapy in reducing the recidivism rates of prisoners at Hageby Prison
in Stockholm, Sweden. Hageby houses "a seriously criminal population," those
with a long history of serious crimes, high recidivism, drug abuse, and disciplinary

problems while incarcerated. Beginning with a pool of prisoners willing to participate, the researchers randomly assigned 30 to an experimental group and 30 to a control group. The experimental group received an average of 5 one- to two-hour sessions of solution-focused therapy, while the control group received no treatment beyond the programming given all prisoners. Outcome data on recidivism were collected at 12 and 16 months after release from Hageby. At 12 months, those in the experimental group had a recidivism rate of 53 percent compared to 76 percent of those in the control group. At 16 months, recidivism rates were 60 percent and 86 percent, respectively. The differences in recidivism between the two groups proved to be statistically significant. In addition, the repeat offenses of those in the experimental group were less serious. The researchers concluded that solution-focused treatment led to lower rates of and less serious recidivism, thus saving the Swedish prison system considerable money.

Part of the challenge of conducting well-controlled research is developing a manualized description of solution-focused therapy (Kim, 2006). While several books, including this one, describe the assumptions and techniques of the approach, so far a manual of the therapy for research purposes complete with adherence measures has yet to be developed. Such a manual is important because it ensures that therapists in any research study of solution-focused therapy are indeed doing the therapy according to a generally accepted standard definition of the approach. As of this writing, members of the European Brief Therapy Association (www.ebta.nu) and the Solution Focused Brief Therapy Association (www.sfbta.org) are creating a manual for solution-focused therapy for use in future research.

It is also essential to continue research on solution-focused techniques and which techniques contribute most to its effectiveness. McKeel (1999) offers the fullest summary of those studies to date. This type of research is important because it offers information about what it is about solution-focused procedures that fosters change in clients. Along the same lines, more micro-analytical research into the coconstruction process in solution-focused conversations is needed to develop additional understanding of how clients change through participating in these conversations (Bavelas, McGee, Phillips, & Routledge, 2000; McGee, Del Vento, & Bavelas, 2005).

NOTES

1. Fewer cases are represented in this table because of incomplete data on progress scores and because clients had to come for at least two sessions for an intermediate outcome score to be calculated.
2. Kim's meta-analysis included 11 dissertations and 11 published studies. Including dissertations generally lowers overall effect sizes.

12

Professional Values and Human Diversity

> The human person has intrinsic value.
>
> (BIESTEK, 1957, P. 73)

Chapter 1 stated that the skills used in solution building represent a different paradigm for professional helping than do those used in problem-solving approaches. If you agree with this view, you may be asking yourself a number of questions:

- How does solution-focused interviewing fit with the values intended to guide practice in the helping professions?

- Is this way of working equally helpful to clients from diverse backgrounds?

- If I decide to use solution-building skills with my clients, how will this be received by my colleagues, supervisors, and the agencies or clinics that might employ me?

- If adopted agency-wide, how would solution building change different aspects of agency practice such as case documentation, case conferences, and supervision of workers?

- I can see that solution building can be helpful to individuals and families, but can it be applied to other levels of practice, such as working with small groups and organizations?

Students and workshop participants regularly pose such questions for discussion. In this chapter and Chapter 13, answers are presented that are informed by conversations with students and practitioners who have been incorporating solution-focused interviewing skills into their practice. In Chapter 14, the experiences of several practitioners, programs, and agencies that have incorporated solution building into their settings are described by these innovators themselves.

SOLUTION BUILDING AND PROFESSIONAL VALUES

The bedrock of any profession is its values. Professional values encapsulate the fundamental commitments of a profession and provide the criteria according to which practitioners must evaluate the acceptability of their work with clients. In the helping professions, all practice procedures, new and old, must be continuously scrutinized for the extent to which they conform with the field's cardinal values.

There are several overlapping but distinguishable helping professions: counseling psychology, marriage and family counseling or therapy, psychotherapy, rehabilitative counseling, social work, substance abuse counseling, and so forth. These various professions and professional associations within the helping field are in close agreement about the principles that should guide interactions between practitioners and clients. This is evident from a comparison of the ethical codes of particular helping professions.[1] This comparison can be made by consulting practice textbooks throughout the field, which typically review the fundamental values of their respective approaches to practice (e.g., Axelson, 1993; Egan, 2002; Hepworth, Rooney, & Larsen, 2002; Ivey & Ivey, 2007; Lewis, Dana, & Blevins, 2002).

The discussion of professional values and solution-focused interviewing procedures draws on the list of values and practice principles formulated by Sheafor & Horejsi (2007) because their formulation is more detailed than others and permits a more complete discussion. The following pages address those values that apply to practitioner–client interaction across all of the helping professions.

Respecting Human Dignity

All persons, by virtue of their humanity, have the right to be treated as valued creatures. This conviction has several implications for how practitioners ought to relate to clients. Foremost among these is the belief that clients must be accepted as they are. According to Biestek (1957), all aspects of any client must be accepted—the client's strengths and limitations, positive and negative attitudes, seemingly healthy and unhealthy behaviors, and attractive and unattractive qualities and habits. As Biestek and others (notably Rogers, 1961) describe it, acceptance must be unconditional. It must not be based on past performance.

Both Biestek and Rogers, however, are quick to point out that acceptance is not the same as approval. A practitioner can accept client attitudes and behaviors as real without approving of them. For example, a practitioner can accept that a client prefers to watch films with graphic violence rather than family movies without approving of that preference. The focus of acceptance is on what is real for a client, not on what is good for the client.

The commitment to respecting human dignity also demands that practitioners remain nonjudgmental. This attitude toward clients means the practitioner has no interest in judging the client or the client's story. Judging involves making legal decisions about the guilt or innocence of a person or moral statements about the rightness or wrongness of a person's attitudes or actions. It amounts to placing blame or making moral evaluations.

While practitioners are committed to remaining nonjudgmental with their clients, they must also recognize that clients live in a family and community context that maintains standards for evaluating individuals' attitudes and actions. In solving their problems, clients must take into account the legal and moral standards of the families and communities in which they live. For practitioners to ignore such standards would leave clients with the impression that their practitioners are unrealistic and not helpful.

Respect for human dignity through acceptance and the nonjudgmental attitude is the foundation for the development of cooperation and trust in the client-practitioner relationship. When a practitioner responds in a judgmental or evaluative way, clients soon sense the practitioner has preferences (and even expectations) about how they will think and behave. The practitioner's acceptance is conditional. Recognizing this, clients begin to feel more awkward and less accepted unless their preferences match those of the practitioner. They come to doubt the practitioner is fully committed to understanding them and lose trust that the practitioner will be helpful.

Solution building effectively operationalizes client acceptance and the nonjudgmental attitude through the use of solution-focused interviewing. Beginning with the fundamental skills presented in Chapter 3, solution building is based on accepting client perceptions and working within clients' frames of reference. Notions of client resistance and challenging or confronting client perceptions play no part in the approach.

The solution-building process also contextualizes any solution that emerges (De Jong & Miller, 1995). As clients answer the miracle question and describe what will be different in their lives when their problems are solved, they are asked how they know such differences can occur in their lives. In their answers, clients describe the family and community contexts in which they live and explain how their goals make sense in those contexts. The relationship questions asked in solution-focused interviewing invite clients to amplify goals and describe exceptions in terms that take seriously their relationships to family members and other important figures in the community.

Human dignity is fostered by relating to others in ways that enhance their sense of worth. Solution-focused interviewing does this by inviting clients to be experts about themselves and their lives. By paying attention to client perceptions, this method of interviewing implicitly conveys to clients that their perceptions are the most valuable and important resource in the solution-building process. Consequently, the process itself not only respects, but actually enhances, each client's sense of personal value and dignity.

Individualizing Service

Each person is unique. Each client wants to be treated not only "as *a* human being but as *this* human being with his [or her] personal differences" (Biestek, 1957, p. 25). All the helping professions emphasize that each person has his or her own constellation of attitudes, beliefs, wishes, strengths, successes, needs, and problems. Clients expect their practitioners to listen to and respect their concerns and be sufficiently flexible to assist them in ways that honor their individuality.

Respecting the individuality of each client is fundamental to solution-focused interviewing. In taking the posture of not knowing and continuously seeking amplification and clarification within the client's frame of reference and in the client's own words, solution-focused interviewing uncovers each client's concept of his or her problems, goals, past successes, and strengths. Solutions are individualized because they are built from exceptions and coping strategies arising out of specific events in each client's life.

Effectively individualizing client services requires optimum flexibility on the part of practitioners. The solution-building process allows practitioners to be very flexible because it depends for specifics (particular goals, coping strategies, strengths, and so forth) on the enormous range of perceptions and experiences brought to the helping relationship by clients. It is not bound by traditional assessment and diagnostic categories, nor does it limit itself to preferred interventions for particular diagnosed problems. Instead, it follows each client from one step behind, as the client develops an individualized solution of his or her own making. In addition, solution building buttresses the practitioner's faith in the inner and outer resources of clients because most clients build realistic and impressive solutions.

Fostering Client Vision

Sheafor & Horejsi (2007, p. 76) write that practitioners must introduce and nurture "a sense of hopefulness and offer a vision that change is possible and that there are new and better ways to deal with the situation." This value implies that practitioners must be careful not to raise false hopes or project unrealistic outcomes for clients.

Solution-focused interviewing fits well with this value, although in a different way than does problem-focused interviewing. A whole stage of solution building—the development of well-formed goals through amplifying answers to the miracle question—encourages clients to develop a detailed vision of what their lives might be like when their problems are solved. This emphasis on inviting clients to create the vision by drawing on their own frames of reference means solution building relies less on practitioner suggestions than do problem-solving approaches. As well as fostering hope and motivation in clients, this approach complements other practice values such as individualizing services and promoting client self-determination.

Solution-focused interviewing also counters any tendency of practitioners to raise false hopes in clients. First, because clients define their own visions for change, the practitioner's preferences for client goals have less opportunity to emerge in the interview. Second, the solution-focused approach asks clients, as experts about their situations, to clarify what parts of their miracle picture can and cannot happen and, in this way, encourages clients to think about and explain what is realistic.

Building on Strengths

Sheafor & Horejsi (2007) indicate that practitioners in the field tend to be preoccupied with client problems, limitations, or deficiencies. They note that client assessments by interdisciplinary teams are often negative and mention few or no client abilities. They lament this "negative way of thinking about clients" and point out that "it is the clients' abilities and potentials that are most important in helping to bring about change" (Sheafor & Horejsi 2007, p. 76).

Building on client strengths is a hallmark of solution building, as illustrated by the emphasis on exploring and clarifying client exceptions and the regular practice of complimenting client strengths and successes.

Encouraging Client Participation

In discussing client participation, Sheafor & Horejsi (2007, p. 77) repeat the well-known maxims of the field that practitioners should "help your clients to help themselves" and "do *with* the client and not *to* or *for* the client." In other words, the helping professions are committed to empowering clients. We believe that solution building not only fits with this value, but also, as explained in Chapters 1 and 2, gives added meaning to client participation and empowerment. By minimizing the role of traditional scientific expertise and maximizing the role of client perceptions, solution building moves toward a different and more complete way of helping clients to help themselves. Clients are asked to help themselves by defining a miracle future, identifying exceptions, and exploring how the strengths associated with past successes can be used to build solutions. Solution-focused interviewing gives added depth to the notion of working *with* clients. To work with clients means to collaborate with them by engaging in dialogues about their concerns and experiences. To truly develop a dialogue with clients means exploring and affirming their otherness. It means acknowledging that, as people distinct from their practitioners, clients probably have different wishes and points of view. In drawing out a client's perceptions during solution-focused interviewing, the interviewer is continually respecting and affirming the client's otherness.

Maximizing Self-Determination

The values discussed complement each other. For example, as you foster client participation, you are also individualizing services and maximizing client dignity. Client self-determination belongs to this same constellation and is probably the most emphasized of the values that should guide practice.

Biestek (1957, p. 103) defines self-determination as "the practical recognition of the right and need of clients to freedom in making their own choices and decisions." As Biestek notes, the helping professions are unanimous in their support of this value because self-determination is not only a basic human right, but also respects the way in which people develop. People mature and develop a sense of who they are through making their own choices. Even though people may get tired and discouraged at times as they struggle with their problems, client self-confidence and satisfaction emerge not when practitioners take over for clients but, rather, when clients exercise responsibility and live as best they can with the consequences of their choices. Even with clients of limited mental capacity, practitioners are expected to work in ways that maximize clients' self-determination.

Solution-focused procedures foster self-determination. Clients are encouraged to take responsibility for their own lives throughout the solution-building process: They are asked to identify their problems and define what is happening in their lives that makes these events problems, and they are asked for their perceptions regarding a more satisfying future, existing exceptions, their levels of motivation and confidence, and so forth. For example, in the conversations between Ah Yan and Peter, she told him she wanted relief from her panicky feelings, and she wanted a future in which she felt happy on the inside as well as the outside and her son, sensing her new composure, would feel free to go outside and play on the swing set and ride his bike. She also described exception times in which she could breathe better with no shakes and worry, and she indicated she had a 10 level of motivation to work and a 10 level of confidence that she would find solutions.

Throughout this process, Ah Yan was taking responsibility for defining her problem and making choices about what to do with her life. Peter invited her to be the expert about problem and solution content. His expertise was primarily limited to guiding the process of solution building through the questions he asked. Working this way with clients brings client self-determination to a deeper level. It is definitely different from approaches in which clients' perceptions are the raw material for professional assessments and suggestions that clients can choose to adopt or ignore.

Fostering Transferability

Ideally, practitioners work in such a way that clients can take what they have learned about resolving their problems during services and apply it to other problems in their lives. Vinter (1985) calls this ideal *transferability*. Sheafor & Horejsi (2007, p. 78) identify an aspect of transferability.

> An important aspect of preparing clients for the future is to teach them how to identify and make use of resources that might be found in their immediate environment. Such resources may include family members, relatives, friends, service clubs, and church or synagogue groups.

Transferability involves increasing clients' awareness of their inner and outer resources. Solution-focused interviewing is able to accomplish this (De Jong & Miller, 1995). By consistently asking clients to explore and trust their own perceptions about what they want and how to make that happen, solution-focused interviewers give clients the opportunity to sharpen their awareness of their past successes and strengths—their inner resources. For example, in Insoo's interview with the Williams family (see Chapter 5), she affirmed Gladys's goal to be a good mother, and she complimented many things Gladys was doing to make that goal a reality. She invited Gladys to put into words those inner resources that she could continue to use in the future.

The relationship questions in solution-focused interviewing also give clients the opportunity to identify outer resources. For example, in exploring with Ah Yan what differences others would notice about her when she was doing better, Peter learned that Ah Yan's husband and sister-in-law were great supports to her. He also learned that she was learning to use these outer resources in new and more effective ways.

The following outcome data bears out the transferability of solution building. The Brief Family Therapy Center (BFTC) telephone survey (see Chapter 11) included this question: "We are also wondering if our treatment program has helped you with personal or family problems besides the one(s) which you worked on with us at BFTC. Would you say that it has helped, hindered, or neither helped nor hindered with other problems?" One half of the former clients responded that the services had helped with other problems. The other half said the services neither helped nor hindered. Kiser's (1988) study of BFTC clients reveals a higher rate of transferability. When he asked former clients the same question, 67 percent reported the services had helped with other problems.

Maximizing Client Empowerment

Sheafor & Horejsi (2007, p. 78) write that empowerment involves "helping people, both individually and collectively, to gain the power needed to change their life circumstances and to gain control over how they live their lives...." They also state that practitioners can help clients to gain control over their life circumstances through connecting them with useful information and resources, and developing the skills needed to make decisions and take actions to increase self-reliance and change the contexts in which they live.

As Chapters 1 and 2 made clear, we agree wholeheartedly with these authors' view that practitioners should be committed to empowering clients. We believe that the solution-focused questions discussed in this book invite clients to take control of their lives by formulating their own goals, marshaling their inner strengths and family and community resources, and clarifying what additional resources would be useful to create more satisfying lives.

Protecting Confidentiality

Confidentiality requires that the practitioner hold in confidence the private information conveyed in the course of professional services. Clients disclose to the practitioner matters and points of view that, if revealed to others, could be awkward or damaging to the clients and those they know. It is the client's right to expect confidentiality. When practitioners meet this expectation, clients are more likely to trust them, feel respected, and work productively with them.

The professional workplace regularly codifies its policies on confidentiality and orients new practitioners to them before they are permitted to see clients. These policies reflect and often exceed client protections included in governmental laws and regulations. Solution-building procedures operate within the law and agency policies. For example, when a team approach is used, clients are fully informed, and the team is not used without signed consent.

Solution-focused interviewing protects confidentiality in another way. There is a longstanding belief in the helping professions that, in order to make progress, clients must express feelings about deeply painful and embarrassing events in their pasts. Some practitioners feel they must probe for such material, even against the client's understandable resistance. By contrast, solution building is committed to the idea, based on experience and outcome data, that clients can make as much or more progress by drawing on their own sense of what their problems are, what they want to be different, and what strengths and resources are available to them. Consequently, clients are not asked to talk about their problems in the same personal detail. They decide what content they need to talk about in order to build solutions. We have found that, when given control over content, clients almost always choose to protect—that is, not to reveal—the intimate details of past failings. This was the case with both Ah Yan and the Williams family.

Creating this context for a deeper protection of confidentiality also results in advantages for you as an interviewer. You no longer worry about helping clients to uncover underlying issues, nor do you encounter client resistance. Instead, you enjoy working with clients more than ever, while allowing them to take greater charge of how they will build their own solutions.

Promoting Normalization

The helping professions participate in delivering services to persons with physical disabilities, long-term mental illnesses, mental retardation, and other disabilities. The tendency has been to isolate such persons. Often they have been required to live in ways that reflect stereotypes of their disabilities and are beneath their capacities. In response, the field has promoted the ideal of normalization, which calls on practitioners to assist such clients, insofar as possible, to live in an environment and in ways considered typical (Sheafor & Horejsi, 2007).

Solution focused interviewing fits well with the ideal of normalization because normalization is the foremost goal of so many clients with disabilities. Clients are encouraged to amplify their vision of their desired living circumstances and to discover their related successes and strengths through exception exploration. They are invited to build additional confidence by asking them how they know that they can repeat and move beyond past successes and who and what will be helpful to them in this process. We have found solution building to be applicable to clients with severe mental illness, those managing the consequences of a debilitating disease such as lupus, those who have recently been diagnosed with a terminal illness, and those with other physical disabilities. Even for clients who seem overwhelmed, solution-focused interviewing can be helpful. Such clients usually become more hopeful when asked coping questions (see Chapter 10) and complimented on their coping strengths and strategies. They often discover additional ideas about how to live with their pain or disability.

Monitoring Change

Because clients and their contexts are always changing, Sheafor & Horejsi (2007, p. 80) state that practitioners and clients together must make a "continuous monitoring and evaluation of the change process" by regularly collecting data about the outcomes of the strategies used to assist the client. If these data indicate that the intended change is not occurring, it is the practitioner's responsibility to take other steps.

In solution-focused interviewing, change is regularly monitored. The client's answers to the monitoring questions are integral to the discovery of client successes and strengths. Scaling questions are used to gain client estimates of change. For example, Peter asked Ah Yan the presession-change question and received an answer of 6, which suggested she was doing considerably better by the time of their first session than at the time she called to make her appointment. In their second session, when he asked her to scale her progress, she chose 7 or 8. In both instances, her answers to the scaling question became the springboard for exploring what was different in her life and what she and others might be doing to make this progress happen. Because scaling is integral to solution building, monitoring progress feels comfortable to practitioner and client.

Solution building also respects the field's commitment to taking other steps when monitoring reveals a lack of progress. In solution building, it is a maxim to try something else when what the client is doing is not working. De Shazer (1985) has identified this maxim as part of the basic philosophy of a solution-focused approach and formulated a suggestion around it: the do-something-different suggestion (see Chapter 7).

Conclusion

Solution-focused procedures fit well with the values intended to guide client-practitioner interactions in the helping professions. In fact, the use of these procedures can often enhance practitioners' ability to bring these values to life in their work with clients. Recalling the discussion of the forces that gave rise to the strengths perspective and recent notions of empowerment (see Chapter 1), contradictions between these values and the procedures adopted in the problem-solving paradigm are what has prompted the call for more collaborative and empowering approaches to practice (Weick, 1993).

DIVERSITY-COMPETENT PRACTICE

Practice textbooks currently in use in the helping professions are calling for more sensitivity to human diversity. Some have gone so far as to build their approach to practice around the concept (Axelson, 1993; Devore & Schlesinger, 1999; Lum,

2004; Sue & Sue, 1999). These books contend that, for too long, the helping professions have operated with built-in preferences for the traits and behaviors of middle-class white males. Such preferences have minimized or ignored the characteristics more common among poor people, women, and people of color. The field is now more committed than ever to preparing diversity-conscious and diversity-competent practitioners.

Efforts to foster diversity-competent practice in the field mainly presume the problem-solving paradigm, in which the practitioner first assesses client problems and then intervenes on the basis of the assessments. The expert practitioner is expected to respect human diversity at the assessment stage and then again at the intervention stage. Practice textbooks (Ivey & Ivey, 2007; Lum, 2004; Timberlake, Farber, & Sabatino, 2002) emphasize that aspiring practitioners must learn about the values, beliefs, and worldviews of different economic, ethnic, and racial groups, along with their different styles of communication and problem solving. They also call on new practitioners to actively examine their own assumptions, biases, and ethnocentric attitudes, so that these can be recognized as personal limitations for professional practice and steps may be taken to lessen their negative effects. Having acquired self-knowledge and expert knowledge about diverse groups, practitioners apply this knowledge sensitively in the assessment stage, so that cultural traits are not assessed as problems or deficits, and again in the intervention stage, so that recommended interventions are inoffensive and effective.

We have definite reservations about this approach. Certainly, it is important for practitioners to learn about the worldviews and preferred lifestyles of different groups, and all practitioners need to become more aware of their own attitudes regarding diversity. However, our preference for a solution-building paradigm makes us uneasy with attempts to address diversity within the context of professional assessments and interventions. Instead, we regard cultural diversity as one aspect of the enormous differences among people and as further confirmation of the need to take a posture of not knowing when interviewing clients.

The field's current approach to increasing diversity competency is incomplete. Imagine you are a white, middle-class male and you are about to interview an African-American female who is unemployed and on welfare. Suppose you have worked hard to soften your class, racial, and gender biases and you have studied the professional literature about the histories, customs, preferences, and patterns of diverse groups. Also suppose you have several years of experience in working with African-American clients. With all these competencies and experiences, you would feel prepared to conduct the interview. However, this background is not enough to ensure you will do a diversity-competent interview because you cannot assume the particular African American you are about to interview will correspond exactly to the characteristics of African Americans described in the literature or represented in your past experience. Moreover, each individual is a composite of several dimensions of diversity (class, ethnicity, gender, physical ability/disability, sexual orientation, race, religion, and so forth), and you have no way of knowing ahead of time how these may interact with one another in any particular client. Consequently, no matter how much experience you may have had with a particular population of clients, you can make few, if any, assumptions about your latest client. Instead, you must make every effort to relate to each client as a human being with particular strengths, experiences, and idiosyncrasies. To do otherwise would amount to stereotyping.

The helping professions need a way of working with individual clients that is effective across diverse groups. We believe that the solution-building process comes closer to this ideal than do problem-solving approaches. Solution-focused interviewing draws on client perceptions and works more fully within the client's frame of reference. Because the client's perceptions will be shaped, in part, by the histories, customs, and problem-solving styles of the groups to which the client belongs, the solution-building process integrates those aspects of diversity as it proceeds. Each aspect of diversity is regarded as a potentially valuable resource.

Outcome Data on Diversity

To examine whether solution-focused interviewing is effective across diverse groups, the following outcome data is included. Chapter 11 presented data on both intermediate and final outcomes for all Brief Family Therapy Center clients who received services between November 1992 and August 1993. Data on intermediate and final outcomes for four categories of diversity follow.

Age   The age of each client was asked on an information form that clients or their guardians completed on their first visit to BFTC. When two adults came for services together, they were asked to choose which one would be the identified client for purposes of recordkeeping and third-party (private insurance or Medicaid) reimbursement. Table 12.1 presents data on intermediate outcome by age categories. As explained in Chapter 11, intermediate outcome is a measurement of progress at the time of services. Table 12.1 includes data only for cases up through 60 years of age because there are too few cases in higher age ranges to permit analysis. The last row of Table 12.1 gives the number of cases in each age category.

If you compare across columns in Table 12.1 within given categories of intermediate outcome, you find that age of client is not significantly related to

T A B L E 12.1 Intermediate Outcome (I.O.) by Age*

I.O.	12 Years and Under	13–18 Years	19–30 Years	31–45 Years	46–60 Years	Total
Significant progress	24%	21%	29%	27%	13%	24%
Moderate progress	44%	58%	38%	56%	50%	49%
No progress	33%	21%	33%	17%	38%	26%
Number of cases	46	24	21	41	8	140

*In Tables 12.1 through 12.8, percentages are rounded to the nearest whole percent.

intermediate outcome. Similar percentages of clients show significant progress for all age groupings. The only exception is for clients of ages 46 to 60 years, where a smaller percentage (13%) shows significant progress by the final session. However, this percentage is based on only eight cases and has little influence on the overall result. When comparing across age categories for clients showing no progress, clients who are ages 13 to 18 and ages 31 to 45 show a lower percentage of no progress, but the differences are not large. Overall, these data suggest that the use of solution-focused interviewing procedures is equally effective for persons of all ages.

Table 12.2 presents the data for final outcome according to age groupings. Final-outcome data were obtained by contacting clients 7 to 9 months after their last session at BFTC and asking them whether their treatment goal was met or not met. Those clients who responded "not met" were also asked whether any progress had been made.

Table 12.2 shows that clients in the 19 to 30 age range are somewhat less likely to state their goal was met and somewhat more likely to say no progress was made toward their treatment goal. Overall, there is little if any relationship between age and outcome. Consequently, the measurements for both intermediate and final outcomes suggest that solution building works equally well for persons of all ages.

Employment Status   Data gathered when clients came for their first sessions at BFTC provide a rough indicator of clients' socioeconomic status. Specifically, clients (or their guardians) were asked about their current employment status. Those who were employed regularly came with authorization for services from private insurance companies. Those who were not employed were, for the most part, on public welfare and their services were paid for under Title XIX. Tables 12.3 and 12.4 present data on employment status and outcomes.

T A B L E 12.2   Final Outcome (F.O.) by Age

F.O.	12 Years and Under	13–18 Years	19–30 Years	31–45 Years	46–60 Years	Total
Goal met	37%	42%	32%	52%	58%	44%
Some progress	40%	47%	36%	24%	17%	33%
No progress	24%	11%	32%	24%	25%	23%
Number of cases	38	19	22	42	12	133

T A B L E 12.3   Intermediate Outcome (I.O.) by Employment Status

I.O.	Employed	Not Employed	Total
Significant progress	22%	25%	24%
Moderate progress	59%	42%	50%
No progress	19%	33%	27%
Number of cases	63	76	139

TABLE 12.4 Final Outcome (F.O.) by Employment Status

F.O.	Employed	Not Employed	Total
Goal met	50%	37%	44%
Some progress	27%	41%	33%
No progress	23%	22%	23%
Number of cases	74	59	133

The data on intermediate outcome indicate that the percentage of those not employed who show no progress from their first sessions to their final sessions is somewhat higher than the corresponding figure for those employed, but the difference is not great (33% versus 19%). In addition, the difference is not present in the data for final outcome. Here, virtually the same percentage of unemployed clients as employed clients show no progress (22% and 23%), although a higher percentage of the employed (50%) report meeting their treatment goal compared with those not employed (37%). Overall, the data suggest a small tendency for the employed to have better outcomes with solution-focused procedures, but there is little, if any, difference in outcome.

Gender   Tables 12.5 and 12.6 present the data on outcomes for clients who are female and those who are male. Here, gender is not correlated with effectiveness. Women and men show equally positive outcomes for both intermediate and final outcomes.

Race   When identified clients came for their first session at BFTC, they (or their guardians) were asked to complete the following question on the client information questionnaire: "What race do you consider yourself/your child to be?" They were given these options: American Indian/Native American; Asian American / Pacific Islander; Black/African American; White/Caucasian; Latino/Latina/Hispanic; and Other. Because there were fewer than five cases for both Native Americans and Asian Americans, data are not presented for these categories. Tables 12.7 and 12.8 present outcome data for the other three groups.

These groups show little difference on intermediate and final outcomes. Latino clients deviate a little from the pattern set by African Americans and Whites, but this difference is small. The Latino group itself is much smaller than the other two.

TABLE 12.5 Intermediate Outcome (I.O.) by Gender

I.O.	Female	Male	Total
Significant progress	28%	20%	25%
Moderate progress	46%	53%	49%
No progress	26%	27%	26%
Number of cases	81	60	141

TABLE 12.6 Final Outcome (F.O.) by Gender

F.O.	Female	Male	Total
Goal met	46%	44%	45%
Some progress	27%	40%	32%
No progress	28%	16%	23%
Number of cases	79	55	134

TABLE 12.7 Intermediate Outcome (I.O.) by Race

I.O.	African American	White	Latino	Total
Significant progress	27%	21%	43%	26%
Moderate progress	45%	58%	29%	49%
No progress	28%	21%	29%	26%
Number of cases	78	48	7	133

TABLE 12.8 Final Outcome (F.O.) by Race

F.O.	African American	White	Latino	Total
Goal met	48%	45%	36%	46%
Some progress	32%	26%	46%	31%
No progress	20%	30%	18%	24%
Number of cases	60	47	11	118

Diversity and Satisfaction with Services

Additional data about outcome 7 to 9 months after services suggest the usefulness of solution building with diverse clients. Former clients were asked the following question: "Overall, would you say that you are satisfied, dissatisfied, or neither satisfied nor dissatisfied with your therapy services at the Center?" Of the 137 who responded, 72 percent said they were satisfied, 16 percent said they were neither satisfied nor dissatisfied, and 12 percent said they were dissatisfied. The level of satisfaction did not change when looking separately at satisfaction level for clients of different age, employment status, gender, and race.

Thus, a wide range of clients makes good progress with solution building. This means that, as an interviewer, you do not need to make assumptions about your clients on the basis of their backgrounds. Instead, if you have a basic knowledge of diversity differences and have worked to rid yourself of diversity biases, you can proceed from a posture of not knowing, in the awareness that, by its very nature, the solution–building process is respectful of diversity and sensitive to people's differences.

NOTE

1. Should you wish to make the comparison, several codes are printed in a supplement (titled *Codes of Ethics for the Helping Professions*) to the textbook *Issues and Ethics in the Helping Professions* (Corey, Corey, & Callanan, 2007).

13

Agency, Group, and Community Practice

SOLUTION BUILDING AND AGENCY PRACTICE

As seen in Chapter 1, the helping professions operate within a problem-solving paradigm. This has definite consequences not only for client-practitioner interactions, but also for how agencies and mental health clinics conduct other aspects of practice. The paradigm requires practitioners to use their expertise to gather case data about client problems and use those data in *problem assessments,* which then provide the foundation for *problem interventions.* Once in agency practice, you will discover that this paradigm has clear implications for the content of your recordkeeping and your interactions with agency colleagues and collaterals.

Case Documentation in Problem-Focused Settings

Case records typically include information about client characteristics, identified problems and their assessment, goals, interventions, services rendered, and documentation of progress. They have several uses (Kagle, 1991; Sheafor & Horejsi, 2007). They help practitioners to stay abreast of case information and progress and to communicate with colleagues, supervisors, and collaterals about cases. They are also important to agencies as documentation of services and sources of information for funding requests and research.

Agencies characteristically require their practitioners to prepare the following documents on each case:

1. An initial assessment. Sometimes called an individual or social history, this document includes identifying information about the client, information about the presenting problem(s), referral sources, the practitioner's assessment of the client and the problem, and (in mental health settings) a *DSM–IV–TR* diagnosis (American Psychiatric Association, 2000).

2. A treatment (or service) plan. This document is a statement of goals in the case and the planned interventions or services intended to accomplish the goals.

3. Progress notes. This document is a brief, often handwritten statement included in the case record after each contact with the client. It describes the degree of progress accomplished toward the goals since the last contact. If new problems have arisen in the case, this document can also include reassessment statements and reformulation of goals.

4. A closing summary. This is a summary statement of the identified problems, goals, interventions, and progress in the case, along with the circumstances under which the client terminated services. In addition, it includes any recommendations for future services or referral to other agencies.

These documents reflect the stages of the problem-solving model. Sometimes, agency procedures go further in their commitment to a focus on problems. They may require practitioners to administer standardized assessment instruments once they suspect certain problems. Practitioners then incorporate the results into the initial assessment and treatment plan.

As you incorporate solution building into your work with clients, you may find certain aspects of this recordkeeping irrelevant to your work with clients. While you will need some information about clients' perceptions of their problems, you will generally find that expert assessment or diagnostic information is not helpful. Practitioners who have become more solution-focused in their work have become increasingly frustrated with their agencies' documentation requirements.

How can you deal with this situation? Some observations and suggestions follow. Let us begin by looking at Peter's experience.

Peter worked for several years in a clinical mental health setting with a problem and pathology focus. His agency had a detailed protocol of categories and questions that practitioners had to follow in order to generate information for incorporation into an initial assessment and treatment plan. The information was also used in a *DSM–IV–TR* diagnosis, which must be submitted with any application for third-party reimbursement for services. Because the initial assessment and treatment plan had to be completed by the end of the second session, Peter felt pressured into adopting an emphasis on problems when he began his work with clients.

He had to follow the protocol. It was an agency policy. He decided to present it to clients for what it was—an agency requirement. As he became more solution-focused in his work, he would begin by making the following proposal to his clients.

> At our agency, it's a requirement to do an initial assessment and treatment plan by the end of our second meeting. The initial assessment involves a lot of questions about the concerns and symptoms which brought you here, as well as questions about your background, family, and personal history. You

may find answering these questions helpful or you may not. It seems to be different for different people. The treatment plan involves talking about what you want different in the future and how you might go about making that happen. It's been my experience that this can be very useful to clients. So I have a suggestion. Let's work today on getting all this information about your concerns down, and next time we can work more on what you would like to have different. You should also know it's important to get this initial assessment information down so that I can make a diagnosis in case you want to receive benefits from your insurance company for your services here. We can talk more about this process today, too, if you wish. Is this plan of action OK with you?

Because clients are usually focused on problems when they first come in, Peter's clients consistently agreed to his suggestion. He then showed them the form the agency used, and he and the client worked through the items one by one. If there was additional time toward the end of the session, he began asking about what the client would like to have different in his or her life. Frequently, he ended the session by giving the formula-first-session suggestion, as a way to turn the client's attention toward solution building. In the next session, he turned to goal formulation by asking the miracle question and its follow-up questions, and he explored exceptions, took a break, and gave feedback at the end of the session.

This agency also required clients to sign their treatment plans, as part of its effort to operationalize clients' right to be informed about their treatment. During the break in the second session, Peter would write out goals based on the goal-formulation dialogue. After the break, he reviewed these with the client and asked if the client would be willing to sign them, once they were typed. Thereafter, he gave his solution-building feedback. After the client left, he used the information obtained in both sessions to dictate his initial assessment and treatment plan.

Peter is still not happy with this compromise solution. First, clients are asked for problem details and history that are not necessary in order to build solutions. Second, committing goals to paper for the client's review and signature pushes clients toward closure on goals when it is more useful for them to be thinking about more possibilities. However, his compromise did allow him to distance himself somewhat from the agency's problem-focused approach, incorporate goal formulation using solution-focused procedures, and include all parts of solution building by the end of the second session.

Another way of dealing with problem-focused recording requirements is to intersperse problem-focused and solution-focused approaches. Thomas's (1995) students have incorporated competency-based questions into their interviewing as they proceed through the client-history and problem assessment questions required by the agencies in their internship settings. For example, when collecting family history data about family problems such as divorces, unemployment, and alcoholism, the interviewer can ask questions such as these:

- Your parents were divorced and at odds with one another all through the years when you were growing up. How did you manage to cope?

- I see a lot of unemployment in your family history, yet you have always held a high-paying job. How did that happen? I wonder what this says about you?

- You say your mom was alcoholic and you're not. Does that surprise you? I wonder what you would say about yourself in this regard?

Although this approach does not necessarily uncover past successes and strengths directly related to what the client might want to be different, it does introduce more balance into the interaction by asking about competencies as well as problems. If the competency data are also included in the initial assessment, that assessment will give a more complete and positive picture of the client to any professionals who might have access to the case file in the future.

Case Documentation in More Solution-Focused Settings

Some programs within agencies are moving away from traditional problem assessments to a solution-focused approach and require fewer client-history and problem assessment questions, except in cases where practitioners suspect physiologically based problems that may necessitate referral to psychiatrists and physicians for diagnosis. This shift changes the practitioners' documentation requirements so that paperwork more closely approximates the stages of solution building. An example is the Family Solutions program, part of a large public service agency for children and families in one of the boroughs of London, England. Family Solutions (described in greater detail in Chapter 14) is an early intervention program with children and their families who are struggling with a range of child protection and other difficulties that may result in child removal and institutionalization. The program's three case-documentation templates closely reflect the stages of solution building.

The first template is a referral form, which is completed by social workers referring families to the program. The form requests information about ethnicity; language spoken by the family and possible need for an interpreter; whether the family is aware of the referral and is in favor of it; description of the difficulties prompting the referral; whether assessments required by the larger agency have been completed; other agencies currently involved with the family; whether there is court involvement with respect to any of the children; any demographic information and information about past sex offenses, violent behaviors, and substance use that the referring worker thinks would be important for the team to know about; the referring worker's "best hopes" for outcomes of the team's work with the family; and whether there are any changes that the referring worker believes must be required of the family to ensure the welfare of the children. Note that this referral form, while it does identify present and past problems of the family, is not intended to gather detailed problem assessment information. It does not, for example, request that any past problem assessment documents be sent to Family Solutions. Instead, it asks for information that tells the story of why the worker is referring the family at this time, what outcomes the worker is hoping for, and information that ensures the team can work conversationally and in physical safety with the family. As such, the form represents the themes discussed in Chapter 4 about the importance of first paying attention to how the client comes to you before launching into solution building.

The second template is the initial session record. This form requires the team to record information about reason for referral; those present; the family's "best hopes" of outcome for the work with the team; the referring worker's best hopes; the family's description of their "preferred future"; exceptions, which are times when the preferred future is already happening; family strengths, and strategies used by the family; scales around progress to date, motivation, and confidence; feedback and compliments given; evaluation of risk; and decisions for further work or a closing summary if the family and team decide on no further work together. This form, which requires narrative content for each of the items in the template, closely approximates the protocol for first sessions presented in this book (see Appendix). It is strikingly different as a formal agency document in that there is no requirement to record detailed problem information. Even the evaluation of risk is based more on the steps the family is able and willing to take to reduce any risk of neglect and violence (that is, a solution built between the team and family) than any detailed assessment of specific problems.

The third template is the session record, which is used for all later sessions. It requires information about the session number; those present; progress achieved; family strengths, and strategies used by the family; scales around progress, motivation, and confidence; feedback and compliments given; evaluation of risk; and decisions for further work or a closing summary if the family and team decide on no further work together. This form requires documentation of an interviewing process very close to that indicated in the protocol for later sessions presented in this book (see Appendix).

The documentation forms designed for Family Solutions, by requiring narrative entries, permit the team to record the family's perceptions using the family's key words. Consequently, the forms allow the team to document each family's unique solution building around its preferred future rather than reducing the family's past experiences and future possibilities to a set of professional categories or a summary score based on a standardized assessment tool or outcome measurement.

An increasing number of agencies recognize that promoting solution-building work with clients requires different documentation. If agency and clinic directors expect their practitioners to be more solution focused, documentation formats must reinforce that expectation. Documentation requirements are one of the most important ways in which agencies tell their practitioners what to pay attention to when working with clients. As such, these requirements, along with the supervision processes that reinforce them, amount to powerful day-to-day training of practitioners in the de facto practice model of an agency.

More and more examples of innovative documentation formats are becoming available. For example, there is a consortium of agencies serving families in Palm Beach County, Florida, dedicated to empowering families through solution-building practice which has created documentation requirements consistent with its practice approach. The consortium is called the Family and Community Partnership. Description of its practice approach and services, along with its documentation forms, are available at www.fcp.org. Yet another example comes from the Department of Human Services in Michigan. This public service agency has required its workers for several years now to complete a "SUCCESS" plan with its public welfare clients. This acronym reflects the shift to strength-based interviewing, and solution-focused questions are used to get details from clients about each of the following elements of their SUCCESS plans.

- **S**eize a vision.

- **U**se your vision to set goals.

- **C**onceive a plan.

- **C**ontemplate resources.

- **E**xpand skills and abilities.

- **S**pend time sensibly.

- **S**tart! Get organized and go!

Other agencies have organized documentation for progress notes around scaling. Forms are devised with space to record concrete details about the meaning of "0," "10," the number the client is currently at, what will be different when things are one number higher, what steps the client is considering or will take to move up the scale, and what resources the client thinks will be most useful to him or her to move up.

Case Conferences in Problem-Focused Settings

In these settings, case conferences generally focus on cases in crisis and chronic or difficult cases. Often, these conferences begin with the supervisor asking whether any of the practitioners have a case they want to bring up that is facing an immediate crisis. After describing the nature of the crisis by giving details about the problem(s) the client is struggling with, the other practitioners and supervisor share ideas about interventions to reduce or remove the crisis. After these emergencies are discussed, one or more practitioners previously scheduled to present move on to describe a chronic or difficult case.

Case descriptions in problem-focused settings begin with lots of description of the details of the client's problems and their history. Formal and informal problem-assessment data are presented, often along with *DSM–IV–TR* diagnoses. The conference then turns to discussing problem dynamics with the aid of genograms, ecomaps, and those theoretical concepts favored by the particular agency or clinic. Finally, participants share ideas about interventions and resources to move the case along.

If you become a solution-focused practitioner employed in this sort of setting, you will quickly sense that minimal attention is given to working with client descriptions of what they want different, related successes and personal strengths, and resources. It is important to think about how you can be most useful in this setting and still be true to the assumptions and procedures of solution building. For example, Peter has mainly practiced in such settings and quickly learned it was no more useful trying to convince skeptical colleagues of the helpfulness of solution building than trying to persuade clients in involuntary situations of complying with directives they do not agree with. It is more useful and consistent with solution building to listen for and ask what the colleague wants different with the case; what has been useful so far, even a little bit; what the colleague has done to make that happen; and what the client would say the practitioner has done that has been useful. It is also very important to affirm the difficulty of the case situation and compliment the colleague on anything the colleague has done to listen carefully and absorb what the client wants and is able and willing to do. As more collaborative forms of practice gain respect in the field, it has become more acceptable in case conferences in problem-focused agencies to ask about what the client says he or she wants. Peter always asks for the words the client uses to describe what he or she wants. Often, others at the case conference then ask the presenter for more details about these words, and the presenter says that question was not asked of the client. The discussion then often turns to what additional useful questions might be asked about client goals and client-designed strategies to achieve those goals. Peter has found that colleagues who are stuck on a case are much more open at that point to try some new solution-building questions with clients. He has also found it productive to be sure to follow up at the next case conference about whether the colleague asked more about client goals, how she or he did this, and what progress, no matter how small, is being made by the client. When the colleague does follow through, Peter offers compliments, giving as much credit as possible to the innovativeness and hard work of his colleague.

You can also remain true to a solution-focused outlook and its practices in these settings by the way you present your own cases. When it is your turn to present a case, besides giving the problem information and history required by the agency, you can present all the solution-building information you have coconstructed with your client to that point, and then raise the questions you wish about possible, fruitful next steps or directions in your conversations with your client. In presenting the solution-building information you have to date, be sure to share the key phrases the client has used so far for what the client wants and the related exceptions and strengths. Presenting case information this way will invite and make it easier for your colleagues to help you formulate additional useful questions to use in additional solution building with your client. Making your case presentations this way is a big step in the direction of conducting a case conference as you might if you were working in the context of an agency structured along solution-focused lines.

Case Conferences in More Solution-Focused Settings

In these settings, case conferences become a primary tool for not only preparing practitioners to troubleshoot but also for learning more thoroughly what to do more of, so that solution building becomes second nature to them. As in problem-focused settings, case conferences in more solution-focused agencies tend to focus on crisis and "stuck" cases. However, the format for the case conference is different, because it is intentionally structured along solution-building lines, just as are interviews with clients in these agencies. We suggest the following guidelines and format based on our experience working with agencies wishing to incorporate solution-building into all aspects of their agencies' functioning. Case conferences structured this way maximize respect among colleagues and make best use of the practice wisdom, specialized skills and knowledge, and other resources that each brings to the table.

One guideline is to ensure case conferences are attended by a mix of experienced and novice practitioners. Doing so offers an excellent opportunity for both groups to benefit. Experienced staff can offer their clinical insights and wisdom gained through long years of practice, while new, young, and inexperienced staff can share some of the knowledge of new developments in the field they gained from classes and newer readings in the field. Although they do not necessarily fall out along the lines of the extent of professional experience, case conferences can become a useful pool of resources and expertise for participating practitioners around their different job experiences, knowledge of resources existing among diverse groups in the community, individual interests and hobbies, personal experiences, and creative, synergistic solutions. An example of the latter is that of a practitioner in a case conference who informed the group that his sister was a registered master gardener and then offered to solicit her help in finding a trained gardener who would volunteer to teach children in a poor neighborhood how to create a community garden.

Another guideline is for the moderator or chair of the conference to lead the group into ways of being helpful and useful to the person presenting cases and guard against participants offering the presenter premature, unnecessary, or unasked-for suggestions. It is important to assume that one's colleagues are competent and doing their best with clients. This means there will be much to ask them about before any suggestions might be offered. Therefore, in case conferences, as in interactions with clients, it is best to take on an attitude of curiosity and discovery and to work through sequences of not-knowing questions. A standardized outline for case presentations is also helpful so that everyone knows what to expect. We encourage creating this outline using solution-building questions so that formal reminders of the desired process for case conferencing are not needed. We suggest the following outline as a guide.

- Ask the presenter for a brief statement of the desired or a useful outcome from the case conference.

- Ask the presenter for a brief description of how the case entered the system.

Next, ask the presenter these questions:

- What would the client say that the practitioner has done so far that's been helpful?

- What is the client's view of the desired outcome?

- How close would the presenter say the client is to achieving these goals? (Use scaling questions.) Would the client agree with this scaling of how far he or she has moved up? If yes, what would the client say is better? If no, what number would the client give, and what would he or she say is happening that leads to that number?

- If the practitioner and client have different goals for the client (or the client's situation has changed), what is the client's current idea of what needs to change?

- What tells the client she or he can achieve these changes at this time? Who would the client say would be most helpful to her or him in this process?

- What are the first small steps the client needs to take in order to move 1 point higher?

- How would things be different in his or her life when things get 1 point higher?

- What else will change then? Who will notice the changes? What would change in the client's interaction with important others in her or his life?

- What additional resources, if any, would the client say would be helpful to reach the desired goal?

In our experience, when a practitioner presents a case as being "stuck," it usually indicates that a clear description of the desired outcome (best hope) has not been coconstructed yet, or the client and practitioner have different goals for the client. When client goals are unclear or not agreed upon, neither client nor practitioner can know whether they are being successful in their work together. We have found that frequent use of scaling questions in sessions with clients is the best way for clients and practitioners to be sure that they share the same perception of the client's goals and are getting a useful reading on whether progress is occurring or not. That being the case, it makes good sense to organize case conferences about "stuck" cases around the same scaling questions that will help to refocus the practitioner on the client's frame of reference about what he or she wants different and how best to make that happen. By using the suggested case conference format, participants are directing themselves toward how far the solution building has come with the case under review and the next, most useful solution-building questions for the practitioner to ask when she or he meets with the client again. In other words, following this format, the presenting practitioner should leave the case conference having gotten the outcome she or he wanted, namely, a clear sense of where to go next in the solution-building conversation with the client.

Because scaling plays so prominently into practitioners staying on track with clients' evolving desired outcomes, we want to add that in our consultations with agencies and their clients, we have found that clients often are quite satisfied to stop at a scale score of 7 or 8, while their practitioners tend to be more ambitious for them. We have met clients who told us how much they appreciated that workers affirmed their stopping at a 6 or a 7 when that was "good enough" achievement for them. They appreciated that their practitioners did not insist on moving up to 10 with their help. When we asked how this was helpful to them, these clients said that by their practitioners allowing them time and space to continue their progress on their own, they could truly take a stronger sense of pride and confidence in achieving the final steps without help. This desire to take ownership of their own successes seems to us to be strong even among the clients commonly thought to be the most resource deprived and economically struggling. This client point of view on scaling scores and when to stop professional assistance has been quite surprising for us to hear, even about the most respectful and committed practitioners. It is a good reminder to ask regularly for client perceptions about what number they need to be in order not to see a practitioner any longer.

Case conferences organized around solution building ought not, in our view, be solely focused on "stuck" cases. Some time should also be devoted to success cases so practitioners can jointly explore strong practice in some detail, and celebrate it. Whether employed around "stuck" or successful cases, case conferencing this way is an essential and effective way to teach and reinforce solution building with clients. One supervisor in child protective services who changed her case conferencing to a solution-building format told us she now recognizes that this form of case conferencing is also a useful group supervision tool. It is so effective, she says, that she has significantly reduced the amount of time she spends meeting one-on-one with workers in individual supervision.

Solution-Building Supervision

The word *supervisor* itself denotes a relationship of expert and non-expert. Traditionally, "super-visors" are assumed to have more knowledge and skill about how to conduct professional practice and hence are given the responsibility and authority to "over-see" and direct the practice of their workers. In fact, in many practice settings, it has been the "super-workers" who have been promoted to supervisors. Several such supervisors told us they went through a range of emotions, from pride to panic to figuring out how to survive, because they found it a very different task to manage a group of professionals, especially one's former peers, than to manage a client caseload. We believe this is definitely the case if one attempts to supervise as the role is traditionally understood.

Whether in a problem-focused or solution-focused setting, if you should become a supervisor and decide to carry out the role using solution building, you will do your work according to the same assumptions and use the same practices. The best description of the role of a competent and respectful supervisor we have heard comes from Peter Cantwell of Melbourne, Australia (Cantwell & Holmes, 1994), who coined the phrase "leading from one step behind." It says volumes about the style and "how to" of a competency-based approach to supervision such as solution building.

A solution-building approach to supervision begins with a set of assumptions that guide the activities used to supervise—or said better, to educate, mentor, nurture, and inspire. The following is a list of core beliefs we hold about those we supervise and hope to inspire to achieve the ambitions that motivated them to enter one of the helping professions in the first place. Until proven otherwise, we assume that those we supervise:

- want to feel that their work makes "a difference" in someone's life

- want to learn the skills needed to achieve this motivation and commitment

- want to be accepted and valued by the organization they work in

- want to identify with the organization's mission and objectives

- already possess problem-solving skills to some degree; thus the task of supervision is to add solution-building skills

- will, when they feel respected and supported by the organization and their superiors, naturally deal with their clients in the same respectful manner

Although some of the details of supervision will vary from setting to setting based on practice matters specific to those settings, the core element of any supervision (including administrative management) is the task of the supervisor to "lead" the practitioner toward greater and greater competency and enhanced skills. We believe this is best accomplished through solution-building conversations that lead both supervisors and practitioners to discoveries about how practitioners are using and can further draw upon their particular strengths and resources to most effectively do the work. For example, one child welfare supervisor who was changing his style of supervision told us what he was now doing differently when workers submitted incomplete case documents: "I always make sure to comment first on what the worker has done well and only then on what further information might make the report an even better one." This opener to a conversation sends workers a very different message about their level of competency and ongoing possibilities to make valuable contributions to the organization and their clients than does a more traditional view of supervision focused primarily on mistakes and figuring out how to avoid them.

The flow of conversation in sessions of solution-building supervision is organized around inviting workers to see clients through clients' eyes, rather than their own. This is so because all the professional activities of the agency or organization should in some sense serve clients. It is the task of supervision, then, to continually teach workers to listen to the client's view of how useful the service is to the client. We encourage supervisors to make extensive use of scaling questions and relationship questions to monitor the progress their clients are making. These questions are useful in discovering and getting details about practitioner successes and also serve as a gentle tap on the shoulder to invite them to wonder about what they may have missed about the client's frame of reference and what else might be done to make their interactions with clients even more solution focused. Here are some of these useful questions:

- What would your client say about how helpful and useful the sessions have been for him or her so far?

- On a scale of 1 to 10, where 10 is the most useful he or she had hoped for and 1 is the opposite, what number would your client give to your work with him or her so far?

- Any guess about what the client would say has been most helpful so far? Would you agree with client's view? If not, what is your view?

- (*If the worker has no idea about what the client believes has been most helpful so far, the supervisor can ask:*) How would you find that out? What else would you do to learn that?

- Suppose the client were to think your usefulness to her or him had improved 1 point. What might she or he notice you are doing differently?

- On a scale of 1 to 10, where 10 is the most satisfied you are with how the work is progressing and 1 the least satisfied, what number would you say you are at?

- What would you notice yourself doing differently when you move up 1 point?

As you can see, these questions are essentially the same as those we suggest for solution-building case conferences. This is not surprising in that the purpose of both activities is the same, namely, to enhance worker competency in solution building with clients. A real-life application of solution-building supervision is that developed by Teri Pichot and presented in Chapter 14. There are also several sources now available for readers who wish to know more about the application of solution building to supervision (Berg, 2003; Pichot & Dolan, 2003; Rita, 1998; Rudes, Shilts, & Berg, 1997; Triantafillou, 1997).

This description of solution-building supervision highlights that we believe the best way to develop solution-building skills in practitioners is in vivo, that is, in a practice setting through the use of solution-building conversations around practice experiences with real cases. We are keenly aware, however, of the realistic constraints of this method of teaching and learning given how labor-intensive and costly it can be. Given modern technologies, supervisors can supplement their teaching by having workers watch videotapes of accomplished practitioners; audiotape or videotape their (workers') own practice and then review it on their own with the purpose of helping to better crystallize their questions for supervision and case conference time; and study the conversations in sources like this book to develop more ideas about how to listen and respond to clients in solution-building ways. One tip for practitioners when self-teaching and -learning is to select what they believe is the best and worst 10 minutes of their recorded interactions with clients and then study them carefully to learn what they are doing well and what else they might do to be even more effective. The Instructors Manual that accompanies this book (De Jong & Berg, 2008) and a publication by Nelson (2005) are also resources that supervisors can use to get more ideas for teaching solution-building skills to practitioners.

Relationships with Colleagues in Problem-Focused Settings

If you choose to become more solution-focused in your work, you will encounter colleagues and supervisors who are unfamiliar and uncomfortable with your approach to clients. Workshop participants and students in internship settings say repeatedly that this happens.

In encounters with skeptical colleagues, you may be tempted to defend your approach and cast the conversation into either/or terms: "Either your way is right, or my way is right." As in your work with clients, we do not recommend that you directly challenge your colleagues' frames of reference, which have probably been developed over long periods of time, are informed by experience, and deserve to be respected. Instead, take a posture of not knowing, and explore their concerns. Pay attention to what they might want from your interaction. Frequently, they may just want to know more about your approach. At other times, they will definitely be skeptical and even critical. In that case, you might ask them what they do differently with their clients and how they know that this is useful. You can respectfully compliment their strengths and successes. If they are interested, you can indicate what you do when you engage in solution-building dialogues with clients and how you perceive these to be helpful. Often, as the dialogue develops, apparent differences become less extreme.

There will be times when differences remain between your views and those of your colleagues. Solution building is different from problem solving. According to workshop participants and students, their skeptical colleagues' major concerns are that solution building deemphasizes the connection between problem and solution, emphasizes the importance of client perceptions, and deemphasizes expert assessments and interventions. You and your colleagues may decide to talk more about the content and consequences of those differences at your agency. You might wish to institute agency roundtable or brown-bag discussions on, for example, the relative importance of problem assessment and solution-focused interviewing in crisis cases at your agency, or designing a study to compare solution-building and problem-solving outcomes with your clients. The point is that differences are best handled through open and respectful dialogue. Direct challenges of deeply held views are rarely helpful.

You may find yourself in circumstances in which your supervisor insists that you follow certain problem-focused procedures. You will have to determine how much leeway you have to also incorporate your solution-building procedures. Several possibilities for doing this were discussed earlier in this chapter.

Relationships with Colleagues in Solution-Focused Settings

If you choose to be solution-focused in your work with clients and have the good fortune to be working with like-minded colleagues, you can make use of your solution-building skills in your relationships with them. As suggested earlier, some of this would be formally structured into the working of your clinic or agency; for example, case conferences and supervision would be conducted along the solution-focused lines just described. In the less structured, but frequent conversations with colleagues around what to do with challenging cases or difficult coworkers, you can informally talk with colleagues using your not-knowing posture, getting their perceptions of any challenging situation and exploring for what they are already doing that is helpful, what they want to see different, what else might be useful, and so forth.

Relationships with Collaterals

Collaterals are professionals at other agencies who have an interest in the outcome of your work with a certain client because they also are working with the client, they referred the client to your agency, or for other reasons. Collaterals can include probation officers, psychiatrists, teachers, religious practitioners, and others. They frequently have definite ideas about your clients' needs and how to go about working with them, and usually they operate within a problem-focused framework.[1]

As with colleagues, assume that collaterals are competent and deserving of your respect. Use your interviewing skills to discover what they might want from you. If they have had contact with the client, find out what they have done that they think was useful to the client. Affirm the valuable work they have done.

Let us illustrate this approach with an example from Peter's experience. Peter has worked with sex offenders referred to him for counseling by their probation officers. The following is a conversation between him and a probation officer named Jackson about a referred client.

PETER: Jackson, I see from the letter you sent that you are referring a Fred Wilson to me. He's on my schedule for tomorrow. How can I be helpful?

JACKSON: You can see from the information I sent that he pleaded guilty to a Fourth Degree CSCC [Criminal Sexual Conduct Code] violation. He had been hanging around the monkey bars in the park, offering to help young girls up and catching them when they jumped off. He also was touching their private parts. Two girls complained to their parents, and there were witnesses who put him at the park at the time the girls claimed the abuse. He touched them through their clothes, and there was no penetration, so it's been processed as a misdemeanor. The guy needs counseling.

PETER: OK. Can you tell me anything more about what you'd like from me?

JACKSON: I met with him a couple of times. I think he is in denial because he said that he didn't do it. He said the only reason he pleaded was because his attorney told him the girls' stories corroborated each others' and would be pretty convincing to the court because they were so specific for an 8- and a 9-year-old. I'm worried he might do the same thing again if he doesn't get it together. He probably has done it before and just never got caught. If he's like the other guys I've dealt with, he's gonna need at least a year of counseling. That's why I recommended a year of it once per week as a condition of probation in my presentence report to the judge. He also has to see me at least once per month.

PETER: So what might tell you that he's coming out of denial? What would he be doing differently?

JACKSON: Well for one thing—admitting that he did it and getting to work on where those sick tendencies in him come from. If you can help him to do that, that would be worth a lot. I talked to him a couple of times, and I think he's got some potential. He still won't admit what he did and that he has to work in counseling, but he's got a family and a good job in sales.

PETER: Knowing what you know about him, how do you think he will be different when he comes around to admitting it?

JACKSON: Like I say, I think he's got a chance. He's got a family and a job, but he's so tied into that job and beating his competition that he's out of touch with his family. He's on the road a lot. I don't know if he even has any friends. He never mentioned any. I think when he starts to see himself for what he has become and admit it to himself and maybe even to his wife, he'll make some changes. He'll get his job more in perspective and get more interested in his family—spend more time with his wife, maybe go to some school activities of his kids. He's got some teenagers in sports, but he doesn't go to their games. He might even make some friends. For sure, he won't go to the parks [cynically quoting the client] "for walks by myself."

PETER: OK, Jackson, that gives me some good information to start with. Seems like you've been doing some serious thinking about this case and what could happen. I think he's lucky you're handling his case. Is there anything else you want me to know right now?

JACKSON: No, I don't think so . . . except that I think that, even though he still denies it, I think he might work in counseling. He listened to me real carefully and says he cares about his family and is thankful that they have stuck with him through this. [pause] He knows I want to talk to you every two weeks at first. He'll sign your releases. Give me a call in two weeks when you have space in your schedule.

PETER: OK, I'll do that. I'll get back to you after I've seen him the second
time. Thanks for the referral.

Peter accepted and explored Jackson's perceptions about his new case. He
invited Jackson to share his expertise about the case. In the process, he affirmed
Jackson for his concern and work and got some specific information about what
Jackson would have to see Fred doing differently in order to gain confidence that
he was making progress and becoming less of a threat to the community.

Peter's interaction with Jackson indicates that, anytime you work with a
collateral, you have at least two clients whose perceptions you will want to
explore—the identified client and the collateral. Be solution focused with both.
Selekman (1997), who has written about how to approach collaterals in children's
cases, offers similar advice.

GROUP AND ORGANIZATIONAL PRACTICE

Solution-focused procedures were developed in work with individuals, couples,
and families and have been most widely practiced and discussed in that area.
However, they are now catching the interest of practitioners in group and
organizational settings.

Group Practice

In group practice, the interpersonal process that develops in small groups is used
to assist clients to achieve their individual goals. Counselors, psychologists, and
social workers all work with groups. There are groups for individuals with
substance abuse problems, pregnant teens, people with AIDS, those recently
divorced, children of alcoholics, those with eating disorders, battered women,
men who batter, incest survivors, and many more. Some groups offer therapy for
behavioral and emotional disorders (for example, an anxiety disorder group at a
mental health facility); others foster personal growth (such as an assertiveness-
training group); and still others are self-help groups (Alcoholics Anonymous).

The organization and process in most small groups has reflected the same
problem-solving assumptions and procedures seen in most individual and family
approaches, so it is not surprising that those who are introducing solution
building into group practice are finding it useful (de Shazer & Isebaert,
2003; Durrant, 1993; Gray, Zide, & Wilker, 2000; Hiebert-Murphy &
Richert, 2000; Lange, 2001; Lee, Sebold, & Uken, 2003; McCollum, Trepper,
& Smock, 2003; Metcalf, 1998; Schorr, 1995; Selekman, 1991; Sharry, 2001;
Uken & Sebold, 1996; Vaughn, Hastings-Guerrero, & Kassner, 1996). There is
also early outcome research suggesting its effectiveness (de Shazer & Isebaert,
2003; Hiebert-Murphy & Richert, 2000; LaFountain & Garner, 1996; Lee,
Sebold, & Uken, 2003; Lee, Greene, & Rheinscheld, 1999; Sharry, 2001;

Zimmerman, Jacobsen, MacIntyre, & Watson, 1996; Zimmerman, Prest, & Wetzel, 1997).

Several agencies have introduced solution-building procedures into their group work after becoming proficient with them in individual and family work. Their groups are customarily set up on a time-limited basis (6 to 12 sessions) because experience has taught that change can occur in a short period of time and that the time limitation encourages more purposeful interaction among group members. In the next chapter, several solution-focused group applications are described by the practitioners who developed them.

Organizational Practice

One of the first known uses of solution-focused principles and practices at the organizational level is that reported by Sparks (1989). She used solution building in place of problem solving in the vehicle maintenance division in a large metropolitan city. Acting as a management consultant, her purpose was to stimulate more openness between managers and subordinates and more team-work among supervisors. She describes her approach as organizational tasking, in which she held five workshop meetings with supervisors and gave them solution-oriented homework assignments to be completed between meetings. The assignments included supervisors meeting with subordinates to ask them to envision the sort of improved work environment they would like to see put in place in the next 12 months, identifying exceptions with subordinates related to these pre-ferred futures, meeting with subordinates to identify and discuss past successes around resolving a conflict or developing an opportunity, asking subordinates to describe an experience with a supervisor that improved the subordinate's work performance and morale, and observing for things they saw happening in the workplace that they wanted to continue to see happen. Supervisors reviewed the results of doing the tasks among themselves in the workshop meetings conducted by Sparks. As a result of their solution-building conversations, Sparks discovered that supervisors listened more carefully to subordinates, interacted with subordi-nates in a more comfortable way, and addressed a greater range of work-related issues between them. Whether coincidental or not, the division manager reported to her that, on all their measures of work performance, the organization had its most productive year ever after her consultation. In addition, Sparks administered her own outcome instruments, which measured four dimensions of successful teamwork: trust, openness, realization, and interdependence. The data led her to conclude "that there was a continual perception of improvement in team functioning over time on all four dimensions of team functioning" (Sparks, 1989, p. 56).

Sparks's work is important because it suggests that a solution-building approach can be useful in realizing organizational objectives. Once problem description and analysis give way to solution-building dialogues among an organization's staff members, hopefulness and motivation seem to increase, and exciting changes can occur. Although practitioners have been applying solution-focused principles and procedures to organizations for several years, this work is just recently reaching print. Cauffman (2001) has published a book in Flemish about his solution-focused consulting with businesses and is exploring prospects for translating and publishing the book in English. Organizational application is also a periodic topic on a solution-focused electronic mailing list, SFTL@ LISTSERV.ICORS.ORG. This group has discussed how practitioners and administrators, working within problem-focused clinics and human service agencies and interested in moving their organizations to a solution focus, can use solution-focused principles and procedures.

There are two websites devoted to organizational applications. Furman and Ahola of the Helsinki Brief Therapy Institute have a website (www.reteaming.com) that describes the application of solution-focused team building to organizations. The site also offers a service to organizations that involves retaining a "reteaming coach" to come into an organization and conduct three to four weekly, two-hour sessions. The sessions focus on turning problems into goals, involve assignments and discussions that build motivation and explore resources, and provide ways of measuring and amplifying progress. Trained coaches are available in several European countries and the United States. Furman and Ahola (1998) have written a reteaming workbook called *Reteaming: Succeeding Together* that has been published in several languages, including English, and is available through their website.

Mark McKergow, based in Great Britain, also offers a website (www .thesolutionsfocus.com) on using solution-focused methods in organizations. He and his partner, Paul Jackson, have been doing management consulting for several years and have written a book about this work (Jackson & McKergow, 2002). Their website also gives information about how to join a related electronic mailing list. In the next chapter, as further illustration of the usefulness of solution-focused thinking and skills at an organizational level, Peter Stam writes about how a large human-service organization in the Netherlands is being transformed through solution building.

NOTE

1.   Note that when you work jointly on a case with colleagues at your own agency, you will essentially be in a collateral relationship with them.

14

Applications

INTRODUCTION

The solution-focused practice model had a humble beginning with a team of creative and innovative practitioners who were dissatisfied with the state of the art of finding solutions to the problems of living. The beginnings of the work was in the heady days of the mid-1970s, when traditionally held beliefs, customs, and mores were being challenged. A ragtag group of practitioners, academics, a social activist, a cell biologist, and a family-practice physician formed a team with an ambitious goal of learning about effective and efficient ways to provide services to those who sought help from an outpatient, community-based mental health service in Milwaukee, Wisconsin. Through methodical experiments using thick-observation, videotaping of sessions, team and case discussions, and the use of a one-way mirror to observe live sessions, the Milwaukee team saw case after case 5 days a week and, at times, on Saturdays and Sundays if clients needed services on the weekend. In addition to seeing clients, the group engaged in lengthy team discussions and review of videotaped sessions, and began to write about the work in a newsletter titled "Underground Railroad," with Steve de Shazer as the first and only editor. When the newsletter circulated, the team received many inquiries, critiques, and suggestions, as well as personal visits, from interested thinkers from around the world. Steve de Shazer's first book, *Patterns of Brief Family Therapy*, was published in 1982, and was the first book-length statement of the team's developing discoveries about a new way of working with people.

Through the '80s, '90s, and up to the present, there has been an explosion of interest in solution-focused practice throughout the world. Innovators and writers including de Shazer, Berg, and others have continued both to hone the model and expand it beyond the therapy room into a variety of fields including child welfare, adolescent offenders and their families, prison work, substance abuse treatment, work with domestic violence offenders, applications in the schools, organizational management and supervision, and coaching and counseling. Like the original Milwaukee team, these innovators were dissatisfied with the results from current, established ways of working and began to creatively apply emerging solution-building principles and practices, especially to their so-called "difficult" and "hopeless" cases. Along the way, they discovered that there are no limits to peoples' creativity or the circumstances in which it can flourish so long as what people want different in their lives is respected and becomes the starting point for collaborative solution-building.

This chapter presents the work of innovators in eight different places around the world who adapted solution-building principles and practices to their client populations and working contexts. As precedes any innovation, the creators were somehow dissatisfied with current models of practice and, much like the Milwaukee team, set out to create something different and more satisfying. Rather than our summarizing their work, we have asked them to tell their own stories. We asked them to describe their contexts, how and why they got started on something different, how their creative efforts unfolded, and what difference their innovations have made for those they work with and themselves. (A brief biography of each and their contact information is printed on pages xix–xxi.)

READING 1

Family Solutions: From "Problem Families to Families Finding Solutions"
Mark Stancer

Family Solutions is a dedicated solution-focused brief therapy team embedded in a public, statutory, children and families social work department in the busy west London Borough of Ealing (Stancer, Sreety, & Britton, 2006). It has been up and running since October 2003. Families are referred to Family Solutions by the agency's social workers working in area-based teams. These families most commonly come from lower socio-economic groups and often have problems in one or more of the following areas:

- Substance misuse issues—alcohol and/or drugs
- Mental health issues—parents and/or children
- Domestic violence/abuse
- One or more parent having a learning disability
- School non-attendance
- Criminal activity
- Other anti-social behaviours

In Family Solutions, we work with a number of families (approximately 25% of our referrals) where one or more children are placed on the Child Protection Register, where they are deemed to be at risk of suffering "Significant Harm" as a result of ill treatment or neglect by their carers. A number of families have experienced their children being taken into care or have themselves been through the care system when they were children. These families are so often perceived by other services as "problem families" having problem saturated histories that no amount of support, educating or therapy will ever put right! What can Family Solutions achieve in six sessions where others have failed? We work with a great many families from minority ethnic groups, both naturalised second and third generation Black African/Caribbean and Asian British families as well as first generation and asylum seekers.

THE NEED FOR SOMETHING DIFFERENT

At a senior management level in Ealing in 2000, the solution-focused brief therapy approach (SFBT) was explored. The aim was to find a more effective, positive and rapid response to families that were approaching crises, with the related aim for the department of reducing the numbers of children and young people coming into care. At that time in the department, there was one "family centre" service that offered families a traditional systemic family therapy service as well as parenting skills training groups, family group conferences and carrying out assessments of parenting, often court directed. By 2002 it became clear that a rapid response team dedicated to carrying out effective therapeutic work was needed. The move toward the creation of Family Solutions had begun.

HOW WE DID IT

Family Solutions took shape through the summer of 2003 once I was appointed to lead and set up the service. I had worked for the department for the previous six years as a frontline social worker and deputy manager of one of the area social work teams. I had undergone the four day introductory SFBT training and at the time was in the middle of the MSc degree in Systemic Psychotherapy at the Institute of Family Therapy. From the outset I had a clear vision of what form the team should take. This was supported by senior management. From my experience of the effectiveness of using SFBT in my social work practice and in supervising staff, it was clear to me that the model worked and clients felt it helped them, often more so than other interventions. Because it is "brief"—in our case up to six sessions—it is also a very efficient use of time and resources. It also means in practice that we are able to offer families who come to our service an appointment the same day, as we have the capacity to do so, which we would not if we were tied up doing long term work. All staff recruited to the team had relevant family work experience but were not necessarily qualified social workers. What I was more interested in was a positive, strength-based approach to supporting families. I wanted them to be optimistic and enthusiastic about enabling change for families. All staff underwent a four day SFBT training as well as Child Protection training in recognising possible abuse. As a team we had a number of team building days before we opened the doors for business.

TECHNIQUES EMPLOYED

SFBT questions form the central basis of the work that we do. A typical initial session would attempt to ask the following:

- Asking clients for their *Best Hopes*—What do they want to achieve from the sessions?
- *The Miracle Question*—What is their "preferred future," what does it look like in as much detail as possible.
- Asking *Scaling Questions*—Using a 0 to 10 scale for clients to identify where they currently rate themselves and how they are able to achieve being at that point and not one lower down the scale.
- Taking a session break to reflect on strengths people are demonstrating and/or "exceptions" that have been identified where the problem is not present.
- Giving feedback to people about the strengths they have demonstrated during the session in the form of "compliments."

Sessions are usually conducted with the family's social worker present for the first part of the initial session. We start by asking the family what their "best hopes" are, what they want to achieve for themselves, before we ask the same of the social worker. Direct supervision and support that each family worker receives is given with a solution-focused emphasis. The whole ethos in the team is one of focusing on strengths, developing skills and confidence for that individual so that they can help families to become more fluent in problem solving, setting their own goals and achieving them.

DIFFERENCES MADE

As Family Solutions continues to develop, we are observing the following positive results.

- Clients having a more positive experience of statutory services.
- More positive and lasting change for families.
- Providing a supportive consultancy role for area social workers.
- Reducing the number of children coming into the care system in an emergency manner.
- More rapid response to families—within 24 hours.
- Offering families with issues of child risk/safety immediate access to a therapeutic service where previously there was none.
- High job satisfaction among workers on the Family Solutions team; they give ratings from 7 through 9 on a 10 point scale of job satisfaction with 10 being the highest level of satisfaction.

CASE EXAMPLES

Katy McKeith

Katy McKeith is a 12-year-old girl who had been brought up by her grandparents in the north of England. She moved to live with her birth family in west London after her grandmother died and her grandfather could no longer look after her due to his increasing ill health. The school and the social services department became increasingly concerned about Katy's mental health as she had started to withdraw from friends and her lessons in school to the point where she would not speak to anyone for days at a time! After assessing the home situation, social services placed Katy on the Child Protection Register concluding that she was suffering "significant harm" as a result of what professionals saw as "emotional abuse." It was felt that her mother was treating Katy very differently from her four siblings (ages from six months to ten years) who had all been brought up by both parents from birth. Katy had also been referred to the local Children and Adolescents Mental Health Service for family therapy at the local hospital. Katy and her parents had attended one session but did not find it helpful. This non-attendance was interpreted by the social services as the parents not engaging or being committed to helping Katy. The child protection process had also made the family very defensive about any professional involvement and support, and they were openly hostile toward the social worker. Katy was not attending school at all, not talking to anyone and staying mostly confined to her bedroom. She was also not eating properly and losing weight, she had been on the Child Protection Register for nine months and the department was thinking that the only option was to go to court to place Katy with foster carers for her own safety. We received a referral at Family Solutions from the social worker as a last chance option.

Session 1: Information Sharing   The initial session was arranged at the family home by the social worker who attended and gave her view on what the problem was. She stated that Mrs. McKeith held resentment toward Katy for having been brought up by Mr. McKeith's parents and now was demanding that Katy had to fit in with this new family and a different way of life. This initial visit was an information gathering session allowing everyone to say what they wanted to improve. Katy did not speak and sat for the whole hour huddled at the end of the sofa. Both parents wanted to hear what she felt the problems were, but the more they asked the more she withdrew. They all felt that the next session would be a chance for Katy to be able to say what was bothering her, and a date was duly arranged. I asked Katy what her best hopes were and she continued to look straight at the floor. I went on to say: "If Katy does not want to talk then that is fine too." Katy then said "I don't want to talk to any more people, they just ask and ask about things . . . and I don't know what the problem is I just want it to get better!"

Session 2: Listening to Clients   Once I arrived at the home one week later, Mr. and Mrs. McKeith ushered the other children out of the lounge and prompted me to sit and talk with Katy on her own. I sat down and saw that Katy was in the same spot on the sofa, huddled holding her knees up to her chest. I asked her what her best hopes were and she just stared at the floor. I said that I was impressed with how she had been able to be clear with me that she did not want to speak and that must have taken some courage to do. She wanted a solution and wanted her parents to sort it out. I wanted to give her the opportunity to tell me her side of things, but it was crystal clear to me that she did not want to at this point. At a bit of a loss to know what to do and finding myself staring at the floor, I suggested that I invite her family back in and we could all have a talk and she could just listen and not say a word if she did not want to. Katy nodded.
I encouraged Mr. and Mrs. McKeith back in who immediately wanted to know what she had told me. I explained that Katy and I had agreed that she did not have to say a word and that I would talk with Mr. and Mrs. McKeith about their best hopes. What followed was a very open exchange with the couple about what had happened in the past, how they felt about Katy having been brought up by her grandparents and how concerned they were about Katy withdrawing into herself. They felt guilty about not being able to care for her when she was young and were feeling powerless to know what to do to help her now. Katy listened intently the whole time but did not say a word.

Session 3: What's Better?   Katy greeted me with a smile when I arrived and Mr. and Mrs. McKeith also looked more relaxed. The family invited me into their living room together with Katy who sat on the end of the sofa as she wanted to continue to observe and listen. They told me that things had improved slightly so I asked them to put it on a scale of 0–10 indicating how it is now. They said 4 out of 10. I asked them what told them that it was 4 and not 0. They noted improvements in terms of Katy becoming more involved in the family and playing more with her siblings. They said the family as a whole was much more accepting and together as a unit with Katy included.

Session 4: What's Next?   By the next session, Mr. and Mrs. McKeith felt there had been tremendous improvement. They felt that Katy was much more settled and happier at home. At this session they rated the situation at home as 7 out of 10, and the improvements had also been acknowledged by the school and the social services department, so much so that at a recent child protection case conference Katy's name had been removed from the Child Protection Register because of the improvements. Mr. and Mrs. McKeith felt that they and Katy needed some longer term therapeutic support and they wanted to return to the medical centre for therapy that they had been to before but this time with clearer ideas about what would be best for themselves and Katy. Their ideas included the following:

- For the therapy to be play-based therapy given that Katy was finding talking about things quite difficult.

- For them all to be part of it as a family because they did not want to focus on Katy as "the problem," which they felt would make her feel more like withdrawing!

- To continue to focus on looking toward future improvements rather than exploring the difficulties in their past, which they felt all other professionals has focused on and did not really get them anywhere further forward.

Katy was in full agreement with the above ideas and the family asked me to attend the initial session in a support role to help them put across these ideas. I attended the session with them and to my great satisfaction I did not have to say a word as both parents put across their ideas clearly and effectively.

Colin James

Colin, a 13-year-old young man of white UK origin, had been placed with his paternal grandparents, Rod and Sue, themselves elderly people, Rod having a severe lung condition that at times made it difficult for him to breathe without oxygen. Colin had lived with them before when his parents' marriage had split, but at that time his grandparents felt they could not cope with his behaviour. He was refusing to attend school, not coming home until late at night and quite possibly getting involved in crime and using drugs. He had spent the previous year placed with foster carers and had returned to his grandparents after his requests to live with them and their acceptance to "give him another try." After about four months with Rod and Sue, they were feeling that it was at breaking point. Colin was still not attending school and he was not adhering to any of the rules and boundaries that were laid down for him. At times he would also become violent and aggressive toward Sue, and she found this situation intolerable and impossible to deal with. The referral came to Family Solutions to "help"!

The initial session was arranged with Colin's social worker to be present with myself as the Family Solutions worker. The initial session went like this:

MARK: (to the family) What are your best hopes, from meeting with us?

ROD: For him (Colin) to behave his-self, to start going to school, to come home at the times he is supposed to and to stop arguing, to stop being rude and stop cheeking his Gran (Sue) . . .! Otherwise we won't have him here and he's going back into care . . .!

COLIN: (remains silent)

SUE: That's right . . . we don't want to but we can't go on like this!

FS: What are your best hopes Colin?

COLIN: I . . . I want to stay with my Nan and Granddad!

MARK: What would you see happening that would mean you can stay here?

COLIN: What do you mean? What do I need to do to stay here?

MARK: Yes.

COLIN: I wouldn't get into trouble at school, I wouldn't shout and argue with my Nan and I would behave myself!

MARK: What would you be doing that would tell you and others you are behaving yourself?

COLIN: Get to school on time, come home on time. You know . . .

Six sessions were held and Colin was able to attend school more often than he had previously done and for a while his behaviour improved at home. The family felt that the six sessions were beneficial because they said Colin would not previously talk to anyone about his problems which made it difficult to understand what was troubling him. It was clear that Colin was desperate to stay living with his grandparents and he clearly wanted to do the "right thing" to stay there. The problem was that he was not always able to do it as his anger would build up and he would "explode" or "lose it completely" as he would say. He often threatened to run away if he was placed back into foster care. Over the next year or so there were still some big ups and downs. Things reached a crisis point again for the family and Family Solutions took a further referral. This referral came because Colin had missed a number of days at school and not told his grandparents. They felt that things had all gone wrong again! We saw it as a setback.

The major change took place during these six sessions. The family made changes in the following areas and continued to build on them:

- Colin came to identify what he was feeling at different times and situations; in the past he was not able to do this.

- As a result of the above, Colin was able to use strategies to manage his anger in better ways, for example, taking himself to his room for a "time out" to cool down.

- Colin made steady improvements in his school attendance and achievements.

- The family saw the effort and improvements Colin had made and they no longer made references to putting him "back in care." At the last session Sue said that whatever problems or ups and downs they encountered, "Colin will stay with us whatever!"

OUTCOMES

In the first two years of service, Family Solutions has taken 598 referrals and held sessions with 83% of these families. Twenty-two per cent of referrals are of a "crisis" nature whereby the family or a child protection worker is saying that the situation at home has become so bad that the child should be removed and placed in alternative care by the Social Services Department—often that same day. In all of these cases we have been completely successful at meeting with the family and the social worker within 24 hours of the request. The remainder of our work is of a more preventative nature—not an immediate crisis. Here, we have succeeded in responding within 24 hours to 87% of these referrals.

Of the aforementioned crisis or emergency referrals, Family Solutions has been successful in resolving the crisis to the extent that in 76% of these cases children can be kept in their families thus avoiding taking them into the care system. Our average number of sessions is 3.5. Seven and one-half per cent of families seen previously come back to us as re-referrals. When this happens, we talk to families as if they have experienced a "setback," not a failure.

Feedback from Families

Closing summaries indicate that 76% of families report that they feel that improvements have been achieved, often quite dramatic ones. The gains families report include improvements in overall family functioning and in children's behaviour. Recently, we have started implementing client evaluation feedback forms. These ask clients to scale "how helpful Family Solutions was to your family" where 0="not helpful" and 10="very helpful." The average score in the early data collected so far stands at 9.1 out of 10! This use of client feedback is something that we aim to develop further in order to improve the work that we do. Below are comments taken directly from the feedback forms. The comments are in response to the question: "Was there anything that you found particularly helpful about the service you received from Family Solutions?"

- "The adjustable timings were really helpful without affecting work and school hours. The family approach has had good effect with problem-solving method."

- "It was nice to have the support there to help me deal with my child."

- "He listened to me, I felt he cared and understood."

- "It was the meeting I had together with the children I was so pleased about. The service they gave to us was really helpful."

- "All of your help was very useful and helpful, (the) only people so far that have helped. You have been my lifeline."

CONCLUSION

I passionately believe Family Solutions is helping families in dramatic and long lasting ways, families who often would not receive a therapeutic service anywhere else, let alone a service that they find consistently helpful. In my view, families are able to make lasting changes as a result of the support for the following reasons. From their first encounter with us they experience a more positive response to them as people with hopes, dreams, interests, passions as well as difficulties and struggles. We strive to convey the belief that they are the "experts" to their own solutions given that they are the "experts" to their problems. The experience of a more positive helping attitude is linked to our commitment to "really listening" to what people tell us; we want to find out what is really important to *them*. Often they themselves may not know, they may have never had the opportunity to think about these things, and they most certainly have never been asked! Often clients come to us with long histories of social services involvement that can span generations. The support they have received has often been "problem driven," most graphically where children have been removed for their safety at the point of family crisis. As a result of these kinds of experiences clients often believe themselves to be a "problem," which keeps them stuck. Through our work we aim to enable people to see themselves in a different, more helpful way, one which has more choices, is strength based and allows people to work toward their goals. This way of working also helps families to separate "problem behaviours" from "the person being the problem" and consequently to identify "solution behaviours." Questions such as, "What are you doing when the problem is not happening" help to reinforce that the problems happen as a result of unhelpful behaviours or beliefs and both these things can be changed to more helpful ones. The use of 0–10 scales is also a really powerful tool to help people break down their solutions into "bite sized" chunks or steps, work toward their solutions, and put things into a "context." I have often listened to a parent talk for some time about things being so difficult and heard how worried and concerned they are about a child's behaviour, and when asked to rate it on a scale of 0–10, 0 being the worst it could possibly be and 10 the best, they might say "currently . . . 7 out of 10!" If I had not have asked I would never have known. Often when we feel in complete crisis we want a magic wand to make everything better at once; anything less can feel like failure or not good enough. Solution-focused scales help people identify where they are now, what number "good enough" is, and what 10 would look like.

Overall, I think that what we do that makes a difference and helps families can be summed up thusly:

- We respond rapidly to families at a time and a place that is convenient to them.

- We welcome people with warmth and look for their strengths from the outset; we see them as human beings who happen to be experiencing difficulties, not as "problem people" or "problem families."

- We are contactable directly by phone and cell/mobile phone; clients do not have to negotiate a busy social work team, and teenagers like to "text"!

- People want and we encourage them to move "forward" by working toward goals and plans for the future. They have often experienced other therapies that they have not found helpful, focusing on past trauma and difficulties, a past that cannot be changed.

- If clients hit a "setback" they can come back to us and we will see them straight away. We have no waiting list!

The most important factor in what makes a difference is the dedication, commitment and passion that all the staff in the team have about the work that we do. They are all inspired by this way of working and give their all to the service. They are all highly competent SFBT practitioners that are ever keen to develop their practice skills. It is a privilege for me to be part of such a committed and successful team, without whom I would not be able to write any of the above story.

READING 2

The WOWW Program
Lee Shilts

WOWW ("Working on What Works") is a program for generating classroom solutions that began in 2002 at the New River Middle School in the heart of urban Fort Lauderdale, Florida. The school receives Title 1 and magnet funds because of its diverse population and the economically disadvantaged backgrounds of many of the children it serves. While it is true that the added funds mean more educational opportunities for the children, it is equally the case that many of the students at New River come from homes where parents are struggling to meet their families' basic needs and to provide a positive learning environment at home.

The whole idea behind WOWW began with working with one child named Ben and a teacher who was utterly frustrated. My long-time colleague and friend, Insoo Kim Berg, was in South Florida doing workshops and happened to be staying at our home for a few days. My wife Margaret, who teaches special education in Fort Lauderdale's middle schools, had had a particularly tough day, largely because of Ben, who tapped, pounded, and drummed on his desk all day long. Our discussion eventually turned to what was normally done with a child in such situations, and Margaret said usually the child is sent to a school counselor for a talk about his behavior. The hope was that the talk with a professional and giving the child and teacher a break from each other would result in the child returning to class a bit calmer. Margaret quickly let us know that this approach was not helpful in the long term, and a child's disruptive restlessness usually re-surfaced and interfered with the learning that the teacher was trying so hard to inspire in the classroom.

As we talked more, it occurred to us that this "removal" approach undermines what teachers are trained to do and are expert at, namely, manage a room full of highly energetic children who are by nature restless, curious, and prone to constant movement. It also ignores what is so important and meaningful to children and critical to their learning, namely, a positive relationship with their teacher. We talked about how children by nature want to learn something new, to be accepted, and to belong to a social group such as a classroom of children. In the long run, they certainly do not want to be separated out and labeled as a "problem child," even though they might seem to get some short-term relief from a difficult math lesson by being sent down to the counselor. Margaret also pointed out that teachers feel overworked and stressed, and filling out the paper work, and conferring with the counselor about the "problem child" only means more time and work and rarely changes the child's behavior or a classroom's atmosphere.

So we were pretty discouraged about the removal approach. Insoo then asked Margaret: "How did Ben *stop* banging on his desk? He must have stopped sometime before the end of the day." That stopped Margaret short and she said: "Oh my gosh, oh my gosh, I never thought of that," and then she drifted off into her thoughts. Since both Insoo and I had the next day free, we decided to visit Margaret's classroom, observe the happenings, and see if we could come up with a better idea of what might be useful to do.

The next morning, Margaret introduced us as visitors who wanted to observe what students do well. She introduced me as her husband and Insoo as "the lady who travels around the world." We sat in the back of the classroom. Soon Ben walked over and began questioning Insoo about whether she had been to different cities he knew of including Boston where his family had come from. After she said "yes" and they talked a bit, he returned to his desk and began working without being distracted by the classroom noise. That evening at dinner, we reviewed our observations and decided to write Ben a note because we realized we had completely forgotten to compliment him on his ability to focus, his curiosity about different cities, and how politely and respectfully he had talked to Insoo. It turned out that Ben carried the letter in his backpack for a week showing it to anybody who would listen. He became the envy of the class. Even Ben's mother, who until then had rarely called or showed up at parent/teacher conferences, called Margaret to ask about the letter that made such a big impression on Ben. Later, Ben sent Insoo a letter written in pencil on torn notebook paper saying that he was ". . . just trying to concentrate on my work" and also asked how Insoo's travel was going.

These events really excited Margaret, Insoo, and myself. We were amazed at what a powerful impact compliments can have on a child! We wondered what would happen if we complimented children like Ben on a more consistent basis. We also asked ourselves what would happen if we found ways to acknowledge and utilize what teachers want and know how to do best—teach and build strong relationships with children. And we dreamed about what could happen if we better tapped into children's desire to please important people in their lives such as teachers, parents, and other children in the class.

Margaret enlisted some other special education teachers in experimenting and discovering new "classroom solutions." I began to devote 2–3 hours per week to classroom visits in order to observe and take notes about what children and teachers already were doing that contributed to children's learning and classroom solutions. Insoo stayed in regular conversation with us about our discoveries via e-mail. We began with compliments to the class after each of my visits. Students looked forward to my visits and, after one year, teachers and the principal began to notice changes: reduced referrals to counselors, decreased absences, and better academic performance. We knew we were on to something important and useful, and energy for the ideas was growing among the teachers and principal, so we decided to give our program a name—Classroom Solutions: WOWW—and continued to forge ahead and adapt more components of the solution-building process to the classroom context. As you will see in the following description of the program, although the original idea for WOWW came from our experience with one student, WOWW has evolved into working with the entire classroom instead of focusing on any one individual or a select few students who are labeled as problems.

THE PROGRAM

As the program developed, we quickly became aware that it must have the support and be accountable to the school's administrator. The administrator sets the tone for the school and should be aware and supportive of the philosophy, agenda, and goals of the program. Once the school administrator has been oriented, the work in the classroom can begin. There are three phases to the program: (1) the observation phase, (2) creating classroom goals, and (3) scaling classroom success.

Observation and Complimenting by a Coach

We begin by introducing the WOWW idea to all students in a way that they can understand. For example, I say: "My name is Mr. Lee and I am going to be visiting your classroom each week to watch what all of you do that is good and helpful to everyone in the class. Once I see all this good stuff, I will report this back to the class and get your feedback on what you think about my observations." I then position myself in the classroom where I have the best chance of observing what is happening. Often I quietly reposition myself a couple of times so I can get a view of everyone by the end of my visit. I make sure to notice all the things the students and the teacher do to contribute to the learning. At the end of my visit, I again introduce myself to the class and thank the students and teacher for allowing me the privilege of being in their classroom and sharing this time with them. I let them know that I plan to be there at least once a week for a minimum of one hour. I then give my feedback, being as honest in my observations as I can. Items of observation often include: (1) students talking politely to each other, (2) students raising hands whenever they want to talk, (3) the teacher complimenting a student, (4) a student sharing a pencil, and so forth. I keep my comments short and to the point. I also only describe what I observed; I do not make interpretations or judgments about the behaviors I saw. The students are usually taken by surprise because they are so used to people telling them what they do wrong, while my observations are always about what they are doing right! I ask if there are any questions and try to answer them as honestly as I can. I also ask if they might have noticed anything else that I missed. After a few visits, the students and teacher often point out some additional positives, including some things that happened between my weekly visits. These added observations are an important sign that the class is beginning to develop the "yes set" of recognizing and accepting those things that are contributing to the learning in the classroom. Their increasing participation in making the observations is also a signal to me that they are ready for the next, goal-setting phase of the program. At the end of my visit, I leave my list of observations with the teacher to become part of an archive for the class to review between my visits and to share with other students, teachers, administrators, and parents.

Creating Classroom Goals

By the third to the fifth week of my visits, I am looking for an opportunity to introduce the concept of setting goals with the class. I make sure I have already discussed the idea of classroom goal setting with the teacher, complimented her for her class being ready to start the next phase, and enlisted her support for the process. As WOWW has developed, we have moved away from students setting individual goals to formulating goals for the classroom that both students and teacher have a voice in defining. This change has led to higher morale and greater cooperation among the students. We now organize the goal-setting discussion with the class around a 1 to 10 point scale where 10 stands for the kind of class that is achieving all their goals and 1 means the class is doing little or nothing in this direction. We then solicit everyone's ideas including the teacher's about what makes for a good classroom. It is important to work for goals that everyone agrees on (joint goals) and that are concrete (simple, small, and easy to do). For example, students might say part of what makes for a good classroom is "to respect each other." We then would ask the class lots of follow-up questions about what they will see and hear when everyone is respecting each other. Here is an example from a WOWW goal-setting discussion:

MR. LEE: So who knows what a goal is?

JASMINE: I do. A goal is what you decide to achieve. I know how to do it.

TAMIKA: I do too. It is something we decide we like doing too.

MR. LEE: That's right. You are both very smart. So, let's talk about what kind of goal you all want to achieve as a classroom. If I was to see this class working at a "perfect 10," what would I see going on?

JIMMY: We will be respectful of each other. And we would want to be seated at our desks when the bell rings.

MR. LEE: That would be terrific. What else might I see this class doing to be a "perfect 10?"

JASMINE: We would also be following the teacher's directions and not talking out of turn.

MR. LEE: That is certainly good. Is there anything else I would see?

DEWAYNE: We will be raising our hands when we want to talk.

MR. LEE: Wow! That would be just terrific. So let me see if I got this straight. I would see everyone being respectful of each other, at their seats when the bell rings, following teachers' directions, and raising their hands to talk. That would be a "perfect 10" and a class that everyone could be very proud of. You all have a very good idea of what it is that you want your class to be like. So suppose everybody was respectful of each other in this class, tell me more about what I would see all of you doing when I come back to observe your class next time?

Once the definition of a 10 classroom is in place, we work on identifying what other points of the scale would look like. We define, for example, what a 1–2 level of "respecting each other" would look like; then a 3–4 level, 5, 6–7, and 8–9. For example, when the class is scoring in the 1–4 range, they would be beginning the idea of respecting each other but certainly not on a routine basis. A scale score of 5–7 would indicate significant progress and perhaps the respecting idea would be occurring almost on a daily basis. Finally, consistent scores of 8–10 would demonstrate that the class is scaling or showing respect on a daily basis. Once these scores are arrived at, the class and coach can begin to move on to other goals to scale. Once the scales for the classroom's goals are in place, the class is ready to begin the third phase.

Scaling Classroom Success

We have found with WOWW that scaling is a wonderful tool to use with children. Children often do not have sufficient language skills to explain to others what they are thinking and wishing to explain. In using a scale of 1 to 10, however, they certainly know that 7, for example, is better than 5 or 6, but not as good as 8 or 9. Talking numbers makes a short-hand way of carrying on a meaningful conversation about almost anything: wishes, accomplishments, hopefulness, confidence, progress, motivation, emotions, and imaginations. In WOWW, the scaling phase has evolved to the point where, at the beginning of each week, the teacher (with the benefit of coaching) asks the class to predict what number they will achieve during the coming week on each goal they have agreed on. The teacher then records this number on a chart prominently displayed somewhere in the classroom. He asks the students what things will look like during the week supposing they do achieve this number, what it will take for them to achieve it, and what tells them they can do it. Throughout the week the teacher compliments the class on successes related to the goals when he notices them. At the end of the week, he and the class return to the predictions and have a conversation about what number they achieved, what tells them they are at that number, and the teacher gives compliments to the class for their successes. Here is an excerpt from a scaling conversation about progress at the end of the week:

COACH: So, on a scale of one to ten (where ten is everyone is sitting and doing their work and one is everyone is running around upsetting the class) where would you put the class right now?

ALICE: At about a four.

COACH: What lets you know that it is a four?

TOMMY: Well, we did not yell as much today. When the teacher told us to sit down and start our work, most of us were able to do that.

COACH: Wow! Most of you cooperated with the teacher and there was less yelling in the classroom.

TARA: Yes, and the teacher seemed to be happy that we were able to do this.

COACH: Yeah. I think she was surprised and she seemed very happy with all of you.

Using scaling questions is teaching us to learn about how teachers and students assess their own progress or lack thereof, and makes it perfectly possible to communicate with children about how they view their own behaviors. We are finding [that] children as well as teachers are able to self-assess and monitor their own behaviors. We believe this is the first, small step in teaching children and teachers to form partnerships around becoming responsible for classroom solutions—not problems.

COACHING

The role of the coach is critical to the success of WOWW by helping to implement the techniques around which WOWW was developed. In addition to the initial observation and complimenting done by the coach, she also gives the teacher instruction and support in how to conduct solution-building conversations around goals and scaling successes. Many people within the school system can qualify to be coaches. It has been our experience that people familiar with solution-focused practices naturally are excellent candidates to coach WOWW. However, it is not imperative that one have an extensive background in the techniques to become an effective coach. More importantly, it is essential that a coach possess the interest, desire, and motivation to work in a classroom setting with a teacher and his or her students with a focus on successes and strengths.

We have often been asked how long a coach needs to be with the classroom before his work is done. There is no set answer to that question. As a rule, a coach can reduce his time when the teacher and students feel comfortable with most aspects of the WOWW approach. Usually, this is the point at which a class has established goals and is routinely scaling quite high on these goals. It is important that the teacher and students decide when and how the coach should reduce his time. Coaching can range from visiting the classroom on a weekly basis to consulting once in a while online with a computer.

OUTCOMES

The WOWW project is just a few years old and outcomes so far are limited to the informal observations of participating teachers and administrators. Below I summarize the typical experience of a WOWW teacher and her classroom.

The following example occurred during the 2004–05 academic year. The students were in a seventh grade science class of approximately 25 students. The class could be described as underachieving students who struggled with their academic success. For example, many of the students had been enrolled in drop-out prevention classes the previous year which means they showed many characteristics of students who are at a high risk of dropping out of school entirely. Several of the students were repeating seventh grade and they often were listless and lethargic. Many of them walked around as if they carried the burden of the world on their shoulders. Additionally, the majority had failed Florida Comprehensive Assessment Test for seventh grade students (FCAT) at least once and had not been promoted to the next grade.

Mrs. G., a recent university graduate with a master's degree in marine biology, stepped into this classroom in the fall of 2004 as a first-year teacher. She soon frankly admitted she felt overwhelmed and became interested in WOWW. She asked for a WOWW coach to visit her class.

The first task of the WOWW coach was to develop a relationship with the teacher and students. On October 13, 2004, the following successes were observed and reported to the class:

- One student helped pass out papers for the entire class.
- The table on the right was very quiet and got to work right away as soon as they sat down at their desks.
- The gentleman in the red jacket (a student) walked in late quietly without disturbing the class.

- Several students remembered to raise their hands when they had answers to a question the teacher posted.
- The students did a great job blowing balloons and working on an assignment.
- One student opened the door for another student who arrived late so that he could come into the class.
- The right side of the room stayed seated and started writing observations right away when asked.

Mrs. G.'s class began with seven goals. These goals came mainly from the teacher. As the school year progressed, however, it was decided by everyone (the teacher, coach, and students) that the goals should be reduced to three. The goals decided by everyone were politeness, doing your work, and listening when someone else is talking. There were a couple of reasons for reducing the number of goals. First, there were just too many goals for the students to maintain. Second, the class was struggling with their behaviors. Therefore, everyone agreed to set aside the more academic oriented goals and concentrate solely on the more behavioral oriented goals. These appeared to benefit everyone in their work toward reaching as well as maintaining any other goals.

The next year, Mrs. G. chose to return to teaching at the school and requested that her class become one of the WOWW classes again. The following are her observations:

As a first year teacher this past year, I found one of my classes to be exceptionally challenging. I was tearing my hair out at night and asking any teachers who would listen if they had any suggestions to better manage this one particular class. After just hearing about the WOWW program, I was ready to start. The WOWW program was first implemented in my class in the early fall. From the very first WOWW discussion the students seemed open and interested in developing goals for themselves. They really enjoyed having the coach in the classroom on a weekly basis. The coach was always so positive and only saw good things in everything children did, in addition to being so enthusiastic. He had good things to say to each child. One of the goals in our classroom was working on politeness to each other. The majority of the students really tried to make this work. On the day that the coach was in the classroom, the students would regularly demonstrate just how capable they all were of "Working on What Works" or working on their politeness with each other and the WOWW coach.

Having the coach in the classroom worked out great for me as well. Another one of our goals was to listen while other people were talking. On the days that the coach was in the classroom, the students seemed more on task with listening. One thing that I really noticed was how much more open the students were to expressing themselves during the scaling part of the class when the coach was in the classroom. They may have been responding to the wrap up encouragement from the coach or just participating more due to the coach being there that day. Regardless of the reasons, both the students and I benefited from the experience. The classroom management issues that were so monumental at the beginning of the year were still present, but to a much lesser degree for the rest of the year. In all, we enjoyed the whole experience of WOWW!

As impressive as they are, we are acutely aware that positive testimonials from school personnel are only one broad measure of effectiveness. Therefore, we are now conducting two, more formal research projects. One study is a qualitative project in which the researcher is interviewing school teachers and administrators about their experiences when working with WOWW. The other is a quantitative study in which we are comparing student outcomes for classes using WOWW and those using traditional behavioral interventions. Outcomes being measured include school tardiness, absenteeism, suspensions, and academic performance.

CONCLUSION

The WOWW approach to classroom learning is described elsewhere in greater detail (Berg & Shilts, 2004, 2005a, 2005b). This program encourages teachers to collaborate with students in setting goals, soliciting students' ideas for solutions, and looking for small successes to build on. Therefore, one can readily see that many aspects of solution-focused practice and philosophy fit with the WOWW approach. It also has been our observation over the past three years that solution-focused practice and philosophy blend very nicely into educational environments and offer school personnel opportunity to interact and converse with students in a different and unique way. We are finding that WOWW offers much promise for increased classroom effectiveness to school personnel by giving them the tools to build positive working relationships with students that promote learning and a positive classroom atmosphere. As one experienced teacher said, "I don't go home with a headache anymore after using WOWW."

READING 3

Solutions for Bullying in Primary Schools
Sue Young

Solution-focused thinking informs everything I do now as a teacher employed by the local authority to support schools. I work in Hull, a port city in the northeast of England. Although once a prosperous community based around the fishing industry, the area now suffers from high levels of unemployment and poverty. As in any inner city, the schools achieve many successes against odds, but from time to time they need to manage difficult behaviour, including aggression and even violence.

In every community, bullying has attracted much attention and many innovative approaches have been tried. Even in the most orderly and successful schools, there are incidents of bullying from time to time. We have found that expanding our understanding of bullying behaviour from a problem behaviour between individual offenders and victims to a socially situated behaviour leads to a better understanding of bullying and more effective interventions (Young, 2002; Young & Holdorf, 2003).

When our anti-bullying project started, the prevailing way of working in this field was problem oriented. The very purpose of the project was to reduce the problem of bullying. However, very quickly we realized that it would be better to concentrate on trying to promote what was wanted rather than trying to stop what was not wanted. The preventative program that was developed and used with whole classes in schools set about to promote friendship, empathy and teamwork through activities such as collaborative group work, mutual appreciation and support. The preventative programme became less about bullying, than its antithesis. Although at the time "solution focused" was not a term familiar in this field, with hindsight it is clear that this is how we had begun to think about our work.

This way of thinking inevitably influenced interventions in individual referrals of children feeling bullied in school. Existing strategies for dealing with incidents of bullying were all problem solving approaches, basically trying to stop the problem, some involving the peer group. I worked with relevant groups of pupils, but left the problem completely behind and concentrated just on making the referred child happier in school. Later, coming across solution-focused therapy literature gave me added confidence in a strategy that I had already found that worked.

While anyone can make a referral to the project, in practice it tends to be the parents or a school. Although it is possible to use this approach with older pupils, this approach has been used most extensively in our project in primary school settings. As a result of using it extensively, it has been honed down to the essential procedure that can be implemented easily by anyone prepared to give it a go.

THE SUPPORT GROUP APPROACH TO BULLYING

Throughout the intervention the word "bullying" is not used because it is implicitly judgemental. It implies the referred child is an innocent victim, being unjustly tormented by others. It is more helpful for the referred child and for the peer group to take an implicitly non-judgemental approach to what has been happening. This also makes it easier to become immediately appreciative of what they contribute later.

The first step is to see the child who is struggling first, with the composition of the support group in mind. There are just three essential questions to ask of the child:

1. *Who are you finding difficult to deal with at the moment?*
    In primary schools usually the child will mention between two and five names. There is no need to ask any details about what has been happening or why it might be—just accept the names they give without comment.

2. *Who else is around when things are difficult?*
    Usually two or three names are mentioned. This is an interesting aspect of school bullying—the presence of bystanders seems to be an essential ingredient.

3. *Who are your friends in school?*

Sometimes, especially if bullying has been going on for a long time, the child may have no friends left, in which case we ask, "*Who would you like to have as friends?*" It is not unusual for a child to give a name that has already been mentioned as a bystander or even a bully.

The child is told that some of these pupils will be asked to help make things better in school for him or her, and then we make arrangements to see the child again in about a week to see how things are improving.

The support group is made up from the names given by the child. If possible, we include all the children the child finds difficult, plus a couple of bystanders and any friends or potential friends. A group of 5 to 7 students works best.

The support group is seen immediately afterwards. The members of the support group are welcomed warmly, and told in straightforward manner that we need their help and we have chosen them because we know they all can help. We say we want them to help make ["child's name"] happier in school. This is the easiest and most accurate way of explaining the selection and the purpose of the group. We avoid implying that the child is unhappy because of anything that anyone in the group is doing because it may make some children feel they need to defend themselves. It is helpful to keep the purpose of the group simple and easy to understand.

We then ask the group members for suggestions for how they might be able to help during the coming week. Some groups are full of ideas, some are not so forthcoming at first, but as each suggestion is welcomed and complimented, usually the rest of the group members can think of their own. Sometimes there may be one or two children by the end of the group meeting that cannot think of something different to contribute. In that case we ask if they would like to help someone else with their idea.

The essential point is that the suggestions for what to do with the target child come from the group members. We do not allow ourselves to be tempted to give anyone a "job," or make them promise to do anything. We do not ask them to be "friends" with the target child. We write down their names with the suggestions as they make them, but only as a means of valuing and validating their ideas. After each contribution, we compliment the child for their thoughtfulness, kindness, good thinking, and so on.

As soon as everyone in the group has had a chance to contribute, we thank them all for their excellent plan and assure them that we think they will be successful at making the target child happier in school. We arrange to see the group again in about a week so they can tell us how they are doing.

About a week later, as arranged, we see the target pupil in school. Although this can be a very short meeting since everything is usually going fine and the student is happy in school, we do make a point of congratulating the child and asking her or him how they have contributed to their improved situation. We then immediately meet with the support group the second time. Although this meeting is usually short, we give enough time so that each member of the support group has a chance to report back what they have done during the previous week to contribute to the target child's happiness at school. We compliment each child as well as the group as a whole. It is better not to compare their suggestions at the previous meeting with what they have actually done. What is important is that the target child is happier and all the children have achieved the outcome together.

Sometimes one or two who have previously had difficulty with the target child can be quiet during this second session, as if they are standing back and just weighing up the situation. By a third session they are usually reassured and are eager to talk about their contributions. Even if they do not volunteer any information, the important outcome is that they have not bothered the target child any further and they can be fully included in the congratulations for this success alone.

It is not unusual for the children to report that there has been some bullying from someone at school, usually someone not in the group. In these cases, the "victim" has usually not mentioned it. The children in the group usually take the initiative and are able to sort any minor troubles on their own without necessarily having an adult intervene for them.

As implied above, if needed, the group can be asked if they would like to continue helping for another week. The children can become very enthusiastic about this; after all, they have not been asked to do anything too onerous or anything that they did not choose to do. If they continue, arrangements are made for them to come back so they can talk again about how they are helping, but we do not specifically ask them to report back any problems. There may need to be a couple of review sessions like this; in a minority of cases we have found helping the target child needs reinforcing for up to 5 reviews. It is very rare for a group to go beyond this.

When the target student is happy in school, the group members are happy with how things are, and the parent and the school are happy that the bullying has stopped, then the referral is closed. When a referral came as a result of a parent's concerns, the parent is kept informed throughout and asked for her or his views on whether the child is happier before the referral is closed.

CASE EXAMPLE

When Mrs. Smith telephoned the anti-bullying project, she was clearly upset as she began to talk about her daughter, Jade. Although Mrs. Smith had been to Jade's school several times and talked to the principal, nothing seemed to be happening. She felt her worries and concerns about Jade were brushed aside even though she knew that Jade was constantly "picked on" by other children. Each morning she had to persuade Jade to go to school, and the mother found herself constantly worrying about what was happening during the day. The first question she would ask when Jade came home was "Have you been bullied today?"

I phoned the school and arranged to meet with the head teacher. She was very concerned that I should be aware of the "whole story." She had personally spent a lot of time on looking into this case, but it was a frustrating business since it was never clear. She had come to the conclusion that Jade was exaggerating and needed to ignore any teasing that happened, and then it would stop. Jade's mother was thought to be exacerbating the situation.

I suggested that a support group would be helpful. In that way the school would be seen to be taking positive action, the children in the group would not feel resentful and they could be seen to be helping out. The head agreed and arranged at my request for a teaching assistant to help by bringing the children and listening in to what happened in the group meeting.

When I saw Jade she was looking very worried and spoke in whispers. I asked her for her name, her age, and about the classes she had just come from. On first meeting Jade I spent a few minutes with general talk so she could become comfortable. I will usually ask about what the child is good at in school, or maybe compliment something she (or he) is wearing or the beautiful beads in her braids, her favourite games, TV programs and so on. I want to make sure to avoid giving the impression that I only see the child in terms of his or her problems. A short time spent getting to know the child better tends to pay big dividends during the rest of the conversation. Then I ask permission, in a sense, to intervene, checking that the child wants some help and she or he is happy for me to work with them. Most children find it difficult to talk about their difficulties, so I usually approach this in an indirect way as I did with Jade:

SY: I have been talking to your mum, she seems very worried about you, is that right?

JADE: Mmm.

SY: Is she right? Are you a bit worried about things too?

JADE: Yeah.

SY: I think I may be able to help, is that ok with you?

JADE: Mmm.

SY: I will need to ask you a few more questions, I notice you're good at answering questions, so I hope that's ok?

JADE: Ok.

SY: I am told that you're finding some other children difficult at the moment, is that right?

JADE: Yeah.

SY: Who is it you're finding difficult?

JADE: Melissa ... and sometimes ... Gary ...

SY: Hmm, I see. (writing down the names only) And who else is around when you're finding them difficult?

JADE: Err ... Jenny and ... Paul sometimes ...

SY: Ok, and who are your friends in school?

JADE: Err ... I don't know ... Jenny is sometimes.

SY: That's great, so Jenny is a friend sometimes. Who else would you like to be a friend?

JADE: I play with Rasheed sometimes, and Sara too.

SY: That's great, Rasheed and Sara too then. (writing down the names only) I am going to ask these children if they can help. I'm sure once they start helping that you will be happier in school. I want you to notice what's going better in school over this next week and I'll come back and see how you're getting on. Is that ok?

JADE: Yes.

I give an opportunity before the end of the conversation for the child to say whatever he or she might wish to tell me. It seems that asking children if there is anything they want to say seems to give them permission not to tell me things that they may have dreaded that I might bring up but they did not want to talk about. I end with a reassurance that things will get better and that I want him or her to tell me next week what he or she notices that is improving:

SY: Is there anything else you want to tell me, or you think I need to know?

JADE: No, don't think so.

SY: I'll see you next Friday then, about the same time?

JADE: Yes.

I met with the support group afterwards, made up from the names Jade had given:

SY: Hi there, come in and sit down here, where I can see you, thanks very much for coming. Are you all comfortable? ... I want to ask for your help, is that ok? My job is to help when children are unhappy in school. Jade is unhappy at the moment. I have chosen you because I know you can all help. Is that ok? (Members of the group were nodding and beginning to feel more comfortable.) We don't want anyone to be unhappy in school, do we? ... Have any of you ever been unhappy at school?

RASHEED: I was unhappy when some kids were calling me names.

SY: Oh dear, are you ok now?

RASHEED: Yes it's ok now.

SY: That's good, I'm glad you managed to sort that out ... You all know Jade, is that right? (Members of the group nod or murmur agreement.) So I'm thinking that you all will have some ideas about what you might be able to do, just a little thing maybe, that would help Jade be happier in school over this next week? Who can think of anything?

JENNY: I can play with her at playtime.

SY: That's a really good suggestion! What is your name? ... right, Jenny (writing it down) so you will play with her ... I'm sure she would like that and it will help her feel happier, thanks very much ... who else has got an idea ... maybe just a small thing they can do?

The conversation continued like this until I had most of the names and suggestions on paper.

GARY: I can help her with her maths when she gets stuck.

SY: That's a great idea, Gary, to help her with her maths. I'm sure she will be pleased if you can do that, thank you, that's very kind. ... Has everyone got something to do to help now?

RASHEED: I don't know what I can do.

SY: Oh, not to worry ... maybe you could help someone else with one of their ideas? (He nods) ... who would you like to help?

RASHEED: I could help Jenny.

SY: Would you like that Jenny, if Rasheed helps by playing with Jade some playtimes too?

JENNY: Yes, we often play together anyway.

SY: Good, that's excellent, thanks very much Rasheed, I'm sure that will help Jade, and Jenny too! Thank you all for coming up with such a good plan! I am sure that these things that you are going to do will make a difference and will make Jade happier in school next week. Would you mind if I saw you all again next week? You can tell me how things have turned out.

ALL GROUP: (Nodding) Yeah! Sure! Mmm, yes.

I telephoned Jade's mother to let her know that everything looked fine and the group of children had all been keen to help. I would be back in touch in a week, by which time she should have noticed an improvement. She sounded somewhat doubtful but thanked me for trying to help anyway.

The following week I saw Jade as arranged. She came into the room smiling broadly. I complimented her lovely smile and asked her how things were going now.

JADE: It's ok now.

SY: Great! What have you been doing to make things ok?

JADE: I've been playing with Rasheed and Jenny.

SY: Oh, that's good, I'm glad to hear that. What else have you been doing?

JADE: Guy gave me a chocolate biscuit.

SY: Gosh that was kind, don't you think?

JADE: Yes, and I brought him some sweets ...

SY: That was very thoughtful of you too ... it sounds like you've been happier in school then?

JADE: Yes, I'm ok now.

> SY: I think I would like to see you again next week to hear what else you've been doing, would that be ok?
>
> JADE: Yes, that's ok
>
> SY: Ok, see you then.

Although Jade seemed happy, I would normally arrange another visit just in case either the group or the parent raised any concerns.

Then I met with the support group:

> SY: It's lovely to see you all again, thank you for coming. I've just seen Jade, but tell me, how do you think things are going?
>
> SARA: She's ok now.
>
> GARY: Yeah, she's ok.
>
> SY: That's great . . . how have you managed that?
>
> JENNY: I have been playing with her at playtimes, so has Rasheed.
>
> SY: That's lovely, thanks very much both of you. Do you think that's helped?
>
> JENNY: Yes, it has helped.
>
> SY: Oh, good, I am pleased. How do know it's helped?
>
> JENNY: She's smiling more and playing more.
>
> RASHEED: She's been laughing too.
>
> SY: That sounds great, well done. Has anyone else managed to help?
>
> SARA: I sat with her at lunchtime and . . .
>
> GARY: I gave her some of my lunch.
>
> SY: Gosh! You have been doing well. Do you think she is happier now?
>
> SARA: Yes, definitely!
>
> SY: You know, I thought you had a good plan and I was right! I'm wondering . . . who would like to carry on helping for another week? (All the group looked at each other and nodded and smiled.)

I phoned Jade's mother who was very relieved things were going well:

> SY: Hello there . . . if you remember I said I would phone to see if you have noticed an improvement this last week.
>
> MOTHER: Oh, things are much better, I've been surprised!
>
> SY: Oh, that's great, how have things improved?
>
> MOTHER: Jade is much happier going to school in the morning, in fact I've had no problem getting her to go this week . . . and she seems to have more friends at playtime.
>
> SY: That's lovely, I've just seen Jade actually and she has been telling me, and the group are saying she seems happier too.
>
> MOTHER: It seems to have worked really well . . . at least so far . . . I am worried it might start again though . . .
>
> SY: I see, well it's looking good to me so far too, I will come back to talk to her next week to see how it's going. I'll give you another ring then if that's ok?

MOTHER: That's good, thanks.

SY: That's ok, thank you for your time, that's been helpful.

At the second review, it was clear that Jade was happy and the group were pleased with what they had achieved. School staff had not noticed any further difficulties and they were happy to give them all a school reward for "working together well." The parent was happy for my involvement to end, given the reassurance that should there be any further difficulties she could get back to me for help in the future.

MAKING A DIFFERENCE

Using this approach proved to have a great deal of advantages over the more traditional problem-solving strategies, for schools, parents, and of course, all the children involved.

Schools can become very defensive when complaints of bullying arise. After all, they are responsible for the care of their students during school hours. Head teachers or vice principals can spend a lot of time trying to find out what's been happening, seeing children individually to try to get to the "truth." The usual response is punishment for the "bully." However, if bullying reoccurs nevertheless, sympathy tends to ebb away. Parents of children who are being accused of bullying come to their child's defence. Blame starts to be pinned on the victim as being provocative, attention seeking or over-protected. Surprisingly often the "victim" ends up being kept in at playtime to avoid further trouble. In using a support group, there is simply no need to make judgements on what has been going on in the past—everyone can agree that things need to change for the better. To have a strategy that can bring about a solution quickly is highly valued and appreciated by school staff and administrators. Following training or watching the support group approach in their own school, many others have used this approach successfully. It is an approach that seems easy to learn and implement.

Administrators can also deal with parents who complain on behalf of their child, confident in the belief that they can sort out the situation quickly and positively for all concerned. As far as parents are concerned, their prime motive is the happiness of their child, not blaming the school for what is happening.

By the time a parent contacts the project about their child, they are often very distressed. Their child's distress is often more apparent to them than anyone at the school. Their child may be wetting the bed, becoming aggressive or withdrawn at home. Usually, they have already approached the school and tried to "get something done" and although the bullying may have stopped for a short while, it has started again. Parents are often sensitive to a feeling that school staff may have begun to blame their child, or even their parenting, for what is happening and as a result feel defensive. They often feel powerless to intervene in case they make things worse; indeed they sometimes feel they have already made things worse for their child just by telling the staff at all. Using a support group concentrates activity on exactly what they want—their child to be happier in school again. In the majority of cases they don't expect to see the results immediately, and it seems remarkable that things could turn around so quickly.

Of course, it is the children involved who gain most from this type of intervention. The child who is supported often appears nervous and worried at the first meeting. It is wonderful to see them again just a week later, relaxed and smiling, looking altogether more confident. However, it is not just the supported pupil who benefits. When I have gone back to review how things are going, children in the groups frequently report how much they have enjoyed doing it. Recently we looked further into the experience of the group members. Children from a primary school were asked if they would join support groups and report back later. All of them said they had enjoyed being in a support group; a couple said they felt proud of what they had done; another said she had been making more friends too during her time in the group. All of them thought that the groups they had taken part in had made a real difference to the child supported, making them happier in school.

EVALUATION

When I first began using this approach, I would often find myself "crossing my fingers" as I left a school, hoping that it would work. After all, in what were seen to be difficult and usually long-term problems such as bullying, change being brought about so quickly was entirely at odds with my previous training in behaviour support. It was traditionally thought to be slow and painstaking. As my confidence grew, it was important to me that I should review all the cases and come to some overall evaluation in terms of the outcomes. This is what I found.

Over the previous two years, the support group approach had been used in 51 primary school cases. All the children involved were between 6 and 11 years old. The approach was very successful in the great majority of cases —the criteria for success being that the difficulties stopped completely and the target child no longer felt in need of support. In one of these cases, a child being supported was excluded from the school, so the intervention was not completed. That left 50 cases:

50 cases	Immediately successful	40	(80%)
	Success delayed	7	(14%)
	Limited success	3	(6%)

I sub-divided all the cases further to distinguish the criteria by which they were judged: "Immediately successful" applied where, from the time the group was set up, the target child reported very minor or no difficulties, the support group agreed, and the parents (when involved) were happy that the bullying had stopped. 80% of cases fell into this category.

In some cases, identified as "Success delayed" in the table, the child was not entirely happy at the first review, or alternatively the support group thought things were not satisfactory, or the parent was not entirely satisfied for some reason. In these cases, the situation improved over the following 3 to 5 weekly review meetings, until everyone felt the difficulties were resolved.

In 3 cases, identified as "Limited success" in the table, even though there had been improvement, the child continued to feel unhappy at times in school. In these cases, reviews continued until there was stability at a "tolerable" level for the child. In fact, these 3 children were re-referred subsequently for being bullied by different students from those in the original group. This small minority continued to need longer term help and was given individual solution-focused support.

It is also important to note that in no case did the situation worsen. Children are often reluctant to report they are being bullied in school. One reason may be that they are concerned that any intervention might make their situation even worse. Anecdotally we know that punishment for bullying can indeed lead to resentment that later leads to further aggravation. Teachers and parents are rightly concerned about this. So any intervention needs to be judged on its safety as well as its effectiveness.

CONCLUSION

Using a solution-focused support group approach is an accessible and effective strategy. No other strategy has been proven to be as successful in responding to incidents of bullying in primary schools.

READING 4

Implementation of Solution-Focused Skills in a Hawai'i Prison
Lorenn Walker

PROGRAM DESCRIPTION

This two-pronged pilot program was designed to decrease inmate recidivism while involving victims of criminal offenses to participate in reconciliation with the offenders and their victims (Walker, 2004). This program uses solution-focused (SF) (Berg, 1994; Berg & Reuss, 1997; De Jong & Berg, 2002; de Shazer, 1985, 1988, 1994) and restorative justice (RJ) (Zehr, 2002) approaches.

Even though SF and RJ approaches originated from two different fields, they both offer many useful tools to achieve the goals of this pilot project. The program is designed to offer both offenders and their victims the opportunity to forge better relationships and a better future whenever possible. The result is a self-directed healing process that restores the dignity of both victims and offenders, and others who may have suffered harm from the criminal behaviors. This process bypasses the involvement of lawyers, judges, and juries, thus focusing on repairing the harm after wrongdoing occurs, away from the criminal justice system that is built on blame and retribution.

Having been a victim of a serious criminal assault and later a practicing lawyer who represented the Hawai'i prison system in lawsuits, I wanted to remedy the system that strips away human dignity and mainly applies a punitive approach to rehabilitation. I was aware of how the system seems to victimize offenders and victims rather than restoring a more peaceful and productive resolution to serious wrongdoings.

Hawai'i, like the rest of the USA, suffers from almost 50% of inmates returning to prisons within two years after release (Department of the Attorney General of Hawaii, 2001). I became concerned that almost 90% of defendants plead guilty to charges before they are convicted and sentenced (Hall, 2003), and that our current system does not encourage reconciliation even though almost 50% of violent crimes committed are between people who know each other (Federal Bureau of Investigation, 2003). Our legal system largely ignores the needs of crime victims who are often the inmates' loved ones. Our program gives inmates and their loved ones an opportunity to address their need to rebuild their lives, beginning with reconciliation.

There are two parts to this program: (1) *Restorative Circles* for individual inmates and their loved ones; (2) *Facilitator Training on Restorative Justice as a Solution-Focused Approach to Conflict and Wrongdoing*, for selected inmates.

The program was conducted at a men's minimum-security prison in 2005 and is being expanded to three medium-security prisons in 2006 including the women's prison.

Restorative Circle

The Restorative Circle is designed to increase and solidify an inmate's support system in the community and family from which he comes and most likely will return to after release. It provides him an opportunity to develop an effective transition plan that he can realistically follow through on after leaving prison.

Eighty-six people participated in 15 Circle sessions offered in 2005. Even though many more wanted to attend Circles, the actual number of participants was limited by the prison. Fourteen Circles were held at the prison and one at a church because the inmate was released before it could be held at the prison. The following is a detailed description of the Circle in step-by-step fashion.

First, inmates who are interested in participating in a Circle complete a one-page referral form and submit it to their social worker or counselor. It is faxed to a Circle facilitator from a non-profit service agency. Second, an interview with the inmate is conducted by the facilitator in the prison. It is designed to gather information about the inmate's successes, competencies, and strengths, however small, and to offer information on what to expect to happen at the Circle (see Lee, Sebold, Uken, 2003). Compliments can include, "How have you stayed so healthy here in prison?" or "Suppose I ask your best friend, what would he or she say how you used your time here productively, what would he tell me?" The facilitator also asks the inmate to identify the people he cares about and who he thinks care about him, as well as to indicate what he wishes to gain from the Circle.

The people important to the inmate are invited to the Circle as well as a prison representative the inmate personally invites. Most often the inmate selects his favorite counselor. Only six people out of 100 invited in 2005 refused to attend, and a few were not allowed to attend due to a difficulty of security clearance.

Next, the tedious task of making the Circle happen begins: contacting all the invited people on the list, explaining what to expect, what will be discussed, how it can be emotional to participate in the Circle, and finding a date and time that will work for all the participants and the prison. These arrangements are made by the facilitator and take an average ten hours of time.

The entire Circle process takes about three hours. The Circle begins with the inmate opening it in any way he chooses: He may begin with a native Hawaiian chant, sing a song, play a guitar or ukulele, say a prayer, a poem, or give a prepared written statement that sets the tone for an apology and reconciliation.

Next, all the participants introduce themselves and the inmate tells his proudest accomplishments since he has been incarcerated. Each person identifies the inmate's strengths that motivated his or her participation in the Circle. It can be a very emotional time for the inmate since this may be the first time anyone acknowledged his positive attributes. We observed many become tearful. Finally, the inmate is asked last, "What other strengths do you have that were not mentioned here?"

The inmate's needs are next considered with reconciliation addressed first. The facilitator introduces reconciliation by telling the group that the inmate's desire for the Circle to seek reconciliation is another one of his strengths.

The reconciliation portion of the Circle follows the three basic restorative justice questions: (1) Who was affected by the past misbehavior? (2) How were they affected? (3) What might be done to repair the harm?

The inmate answers the first two questions, and then each of the inmate's loved ones addresses the second and third: "How were they affected? What might be done to repair the harm?" One universal condition that all participants address is that the inmate must stay away from drugs and alcohol. Not surprisingly, all participating inmates have agreed to either stop drug or alcohol use altogether or reduce its harmful effects.

SF language skills are applied throughout the Circle by the facilitators including scaling questions, SF listening, and re-framing deficits into strengths. During the agreement phase for reconciliation, inmates are often asked, "What gives you hope you can stay clean and sober?" and "On a scale of 1 to 10, where are you on staying away from drugs and alcohol?"

After the inmate and his loved ones make an agreement for reconciliation, his other practical needs are addressed: housing, employment, transportation, needed documents (i.e. social security card, birth certificate, etc.), maintaining his emotional health, and maintaining his physical health. A date for a follow-up Circle is also set by the group at the first Circle.

During the Circle, notes are kept on large sheets of butcher paper recording everything the participants say. From this information a Circle Summary is prepared after the Circle, which includes a detailed Transition Plan describing who will take what steps in order to complete a successful transition into the community. For example, it might be, "Clayton will write a letter apologizing to Shantel by November 2, 2005" or "Uncle Joe will write a letter to Mikka by December 4, 2005, about a possible job working in construction," and so on.

The Circle concludes with each of the participants complimenting the inmate on anything they observed during the Circle or on any changes they noticed about the inmate. Often the compliments are included as strengths in the Circle Summary. After the Circle ends there is time for the group to have refreshments and to socialize.

Inmate Training in SF Skills

In 2005 eighteen (18) inmates were trained in *Restorative Justice as a Solution-Focused Approach to Conflict and Wrongdoing*. They met for 12 weeks, two hours each week.

The inmates were introduced to a number of important SF skills by engaging in carefully designed activities. They worked in large groups, small groups, and dyads to learn the following skills.

Identifying Strengths   In order to identify their own strengths, competencies, and resourcefulness, participants were introduced to ways to recognize these in themselves and in others. For example, they were asked to notice what is going right in their own lives, and to look away from "What's wrong with me?" Even though life in prison is not what they want, many participants are able to find pleasant experiences and some things were even going well for them. Every week the training began by asking each to tell the group a different version of "What is better?" and respond to, "What happened positive for you this week?" Major events such as, "My father finally wrote me a letter after three years!" to more simple appreciations such as "I'm still here," or "I didn't get in any trouble this week" were mentioned.

After a few weeks of training, the group began commenting on how much they appreciated the opportunity to learn the skills they were being introduced to at the training and using outside the training sessions. Some inmates were surprised at how they appreciated being in prison and having the opportunity to learn so much there! One said, "This is really like a retreat to learn from." Each trainee received a paperback copy of *Man's Search for Meaning* by Viktor Frankl to keep.

Listening   Listening was introduced to the inmates as a gift that one gives another—that listening is honoring and respecting someone else. True listeners focus on the speaker's concerns and ideas, and not their own. Out of 15 inmates who completed surveys on the training, 11 specifically stated that learning the *listening* skills was the most helpful thing they learned during the training. One inmate stated, "We were all given a gift: the gift of listening."

A great deal of hands-on training and listening practice was necessary in the beginning. For example, one exercise was designed to look for the strengths of a speaker who complained about life a great deal. This was practiced in small and large group and pairs as well as listening intently for the speaker's exact words and formulating responses by using the speaker's exact words. Inmates were also introduced to compassionate listening as developed by the Compassionate Listening Project (Hwoschinsky, 2001), where they learned that identifying the underlying values of people who are angry or upset can help to defuse hostile situations.

Inmates worked on mindfulness by practicing being present and returning to listening when they found their minds wandering. A number of trainees commented, "I never realized how much I just tell people what to do and that I don't listen to them much." "I always thought listening just meant to solve problems for people and just to give them advice."

Responding   In addition to using a speaker's exact words, trainees were introduced to the use of open-ended questions (i.e. what, when, who, where, and how) for responding when listening. They practiced this skill frequently and they commented on how valuable it was. As the training progressed some said, "I never knew someone had so much to say about something!" "When he listened to me like that I just felt good at the end, like I took care of my own problem and he was just there listening to me."

Complimenting   Inmates practiced noticing what others were doing well and complimenting them on it. At the end of each training session, each inmate complimented another inmate in the large group circle on some observations, always based on factual information. Frequently these compliments were about something the others did during the week. For example, "I want to compliment Frank for defusing a situation by listening to two angry people in our dorm last week." Several times inmates got up and hugged each other or engaged in a special friendship handshake (putting their hand into a fist and touching the other person's fist—like the "high five" hand clap together, but instead fist to fist).

Scaling Questions   Frequently, the use of scaling questions in large group discussions was helpful, for example, for inmates to self assess their progress in interacting with others: "On a case of 1 to 10, how close would you say you are to staying calm in spite of being angry, where 10 is you are very confident and 1 is you are back to your old ways? What number would you say you are at right now?" Trainees found many ways to adapt these scaling questions to their daily life in the prison.

CASE EXAMPLE: RESTORATIVE CIRCLE

"I want Ken to stay off drugs when he gets out. That's the most important thing for me. Me and the kids need him, and we need him clean and sober," says the young woman with long dark hair falling around her face. Tears are welling up in her red puffy eyes. Her name is Rachel. She is Ken's girlfriend and the mother of his children. She sits in a circle with Ken, Ken's aunt Martha, a prison counselor, and a facilitator, in old beat up metal chairs that are covered with plastic bursting at the seams in many places from wear and tear.

A recorder is busy writing everything said on large white sheets of butcher paper in one corner. About twelve windows around the room are open. Bright green palm trees and other tropical vegetation dot the mountains surrounding the building. Although the building and furniture are old and rickety and there are only dirt roads around the place, this is probably one of the most beautiful minimum-security prison settings in the United States.

The facilitator picks up on what is important to Rachel and the reconciliation process:

F: Is that something you can do, Ken? Stay off drugs like Rachel wants?

K: (Turning toward Rachel and taking both of her hands in his) For sure. I learned a lot here. I'm different now. I never want to go back to my old life. I'm over it, Rachel.

F: What gives you hope you can do that, Ken?

K: (Responding quickly, without any hesitation) I just know I can. I've been through the worst of my life already. I'm only 24 years old and sometimes it seems like I'm 100. So much has happened. My family is all that matters to me. I know I can do this.

F: (Complimenting and asking for details). I think it's wonderful that you want to really prove to Rachel that you want to turn your life around, and what tells you that you can do it this time?

K: Ya know, I really felt like quitting KASH BOX [drug treatment program at the prison] when it got hard, but I didn't. I hung in there and kept going. I really have changed.

F: What will you do different when you get out of prison, Ken?"

K: Well, one thing is I'm not going back to my old places and hanging out with a lot of my old friends no more. I'm gonna work my music and take care of my family. I've only seen the baby once and I don't want to miss any more of my girls' lives.

F: That's great, Ken. So on a scale of 1 to 10, how sure are you about doing these different things when you get out?

K: Ya know, I really think I'm 100% sure I'm never going back, but just to be totally honest I'm gonna say I am at 8.

F: That's great Ken! What do you need to do to push yourself up one point, to a 9?

K: I dunno. I guess I'm gonna need to stay good with my recovery and stay going to meetings on the outside. I don't wanna slip.

F: Okay. Great. Rachel said she needs you to stay clean and sober to help repair some of the harm that happened from your past behavior, and you said that you can do that. You also said that to stay with your recovery you will need to go to meetings and away from your old hangouts and friends. Is there anything else you will need to do that will help you stay clean and sober?

K: I think I need to stay close with my auntie and we should live by her.

F: Okay. How does that sound to you, Martha? Having Ken and his family living with you?

M: (Martha, with tears dropping off her cheeks) He knows he's always welcome. I have a place waiting for them to live and a car too. It's just all waiting till Ken gets out. They're my family and I want them with me as along as they want.

EVALUATION

After two years have passed, we plan to do an analysis of the recidivism rate for the 15 inmates who had the Circles and the 18 inmates who participated in the inmate training. In the meantime we obtained and analyzed satisfaction surveys of the inmates and of the prison staff on their perceptions of what the inmates learned from the Circles and from the inmate training.

Satisfaction with Restorative Circles

Surveys of 86 participants at the 15 Circles were reviewed, and show overwhelming satisfaction with the Circle process. Participants ranked eight different aspects of Circle as "very positive," "positive," "mixed," "negative," or "very negative." The measured variables included what participants believe about the Transition Plan developed at the Circle, if they think the Circle expanded the inmate's support system, and whether the Circle helped them with reconciliation and forgiveness concerning the inmate. The inmates' survey also asked if the "Circle helped me forgive myself and others."

Review of the 86 surveys showed that almost all participants found the process to be very positive or positive. An inmate's ex-wife, two prison counselors and one inmate indicated that their experience with the Circle was less than positive. The ex-wife said it was "negative" learning about the inmate's strengths at the Circle (the only negative rating on any of the 86 surveys). One counselor was "mixed" about whether he was "more optimistic about the inmate's success to stay out of prison as a result of the Circle." Another counselor felt "mixed" regarding his reconciliation and forgiveness toward the inmate. The inmate found that he was "mixed" about whether "the Circle helped me forgive myself and others." Otherwise all other surveys indicated "positive" and "very positive" results with the Circle.

Survey respondents were also invited to write comments about what they liked best, and what could be improved on, concerning the Circles. Almost all comments were overwhelmingly positive. One 36-year-old inmate said, "I found out my strong points, people can help me, I have a good support system and my Dad said he loves me." The only slightly critical comment came from an inmate's sister who said the process could be improved if "It wasn't so structured and I didn't feel obligated to say something." Her mother at the same Circle said, "Issues were brought out that had not been discussed in the past." Several Circle participants indicated relief that their families talked about things during their Circles that they never had before.

Satisfaction with Inmate Training

The inmates were overwhelmingly satisfied with the training. They were asked five questions concerning the training about whether they learned valuable information about themselves from it, good ways to deal with others, whether they understood forgiveness and reconciliation more, if the activities were good learning tools, and if they learned things that were helpful for them to stay out of prison in the future. These questions were answered with a 5-point scale scored as follows:

Very Positive [5]   Positive [4]   Mixed [3]
Negative [2]   Very Negative [1]

The 15 inmates who filled out the surveys found that they believed the training mostly very positive in all areas—they especially thought the activities they engaged in during the training were effective learning tools. The results of the survey were as follows:

Learned valuable information about self:	4.87
Learned good ways to deal with others:	4.87
Helped with forgiveness & reconciliation:	4.93
Activities were effective learning tools:	5.00
Learned how to help me stay out of prison:	4.87

The inmates also had the opportunity to write what they found most useful about the training. In addition to the 11 inmates who found the listening skills most helpful, one inmate said "forgiveness and understanding" and another said, "Feeling my emotions, and learning how to let it go after feeling it, not acting out on it."

The warden of the prison, with 30 years' experience working in corrections, found the training "Superb. It has the potential of positively impacting prison management by shifting the inmate culture from an adversarial stance to one based on understanding."

CONCLUSION

So, while we have no data on recidivism yet because the program is too new, we do see many encouraging results from both the inmate trainings and the Restorative Circles. Some of these results have amazed us. For example, one inmate who could have been released decided to stay in the prison in order to participate in future training programs including becoming a tutor for a solution-focused inmate training program to be offered in 2006. Especially satisfying has been that many family members who had not seen or communicated with inmates for many years have participated in Circles. This is strengthening the family support for the inmate, which can only make transition out of prison easier. Having a concrete plan that describes exactly what an inmate and others will do to assist the inmate make a successful transition is badly needed throughout the prison system for all those being released.

Our program is being expanded to more prisons in 2006 in collaboration with the Hawai'i prison system. Legislative mandate and funding in support of this program is being sought at this time.

READING 5

It's a Matter of Choice
Steve de Shazer and Luc Isebaert

The alcohol (problem drinking) treatment program described here is run as part of the Psychiatric and Psychosomatics Department, St. John's Hospital, Bruges, Belgium (de Shazer & Isebaert, 2003). St. John's is a large, public hospital serving the western part of Flemish speaking Belgium. Since all patients are covered by Belgium's health insurance, all social classes, employed, unemployed, pensioners, and people on welfare, are admitted. Approximately 1/3 of the patients in the alcohol treatment program are involuntary, most frequently brought in by the police. Belgian law allows, and indeed requires, that these patients be kept on the ward for as long as they are confused as a consequence of alcohol withdrawal. This may last only 24 hours or, if delirium is present at admission, up to ten days.

Prior to 1983, when Dr. Luc Isebaert became chief psychiatrist, everyone—patients and staff alike—was dissatisfied with the traditional approach to working with alcohol problems. Simply, the approach was ineffective with frequent and early relapse episodes. Dr. Isebaert, in addition to traditional training (Lacanian), was trained in family therapy and Ericksonian hypnosis. He decided that there must be a better, more effective and efficient way of working. He began to train the entire ward staff to work in a different way primarily based on the approaches of Milton H. Erickson, the Mental Research Institute (MRI), and the existential therapy of Ludwig Binswanger and Viktor Frankl. Then, in 1990, he invited Steve de Shazer to come and do the first of a yearly series of workshops on Solution-Focused Brief Therapy (SFBT) for his staff and others. There was an immediate fit between SFBT and the new approach the therapists had begun to use, which focused on the patients' choices.

THE PROBLEM DRINKING TREATMENT PROGRAM

1. After 24 hours on the ward, each patient can choose to (1) remain an inpatient, (2) go to the day hospital, (3) become involved in an outpatient treatment, or (4) leave the program. They can change their minds at any time.

2. Sometime during the first week the patients receive extensive information on the biological, psychological, sociological aspects of drinking from the nurses, who are their primary therapists. They also are given a choice of (1) SF group therapy, (2) individual SF therapy, (3) SF therapy with their spouse/partner, (4) SF therapy with the whole family, or (5) none. Again, they can change their minds at any time.

3. The nurses will help the patients (and their families) decide between joining the abstinence-oriented treatment group (AB) or the controlled drinking-oriented treatment group (CD). Since abstinence is not seen as the only approach to handling problem drinking, the nurses and doctors will accept the patient's choice. Again, they can change their minds at any time.

Techniques from SFBT

Clearly, much of the "standard" SFBT practice fits into this program with its focus on the patients' choice.

1. The miracle question clearly focuses on the patients' choice of how they want things to be when the problem disappears. Once the patient and therapist have explored (in a therapy session) the patient's description of the day after the miracle in detail, the next step is for the patient to figure out which approach, AB or CD, will most likely be most useful to the patient in achieving his miracle picture. Frequently scales will be used to help the patient in making this choice.

2. Scaling questions are a central technique for both treatment groups. Of course, 10 can be used to represent how confident they are to achieving abstinence or controlled drinking. Another scale might be used for patients in the CD group, how difficult/easy it was to stop after three or fewer drinks. For patients in the AB group, how difficult/easy was it to overcome the urge to have even one drink.

    In therapy sessions, scales are also used as part of the miracle question, with "10" standing for how things are the day after the miracle and "0" standing for how things were at admission. The patient and therapist can thus assess progress from session to session.

3. Of course, exceptions—often defined as times when the patient could have had a drink but did not—are explored in detail in both therapy sessions and group meetings. As usual, who was involved, what was the situation, when did this happen, and where, are looked at for keys to furthering progress.

4. Relapse management is an important element in the treatment. Relapse is seen as an exercise in controlled drinking that has failed up to a point but that also has been partly successful. These partial solutions are discussed in detail. To prepare them to better manage future difficulties, patients are asked:

    ▪ When you wanted to drink alcohol in the past and you succeeded in overcoming the urge, what helped not to drink the first glass?
    ▪ Have there been occasions where you had just one glass and stopped after that? How did you do that? What else might be useful?
    ▪ If you have been drinking three glasses in a row, are there still things you could do to stop at that point?
    ▪ If you have been drunk one day in the past, what has helped to stop again the next day? What else might help? Who could help you and how?
    ▪ If you have been drinking too much three days in a row, and you consider you are in relapse, what could you do on the fourth day to pull yourself together and start again living the life you want to live?

These questions are discussed with the patient, his/her partner, and in the group sessions. The patient then writes down all the answers (often on the back of the picture of a loved one) and keeps them in his wallet.

A CASE

Franz, a man in his mid 40s, described—in his second therapy session—how he had had a setback on the weekend when he had gone home. He had a long history of drinking too much too often and wanted to control his drinking. He continued to hold a job and wanted to keep his marriage together and thought that controlling his drinking would permit both of these to happen.

T: So, how many beers did you have?

F: Far fewer than normal. But certainly more than the limit of 3 beers I had given myself.

T: Glad to hear it was less than usual. And, how many would you say?

F: Let's say around 8. That seems about right.

T: And you could have had more?

F: Sure.

T: So, how did you stop at 8? How come not 9?

F: Well, I was at the village pub with my neighbors—which I've done every Friday evening for the past 20 years or so. Around 9:30 I had to go to the toilet, so I got up from the table. Next thing I knew I found myself outside—I must have taken the wrong door. So I decided that, since I was outside, I might as well go home. I went right to bed and slept till noon Saturday morning.

T: You could have gone back in. How did you decide to just go home?

F: Actually, I thought that since my wife was gone I could get away with having broken my promise of limiting to 3 beers if I went to bed before she got there. But she stopped at the pub on her way home and found out from the neighbors that I left.

T: Hmm.

F: I guess it is easier than I thought to get up and go home. It never even crossed my mind to go back in for more. Next time I want to stop after 2 or 3.

T: On a scale, with 10 standing for you are as confident as anyone can be about anything that next time you will stop at 2 or 3 beers, where are you now?

F: If you had asked me that last week, I would have said 8, but now I have to say it's no higher than 2. At least now I know what to do.

T: Get up and walk back home.

F: Right.

T: Where do you think your wife would put you now?

F: She would say 0. She's really upset.

T: So, how will she know you've gone up from 0 to 1?

F: She's not talking to me right now, so saying something won't help. Perhaps if I got up and made breakfast for her tomorrow . . .

T: Perhaps she'd like that anyway.

F: It would shock her.

T: In a pleasant way, I hope. So how will you know you've gone up to 3?

F: I don't know . . . perhaps if I don't even have 1 beer between now and Friday. Yeah, that would do it. That might even be a 4!

T: You've made promises like that before, I assume.

F: Often and always broke them, too. So this time, no promise.

T: Perhaps you might even keep it a secret.

F: Yeah, just do it.

T: Who'd be most surprised by it, you or your wife?

F: Me!

Over the next two sessions, Franz learned more and more about how to control his drinking. He held his marriage together and even had the impression that things were getting better between them. His work continued to go well and, in general, things were much improved.

FOLLOW-UP

An attempt was made to contact each of the patients who completed treatment at St. John's during an 18-month period (n=132) four years prior (de Shazer & Isebaert, 2003). Four year follow-ups are standard. The interviews were done by graduate students in psychology who had no connection with the program or the hospital. When possible, collateral interviews were held with family members, family physicians, and the referral sources including the police.

Eighty-nine (67%) of the patients were males, 43 females. Their ages ranged from 19 to 74, with an average age of 46.2. Out of the original 132 patients, 13 had died. Sixty (45%) reported being abstinent, 40 (30%) reported successfully practiced controlled drinking, and 19 (14%) reported not to have reached their goals of either abstinence or controlled drinking. An additional group of outpatients (n=72) gave similar reports: 36 (50%) reported being abstinent, 23 (32%) reported success at controlled drinking.

No statistical differences were found in success rates between: (1) patients who initially chose controlled drinking vs. abstinence; (2) males and females; (3) married or unmarried males or females; (4) patients who were working and those unemployed or on a pension; (5) high and low socio-economic class; (6) patients who saw their spouses as supportive or non-supportive; or (7) patients who saw their families as harmonious vs. non-harmonious. The degree of severity of the alcohol problem (on a standardized measure) at admission had no impact on outcomes.

Inpatients typically stayed in the hospital for 10 to 14 days and in the day hospital for another one or two weeks; the average duration of hospitalization (including day hospital) was 21 days. Outpatients averaged 4.2 sessions each.

CONCLUSION

Clearly, this approach to working with problem drinking differs markedly from more traditional approaches. SFBT, which focuses on patients' ability to make the changes they want to make and to make the necessary choices along the way, seems to be useful to both patients and therapists working with problem drinking. Of course this program evaluation follow-up can only be suggestive. More controlled research is necessary, but these results provide some optimism for those working with problem drinking.

READING 6

The Plumas Project : Solution-Focused Treatment of Domestic Violence Offenders
Adriana Uken, Mo Yee Lee and John Sebold

HISTORY

In 1989, a local superior court judge approached John Sebold and me, Adriana Uken, at the Plumas County Mental Health Department to ask if we could provide a treatment program for domestic violence offenders. We had no previous experience doing groups for offenders and started looking for what was being done in the field. We found a popular psycho-educational model, requested the materials, and began our own program. The materials were heavily slanted toward a cognitive-behavioral–feminist perspective and included graphs demonstrating the many types of domestic violence, control logs, video tapes of couples fighting, and a major emphasis on getting offenders to take accountability for their behaviors. Although not explicitly stated, most of the information implied that domestic violence is something men do to women, not the other way around.

After running this program for two years, we became increasingly disenchanted. We were having difficulty convincing offenders to take responsibility for their behaviors. Although we were both experienced practitioners, trying to talk men into admitting that their behavior was dysfunctional, wrong, and illegal became very frustrating. The relationship between us and the group members seemed to be part of the problem. We felt our job was to gain control and get offenders to say and do what we thought was right for them, perhaps not unlike what they were already doing in their relationships with others. Despite our hard work, it seemed we were not making a difference. In addition, we had problems of high drop-out rates, continuance of violent behaviors, and people not paying for services. We came to the conclusion that we needed to do something drastically different.

SHIFTING TO A SOLUTION FOCUS

"Participants take ownership of their problems not by talking about or reaffirm-ing the problem but by defining goals of therapy and constructing solutions."
(Lee, Sebold, & Uken, 2003, p. 9).

About this time we had started reading some of Steve de Shazer's work on solution-focused therapy. We read that if something doesn't work—don't keep doing more of it—do something different. Our original attempt to do this was to shorten the program. We realized that demanding offenders to come 26–52 weeks was unrealistic, and gleaned from the literature that people can change in a short amount of time. We shortened the group to 8 weeks. We had been reading about the miracle question and well-formed goals and wondered if group members might be more focused and committed if they were required to work on a goal. We decided the goal must be for group members to improve a relationship in their lives. We came up with a list of rules that required members to figure out what relationship each wanted to make better and specifically how each thought that could be done. We also specified that, once the goal was formulated, we would ask questions each week about whether the new behaviors were helpful in reaching the goal. If they were, we would encourage the member to continue doing them; if not, we would ask what could be done instead.

It seemed to us that if group members were able to choose their own goals, express them in their own language, and figure out for themselves what they might do different to make them happen, members might be much more motivated to change. We saw our task mainly as asking the questions that elicited the search for what might work and what might not work. Once members discovered what was helpful, our job became complimenting successes, encouraging more of the same, and helping them discover what differences these changes were making in their lives.

Initially the court sent us only first time offenders but gradually, after seeing how effective our program was, sent us all domestic violence offenders including repeat offenders, those coming out of prison, and both men and women. One of the striking differences, we think, between our treatment program and others in the field of domestic violence is that we chose not to receive information about the nature or details of various group members' offenses. While many in the field might doubt the wisdom of this decision, our previous experience had taught us that focusing on problems did nothing to help offenders figure out what to do different in their lives and, until they figured that out, nothing could change.

OUR PROGRAM

Assessment Interview

All participants are given an individual "assessment" prior to starting the group (see Lee, Sebold, & Uken, 2003; 2004). However, instead of focusing on problems we do two things. First, we explain the group's requirements including coming up with a goal to improve a relationship. While it is up to the person to choose whether to join the group or not, there is no choice about working on a goal. We encourage potential members to begin thinking about a goal because we will ask about their ideas for a goal at our first session. We believe this suggestion creates the seeds for change at the initial contact. We also explain other group rules such as there being eight sessions with only one excused absence permitted, dismissal from the group if a member arrives at group under the influence of alcohol or drugs, completion of written assignments, participation in group discussion, no blaming talk, and required attendance reporting by us to participants' probation officers. We believe that explaining what the requirements of the group are and what members can expect helps to resolve fears about how they might be treated. We know from past experience that many offenders are intimidated by the prospect of being in a treatment group, and giving them as much information as we can helps to allay some of their concerns.

The second part of the individual assessment involves us asking questions about their strengths and resources. Some of the questions we ask are:

- What are some of your recent successes?
- What have you done that you are proud of?
- What have you done that required a lot of hard work from you?
- Have you ever broken a habit that was hard to break?
- What kinds of things do people compliment you on?

Beginning by discovering a participant's successes and strengths creates an environment where the individual can recognize that they have been competent in the past and helps to instill hope that they can be competent in the future. It also gives us the opportunity to begin complimenting the participant and developing rapport by signaling to the client that this is going to be a different experience than what he/she might have expected. While the assessment is clear that there will be requirements, it also demonstrates that there will be support and belief in the participant's competence to succeed.

Focusing on and emphasizing competencies, however, must never be equated with minimizing the destructiveness of offenders' violent behaviors. Solution-focused domestic violence treatment does not deny or minimize aggressive or violent behaviors, but recognizes that treatment programs are part of a coordinated community response to reduce domestic violence. Our program's role is to be an agent of change and reduce the likelihood of recidivism. We feel that we have an ethical responsibility to end violence in intimate relationships as quickly as possible and a moral challenge to develop programs that can do that.

Sessions 1–3

The first group session starts with a sign-in sheet used to report attendance to the probation department. Next we go over the group rules and each participant is given an opportunity to ask questions or express disagreement about the rules. Utilizing this time to talk about group rules prevents any problems about the rules coming up later. Thirdly we start working on goals. The real work of the group now begins in earnest. Our task is to ask questions that help members figure out what they can do in a behavioral way (so that it can be seen or heard by others) that might improve a relationship. Useful goals neither come easily nor effortlessly, so we devote the first three sessions to goal formulation. Here is a partial transcript from a second session where a group member we will call Brandy tries to figure out what she can work on.

> JOHN: ...do you have an idea of what you want to work on?
>
> BRANDY: It's just that my goal is not...I overreact with my spouse and just assume the worst, and so my goal would be to not overreact in a given situation.
>
> ADRIANA: What do you want to do instead?
>
> BRANDY: I honestly don't know. I guess not to think the worst, give him the benefit of the doubt.
>
> ADRIANA: How would you do that?
>
> JOHN: Before we get into that, I want to explain to you that this goal has to be something that you do, as opposed to something that you don't do. So we will ask you questions that might help you to a place where you can see what you need to be doing instead. If we're moving too fast, tell us and we will try and back off and approach it in a different way...
>
> ADRIANA: So Brandy, if I was a fly with a video camera on the wall in your house, and last week I would have seen you overreacting, what would I see and hear you doing next week, what would be different?
>
> BRANDY: It's just my communication because I am like—I would be communicating calmly about it rather than just freaking about it.
>
> ADRIANA: So what would you be doing different, something that I could see or hear?
>
> BRANDY: I can start being calm.

ADRIANA: How would I notice you *doing* that? So what would be different about your voice?

BRANDY: I would be calm, I wouldn't be hollering and high pitched.

ADRIANA: Can you give me an example of that tone, of being calm?

BRANDY: This is calm right now.

ADRIANA: So you will be talking in this tone of voice?

BRANDY: Yeah.

ADRIANA: So will you be saying something different as well?

BRANDY: Well, I'm going to be more positive as opposed to being more negative . . . I always just assume the worst.

ADRIANA: So what will you do instead of assuming the worst?

BRANDY: So instead of always saying when he's late, "oh, you stopped at the bar!" so instead of saying that, I would try and be calm about it, I could think that there is a good reason, like maybe there was a lot of traffic, or road construction.

ADRIANA: So, when he's late you will think there is a logical reason for him being late?

BRANDY: I wouldn't be reaming his ass. (group laughs) That's the truth. That's what I normally do.

ADRIANA: How would you greet him when he comes home?

BRANDY: Like just hug and kiss. I wouldn't be upset . . . This is really different. We already talked about it.

ADRIANA: You did? You and him together? And he said?

BRANDY: Yeah, I overreact.

JOHN: I kind of want to understand what you are saying right now. So you will be at home, and he will be coming home late, and you normally think that he's doing something that he shouldn't be doing and that's why he's late? So in the past you overreact before he even comes in the door?

ADRIANA: Does he give you a reason to think this?

BRANDY: Never.

ADRIANA: So he has not given you any reason?

BRANDY: No, that just comes from past relationships.

JOHN: Okay, so what I hear you saying, before he even gets home you're going to be doing something different on how you think about this whole thing. So this time what are you going to be doing and thinking about?

BRANDY: I don't know, I mean it could be that he just got stuck in traffic. He comes all the way from Reno.

JOHN: So stuck in traffic might be real—he comes from far away.

ADRIANA: I think this could be a great goal for you.

JOHN: It's a tough goal.

BRANDY: Yeah.

ADRIANA: It's going to take a lot of hard work.

JOHN: I'm curious, this brings us to the other question. If it's so automatic, how are you going to shift from being automatic to doing this other thing? What kind of messages are you going to give yourself so you go down a different road?

BRANDY: I have no idea.

OTHER GROUP PARTICIPANT: Maybe if he went out and bought you a ring, and you could twist it every time you got angry to remind yourself to do something different.

ADRIANA: Yeah, but that would require (him) *your husband* to do something different, and if he did not do it, then you would be stuck.

BRANDY: Right. Maybe what Joe said, that childhood thing that girls do, when they pick petals off a daisy and say "he loves me, he loves me not," and instead say to myself that "he loves me, he loves me, he loves me," and—say that to myself over and over. There is no indication that he will hurt me.

OTHER GROUP PARTICIPANT: And have notes all over the house to remind you.

JOHN: Let's just say you are confident that it can really work, I don't mean solve it, because it's going to take a lot of hard work—but 10 is that it can really work, and 1 is that it will not work, where would you stand on that scale?

BRANDY: I am on 9. I am pretty sure it's going to work out.

Sessions 4–8

After goal formulation, successive group sessions focus on what participants have been doing differently the previous week to work on achieving their respective goals. We ask questions, give compliments, and focus on what the next step might be. Below is a dialogue with a client we call Bill that illustrates some of this process. Bill had said he wanted to be less angry with his partner, trust more that she is "not messing around," and not fight anymore. Bill had admitted that she had never given him reason not to trust her. One of the things he had decided he wanted to do differently was to think more positively about her. The following transcript is from session 7:

ADRIANA: So Bill what has been happening with your goal?

BILL: I'm still where I was last week, I've been kind of a hermit working out of town, but I talk to my wife every day.

ADRIANA: So do you have opportunity even at work?

BILL: Yeah, of course. You know, there's one thing I've kind of noticed, being complimentary and everything even just over the phone to my wife, it kind of gives me a little more trust. I didn't even see that that would affect it at all though, you know—that kind of blew me away.

ADRIANA: Yeah?

BILL: Because before I always just kind of wondered what is she doing? What is she up to while I'm gone? Is there a big party going on at my house or something like that? But being complimentary saying "you know you're so helpful, I believe in you," and all this other stuff, I guess it's kind of bull-shitting me into believing it.

OTHER GROUP
MEMBER: It works man! (Group laughter)

BILL: Yeah, so whether she is or she isn't—it's out of my head you know. I don't sit there and wonder about things.

ADRIANA: So what do you notice when you compliment her?

BILL: By complimenting her, I tell her she's a good person, she does good things and stuff, and she seems to react positively back, and for some reason I don't wonder about her when I'm out of town.

ADRIANA: Wow!

BILL: And that kind of blew me away.

ADRIANA: So, the complimenting makes you have more trust? *You* do the complimenting and it makes *you* trust the other person more?

BILL: It does in a way. It's kind of a weird feeling.

ADRIANA: Isn't that interesting?

OTHER GROUP
MEMBER: So, do you think listening to their goals (points to two other group members) which were kind of similar, has helped...

BILL: Oh, yeah. You know I'm one of the most imperfect people in the world probably, and you know his goal (pointing to another group member) that he's got going that makes him take more responsibility, it helps me with my responsibility, and what she's doing to "just block it out" sometimes that works for me too. You know everyone has a good opinion about what they're doing—I'm always thinking about what you guys are saying and trying to see how I can use that.

JOHN: I'm still really interested in your compliment here and what I kind of hear you saying is that it's hopeful for you when you think about yourself and your relationship?

BILL: You know there *have* been times in the past, especially with trust, I just never could see myself really trusting. But that's how it kind of worked out to be, in a way.

JOHN: Yeah, life kind of comes back to that, in relationships especially.

ADRIANA: So, the more you compliment, the more you trust?

BILL: Yeah, it seems to be turning out that way.

OTHER GROUP
MEMBER: I'm going to try that.

ADRIANA: You're going to try that?

OTHER GROUP
MEMBER: Yeah, it seems to work.

BILL: ...Do I have to say any more? I don't like talking in front of people.

ADRIANA: Well, my original question was have you found opportunity at work to...

BILL: Yeah, I kind of hit on that last time, and it's been pretty much the same. You see someone doing something a certain way and you say, "Hey that's better than the way I've been doing it, you know. I've been wasting time." And I give them a little step up and also encourage the people that work around you. I work with this one guy, and he never thinks too much. He just comes in and puts in his hours, and then wants to leave. Sometimes I tell him, "Hey, I think you put yourself down too much. You're a pretty hard worker and stuff." He kind of looks up, and I get a better helper that way you know.

ADRIANA: Yeah?

BILL: Before he was just kind of lazy and just putting his hours in—and I say to him, "What do you think about that?" and he says "I think we could do it this way," and I say "You know that's a pretty good idea, let's try it your way."

ADRIANA: So you see him more committed?

BILL: You see him thinking more and at least trying hard. Before I may have resented him for lagging on me, having to help him with his part, and not *wanting* to say anything. Now I've found another way of getting him to do 50/50 you know, instead of getting angry at him.

Assignments

Depending on the size of our group and time constraints, we sometimes give written assignments to the group members. At the end of a session, we ask a question, such as, "Write a page on someone who had a positive influence on your life and be prepared to discuss it next group session." Another assignment we might give is: "Write down all the small things that you think make a relationship work," or "write a page on how you show your partner that you care about her, and how she shows her caring for you."

The assignments are all directed at positive behaviors, and a wonderful opportunity for good group discussion. They are designed to help participants focus on specific behaviors that improve relationships, and perhaps most importantly they describe behaviors that are in the context of their own lives. The assignments also give us the opportunity to ask good questions, for example, Chad had written about his grandmother, who had been the most important influence in his life, and taught him "right from wrong." We were then able to ask Chad at a later time what he thought his grandmother would say about him, and what difference it would make to her if she could see how much better he was doing at home.

We consistently give an assignment at session 7. Each participant is to write down what they learned from the group, what goals they intend to keep working on after the group is over, and how confident they are on a 1–10 scale that they will keep working on that goal. Three months after completion of the group we send them a letter thanking them for attending the group, complimenting them on their hard work, and return their session 7 assignment. We suspect that the return of the assignment might be a good reminder to continue their goal work. This assignment has given us hundreds of wonderful personal statements of how participants are impacted by the program, and their commitment to improving their relationships.

PROGRAM OUTCOMES

We believed from the beginning that it is important to carefully accumulate empirical evidence about what works with offenders so that more effective treatment could be developed. We gathered quantitative data to measure behavioral changes such as cessation of violent behaviors, respectful and caring behaviors in intimate relationships, and behavioral indicators of increased self-esteem. We accumulated qualitative data to identify components within the program that contribute to positive changes in participants.

Recidivism Rates

Reviews of domestic violence offender treatment programs generally report recidivism rates ranging from 20% to 50% in the year after completion of the program (Lee, Sebold, & Uken, 2003). Studies that measure recidivism through partners' reports and arrest records find recidivism rates of 40–50%. Rates of early dropouts from these programs also have been very high, ranging from 50 to 75%. (Lee, Sebold, & Uken, 2003, p. 8). In comparison, recidivism rates for our program participants obtained from the district attorney's office, probation department, and victim witness office have averaged 16.7% after 14 years of data collection along with a program completion rate of 92.8%.

Partners' Comments

In their evaluations, most partners of participants focus on the issue of anger control when describing changes they have noticed. Characteristic comments include "I can't remember when he blew up the last time," "... hasn't hit the children," "... not violent," "... (handles) anger issues better," "... (is) less aggressive," "he controls his temper a lot more," "... he takes time to think through things," "he learn(ed) how to deal with anger in different ways." One representative partner commented that her spouse now "drives a lot slower, (is) more considerate and less impulsive." Another said: "She is easier to get along with, she's easygoing, (and) has slowed down." Spouses also describe their partners as more involved and engaged in their families' lives, helping around the house more and spending more time with spouses and children. Some said their partners are "not using any substances (anymore), and "(keeping) his job for more than a year." Other partners said "he doesn't try to blame others for his actions" and "she tries to keep positive instead of negative."

Group Members' Comments

The following is a transcript from a session which addresses the question of what participants see as helpful. Insoo Kim Berg attended this particular session and asked the following question:

> INSOO: I want to ask you this—John and Adriana don't know I'm going to ask you this. What occurred to me, I'm curious about this, what do you suppose you will say if you were to tell your friends, or family or mate about what they (John and Adriana) are doing since you came to this meeting, is this the fifth meeting? What are they doing that is helping you? What is useful to you?

GROUP MEMBER: They ask a lot of questions.

INSOO: That's helpful?

GROUP MEMBER: Yeah. They help you say what you're trying to say, well for me what I am trying to say—they help a lot. By keep asking questions and putting them in different ways and asking the same question different ways.

GROUP MEMBER: Rather than tell you or direct you in a direction or something like that, they ask you, you do it yourself. You pull it out—you define your own position rather than there being, it's not really like a guideline they make you follow...it's something...

INSOO: You like that?

GROUP MEMBER: Yeah, it's not like you have to do this and you have to go and do this to make this thing work. They ask you questions and make you come up with it yourself. I think that's really helpful because each person is different and they each find their own way.

INSOO: It sounds like what you are doing is all different.

GROUP MEMBER: In its own way, that's how you feel.

GROUP MEMBER: I like the way you guys both make each of us individually feel that no matter what we say or have done over the last week, you make us feel good about it. That somehow or something about whatever each of us have said or brought to the class. That's something we all take away from here, feeling a little better with the positiveness you both put toward us and comments and remarks that have been made.

INSOO: The question I am asking all of you is, what [are] John and Adriana doing since you've been coming to this class?

GROUP MEMBER: Actually they give you a lot to think about when you leave the class. They keep you in focus, you know why you're out here. And they never bring it up why you're here, which is great to me. I mean really. A lot of people will bring it up why you're out here, but they never bring it up. They always stay focused on other things to make you better. And for me it has been very helpful. It really has been.

GROUP MEMBER: I think one of the most helpful things they contribute to this whole group, in fact I see it as the most helpful is—we all have our goals and everything, and we all bring it out, we discuss our goals, but they always ask us—and they bring it up every time, "How are you putting this into action? How are you making it work for you? How are you going about it? And what are the results you are seeing from it?" rather than just sit here and talk about what the goal is, and what's going on. I think that it's harder to come out and answer these questions—rather than just talk about it.

INSOO: Can anyone think of anything else they do that seems to make it helpful?

GROUP MEMBER: All their questions helps me, keeps me going.

INSOO: It does? What about their questions?

GROUP MEMBER: Helps me to stay in focus.

INSOO: You mentioned questions and you did too.

GROUP MEMBER: It helps open your mind up. It broadens you, to me it does, broaden my mind about the bigger picture of things, than the small part of things.

GROUP MEMBER: It's always what you can do to help out your situation and you know you can't do nothing about what everyone else did—it's about you.

INSOO: You like that?

GROUP MEMBER: Yeah.

INSOO: O.K. well, thank you very much for taking extra time.

IMPACT ON PRACTITIONERS

Using solution-focused practice has made a tremendous difference for us as practitioners. We use it with domestic violence groups, groups for adolescent substance abuse offenders, parents of adolescents who were on probation, but also with the entire range of clients in a community mental health clinic. When we used to do problem-focused work, it seemed we were tired all the time. We never seemed to know when a client was done with therapy, and often felt that we were doing all the work, and had to be the "expert" and figure out how to "fix" or "cure" the client. We spent hour upon hour listening to people's stories about what was wrong with their lives, and felt that in order to be effective, we needed to ask more and more questions about what was wrong.

Solution-focused therapy was a breath of fresh air. All of a sudden, it was the client who determined when they were done with therapy. There were clear behavioral indicators when the goal was reached. We no longer had the burden of being "an expert," but worked in collaboration with the client to figure out together what would be helpful. We no longer listened to months of problems, but were listening to strengths, and competencies, and abilities. We were watching miracles in the making. That didn't mean we just sat back and listened. It certainly wasn't easy or simple. We had to learn how to look for people's strengths, and learn how to ask the questions that helped them build the bridge from the problem they came in with to the future that they wanted. We had to train ourselves to listen exquisitely to anything the client might be doing that was different, which they might not have noticed or paid attention to, and that might be useful. At the end of the day we felt we had made a difference and felt enthused about how amazing people really are. As you might be able to detect from the transcripts, we are totally impressed by the changes our domestic violence offenders are making and are sincere in our respect for them. We no longer saw clients as *DSM* labels but as incredible beings full of possibilities. Work became fun and felt empowering. Our life outside of work was affected as well. We found ourselves complimenting others more often, in fact even each other. What a difference it makes when you are looking for what is positive, and recognize that it is your own behavior that determines the quality of your life. We discovered that current reality gets created through the use of language in conversation with others, not by what happened to you in the past. We found we were living life in the present and were definitely having more fun.

IMPACT ON OUR AGENCY

As an agency, solution-focused therapy changed not only the way we related to our clients, but also how we worked together. The agency became much more of a team, sharing responsibilities, and noticing each other's strengths. Staff meetings became a shared event, not a hierarchical process, where the "boss" dictated to his staff what they needed to do. During clinical meetings, staff would describe client's successes, instead of just their problems. Compliments for each other's work came easily. The boundaries between clinical staff and support staff seemed to lessen. Staff worked harder, did what needed to be done to do the job, and went out of their way to help each other out. Clients were not referred to by diagnosis, but rather as people capable of change. The challenge became how to most quickly find the "diamond in the rough." John and I looked forward to our domestic violence groups, and described it to others as "fun." We would talk about how impressive these group members were and how much we were learning from them. We would compliment each other on the "good questions" the other had asked. We would frequently wonder whether we would be able to do what we saw our group participants doing— having courage, strength and persistence.

There have also been challenges, especially in dealing with other agencies that live in a more problem-focused world. We saw that in order not to create barriers or defensive responses, we needed to acknowledge and appreciate what others are doing and to find out what works for them. Although our agency is committed to being solution-focused, we still have the requirements of larger systems, such as state and local governments. We are required to give *DSM* diagnoses and need to specifically list exactly what problems clients have and continue to have in order to receive payment. Dealing with these larger systems can require incredible patience and the ability to shift back and forth. It helps to recognize that politics plays a huge role, especially in the area of domestic violence.

CONCLUSION

The shift from problem-focused to solution-focused work with domestic violence offenders has been an eye-opening adventure for us. It has transformed how we think about treatment, our clients, our co-workers, and our relationship to collateral systems. Fourteen years of experience with the offenders in our groups have persuaded us of three core beliefs that now guide our professional practice:

1. that people can create their own solutions,
2. that the element of choice in treatment creates a powerful force for change, and
3. that focusing on small, goal-related behaviors can provide a powerful catalyst for developing meaningful and lasting change in a relatively short time.

READING 7

Transforming Agency Practice through Solution-Focused Supervision
Teri Pichot

I began my career as a substance abuse counselor in 1989. I was in the process of obtaining my bachelor's degree from a local state college, and part of the requirements was to complete two field practica and an internship. It was through these hands-on experiences that I got my first glimpse of traditional substance abuse treatment. I chose residential treatment as the setting in which to complete my field practica since that was the most widely used treatment modality of the day. In these settings clients attended multiple treatment groups and 12-step meetings; the curriculum was predetermined, and the belief that the clients were suffering from a disease permeated every intervention. Clients who disagreed with the prescribed treatment were labeled as in denial, and confrontational-style interventions were designed to break through the clients' defenses. Tears and anger were a common part of the clients' day as interventions unfolded, and the environment was emotionally draining as therapists viewed such client outbursts as signs of necessary break-throughs. The therapists frequently strategized behind the scene, searching for the ideal intervention to address the clients' problems. The therapists were quick to self disclose their own recovery from addiction, and these recovering therapists were viewed by the clients and staff as role models. Not ever having suffered from a chemical addiction myself, I viewed myself as lacking the potential effectiveness that these recovering therapists had, sensing a need to be more effective with the other forms of interventions to compensate, and always feeling a sense of inadequacy when clients asked me directly about my past.

These early experiences reinforced how little I truly knew about people and the change process. I quickly enrolled in graduate school hoping to get the needed education to boost my professional confidence. Throughout my education, I worked in various outpatient and residential settings with a variety of clients; domestic violence and substance abuse issues seemed to dominate the presenting problems. The staff in all of these agencies suffered from burnout, was looking for better jobs, or was pessimistic about the clients' futures as clients cycled through the agencies at a discouraging frequency. My enthusiasm and energy was seen as a symptom of inexperience and naïveté.

WHY CHANGE WAS NECESSARY

As I began to practice therapy independently, I soon learned that the confrontational approaches and expert-based stance that I had been taught were not as effective as I had hoped. Clients challenged me at times when I took an authoritative stance, and I caved under the pressure knowing even I wasn't sure that what I was saying was true for them. Their arguments and explanations of why they didn't have a disease or what would work better for them actually made sense to me. Embarrassed to admit such a thing publicly for fear that I was truly naïve, I quietly began changing my approach with clients. I began to listen more than tell, look for clues of possible answers within the clients' own statements, and hear what mattered to the clients and then seek to help them obtain it. I wasn't sure if my new approach was any more effective, but I felt a greater sense of connection with my clients and more energy and joy in my job. My clients and I seemed to have found a new sense of partnership and to have abandoned the prior, adversarial way of working. I saw clients making changes, and they no longer seemed to hide who they were and how they thought from me.

It was during this time of experimentation that I was first introduced to solution-focused therapy in a workshop. Of all of the approaches to which I had been exposed, this one resonated with me. While my colleagues in the workshop questioned and challenged the new concepts, I eagerly embraced them and only questioned why this approach was not more widely used. I became a sponge, seeking to absorb anything I could find about this way of working with clients. My supervisor was supportive of my new way of thinking and gentler approach, but I could tell that she wasn't convinced that this way of working was entirely correct. I worked in an environment in which value was placed on understanding and knowing the etiology and therefore the answers to problems. Ironically, it was through embracing my "not knowing" rather than trying to disguise it, that I began to gain the needed professional confidence. And when a position became available in 1995 as the clinical supervisor of an outpatient substance abuse treatment program at a local county health department, I applied. I had no experience as a clinical supervisor and I wasn't convinced that I could really do the job, but I saw this as a career advancement that I just couldn't pass up. And so began the journey that has forever changed my professional life.

The clientele at the Jefferson County Department of Health and Environment Substance Abuse Counseling Program is similar to that of other publicly funded programs: frequently low income, ethnically diverse, legally involved, mandated clients. In other words, they are clients who have been in the system for some time, who are frequently angry and mistrustful, and who many professionals view as not their desired clientele. Many of our adult clients come from the department of social services due to accusations of child abuse or neglect, their children currently in foster care, and substance abuse treatment a requirement of the Family Service Plan. The families are categorized as "multi-problem" and they are being asked to attend many forms of treatment to address the areas of concern (e.g., substance abuse, mental health, domestic violence, anger management, and parenting). In addition we have clients—adults and adolescents—who are referred from the legal system (probation, diversion, etc.) as well as from other community agencies. Clients come to our agency due to the financial affordability of our services. Although our clients frequently insist that they were unjustly accused and that they do not have a problem with substances, their referral sources provide evidence to the contrary such as methamphetamine labs and countless substance-related legal charges. The majority of our clients qualify for *DSM–IV* diagnoses of dependence on multiple substances as well as major mental health disorders such as Major Depressive Disorder, Bi-polar Disorder, Schizophrenia, and Borderline Personality Disorder. By no accounts is this an easy group of clients to treat. Professionals frequently see working in this type of treatment setting as an undesirable but sometimes necessary stepping stone toward the more rewarding and less taxing privately funded sector. Burnout and high turnover are commonplace in such settings.

HOW I INTRODUCED SOLUTION-FOCUSED PRACTICES

As I began my work at this agency, I was painfully aware of how much I didn't know. At the time, I saw this as a weakness. I now know that it was this awareness and the resultant stance of not knowing that was probably the most instrumental to my success. I am a therapist by trade, and I used the same approach that had been successful with my clients with my new team of therapists. (In retrospect, I now know that this approach is incredibly effective, and is one that I highly value to this day. Then, I simply used it because it was all I knew.) People are people, and the same process that results in change in clients will result in change in professionals. I believed that by being genuine and treating staff as I would treat clients, not only would I create a positive change in my therapists' work, but I would also teach these principles and interventions to my staff through their demonstration. I began by getting to know my new staff of six therapists, asking them what they were doing with their clients that was working, what they needed from me as a supervisor, and how I could best help. I took a curious, learning stance. They were the experts about their job and their agency, not me. This served as an excellent way for me to work in partnership with the team members. Now I should mention that this was far from an easy process. Staff members were skeptical of this new approach, and they frequently responded in a similar fashion as my previous, mandated clients. However, they also gradually began to become more open and work in partnership just like my previous mandated clients, reaffirming that there is little difference between professionals and clients in this regard.

Once I obtained a good understanding of how the staff members saw their work, I gently began to question and ask for their thinking behind their interventions. My goal in doing this was to insist that they have a purpose behind their interventions so that they could then evaluate the effectiveness of their interventions by comparing the outcome to their initial intent. This was a new concept for them since the majority of my staff considered themselves as "eclectic" and operated on "gut instinct." Therapist self dis-closure was common, and all of my newly acquired staff strongly viewed themselves as the expert in their clientele and the problem of addiction. This part of our journey was extremely challenging, for at times my questions were viewed as a challenge to their authority and expertise rather than a genuine invitation for curiosity and accountability. However, once the staff understood my motivation, we were able to explore the answers together. This was a difficult time in the history of the transition. Approximately half of the therapists left the agency since they did not like to be questioned and saw no need for my insistence upon an open evaluation of client care. I did not yet consider myself to be a solution-focused supervisor, nor did I have the intent to change the agency's theoretical orientation. I was simply doing the only thing that made sense to me; questioning everything. However, upon reflection, the basic tenets of solution-focused therapy became a solid part of the program's foundation and my way of supervising staff during this time period. Here is an example of the sort of conversations I was having with staff at that time and still today with therapists new to our staff:

TERI (SUPERVISOR): I'm glad we have a chance to meet privately since I have so much that I would like to learn about you and your work with clients. Is it O.K. with you if I spend some time getting to know you better?

THERAPIST: Sure. I guess [clearly suspicious of this unexpected approach].

TERI: You work with some challenging clients. You must be very good at your job to have been here working with such tough clients for so many years. So tell me what you have discovered that works best with them.

THERAPIST: Well, I teach them about addiction and the stages. Once they understand they are in denial and become more open to accepting the fact they have a disease they really aren't that difficult to work with.

TERI: Wow! So you have found a way to make them easier to work with! How do you get them to listen to the stages of addiction and get through the denial?

THERAPIST: The clients really do want their lives to change, so once they under-stand the problem, they are really motivated to go along with the program.

TERI: How did you discover that the clients really do want something? That is an amazing insight that you have about these mandated clients!

THERAPIST: Well, they do tell you if you just listen.

TERI: So, you are a very good listener. [This is a very important concept for the supervisor to note and use for future supervision sessions since listening (combined with the therapist's earlier insight that clients really do want something) is a key commonality with solution-focused therapy. By asking the therapist questions during future supervision sessions about what the client really wants and what the client is really saying about what he wants, the supervisor can begin the process of shifting what the therapist is listening for.]

THERAPIST: Yeah, I guess so.

TERI: You have been around quite a bit, and I would like to know, how I can help you in your job?

THERAPIST: What do you mean?

TERI: Well, my job is to be a support to you and help you be the best therapist you can be. How can I best do that?

THERAPIST: I guess just be there if I need help.

TERI: O.K. I can do that. Please let me know as you think of other things I can do. [The therapist has now given the supervisor a form of permission to "be around." While this may not seem like much, it is the beginning of a change in relationship. The supervisor can now use phrases such as, "How's it going? Is there anything you need?" and the therapist is more likely to interpret the supervisor's presence as a positive thing rather than a threat. The best supervision happens during these impromptu moments; what I call "hallway supervision."]

Even the therapists who remained struggled with this transition. While they were more comfortable with the questions and were energized by the new way of thinking, they frequently did not have answers and were not yet comfortable with this feeling of not knowing. They had never thought about treatment from the clients' view point nor had they ever considered the value of such an approach. My questions such as, "What would your clients say was helpful about group?" or "What would your client say is most important to him?" challenged the fundamental concepts about whose opinion matters the most in the therapeutic relationship. These questions also gently taught the therapists that they were not an expert on the clients themselves, only on the process of change. However, the therapists soon discovered that it was the answers to these difficult questions that held the keys to discovering the most effective paths during client interactions.

Creating a culture of accountability and openness was the most important aspect of this transition. Most of our scheduled clinical interactions (i.e., group sessions) were done on Tuesdays, Wednesdays, and Thursdays, so I began to seek out the therapists after they finished their sessions and retreated to their offices to complete their paperwork before leaving for the day. It was common for me to casually appear in the evenings and to ask as unobtrusively as possible from the doorway, "So, how was group?" My question was intentionally vague as well as compassionate, as I hoped to begin a dialogue with the staff and create a safe environment in which they could explore their clinical work or gain some professional emotional support. As we talked, other staff members became curious about our conversations and would join us.

It was in these impromptu moments that the therapists first began to expose their uncertainty, mention their frustrations with clients' apparent lack of progress, and first become open to new ideas for ways to view and approach clients. As a way to reinforce this newly formed norm, I even telephoned the therapists when I was unable to be in the office in the evenings, playfully asking them, "How was group?" The casual debriefing of the clinical aspects of the day became part of our routine, and the therapists began to gather spontaneously in my office expecting time in the evenings together before going home. It is a tradition that continues to this day at the agency and serves several important roles including providing a time in which staff can leave the frustrations of the day behind, a place for learning from one another, and an opportunity that I as a supervisor can hear possible needed areas of learning for individual therapists or the team as a whole. Here is an example of this solution-focused debriefing at the end of the day:

> TERI: So what would be helpful to talk about tonight?
>
> THERAPIST 1: I have something...I had to take Joe out of group tonight. He wasn't working on anything. Why is he here, anyway? [looking at therapist 2 since she is the client's primary counselor]
>
> THERAPIST 2: Well there is really a lot going on that he needs to work on...
>
> TERI: So without going into all the history right now, what let you know that pulling Joe out of group was a good idea?
>
> THERAPIST 1: He was much more talkative one-on-one.
>
> TERI: Good! So were you able to get a better sense of why he came tonight and what he wanted?
>
> THERAPIST 1: Yeah, I guess so. He said he had court today, and he was really upset about it.
>
> TERI: Wow! And he came to group anyway! That's impressive.
>
> THERAPIST 2: Yeah, he is really committed to getting his children back. I didn't know he had court today. No wonder he had a rough time.
>
> TERI: Did you end up having Joe go back into group, or what did you ultimately decide was best for tonight?
>
> THERAPIST 1: Yes, he agreed to participate more.
>
> TERI: Looking back, was it a good decision?
>
> THERAPIST 1: I guess so. He was still really quiet.
>
> TERI: How about the rest of the group members. What let you know that pulling Joe and then allowing him to return was a good decision for everyone else?
>
> THERAPIST 1: I really don't think they were very bothered by Joe.
>
> TERI: What let you know?
>
> THERAPIST 1: They were talking about really meaningful stuff and seemed focused on their own things. [It is important for the supervisor to take note here that Joe's behavior did not appear to have a negative impact on the group norms. This may be something for therapist 1's individual supervision.

The therapist could possibly help him to explore alternative ways to measure if a client is benefiting from group other than vocal participation. Alternative ways might increase the therapist's curiosity about what is going on with the client rather than responding out of frustration, questioning why the client was even there. It is important that the therapist come to believe that every client who shows up only does so because there is something very important that he/she wants. This leads to a curious stance rather than a frustrated stance.]

TERI: Good. It sounds like you handled it well. Is there anything else that we need to do to help Joe?

THERAPIST 2: I'll call him tomorrow and touch base with him.

In time, therapists shared with me that this processing at the end of the day led them to begin to question themselves in a fashion similar to what I had done in the past and continue to this day. One therapist even told me that she and other therapists would linger behind in the parking lot after we left and continue the questions; frustrated by the lack of answers to the questions, but intrigued by the power of the exploration. She went on to say that during this transition, she had had countless "arguments" with me in her mind as she tried to discredit this new way of thinking, but that I somehow always "won the arguments" even though I had no idea of my involvement in her internal battle.

Once the therapists became open to thinking from the clients' point of view, and once they became comfortable exploring areas of possible growth, they became curious as to how I would handle difficult situations. Initially it was from a place of challenge and then it gradually changed to genuine curiosity. For example, during a supervision session with one of the therapists, I asked her what was most important to the client she was discussing and how the client wanted his life to be. I could tell that the therapist was becoming frustrated with my line of questioning and would much rather that I remained focused on her well-intentioned group lecture. Despite the growing tension, I gently pressed on, asking her what mattered most to her client. She then said in exasperation, "Oh, I don't know! I didn't ask. What would you have done?" Although I wasn't convinced that she really wanted to know, it was the first time she had ever blatantly asked me for a suggestion, so I took the opportunity. I then told her about a seemingly unusual intervention called the miracle question and explained how this question held the power to suspend a client's disbelief and tap into a powerfully creative part of the client's way of thinking. I went on to explain that by asking this question, the client then becomes the expert and we as professionals can then discover what truly matters and therefore motivates the client for change. The therapist then responded with why she didn't think such a question could ever work, how stupid the intervention was, and so forth. I agreed that maybe she was correct in this case and let the matter drop. In a subsequent supervision session, this therapist disclosed that she had actually tried the miracle question (admittedly just to prove me wrong), and that she had been pleasantly surprised by the response. As the therapist explored the outcome of the intervention and what she learned, other therapists began to hear about the "crazy question" and others became curious. It was through interactions similar to this that all of the solution-focused interventions were introduced to the therapists and they began to experiment with scales, compliments, difference questions, exceptions, and relationship questions. Although they couldn't have told anyone the names of the interventions, they had become curious and the new way of working with clients had taken hold.

THERAPISTS' VIEWS

I asked the therapists I supervise to share their views on what difference they think solution-focused supervision makes. Here is what they said:

Therapist 1

What I have experienced with supervision with Teri is that there isn't the feeling of top down. It does feel like we walk together and that she is not only my supervisor but my peer who cares about my goals and aspirations and wants to do everything she can to nourish those goals. Teri understands that there are certain things where she has to make the ultimate decision, but for most things she asks the team for feedback and takes into consideration the feedback when making decisions that impact the team. The team she has created works as a team. Even when making vacation plans or arranging our schedules we take into consideration others' needs. She expects that each team member take responsibility and when needed, to ask co-workers for help and then if this doesn't work to go to her. She encourages us to work through things together. With Teri, if I make an error, I don't hesitate to go right to her because I know she will know I did not make the error on purpose and will sit down with me to figure out a solution rather than reacting to it.

My experience in supervision with non–solution-focused approaches was a feeling of division. I was definitely aware that my supervisor was my supervisor who made the decision for the team. It didn't feel like a collaboration. I felt more checked up on, and if I had done something wrong I wasn't sure the response I would get. I also never experienced a true team. It was more like each person worked individually and didn't take other team members into consideration much when making individual plans.

I love that our team is open about feedback and that we prevent cliques. It is refreshing to have everything out in the open so we can figure out as a team how we can make our team stronger.

Therapist 2

Working with a solution-focused supervisor has helped me explore and define my professional goals and what are "our team" goals. Supervision is weekly and quarterly as a team. I have appreciated that I have unique talents that I bring to the agency and that my supervisor has embraced those strengths and allowed me to utilize those abilities more often. For example, I tend to lean more toward the administrative side of things in my job and I have been allowed to pursue more of that type of position and that keeps me intrigued and curious about learning more. Questions and accountability are a huge piece of this. It is both valuable and empowering. I believe this approach creates and promotes a strong staff that is dedicated, creative, and has mutual respect for ourselves and others. I know that our agency as well as myself have benefited from this type of supervision.

In working with past supervisors, supervision was random and I often felt like my supervisors' goals were my goals. At times I can remember that I wasn't really valued and that I may be replaced at any time. It definitely was not a relationship of mutual respect.

Therapist 3

It helps me take more responsibility for my role in the work environment. My SFT supervisor encourages me to look at what works and what doesn't work in my therapy sessions. It makes me really think about what I'm doing as a therapist. It's a good example of how I want to be with clients. I am encouraged to come up with goals in supervision. I am held responsible for my time/actions. Some SFT techniques have been used during supervision, and I am able to take what I have learned and apply it to clients. I have learned to hold people accountable through being held accountable in supervision.

Therapist 4

I believe that this type of supervision is helpful in regards to people's investment in their futures. When you can create a safe environment for people to explore how they want their futures to be, it allows a person to outwardly work with their supervisor on gaining skills to accomplish long term goals yet it also impacts the current workplace for the better more immediately.

There is a tremendous amount of peer accountability which I believe is so lacking in the workplace and this world. I think that learning how to hold people accountable helps create a better workplace and society. It is not as easy to blame one person if you are hearing the same thing over and over.

FURTHER DEVELOPMENTS

As the years went by the staff began to embrace solution-focused therapy, and we discussed the interventions and principles openly. We adopted the principles and practices of solution-focused therapy as the driving approach at all levels of our organization's functioning. We now hire only new staff members who are open to learning and practicing it. As a treatment program there are four primary areas in which we actively integrate it: (1) individual and group therapy sessions with clients, (2) case management and relationships with collateral professionals, (3) supervision, and (4) management.

As with supervision, there is a story to be told about how our staff has integrated solution-focused practices into each of our other areas of functioning. We have written about this in detail in another publication (Pichot & Dolan, 2003). I invite the reader to study this source as an example of how to transform all human relationships in an organization in a solution-focused direction.

DIFFERENCES WE HAVE NOTICED

It has now been ten years since I first started working at the Substance Abuse Counseling Program, and the differences to staff and clients have been incredible. When visiting therapists observe our treatment groups behind our one-way mirror, they frequently comment, "These don't seem like mandated clients." The clients readily identify things that are important to them and talk about these things in the treatment groups. When they do have difficulty identifying something that matters to them, we respectfully ask them to speak with a staff member privately to ensure that their time spent in group is beneficial and that we are really able to hear who they are and what they want.

While substance-related concerns bring all of our clients to us, the content of treatment is about parenting, self-sufficiency, hope, and relationships. Even when the subject of substances comes up, our focus is on how life will be once the substance abuse is resolved. One client stated, "This is not drug and alcohol treatment. This is a life group." While we still encounter our share of disgruntled clients, we are most often able to help those clients to shift away from their frustrations toward what they want and how we can help them achieve it. We don't see tears as a sign of success or a breakthrough as I was originally taught, but as a sign that the client is ready for something to be different. It is our role to hear what it is that they want to be different and to take action. This results in a strong sense of hope in both the clients and the staff members.

The change in the staff members has been marked. The therapists have an increased sense of purpose. They are less discouraged by client failure and are able to better focus on the change process rather than the events. For example, relapse is a normal part of recovery for substance abusing clients. In the past, therapists would see a positive urine screen as a sign of failure and discredit all of the other apparent work the client had done. Now, the therapists are able to see that clients are able to make and maintain changes even during times in which the client uses substances. This allows both the client and the therapist to maintain hope and to focus on what is working even when problems or setbacks occur. This decreases the risk of burnout for the staff, which is a common problem in substance abuse treatment programs.

In addition, the therapists are better able to view the treatment program in the context of referral sources and regulatory agencies. This allows them to have a sense of investment in the outcome and to drive the future direction of the program. During the past ten years we have had the opportunities to present solution-focused therapy on a national level as well as participate in several publications. Staff who have had an interest in these kinds of professional endeavors have benefited from these projects and have gained not only professional experience but a sense of empowerment and ownership in the program. The agency as a whole has benefited greatly from their ideas and enthusiasm. Staff turnover is very low, with the majority of staff members remaining employed five to ten years before leaving the agency for additional opportunities.

Some of the most unexpected differences have been within the larger agency itself. Other supervisors have noticed the changes in the Substance Abuse Counseling Program, and they have inquired about learning solution-focused concepts to use within the nursing programs. As a result, I have taught multiple classes on solution-focused therapy to the nurses and health educators, and they have in turn taken these concepts into their programs to use with their clients. I even received a phone call from the Food Inspection Program wondering how they could use these concepts when working with restaurants who are resistant to necessary change.

A wise person once said, "There is nothing more worthless than the answer to an unasked question" (author unknown). My experience has shown this to be very true. While it is tempting on occasion to share solution-focused therapy with other professionals out of enthusiasm, I have found that solution-focused therapy is best taught by simply quietly practicing the principles. I think this is the secret to successful supervision and organizational change. The changes in others from asking solution-focused questions about their work are quickly noticed and they become pervasive.

It has been an incredible journey over these past ten years as we integrated solution-focused therapy into our agency and into my heart. I have learned many valuable lessons from both my staff and clients. It is a journey of which I am truly blessed to have been a part. This journey has taught me that "not knowing" is something not of Which To Be Afraid Or Embarrassed, but to be embraced. For it is not a sign of naïveté, but of experience and trust.

READING 8

Youthcare Drenthe
Peter Stam

The province of Drenthe is located in northeastern part of the Netherlands. It has a population of 450,000. Our agency provides services to families with children ages 0 to 18. We have a total staff of 375 and provide services to 1600 clients per year. Families come to us with severe problems related to raising children with physical, psychiatric, social, and other serious family relationships difficulties. Our services include outpatient services, residential care, daycare, in-home treatment, foster care and addressing child safety concerns, parent training, and family dispute mediations.

BECOMING A SOLUTION-FOCUSED ORGANIZATION

Adopting a Paradigm Change

My educational background includes social work and economics. I also took a year-long course in the solution-focused treatment model about two years after I became the director of Youthcare Drenthe. What attracted me to the model was the shift in paradigm from the traditional view of the relationship between problem and solution. My practical experience in dealing with everyday problems that clients brought to our agency seemed to indicate that problems and solutions often were not related and did not seem connected to each other. I was attracted by the view of human beings which was very respectful in that people are viewed as having good intentions as well as having sufficient insight into their lives that they know what is good for them when they are respectfully asked. I specifically liked the pragmatic view that every family—even those with difficult children—behaved positively sometimes.

I was also acutely aware that all organizations change all the time and it is a leader's task to point in the desired direction of the change to maximize opportunities for both staff and client families to prosper and continuously evolve toward being their own agents of positive changes. Also, for families, I wanted families to gain a sense of the best possible life they can create on their own.

I believe that the task of a leader is not to manage, but to create an organization that will maximize client resources as well as that of the staff. I was very attracted to the model's simple rules:

- If it works, do more.
- If it does not work, stop. Do something different.

Swarm Phenomenon

In addition to the solution-focused model, another important influence in shaping my view of an organization comes from the swarm phenomenon, which provided me a good way to imagine the systemic nature of an organization (Kennedy, Eberhart, & Shi, 2001).

Swarms of birds have specific goals and fly simultaneously toward that goal, for example, seeking a particular location in France. At the same time, an accident to one bird will not detract the swarm from its goal. Swarms work according to these principles:

- They have a goal such as reaching a particular meadow in France.
- They share a sensibility; for birds this is related to the way they respond to magnetic fields.
- They share a few simple rules:
  - Pull away before you crash into one another.
  - Try to go about the same speed as your neighbor in the flock.
  - Try to move toward the center of the flock as you perceive it.

One can apply these principles and rules to organizing an agency in a solution-focused way. For our organization, the goal was very clear—build an organization that makes the most meaningful difference for our clients. (In order to know whether we are getting closer to this goal, we must conduct follow-up studies, which I will address later.) The sensibilities we as human beings can draw on are our capacities to communicate through language and respect and respond to the thoughts and reactions of others, as well as our related ability to scientifically measure outcomes and use that knowledge to improve the help we offer our families. Our rules for interacting together are drawn from the solution-focused model and are very pragmatic:

- If it works, do more.
- If it does not work, stop doing it and do something different.

We added one more of our own:

- If it works, teach it to others and learn it from others. (Stam, 2004)

These rules gave us all the necessary tools to launch our re-making of Youthcare Drenthe into a swarm of professionals all moving in the same direction.

My Vision for the Miracle Organization

At the European Brief Therapy Association conference in Amsterdam in 2004, I gave a plenary speech in which I defined a solution-focused organization as "an organizational context in which the most effective interventions will triumph over the less effective ones" (Stam, 2004). I continue to hold this view. About five years ago I set out to change the nature of Youthcare Drenthe into a sort of a miracle human service organization built around that vision. I realized that any time a new idea is introduced into any setting from the top, many staff immediately are suspicious that somehow management is de-valuing and negating what they have been doing and naturally become reluctant to go along with the management's vision of needed changes. Therefore, I knew I faced a very challenging task. I knew I would have to lead the organization toward my miracle vision, but I could not do it by "managing" my staff. I had to both provide energy and vision for change but, at the same time, provide respectful space and opportunity to involve everyone in the ongoing creation of the vision for this miracle organization that they could agree with and accept.

The first step was for me to decide how I was going to present the way clients are viewed in my vision of the miracle organization. Drawing on the solution-focused model, I decided to emphasize that:

- Each client has strengths, abilities, talents, and resources that can be used to arrive at workable solutions.

- However, at the time of our organization's contact with clients, many clients are struggling and unaware of all they bring to developing workable solutions for them.

- Therefore, in our work with clients, we should discover first of all what they are doing that is working and then:
  - If something they do works, encourage them to do more of it.
  - If something we are doing with clients is not working for them, stop, and do something different.

In my opinion, this way of viewing and talking about clients was a big departure from the way our staff traditionally had been viewing and interacting with our families. However, I also knew that nobody could object to these pragmatic statements. Not even the most dic-hard, problem-focused worker would claim to continue to do what does not work. So this pragmatism was a strong point from which to start because it could be offered to all staff without any objections.

As an administrator, I also knew I needed to have and present a clear view of my assumptions about our staff and their work, one that is consistent with the view I expected my staff to hold about the families they serve. The following captures what I assume about workers and other staff that I shared with them as part of my vision for our organization:

- *At this very moment every worker already makes a difference for their clients.* This means that I begin my work by acknowledging that every worker is doing whatever they are doing the best they know how, and they need to know as clearly as possible what of whatever they are doing is working so that they can do more of it.

- *However, not every worker makes their difference the same way.* This assumption emphasizes that while all workers make a difference, they do not all do it in the same way(s); each worker does so in his or her own unique way.

- *We all want our organization to be the best for our clients.* This assumption makes transparent a couple things. First, by saying "our organization," I make it clear that all staff work first of all on behalf of the organization and its goals versus any individual wishes that might or might not be realized through their work. Second, I am making it clear that the organization exists, first of all, for the good of the clients, not ourselves or any other organizations or political bodies that might have an interest in what we do with our clients.

- *In order to achieve the organization's goal of more effective interventions triumphing over less effective ones, there must be a discovering of what is working now and it should be spread throughout the entire organization.* This last assumption directs our attention to needing to teach it to others, again something so self evident that nobody could disagree.

The third aspect of my beginning vision of the miracle organization involved a view of the systemic working relationship with clients. In general, clients come to us because they have decided that they need help. Therefore, I believe, it is their right to define when this help is no longer needed. That is, the client—not the worker—should decide on what needs changing and the particulars of how to make that happen. By defining these parameters of change, clients choose the *direction* of the change that will take place. The caseworker's task, on the other hand, is to help clients regain their resources, figure out how to use them, and, if necessary expand them in order to achieve the desired solutions; that is, give assistance with the *process* of change. So I emphasized to my staff that in asking for help, clients mandate the caseworker only in the design of the process of change, while they keep responsibility for working out the direction of the changes.

Making the Vision Happen

Including Others   Once I knew how I wanted to articulate my vision for the organization, the next step was to start involving staff and create the same interactive process in the organization that I envisioned would happen between the organization and its clients. The first thing I did was to send out my statement of vision to program directors and other managers within Youthcare Drenthe, soliciting their opinions and reactions. They began contributing to shaping the vision by suggesting word changes and helping to make things more clear. Once we began working on the implications of the vision for conducting our programs, their suggestions became more substantive, detailed, and valuable. For example, we re-formulated our educational programs for staff. We re-worked how we deal with worker absence due to illness and how we respond to worker "trauma" and fatigue related to working with very difficult youngsters and their families. We also designed and established "learning groups" which have become a major contributor to making our miracle vision a living and breathing reality for every member of our organization.

Learning Groups   All staff now are randomly assigned to a learning group that meets every seven weeks. Each group is led by a leader trained especially for that role. Participants in learning groups do not have a leader who otherwise might supervise them. Originally, when they began, the groups focused on learning the solution-focused model of client and organizational change, its associated practices, and explored and designed how each task in the organization could be accomplished using these practices. As expected, there were a few employees who left the organization voluntarily as this work and associated changes unfolded. These departures actually helped our change process become more efficient and effective. The learning group gave a place and motivation for people to meet and get to know each other because all staff were a meaningful part of defining the "what" and "how" of our organizational change. I could not have been more pleased because this meant we were developing a joint vision that was spreading to all parts of the organization with everyone's participation instead of the vision just being several slogans posted on the wall in the director's office. For myself, I had to keep thinking about how to trust the solution-focused process and let the vision come alive in the interactions of the staff working together, and not try to structure those interactions from the top down from the director's office.

The learning groups soon realized that they could benefit by our organization, inviting many leading trainers in the field of solution-focused therapy to our agency to teach us more about the practices. Through these trainings and the learning groups, all the staff learned the implications of the model for their daily work. They learned to speak the same language about clients and their working relationships in the organization. Since the learning groups were heterogeneous, being made up of staff from different programs and in different positions in these programs, they began quickly to translate good ideas about what works throughout all the programs and levels in the organization, from foster care to outpatient mental health to residential care to in-home services to parent training and so forth. Because of the learning groups, the staff started to look more and more like the swarm of the miracle organization that I originally envisioned.

Consequences   These changes had important consequences for our clients and our staff. Regarding clients, the average treatment time per case has been reduced 20 percent. With our greater emphasis on exploring and drawing on client resources and developing family-based solutions, we are seeing a reduction in the need for residential care. We also are noticing that clients are making fewer complaints about our workers and services. For example, in 2003, we received 45 complaints; in 2004 that number was down to 17. Regarding staff, we are observing less resistance and more cooperation in the worker/client relationship. We see this both in our outpatient treatment, in-home service, and residential programs. Workers report more satisfaction in working with clients and there is a reduction in sick leaves taken by workers

Role of the Director

Looking back on how far we have come and how it happened, I can see five essential responsibilities for a director of a solution-focused organization:

1.   **Attending to Context** Every organization performs in a context and needs the ability to intelligently adapt to the cultural, political, and financial environment. Neglecting this context would severely harm the organization and can even lead to its downfall. The basic responsibility here is that the organization is well managed financially so that employees do not have to worry about stability and security in their workplace. The director must know the organization's context and take the lead in dealing with external systems to create the needed stability. In addition, the director must also lead in fostering relationships among staff that reflect the paradigm shift and so increase the meaningfulness of their work and contributions to the organization, as well as take steps to demonstrate appreciation and celebrate these contributions.

2.   **Taking a Systemic Approach to Clients and Staff** In order to activate and reactivate the client's resources and avoid the organization giving unnecessary services to clients (which may in fact risk damaging the client's own resources), the director should take the lead in redrawing boundaries away from traditional, "expert" ways of working for clients. For example, family conferences that include all important members of the client's support network, as the client defines these, are a way of redrawing boundaries for finding solutions that fits the new paradigm. We found changing to this way of practice enhanced client motivation and client-driven solutions. So we continued to do and find new ways to expand it because "if it works, continue to do it and do more of it." The learning groups are an example of the same systemic approach to involving staff.

3.   **Building a Miracle Vision** If a director dares to ask staff to ask the miracle question of clients, that director should be willing to build a demand-driven organization. In most settings, human service organizations decide what kind of services they will offer to clients. In other words, clients must adapt to what the organizations decide to offer, rather than services adapting to what the clients need and would find useful. I believe it should be the other way around. From an organizational leadership point of

view, I believe this is the most challenging part of shifting to the new paradigm. However, it is so important that I now include it as part of my definition of a solution-focused organization; namely, a *demand-driven organization providing only the help that supports clients in reaching their own solutions—and not anything more than that.* Organizational principles and procedures for supervision, financing and documentation of any help offered are of secondary importance to this defining principle that requires staff to always be learning from clients what would be useful to them. The client does not need to adapt to the organization, but the organization must adapt to the client (Stam, 2004).

4. **Teaching Solution Talk** If you want the organization to be solution-focused, a leader must make provision to teach all staff the solution talk needed to make the vision a reality. Teaching everyone in the organization these skills also means teaching the importance of language structures and the necessary systemic knowledge described above.

5. **Measuring Outcomes** There is an increasing tendency to measure outcome in the field of service providers. This reflects the trend of developing and moving the field toward using evidence-based programs such as Functional Family Therapy and Parent Management Training of Oregon. I agree that measuring outcomes is necessary to improving programs, and we too at Youthcare Drenthe have been measuring outcomes. Our organization is partnering with the Universities of Utrecht, Nijmegen, & Groningen in designing and conducting outcome studies so there is and will continue to be ongoing independent, external evaluation of Youthcare Drenthe. We are using the Child Behavior Check List, the Youth Self Report form, and a Teachers Report Form to measure problem reduction in children and youth. We also are gathering stress reduction data from children and parents using other standardized tools. And, finally, we use a tool developed between clients and university researchers to measure client satisfaction with our services. The results so far have been encouraging and we review these in our learning groups to make decisions about services. For example, we have discovered that parenting skills exercises and rehearsals with families produce better results than just talking about new parenting skills. Our most recent study indicates that we are becoming more efficient. In 2005 we delivered services to 1570 families with the same number of workers (260) that it took to serve 1050 families in 2002. At the same time, our data indicate our outcomes have improved over the same period. Besides looking at outcomes at the program level, I believe we also have to examine outcomes at the level of the individual worker. This is very important for assuring treatment integrity for clients across our organization's many workers. Although this can be a delicate subject with workers, I believe workers should be comparing their work to that of other workers doing the same work. Doing this will add to our knowledge of what works best with families and ensure that workers continue to develop the skills that are most useful to families. We have made the decision to use our learning groups for this purpose. Workers will bring audio and video tapes (with signed permissions) of their interactions with the families they serve. Our idea is to play these tapes in the learning groups and pay attention to which clients make progress, what seems to be most useful to clients, and what the worker needs to do more of and do differently in interaction with future families. Also, by comparing the recordings of a worker from one year to the next, we will have a useful way to document a worker's gains in skills and inspire other workers to keep building their skills. I believe doing this in the context of cooperative learning groups in the context of a solution-focused organization that is always looking for what is most useful to families should go a

long way toward reducing any anxiety workers may feel at the prospect of having their work viewed carefully by their colleagues.

CONCLUSION

To summarize, on a level of an individual client family at Youthcare Drenthe, we work with the motto "if it works, do more." At that level, the motto has been quite valid and useful. On the level of our organization, however, my experience in leading us toward doing all our work as a solution-focused organization leads me to want to change the motto to "if it works *better*, do more." I have learned it is most useful to always stretch for better ways of doing things. A humble metaphor expresses it well: One can drink milk out of a bucket and because it works, one could go on this way forever. However, I now prefer that I, and my staff, look around for an opportunity to find a glass and discover this works even better as a way to drink milk.

15

Theoretical Implications

In fact, we are such inveterate meaning-makers that when we do not
have an explanation for something, we make one up.
(SAARI, 1991, P. 14)

I thought I was depressed, but after my visits to Brief Family Therapy
Center, I came to realize that I was only having blue spells.
(A FORMER CLIENT)

So whether the client discovers, on one hand, abilities and positive
qualities or, on the other hand, disabilities and pathology, he or she has
been intimately involved in co-constructing this new common ground.
(MCGEE, DEL VENTO, & BAVELAS, 2005, P. 381)

If you are like most people, you want to understand, and will make great
efforts to figure out, the *meaning* of life's events. If an event is important to
you, you reflect on it, put your impressions into words, and talk about it with
other people. To do so is our most obvious and unique human characteristic
(Mead, 1934).

Clients are no different. They want to know the meaning of what is
happening in their lives. Immersed in a culture that emphasizes problem-solving
thinking, clients typically want to talk to their practitioners about *why* they are
having their problems. They regularly seek the meaning of their problems in
supposed causes, in the same way people in Western societies make sense out of
diseases by trying to discover the agents that give rise to them. Ah Yan, whose
case was presented in Chapters 5 through 8, is an example. When she first told
Peter about her panicky feelings, her question was: "Why? Why is this?" She told
him, "I gotta figure out what's wrong with me."

As you may recall from Chapters 3 and 10, and as demonstrated by
the dialogues throughout this book, in solution building with clients, we never
ask why. We do not ask the why of client goals or exceptions, much less of their

problems. Experience has taught us that asking why is not useful. Clients build solutions more efficiently when practitioners do not encourage them to analyze why they have problems and why solutions might work. Similarly, it is generally not useful for practitioners to try to figure out why clients have their problems. Clients build solutions more efficiently if practitioners remain not knowing toward client problems, goals, and exceptions and deemphasize problem assessment. Regardless of whether it is useful, however, clients and practitioners alike keep trying to figure out the meaning of their experiences.

In Chapter 1, two points may have struck you as odd. First, we indicated that solution-focused procedures were mainly developed inductively by observing client-practitioner conversations and paying attention to what seemed to be useful. They were not deduced from existing theory. Second, we noted Steve de Shazer's comment that although he knows solution-focused procedures are useful, he does not know why. Although our observations must remain tentative, this chapter reflects on the meaning of what happens in the solution-building process and what that may teach us about how best to go about helping others.

SHIFTS IN CLIENT PERCEPTIONS AND DEFINITIONS

Observers at Brief Family Therapy Center noticed that as clients talked about their problems and how to solve them, their perceptions of the meaning of both problems and possible solutions shifted regularly. Some clients came in with several problems and were not sure about which was their real or underlying problem. Over time, their focus became clearer. Clients would begin to describe the characteristics of their problems in new ways. The observers noticed consistently that over the course of several sessions, or even during just one session, clients would redefine their problems.

Ah Yan's problem definitions offer a good example. At the beginning of her first session, she viewed her problem—feeling panicky—in biological and psychological terms. She said she thought she was crazy, noticed her hair falling out, and sought out a physician to discover the causes through medical testing. The tests were inconclusive. Peter began a conversation with her about what she wanted to have different. He also worked with her on developing a vision of an alternative future and explored whether there were any exception times that resembled parts of her miracle picture. She was able to describe exceptions that were random, not deliberate, and she emerged from this conversation with a vague definition of her problem.

> Ah ... maybe ... I don't know.... I can't figure it out—what's wrong with me. I don't know what to do.... I got all these feelings.... I gotta figure out what's wrong with me.

In their second session, as Ah Yan and Peter talked about what was better, Ah Yan identified several successes. She indicated that by leaving a dance for a short time, she had been able to recompose herself when she felt her panicky feelings coming on. She implied her problem might be tied to situations with a lot of people, where it is too stuffy. This description is more circumscribed than the all-encompassing definition of her problem in the first session. As Ah Yan and Peter explored additional exceptions, she was able to describe several successes and strategies she used to brush her problem off. In exploring these successes and what she might be doing to make them happen, Ah Yan shifted her focus from figuring out the causes of her panicky feelings to figuring out more strategies she could use to keep the problem under control. Toward the end of the second session, in discussing the next steps, she again reshaped her perspective: She told Peter she needed to find more ways to let her children "learn how to do things by themselves." Having started with a biological and psychological definition, Ah Yan worked her way toward a more interpersonal problem definition by the end of the session.

> Yeah, I felt alone. I felt trapped. I don't know. I just felt so lonely, and now that I'm talking—like, my sister goes, "I heard that you didn't feel good," and she says, "I told mom you worry too much. You think too much." You know, now that I talk to people, it's like I can talk to anybody, you know . . . .
>
> Yeah, it's different [now]. I'm always listening and never talking; maybe that's my problem too: I never talk, always keeping everything inside. And, now, I'm starting [to talk], . . . and it kind of makes me [think], "Oh, someone's listening to me." It makes me feel better.

In addition, by the end of the second session, she was coming to define herself as an important part of the problem. She was giving up the idea that the problem was some mysterious biological or psychological factor outside of her control. She said:

- You know, it's like I'm trying to figure out if I can control it, if it's just me.
- Now I'm noticing I can control it if I want.
- I feel like it's really me that's making myself feel like this. I feel it's me.

This dramatic shift in problem definition occurred in the context of conversations about several other matters: what Ah Yan wanted to have different, the details of her miracle picture, occasions in her present life that resemble her miracle picture, what was better by the time of the second session, and the strengths she used to make her successes happen. As she and Peter talked about these other topics, her definitions of her problem shifted.

These different areas of conversation between Peter and Ah Yan are equally important for successful solution building. As Ah Yan's definition of her problems shifted, so did her perceptions and definitions of what she wanted to be different, her successes, and her strengths. By reviewing the dialogues with this in mind, these shifts become apparent. First, regarding what she wanted, Ah Yan began by saying she wanted relief from her panicky feelings. By the second session, however, her attention had shifted to strategies that worked for her (such as leaving a stuffy place for a break, rolling down the window in a moving car, and deep breathing), to finding more ways to "let my kids go a little bit," and to talking more to others about what is going on inside of her. Second, regarding her successes and strengths, she first talked about feelings of powerlessness.

> Yeah, last year for a while I thought I was crazy or something. I was gonna get up and get out of bed and my hair is falling out and, like, when I took a shower, there's a bunch of hair in my hand. And I went to the doctor and said: "Doctor, why? Why is this?" And they did tests, lots of tests.

However, by the end of her first session she was talking very differently. Her sense of competency and strength was building. When asked to scale her level of confidence about finding a solution, she chose 10 and commented, "I'm not gonna stop until I'm all the way." In her second session, she said: "I read that book: 'Who's in charge, you or your mind?' ... *I am.*" With further conversation, she was able to describe the successes and strengths that warranted her growing sense of competency and personal agency.

The same pattern of shifting perceptions and definitions occurs in the conversations between Insoo and the Williams family. Reread those dialogues and trace the shifts in perceptions and definitions.

In some cases, the shifts in clients' perceptions are dramatic and easy to identify (de Shazer, 1991). In others, they are more subtle and difficult to identify. However, if you carefully review what clients say over the course of their solution-building conversations, you will always find examples of these shifts (Berg & De Jong, 1996). Note that your skill as a solution-building interviewer depends on learning to listen for these shifts and inviting your clients to explore them as they occur.

SOCIAL CONSTRUCTIONISM

Client perceptions and definitions shift in the solution-building process. How can we make sense of this observation?

The theoretical perspective that, we believe, comes closest to accounting for these shifts is social constructionism (Cantwell & Holmes, 1994; Gergen, 1985, 1999; Goolishian & Anderson, 1991; Laird, 1993; Parton & O'Byrne, 2000). This perspective maintains that individuals' sense of what is real—including their sense of the nature of their problems, competencies, and possible solutions—is constructed in interaction with others as they go through life. People *make meanings* as they interact with others. Many authors (for example, Berger & Luckmann, 1966; Gergen & Kaye, 1992; Hoffman, 1990; Mead, 1934) have pointed out that, as human beings, we are always trying to figure out the meaning of our experiences. "We are such inveterate meaning-makers that when we do not have an explanation for something, we make one up" (Saari, 1991, p. 14). In the conversations between Ah Yan and Peter and between Insoo and the Williams family, the clients' meaning-making tendencies showed again and again. For example, reflecting on her problem of feeling panicky, Ah Yan asked, "Why?

Why is this?" She told Peter, "I gotta figure out what's wrong with me." She also reshaped meanings for her problems, competencies, and solutions as she conversed with others, including her husband, her sister-in-law, and Peter.

What are the theoretical implications of the observation that client perceptions and definitions, or meanings, shift over time and in interaction with others? Answering this question is an enormous undertaking; the question cuts across the fields of literary interpretation, philosophy, social sciences, and humanities. Central to any answer is an understanding of language, the means by which human beings converse. Theoretical writings are beginning to give more attention to the role of language in the helping or therapeutic process. For example, de Shazer (1991, 1994), de Shazer et al. (in press), Gergen (1999), and Miller (1997) work with the linguistic insights of philosophers including Derrida, Foucault, and Wittgenstein to analyze the interrelationships among the use of language, client meanings, and solutions in the therapeutic process. Also relevant here is the work of McGee, Del Vento, and Bavelas (2005) who, through communication analysis, generate several theoretical propositions about how the use of language by therapists in solution-focused conversations leads both therapists and clients to coconstruct clients as their own agents of the unfolding positive changes in their lives.

Social constructionists emphasize that shifts in client perceptions and definitions occur in contexts—that is, in communities. Consequently, meaning-making is not entirely an individual matter in which clients develop private meanings (including solutions) without regard to others. Instead, individuals always live in ethnic, family, national, socioeconomic, and religious contexts. They reshape meanings under the influence of the communities in which they live. In solution building, relationship questions provide a useful way in which the interviewer can explore clients' perceptions of their contexts.

Besides emphasizing that clients must develop their individual meanings in the context of community, social constructionists draw attention to the wide diversity of communities from which clients come. Clients' backgrounds reflect different racial groupings, ethnicities, nationalities, socioeconomic statuses, and so forth. Individual clients reflect the multiple realities of these communities.

What are the implications of social constructionists' views for practitioners in the helping professions? The practitioner is a collaborative partner as clients reshape their meanings and create more satisfying and productive lives. As Goolishian and Anderson (1991, p. 7) write, working with clients becomes:

> a collaborative and egalitarian process as opposed to a hierarchical and expert process. The therapist's expertise is to be "in" conversation with the expertise of the client. The therapist now becomes the learner to be informed, rather than a technical expert who knows.

As you begin to understand the social constructionist view of definitions of reality and how people acquire these definitions, you will see how these theoretical ideas make sense of the usefulness of solution-building procedures, which encourage clients to explore their definitions of reality (problems, miracles, successes, strengths, and solutions) as they struggle to create more satisfying and productive lives.

SHIFTING PARADIGMS

The recognition that client perceptions and definitions shift and that there are multiple definitions of reality among clients poses a challenge to the assumptions of a scientifically based, problem-solving approach to working with clients. If clients' definitions of their problems and solutions change over time and in collaborative interaction with others, how can those problems be real in an objective, universal, and scientifically knowable sense? As explained in Chapter 1, the scientific approach to problem solving rests on the assumption that client problems are objectively real and universally the same, much like a stomach tumor or air pollution. It also implies that client problems are as accessible to the systematic observations of the scientist as are the human kidneys or the planets. The problems that Insoo and the Williams family worked on and those that Ah Yan and Peter worked on do not seem to be real in that sense.

Once you start to think of clients' problems as a function of their current definitions of reality rather than as something that is objectively knowable, you must shed the role of expert about clients' problems and solutions. To quote Goolishian and Anderson (1991) again, "the therapist now becomes the learner to be informed, rather than a technical expert who knows."

As seen in Chapter 1, reliance on scientific expertise is one of two fundamental aspects of the problem-solving approach to working with clients. The other is a problem-solving structure that assumes a necessary connection between a problem and its solution, as in modern medicine, where it is believed a disease and its treatment are necessarily linked. This assumption underlies the field's emphasis on assessing problems before making interventions.

This second assumption does not fit well with the observation that clients have multiple and changing definitions of reality, nor does it fit with BFTC practitioners' finding that different clients build very different solutions to what seem to be the same problems. Finally, it does not fit with outcome data on this topic that we have collected.

Outcome Data

Practitioners at BFTC have observed that clients' answers to the miracle question sometimes seem logically connected to their problems but at other times are completely unrelated. In later sessions, when clients begin to talk about what is going better in their lives and how they made those things happen, these successes and strengths often have no apparent logical relationship with their problems (de Shazer, 1988, 1991, 1994). Many clients are as surprised about the solutions as any problem-solving practitioner might be. In this connection, de Shazer (1988, pp. 5–6) has written that clients' concept of solution often precedes a definition of problem. Having figured out a solution, the client will go back and define or redefine the problem to fit the solution. If correct, de Shazer's observation gives insight into part of the process by which people develop their sense of reality.

In solution building, the practitioner works in the same way with each client, regardless of what the client might say is the problem. However, if solution building can be regarded as an intervention with clients in traditional problem-solving terms and there is a necessary connection between problem and solution, then solution-building procedures should not work equally well with all client problems. To test this reasoning, we reviewed intermediate and final outcomes in terms of *DSM* diagnosis and client estimates of their problems.

DSM Diagnosis and Outcomes   Practitioners at BFTC have been trained in giving *DSM* diagnoses (diagnoses based on the American Psychiatric Association's *Diagnostic and Statistical Manual of Mental Disorders*), which they submit in order to receive third-party remuneration for services. Table 15.1 presents data from the 1992–1993 BFTC study for intermediate outcomes by diagnosis, and Table 15.2 gives the data for final outcomes by diagnosis. Diagnoses are given according to the revised third edition of *DSM* (*DSM–III–R*), which was current at the time the diagnoses were given. Only diagnoses for which there are more than five cases are reported. The names of the diagnoses corresponding to the *DSM* numeric code in Tables 15.1 and 15.2 are as follows: 300.40, Dysthymia; 309.00, Adjustment Disorder (AD) with Depressed Mood; 309.23, AD with Work Inhibition; 309.24, AD with Anxious Mood; 309.28, AD with Mixed Emotional Features; 309.30, AD with Disturbance of Conduct; 309.40, AD with Mixed Disturbance of Emotions and Conduct; 313.81, Oppositional Defiant Disorder; and 314.01, Attention-Deficit Hyperactivity Disorder.

Looking first at intermediate outcomes, the data in Table 15.1 indicate a majority of clients receiving solution-building services showed improvement over the course of their services. The percentage of outcomes with no progress was highest for clients with diagnoses of Adjustment Disorder with Anxious Mood and Attention-Deficit Hyperactivity Disorder.

Table 15.2 on final outcomes by diagnoses indicates the same result: Diagnosis does little to predict outcome. The percentage of outcomes with no progress was somewhat higher for clients with diagnoses of Dysthymia (note the small number of cases) and Oppositional Defiant Disorder.

Clients' Self-Reported Problems and Outcomes   We also gave clients an extensive checklist of problems when they made their first visit to BFTC. Before they began their first session, they were asked to indicate each of the "problems that you feel apply to you." Among the problems on the list were depression, suicidal thoughts, eating disorder, job-related problems, parent-child conflict, family violence, alcohol/other drug abuse, sexual abuse, death of a loved one, self-esteem problems, and blended-family issues. We analyzed the data for possible relationships between any of these self-assessed client problems and our measurements of intermediate and final outcomes.

Table 15.3 presents a summary of these data. We have calculated a success rate on intermediate outcome and final outcome for each type of client problem for which we have more than five cases. The success rate for intermediate outcome is a combination of the categories "significant progress" and "moderate

T A B L E 15.1 Intermediate Outcome (I.O.) by *DSM-III-R* Diagnosis*

I.O.	300.40	309.00	309.23	309.24	309.28	309.40	313.81	314.01	Total
Significant progress	27%	20%	17%	14%	29%	8%	33%	6%	20%
Moderate progress	46%	80%	50%	43%	46%	62%	42%	47%	51%
No progress	27%		33%	43%	25%	31%	25%	47%	29%
Number of cases	11	10	6	7	24	13	12	17	100

*In Tables 15.1 through 15.3, percentages are rounded to nearest whole percent.

T A B L E 15.2 Final Outcome (F.O.) by *DSM-III-R* Diagnosis

F.O.	300.40	309.00	309.24	309.28	309.30	309.40	313.81	314.01	Total
Goal met	33%	67%	14%	48%	33%	53%	18%	31%	39%
Some progress	17%		71%	35%	50%	40%	45%	54%	40%
No progress	50%	33%	14%	17%	17%	7%	36%	15%	21%
Number of cases	6	6	7	23	6	15	11	13	87

progress." The success rate for final outcome is a combination of "goal met" and "some progress."

These data suggest that solution building with clients is consistently success-ful, regardless of the client's problems.[1] With the exception of panic attacks on final outcome, Table 15.3 indicates success rates between 60 and 89 percent.

The data on clients' estimates of their own problems and those on practitioner diagnosis and outcomes do not support the theory of a necessary connection between problem and solution. It does not appear from these data that clients need specialized interventions based on professional assessments in order to make progress. In solution building, clients have successful outcomes when exposed to a uniform set of procedures, without regard for any purported connection between problem and solution.[2]

These findings have some important implications. First, they suggest that practitioner preparation could be greatly simplified. Currently the helping professions expend considerable resources on conceptualizing problems, devising problem-assessment procedures and instruments, developing specialized interventions, and teaching that content to aspiring practitioners. Our findings suggest they could focus instead on observing more carefully how clients use personal strengths and environmental resources to make changes happen and teaching new practitioners how to respect and foster self-determined change in clients. This conclusion refers back to certain recommendations arising from the empowerment and strengths perspective cited in Chapter 1 (Rappaport, 1981, 1990; Saleebey, 2007).

Second, if solution-building procedures are equally effective across different problems, then learning to become an effective practitioner need not be such a

T A B L E 15.3 Success Rates on Intermediate (I.O.) and Final (F.O.) Outcomes for Different Types of Client Problems

Type of Problem	I.O. Success Rate	F.O. Success Rate
Depression	75% (79)*	75% (60)
Suicidal thoughts	74% (34)	79% (19)
Anxiety	72% (50)	74% (42)
Panic attacks	80% (10)	50% (10)
Sleep problems	75% (59)	76% (49)
Eating disorder	80% (40)	73% (26)
Withdrawn behavior	67% (58)	80% (39)
Health problems	72% (18)	60% (10)
Job-related problems	84% (19)	80% (15)
Financial concerns	74% (43)	74% (31)
Parent-child conflict	71% (35)	76% (25)
Communication problems	65% (57)	76% (46)
Family violence (actual or threatened)	60% (20)	77% (13)
Sexual abuse	64% (11)	75% (8)
Physical abuse	67% (12)	89% (9)
Alcohol/other drug abuse	67% (12)	63% (8)
Marital/relationship problems	76% (45)	81% (47)
Sexual problems	72% (21)	89% (18)
Death of a loved one	72% (18)	79% (14)
Self-esteem problems	77% (48)	73% (40)
Brother/sister problems	78% (36)	78% (31)
Blended-family issues	74% (27)	71% (21)

*Figures in parentheses indicate the number of clients who indicated having the particular problem. The total number of cases is 141 for I.O. and 136 for F.O.

complex undertaking. If you decide to become proficient in the use of solution-building skills, you can expect to be consistently useful to clients, regardless of the problems they bring to you.

SHIFTING PERCEPTIONS AND DEFINITIONS
AS A CLIENT STRENGTH

Our observations and outcome data indicate that when they come to us for professional assistance, our clients are teaching us some important things about the nature of their humanity and, therefore, how we can best work with them.

They teach us that as they encounter life's struggles, other people, and a variety of experiences, they regularly reflect on these encounters. In reflecting, they are continuously conceptualizing and organizing their experiences through their capacities for abstract thought and language. They create interpretations and frames of reference that make sense out of what they experience.

People create meanings or definitions of reality through their use of words and talking to one another. This does not imply that their experiences and definitions are not real. Several authors (Berger & Luckmann, 1966; Watzlawick, 1984) have emphasized that definitions of reality, although in a certain sense constructed or invented, are completely real to the person. For example, when Ah Yan was experiencing nervousness, shortness of breath, and physical tremors, her problem of panic was fully real to her. Ten days later, her sense that she was in charge of her problem ("I can control it if I want") was no less real. As Efran, Lukens, and Lukens (1988, p. 33) put it, "An invented reality—once it has been invented—is as real and solid as any other." Clients' capacity to reshape and shift their perceptions and definitions of reality is a critically important resource in their efforts to deal with their problems.

Clients' capacity to change is connected to their ability to see things differently. As George Kelly, an early constructivist practitioner, wrote, "There is nothing so obvious that its appearance is not altered when it is seen in a different light. . . . *Whatever exists can be reconstrued*" (cited in Efran, Lukens, & Lukens, 1988, p. 32). Gladys's efforts to create a better life for herself and her children are connected to her ability to expand her perception of her own childhood abuse from something ugly and despicable to something that could teach her how she wanted to treat her own children. Ah Yan's ability to make differences in her life is connected to her capacity to shift her perception of her panicky feelings from a sense of victimization ("I don't know . . . . I can't figure it out—what's wrong with me") to a growing sense of power ("Now I'm noticing I can control it if I want").

These shifts in client perceptions and definitions of reality, which are a part of clients' solution building, occur most readily in conversations about alternative futures and useful exceptions. Solutions depend more on clients' capacity to develop and expand their definitions of what they want and how to make that happen than on scientific problem definition, technical assessment, and professional intervention. If that is so, the role for you as a practitioner is to be what Anderson and Goolishian (1992) call a conversational artist. By using your skills to sustain purposeful conversations, you allow clients to develop the expanded perceptions and definitions they need to live more satisfying and productive lives. Strictly speaking, practitioners do not empower clients or construct alternative meanings for them. Only clients can do that for themselves. However, practitioners can assume and respect clients' competencies and artfully converse with clients so they can create more of what they want in their lives (Berg & De Jong, 1996).

In the end, believing is seeing. If you are to escape the longstanding belief in the field that client perceptions and definitions are not rich resources but instead signs of underlying problems and deficiencies that the practitioner must treat as well as sources of avoidance and resistance the practitioner must overcome, it will be through your experiences in solution building with clients. If your experiences are anything like ours, you will see clients build solutions you never could have envisioned or designed for them. You will see a Gladys transform past abuse into motivation to be a good mother, a family create a spaghetti fight to reestablish connection and commitment to one another, or a Jermaine recover from a horrific experience by listening to his wife's breathing during the night. If you remain patient and purposeful in your solution-building procedures, your clients will impress and amaze you with their resilience, creativity, and competence.

NOTES

1. Although, strictly speaking, we did not have a probability sample of a larger population in the BFTC study whose data we are reporting, we still ran tests of significance. We ran the Pearson chi-square test for the bivariate relationships in Table 15.3 and for the other relationships in the tables in Chapters 11, 12, and 15. None of the differences were found to be statistically significant.

2. Additional studies reveal the same lack of connection between problem and solution when using solution building with clients; see de Shazer & Isebaert (2003) and Lee, Sebold, & Uken (2003).

Appendix:
Solution-Building Tools

GOAL-FORMULATION PROTOCOL

Role Clarification

(Working with a team; team may interrupt with a question; break, then feedback.)

Problem Description

How can I help?

How is this a problem for you? (Get problem description; if more than one, which is most important to work on first?)

What have you tried? (Was it helpful?)

Goal Formulation

What would have to be different as a result of our meeting today for you to say that our talking was worthwhile?

Miracle Question

(Once asked, focus on *what will be different* when the miracle happens.)

Regarding client: What will you notice that's different? (What will be the first thing that you notice? What else?)

Regarding significant others: Who else will notice when the miracle happens?

What will he or she notice that is different about you? What else?

GOAL-FORMULATION PROTOCOL
(continued)

When he or she notices that, what will he or she do differently? What else?

When he or she does that, what will be different for you?

Moving toward a Solution

(Use when client can answer the miracle question.)

Suppose you were to pretend that the miracle happened. What would be the first small thing you would do?

How might that be helpful?

Or: What's it going to take for a part of the miracle to happen?

Is that something that could happen? If so, what makes you think so?

Ending

1. If the client is concrete and detailed in answer to the miracle question, give compliments and suggest: "In the next week, pick one day and pretend that the miracle has happened and look for what difference it makes."
2. If the client is *not* concrete and detailed in answer to the miracle question, give compliments and suggest: "Think about what's happening in your life that tells you that this problem can be solved. And I'll do some thinking too."

(If a second session is a possibility, you can ask the client to meet with you again to continue working on the problem.)

QUESTIONS FOR DEVELOPING WELL-FORMED GOALS

To the interviewer: When using these questions, remember that you most want to explore for the client's perception of *what will be different* when either the miracle happens or the problem is solved. Also remember that developing well-formed goals is hard work for clients. Be patient and persistent in asking the interview questions.

The Miracle Question

Suppose that, while you are sleeping tonight, a miracle happens. The miracle is that the problem which brought you here today is solved. Only you don't know that it is solved because you are asleep. What difference will you notice tomorrow morning that will tell you that a miracle has happened? What else will you notice?

Amplifying Around the Characteristics of Well-Formed Goals

Small   Wow! That sounds like a big miracle. What is the first small thing you would notice that would tell you that things were different?

What else would tell you that things were better?

Concrete, Behavioral, Specific   You say that the miracle is that you'd feel better. When you feel better, what might others notice different about you that would tell them that you feel better?

What might you do different when you feel better? What else?

Start of Something Different/Better   You say that the miracle is that you'd weigh 50 pounds less. OK, what will be different in your life when you lose that first pound? What else?

Presence of Something Different/Better   You say that, when the miracle happens, you'll fight less with the kids. What will you be doing *instead*?

QUESTIONS FOR DEVELOPING
WELL-FORMED GOALS
(continued)

Amplifying Around Perceptions of Significant Others

When the miracle happens, what differences will your husband (children, best friend, coworkers, teachers, etc.) notice? What differences will your husband notice about you? What else will they notice that's different?

Amplifying Around the Client's System of Relationships

When your husband (children, best friend, coworkers, teachers, etc.) notice _____ (the difference that the client mentions in answering the previous question), what will your husband (they) do differently? What else? And when he does that, what will you do? And when you do that, what else will be different?

Tips

If clients say "I don't know," say:

Suppose you did know. What would you say?

Or, go to relationship questions, for example:

Suppose I were to ask your husband (children, best friend, etc.), what would he (they) say?

If clients struggle with the questions or say they are tough, agree with them and say:

I'm asking you some tough questions; take your time.

If clients cannot work with the miracle question, work with questions phrased along the lines of "when the problem is solved."

When clients get unrealistic ("I'd win the lottery!"), just agree with them by saying:

That would be nice, wouldn't it.

If they persist, ask:

What do you think the chances are of that happening?

Or, ask:

What tells you that _____ could happen in your life?

QUESTIONS FOR DEVELOPING
WELL-FORMED GOALS
(continued)

When clients give you a concrete piece of the miracle picture or potential solution (for example, "When the miracle happens, I guess I'd be taking more walks"), be sure to build by asking, for example:

> What's different for you when you take more walks? (and continue to build from that answer)

Part of respecting the client's perceptions is to respect the words that they use for their perceptions and adopt them in your interview questions. Thus, the preceding question picks up on the client's reference to taking more walks.

VERY IMPORTANT: If, despite your best efforts, clients are unable to work with the miracle question or define how things will be different when the problem is solved, ask:

> How do you know this problem can be solved?

Goal Formulation in Later Sessions

Work from the scaling question about progress:

> On a scale of 0 to 10, where 0 is where you were at when we began working together, and 10 means that the problem is solved (or the miracle happens), where are you at today?

> OK, so you're at a 5. What is happening in your life that tells you that you are a 5?

> So when you move up just a bit, say from 5 to 6, what will be different in your life that will tell you that you are a 6? What else? What will be different when you move on to a 7?

Thereafter, amplify just as you would for the miracle question, for example, around significant others. For example:

> When you move up to a 6, what will your best friend notice that will tell her or him that you are doing just that much better? What else?

PROTOCOL FOR FORMULATING
FEEDBACK TO CLIENTS

Finding the Bottom Line

Does the client want something? What is it?

Is there a well-formed goal? What is it?

Are there exceptions? What are they?

If yes, are they deliberate or random exceptions?

The Feedback

Compliments

Bridging Statement

Suggestion(s) (Based on the client meanings coconstructed in the interview)

COMMON MESSAGES
(END-OF-SESSION FEEDBACK)

When Clients Do Not Perceive a Problem and
Do Not Want Anything

Here is an example of a message to a client sent for services by his probation officer (from Berg and Miller, 1992, p. 99):

> Curtis, we are very impressed that you are here today even though this is not your idea. You certainly had the option of taking the easy way out by not coming. . . . It has not been easy for you to be here today; having to give up your personal time, talking about things you really don't want to talk about, having to take the bus, and so on. . . .
>
> I realize that you are an independent minded person who does not want to be told what to do and I agree with you that you should be left alone. But you also realize that doing what you are told will help you get these people out of your life and you will be left alone sooner. Therefore, I would like to meet with you again to figure out further what will be good for you to do. So let's meet next week at the same time.

When Clients Perceive a Problem but Not a Role
for Themselves in a Solution

1. **Client cannot identify exceptions and does not have a goal**

    > Pay attention to what's happening in your life that tells you that this problem can be solved.

    Or, since the client does not have well-formed goals, use the formula-first-session task (de Shazer, 1985, p. 137):

    > Between now and next time we meet, we (I) would like you to observe, so that you can describe to us (me) next time, what happens in your (pick one: family, life, marriage, relationship) that you want to continue to have happen.

COMMON MESSAGES
(END-OF-SESSION FEEDBACK)
(continued)

2. **Client can identify exceptions**

> Between now and the next time we meet, pay attention to those times which are better, especially what is different about them and how they happen—that is, who does what to make them happen. Next time I'd like you to describe them to me in detail.

Or, a variation of the same observation suggestion when the client says that the exceptions are due to someone else doing something different:

> Alice, pay attention for those times when your boss is more reasonable and open. Besides paying attention to what's different about those times, pay attention to what he might notice you doing that helps him to be more polite, reasonable, and open toward you. Keep track of those things and come back and tell me what's better.

A final variation adds the element of prediction:

> Alice, I agree with you; there clearly seem to be days when your boss is more reasonable and open and days when he is not. So, between now and the next time that we meet, I suggest the following: Each night before you go to bed, predict whether or not tomorrow will be a day when he acts more reasonable and open and polite to you. Then, at the end of the day before you make your prediction for the next day, think about whether or not your prediction for that day came true. Account for any differences between your prediction and the way the day went and keep track of your observations so that you can come back and tell me about them. (de Shazer, 1988, pp. 179–183)

When Clients Want Something and See Themselves as Part of a Solution

1. **Client has a clear miracle picture but cannot identify exceptions**

> Between now and the next time we meet, pick one day and pretend the miracle. Go ahead and live that day as if the miracle has happened—just like you described it to me. Then come back next time and tell me what's better.

2. **Client seems highly motivated but does not have well-formed goals and cannot identify exceptions**

> We are so impressed with how hard you have worked on _____ (the client's concern) and with how clearly you can describe to us the

COMMON MESSAGES
(END-OF-SESSION FEEDBACK)
(continued)

things you have tried so far to make things better. We can see why you would be discouraged and frustrated right now. We also agree with you that this is a "very stubborn" (client's words) problem.

Because this is such a "stubborn" problem, we suggest that, between now and next time we meet, when _____ (the client's concern) happens, that "you do something different ... no matter how strange or weird or off-the-wall what you do might seem. The only important thing is that whatever you decide to do, you need to do something different." (de Shazer, 1985, p. 123)

3. **Client has well-formed goals and deliberate exceptions of her or his doing**

Ralph, I am impressed with you in several ways: First, how much you want to make things go better between you and your children. Second, that there are already several better times happening like _____ (give examples). And third, that you can describe to me so clearly and in such detail what you do to do your part in making those times happen, things like _____ (give examples). With all that you are doing, I can see why you say things are at a 5 already.

I agree that these are the things to do to have the kind of relationship with your children that you want to have. So, between now and when we meet again, I suggest that you continue to do what works. Also, pay attention to what else you might be doing, but haven't noticed yet, that makes things better, and come back and tell me about them.

Other Useful Messages

When a client wants to overcome a compulsion

Pay attention for those times when you overcome the urge to (overeat, drink, hit your child, use pornography, get panicky, etc.). Pay attention for what's different about those times, especially what it is that you do to overcome the urge to _____ . (de Shazer, 1985, p. 132)

When there are competing views of a solution

There are two possible situations here. In the first situation, individuals have different views. For example, if parents disagree about how to handle a child who steals, you might say:

We are impressed by how much both of you want to help your son "not to steal." The team is also impressed by what different ideas the two of

COMMON MESSAGES
(END-OF-SESSION FEEDBACK)
(continued)

you have about how to help your child through this difficult time. We can see that you were brought up in different families and learned different ways to do things (the parents had said they could see their different family backgrounds at work in their conflicting views).

The team is split on which way to go—one half feels like you ought to go with John's ideas and the other half feels like Mary's might work best. Therefore, we suggest that each morning, right after you get up, you flip a coin. Heads means that Mary is in charge and you do things her way with Billy while John stays in the background. Tails means John is in charge that day. And also—on those days when each of you is not busy being in charge—pay careful attention to what the other does with Billy that is useful or makes a difference so that you can report it to us when we meet again.

In the second, an individual is aware of more than one option and cannot decide which is best; for example, if a client is struggling with the decision whether to leave her boyfriend, Bill, you might say:

I am unsure about whether it would be best for you to "stay with Bill or leave him and begin a new life" (her words). I agree that this is a tough decision and figuring it out is going to take more hard work. As you continue to work on it, I suggest that each night before you go to bed, you flip a coin. If it comes up heads, live the next day as much as possible as though Bill is no longer a part of your life. Don't contact him, and start to take the first steps toward the things you said you would do differently if you were on your own, such as spending more time with your friends and family and so forth. If it comes up tails, live the next day as though he is still a part of your life—all those things you described to me about what that means for you. Then, as you do these things, keep paying attention to what's happening that tells you that you are becoming more clear about whether to leave him or stay in the relationship. Remember, though, that usually a person cannot be 100 percent sure. And then come back and tell me what's better.

PROTOCOL FOR FIRST SESSIONS

Client Name(s): _____   **Date:** _____

Client Concern/History: (How can I help? What tells you that _____ is a problem? What have you tried? Was it helpful?)

Goal Formulation: (What do you want different as a result of coming here? Dialogue around the miracle question.)

Exceptions: (Are there times when the problem does not happen or is less serious? When? How does that happen? Are there times that are a little like the miracle picture you describe?):

Scaling:

How close things are to the miracle:

Presession change:

Willingness to work:

PROTOCOL FOR FIRST SESSIONS
(continued)

Confidence:

Compliments:

Bridge:

Suggestion(s):

Next Time:

PROTOCOL FOR LATER SESSIONS

Name: _____ **Date:** _____

What's Better?
Elicit: (What's happening that's better?)

Amplify: (How does that happen? What do you do to make that happen? Is that new for you? Now that you are doing _____, what do you notice different between you and [significant other]? What's different at your house?)

Reinforce/Compliment: (Not everyone could have said or done _____. So you're the kind of person who is/does/believes _____ ?)

Start Again: (What else is better?)

Doing More: (What will it take to do _____ again? To do it more often?)

If Nothing Is Better: (How are you coping? How do you make it? How come things aren't even worse?)

Scaling Progress:
Current level:

Next level(s): (When you move from _____ [number for current level] to _____ [one number up the scale], what will be different? Who will be first to notice? When she or he notices, what will she or he do differently? What would it take to pretend a _____ [one number up the scale] has happened?)

PROTOCOL FOR LATER SESSIONS
(continued)

Termination: (What number do you need to be at to not see me any more? What will be different then?)

Compliments:

Bridge:

Suggestion(s):

Next time:

◈

EXCEPTION-FINDING QUESTIONS

To the interviewer: When exploring for exceptions, be aware that such questions can be phrased to ask for the client's perceptions of exceptions (individual questions) and the client's perception of what significant others might notice (relationship questions). Examples of each are included below.

Exceptions Related to the Miracle

1. **Elicit**

   So when the miracle happens, you and your husband will be talking more about what your day was like and hugging more. Are there times already which are like that miracle—even a little bit?

   If your husband was here and I were to ask him the same question, what do you think he would say?

2. **Amplify**

   When was the last time you and your husband talked more and hugged more? Tell me more about that time. What was it like? What did you talk about? What did you say? What did he say? When he said that, what did you do? What did he do then? How was that for you? What else was different about that time?

   If he were here, what else might he say about that time?

3. **Reinforce**

   Non-verbally: Lean forward, raise eyebrows, take notes (do what you naturally do when someone tells you something important).

   Verbally: Show interest. (Was this new for you and him? Did it surprise you that this happened?) And compliment. (Seems like that might have been difficult for you to do, given everything that's happened in the relationship. Was it difficult?)

EXCEPTION-FINDING QUESTIONS
(continued)

4. **Explore how the exception happened**

   What do you suppose you did to make that happen?

   If your husband were here and I asked him, what do you suppose he would say you did that helped him to tell you more about his day?

   Use compliments: Where did you get the idea to do it that way? That seems to make a lot of sense. Have you always been able to come up with ideas about what to do in difficult situations like this?

5. **Project exceptions into the future**

   On a scale of 1 to 10, where 1 means no chance and 10 means every chance, what are the chances that a time like that (the exception) will happen again in the next week (month, sometime in the future)? What will it take for that to happen?

   What will it take for that to happen more often in the future?

   Who has to do what to make that happen again?

   What is the most important thing for you to remember to do to make sure that _____ (the exception) has the best chance of happening again? What's the next most important thing to remember?

   What do you think your husband would say the chances are that this (the exception) will happen again? What would he say you could do to increase the chances of that happening? Suppose you decided to do that, what do you think he would do? Suppose he did that, how would things be different for you . . . around your house . . . in your relationship with him?

Exceptions Related to the Problem

If the client cannot define a miracle and relates to you only in terms of problem talk, phrase your questions in terms of the *problem* instead of the miracle. Example:

   Can you think of a time in the past day (week, month, year) when you and your husband fought less or not at all?

Then proceed with the five steps given for exceptions related to the miracle.

EXCEPTION-FINDING QUESTIONS
(continued)

What's Better?

You can begin all later sessions with this exception-exploration question. Be sure to follow all five steps given for exceptions related to the miracle and to use both individual and relationship questions.

Always ask "What else is better?" after you finish exploring an exception.

Coping Questions

In rare cases, the client cannot identify any exceptions and seems overwhelmed. You can ask coping questions to uncover what the client is doing to make it in such difficult circumstances:

> I'm amazed. With all that's been happening, I don't know how you make it. How do you do it? How do you get from one minute to the next?

If a client describes a longstanding depression and one discouraging event after another, you might say:

> I can see that you have many reasons to feel depressed; there have been so many things that haven't worked out the way you wished. I'm wondering, how you have managed to keep going? How have you been able to get up each morning and face another day?

If the client says she or he has to keep going for her or his kids, you might say:

> Is that how you do it? You think about your kids and how much they need you? You must care a lot about them. Tell me more about what you do to take care of them.

PROTOCOL FOR INTERVIEWING CLIENTS IN INVOLUNTARY SITUATIONS

Role Clarification

(Introduce yourself, describe your role briefly, and describe structure of session: taking a break, etc.)

Problem Description and Attempts at Solution

(Throughout, pay attention for clues about what the client might want, and what he or she might be able and willing to do.)

What is your understanding of why we are talking today? (Be prepared to share what you know about the case.)

What have you done about this situation so far?

What have thought about trying but haven't done yet? How might that be helpful?

Goal Formulation

What does _____ (pressuring person or mandating agent) think you need to do differently? (Use these questions when the client starts out negatively and seems to be unmotivated.)

> Suppose you were to decide to do that, what would be different between you and _____ (pressuring person or agent)? (Continue with: What would be different between you _____ [significant others]?)

> Is that something you could do?

PROTOCOL FOR INTERVIEWING CLIENTS IN
INVOLUNTARY SITUATIONS
(continued)

What at a minimum would you say that you have to do differently?

When was the last time you did that? Suppose you were to decide to do it again, what would be the first small step you would take?

Miracle Question

(Once asked, focus on *what will be different* when the miracle happens.)

Regarding client: What will you notice that's different? (What will be the first thing that you notice? What else?)

Regarding significant others: Who else will notice when the miracle happens?

What will she or he notice that is different about you? What else?

When she or he notices that, what will she or he do differently? What else?

When she or he does that, what will be different for you?

Moving Toward a Solution

(Use when the client can answer the miracle question.)

Suppose you were to pretend that the miracle happened. What would be the first small thing you would do? How might that be helpful?

Or: What's it going to take for a part of the miracle to happen? Is that something that could happen? If so, what makes you think so?

PROTOCOL FOR INTERVIEWING CLIENTS IN

INVOLUNTARY SITUATIONS
(continued)

Or: On a scale from 0 to 10, where 0 equals the worst the problem has been and 10 equals the miracle you described, how close are you to the miracle right now? What tells you it is that number? Suppose it was one number higher, what would be different? What would it take for that to happen? (And so forth.)

Ending

1. If the client is concrete and detailed in answer to the miracle question, give compliments and suggest: "In the next week, pick one day and pretend that the miracle has happened and look for what difference it makes."

2. If the client is *not* concrete and detailed in answer to the miracle question, give compliments and suggest: "Think about what's happening in your life that tells you that this problem can be solved. And I'll do some thinking too."

(If a second session is a possibility, you can ask the client to meet with you again to continue working on the problem.)

USEFUL QUESTIONS FOR USE WITH CLIENTS IN INVOLUNTARY SITUATIONS

- Whose idea was it that you need to come here?
- What is your understanding of why you are here?
- What makes _____ (pressuring person or mandating agent) think that you need to come here?
    - What does _____ think you need to do differently?
    - What does _____ think is the reason you have this problem?
- What would _____ say that, at a minimum, you have to do differently?
- What do you have to do to convince _____ that you don't need to come here?
- When was the last time that you did this (i.e., whatever the client said [pressuring person or mandating agent] said needs to be different)?
    - What was different in your life then?
    - How did you manage to do that?
    - What do you think _____ (significant other) would say he or she noticed different about you then?
    - Suppose you were to decide to do that again. What would be the first step you would have to take to make it happen?
    - How confident are you that you could do that again?
    - What would it take to raise your confidence a bit?
    - What would _____ (significant other) say the chances are that you will do this again?
    - Suppose you were to decide to do this. What would be different between you and _____ (significant other)?
    - What would be different between you and _____ (pressuring person or mandating agent)?
    - Suppose you were to decide to do it. What other differences would that make in your life?

USEFUL QUESTIONS FOR USE WITH CLIENTS IN INVOLUNTARY SITUATIONS
(continued)

- What would be going on in your life that is not going on now?
- How will you know when you have done enough?
  - Who will be the first to notice when you make those changes?
  - When _____ notices the changes, what will he or she do differently from what he or she does now?
  - And, when he or she does that, how will that be for you?

PROTOCOL FOR CRISIS INTERVIEWING

Role Clarification

(There may be times when you would not start this way, but be prepared to state your name and what you do in this setting)

Say: I'm glad you came here today. I think you are in the right place. What kind of help do you need first?

Go slowly; accept and affirm the client's perceptions.

Current Coping Efforts

(Assume competency.)

Find and compliment strengths, say:

I'm glad you called (or, I'm glad you made it here). I wonder how you did that.

What else are you doing to take care of yourself in this situation? (Get details: what, when, where, who and how.)

What else has been helpful to you?

Could it be worse than it is? How come it is not worse? (Notice and compliment strengths.)

PROTOCOL FOR CRISIS INTERVIEWING
(continued)

Who (and what) do you think would be most helpful to you at this time?

What about them (and that) would be so helpful to you?

Scaling Coping Progress

Suppose 10 means you are coping as well as you could possibly imagine, and 0 means you are not coping at all, where would you say you are at right now?

(If the number is 2 or above, be amazed/compliment and ask how he or she got all the way up to that number; if it is 0 or down to –2, ask what he or she is doing to prevent it from sliding further. Get details of coping thoughts and behaviors.)

Goal Formulation: Coconstructing the Next Step

Suppose things moved up one number on the scale. What would be different that would tell you that you were coping just that much better?" (Ask for small signs of improvement.)

What would _____ (significant other) notice different about you that would tell her or him that you were coping better? What else?

What would it take for that to happen?

Suppose things moved up 2 or 3 numbers on the same scale. What would be different that would tell you that you were coping that much better? What else? What would it take to make those things happen? What else? (Or, if the client is becoming more hopeful, ask the miracle question around "coping as well as anyone could imagine, considering what you have been through.")

What is the single most important thing for you to remember to continue coping with this situation?

PROTOCOL FOR CRISIS INTERVIEWING
(continued)

Ending

Summarize what the client is doing that is useful for herself or himself. Be sure to point out small details using the client's own words. Compliment the client for his or her strengths and successes. Suggest that the client continue to do what works and pay attention to what else she or he may be doing that is useful for coping.

USEFUL COPING QUESTIONS

- How did you manage to get out of bed this morning?
    - Was it difficult for you?
    - What else was helpful so that you could do it?
- How long has it been since you last ate?
    - How has that been helpful to you?
    - How do you get yourself to eat?
- When is the last time that you got some sleep?
    - Has it made a difference?
    - With all you've been through, how do you manage to get to sleep?
- What has been helpful that got you through so far?
- What do you think we can do that would be most helpful?
- Have you been in this situation before?
    - What did you do to get through it then?
    - What was the most helpful to you?
    - Who helped you the most then?
    - How did you know that _____ would be helpful?
    - What did you do to get _____ to help you?
    - What did _____ do that was so helpful to you? What else?
    - What would it take for _____ to help you again? What else?
    - When you get that help again, what difference will it make for you this time?

References

Alcoholics Anonymous. (1976). *Alcoholics Anonymous: The story of how thousands of men and women have recovered from alcoholism* (The Big Book). New York: Alcoholics Anonymous World Services.

American Psychiatric Association. (2000). *The diagnostic and statistical manual of mental disorders* (4th ed.–TR). Washington, DC: Author.

Andersen, T. (1987). The reflecting team: Dialogue and meta-dialogue in clinical work. *Family Process, 26,* 415–428.

Andersen, T. (Ed.). (1991). *The reflecting team: Dialogues and dialogues about dialogues.* New York: Norton.

Anderson, H., & Goolishian, H. A. (1992). The client is the expert: A not-knowing approach to therapy. In S. McNamee & K. J. Gergen (Eds.), *Therapy as social construction* (pp. 25–39). London: Sage.

Axelson, J. A. (1993). *Counseling and development in a multicultural society.* Pacific Grove, CA: Brooks/Cole.

Bateson, G. (Ed.). (1972). *Steps to an ecology of mind.* New York: Ballantine.

Bateson, G., Jackson, D. D., Haley, J., & Weakland, J. H. (1956). Toward a theory of schizophrenia. *Behavioral Science, 1,* 251–264.

Bavelas, J. B., McGee, D., Phillips, B., & Routledge, R. (2000). Microanalysis of communication in psychotherapy. *Human Systems, 11,* 47–66.

Benjamin, A. (1987). *The helping interview with case illustrations.* Boston: Houghton Mifflin.

Berg, I. K. (1994). *Family based services: A solution-focused approach.* New York: Norton.

Berg, I. K. (2003). *Supervision and mentoring in child welfare services: Guidelines and strategies.* Milwaukee, WI: BFTC Press.

Berg, I. K., & De Jong, P. (1996). Solution-building conversations: Co-constructing a sense of competence with clients. *Families in Society: The Journal of Contemporary Human Services, 77,* 376–391.

Berg, I. K., & De Jong, P. (2005). Engagement through complimenting. *Journal of Family Psychotherapy, 16,* 51–56.

Berg, I. K., & de Shazer, S. (1993). Making numbers talk: Language in therapy. In S. Friedman (Ed.), *The new language of change: Constructive collaboration in psychotherapy.* New York: Guilford.

Berg, I. K., & de Shazer, S. (Eds.). (1997). Special issue: Solution-focused brief family therapy: Across the spectrum—around the world. *Contemporary Family Therapy: An International Journal, 19,* 1–141.

Berg, I. K. & Dolan, Y. (2001). *Tales of solutions: Hope-inspiring stories from around the world.* New York: Norton.

Berg, I. K., & Kelly, S. (2000). *Building solutions in child protective services.* New York: Norton.

Berg, I. K., & Miller, S. D. (1992). *Working with the problem drinker: A solution-focused approach.* New York: Norton.

Berg, I. K., & Reuss, N. (1998). *Solutions step by step: A substance abuse treatment manual.* New York: Norton

Berg, I. K., & Shilts, L. (2004). *Classroom solutions: WOWW approach.* Milwaukee, WI: BFTC Press.

Berg, I. K., & Shilts, L. (2005a). *Classroom solutions: WOWW coaching.* Milwaukee, WI: BFTC Press.

Berg, I. K., & Shilts, L. (2005b). Keeping the solutions within the classroom: WOWW approach. *School Counselor,* July/August, 30–35.

Berg, I. K., & Steiner, T. (2003). *Children's solution work.* New York: Norton.

Berg, I. K., & Szabo, P. (2005). *Brief coaching for lasting solutions.* New York: Norton.

Berger, P., & Luckmann, T. (1966). *The social construction of reality: A treatise in the sociology of knowledge.* Garden City, NY: Anchor.

Biestek, F. P. (1957). *The casework relationship.* Chicago: Loyola University Press.

Blundo, R. (2001). Learning strengths-based practice: Challenging our personal and professional frames. *Families in Society: The Journal of Contemporary Human Services, 82,* 296–304.

Cade, B., & O'Hanlon, W. H. (1993). *A brief guide to brief therapy.* New York: Norton.

Cantwell, P., & Holmes, S. (1994). Social construction: A paradigm shift for systemic therapy and training. *The Australian and New Zealand Journal of Family Therapy, 15,* 17–26.

Carkhuff, R. R. (1987). *The art of helping* (6th ed.). Amherst, MA: Human Resource Development.

Carkhuff, R. R., & Berenson, B. G. (1977). *Beyond counseling and therapy* (2nd ed.). New York: Holt, Rinehart & Winston.

Cauffman, L. (2001). *Oplossingsgericht management: Kan het zo eenvoudig?* Utrecht, Holland: Uitgeverij LEMMA.

Cecchin, G. (1987). Hypothesizing, circularity, and neutrality revisited: An invitation to curiosity. *Family Process, 26,* 405–413.

Conrad, P., & Schneider, J. W. (1985). *Deviance and medicalization: From badness to sickness.* Columbus, OH: Merrill.

Corey, G., Corey, M. S., & Callanan, P. (2007). *Issues and ethics in the helping professions* (7th ed.). Belmont, CA: Thomson Brooks/Cole.

De Jong, P., & Berg, I. K. (2001). Co-constructing cooperation with mandated clients. *Social Work, 46,* 361–374.

De Jong, P., & Berg, I. K. (2002). *Interviewing for solutions* (2nd ed.). Pacific Grove, CA: Brooks/Cole.

De Jong, P., & Berg, I. K. (2008). *Instructor's resource manual with test bank: Interviewing for solutions* (3rd ed.). Belmont, CA: Thomson Brooks/Cole.

De Jong, P., & Miller, S. D. (1995). How to interview for client strengths. *Social Work, 40*, 729–736.

de Shazer, S. (1982). *Patterns of brief family therapy*. New York: Guilford.

de Shazer, S. (1984). The death of resistance. *Family Process, 23*, 79–93.

de Shazer, S. (1985). *Keys to solution in brief therapy*. New York: Norton.

de Shazer, S. (1988). *Clues: Investigating solutions in brief therapy*. New York: Norton.

de Shazer, S. (1991). *Putting difference to work*. New York: Norton.

de Shazer, S. (1994). *Words were originally magic*. New York: Norton.

de Shazer, S., Berg, I. K., Lipchik, E., Nunnaly, E., Molnar, A., Gingerich, W., & Weiner-Davis, M. (1986). Brief therapy: Focused solution development. *Family Process, 25*, 207–221.

de Shazer, S., Dolan, Y. M., Korman, H., Trepper, T., McCullom, E., & Berg, I. K. (in press). *More than miracles: The state of the art of solution-focused brief therapy*. New York: Haworth Press.

de Shazer, S., & Isebaert, L. (2003). The Bruges model: A solution-focused approach to problem drinking. *Journal of Family Psychotherapy, 14*, 43–53.

Research and Statistics Branch, Crime Prevention and Justice Assistance, Department of the Attorney General of Hawaii, & Social Science Research Institute, University of Hawaii at Manoa. (2001). *Parole decision making in Hawaii*. Honolulu, HI: Author.

Devore, W., & Schlesinger, E. G. (1999). *Ethnic-sensitive social work practice* (5th ed.). Boston: Allyn & Bacon.

Dolan, Y. M. (1991). *Resolving sexual abuse: Solution-focused therapy and Ericksonian hypnosis for adult survivors*. New York: Norton.

Durrant, M. (1993). *Residential treatment: A cooperative, competency-based approach to therapy and program design*. New York: Norton.

Durrant, M. (1995). *Creative strategies for school problems: Solutions for psychologists and teachers*. New York: Norton.

Efran, J. S., Lukens, R. J., & Lukens, M. D. (1988). Constructivism: What's in it for you? *The Family Therapy Networker, 12*, 27–35.

Egan, G. (2002). *The skilled helper: A problem management approach to helping* (7th ed.). Pacific Grove, CA: Brooks/Cole.

Epstein, L. (1985). *Talking and listening: A guide to the helping interview*. St. Louis, MO: Times Mirror/Mosby.

Federal Bureau of Investigation. (2003). *Crime in the United States, 2002*. Washington, DC: U.S. Department of Justice.

Franklin, C. (2006). Outcome studies on solution-focused therapy. Retrieved August 1, 2006, from http://www.utexas.edu/courses/franklin

Franklin, C., & Streeter, C. L. (2006). Solution-focused accountability schools for the twenty-first century: A training manual for Gonzalo Garza Independence High School. Retrieved November 1, 2006, from http://www.austinisd.org/schools/website.phtml?id=024focused.html

Freedman, J., & Combs, G. (1996). *Narrative therapy: The social construction of preferred realities.* New York: Norton.

Freud, S. (1966). *The complete introductory lectures on psychoanalysis* (J. Strachey, Trans.). New York: Norton.

Furman, B., & Ahola, T. (1992). *Solution talk: Hosting therapeutic conversations.* New York: Norton.

Furman, B., & Ahola, T. (1998). *Reteaming: Succeeding together.* Helsinki, Finland: Reteaming International—The Brief Therapy Institute of Helsinki.

Garfield, S. L. (1994). Research on client variables in psychotherapy. In A. E. Bergin & S. L. Garfield (Eds.), *Handbook of psychotherapy and behavior change* (4th ed., pp. 190–228). New York: Wiley.

George, E., Iveson, C., & Ratner, H. (1999). *Problem to solution: Brief therapy with individuals and families* (2nd ed.). London: Brief Therapy Press.

George, E., Iveson, C., & Ratner, H. (2006). *Briefer: A solution focused manual.* London: Brief.

Gergen, K. J. (1985). The social constructionist movement in American psychology. *American Psychologist, 40,* 266–275.

Gergen, K. J. (1999). *An invitation to social construction.* London: Sage.

Gergen, K. J., & Kaye, J. (1992). Beyond narrative in the negotiation of therapeutic meaning. In S. McNamee & K. J. Gergen (Eds.), *Therapy as social construction* (pp. 166–185). Newbury Park, CA: Sage.

Germain, C. B., & Gitterman, A. (1980). *The life model of social work practice.* New York: Columbia University Press.

Germain, C. B., & Gitterman, A. (1996). *The life model of social work practice: Advances in theory and practice* (2nd ed.). New York: Columbia University Press.

Gilligan, S., & Price, R. (1993). *Therapeutic conversations.* New York: Norton.

Gingerich, W. J., de Shazer, S., & Weiner-Davis, M. (1988). Constructing change: A research view of interviewing. In E. Lipchik (Ed.), *Interviewing* (pp. 21–32). Rockville, MD: Aspen.

Gingerich, W. J., & Eisengart, S. (2000). Solution-focused brief therapy: A review of the outcome research. *Family Process, 39,* 477–498.

Gingerich, W. J., & Eisengart, S. (2001). Solution-focused brief therapy outcome studies. Retrieved August 1, 2006, from http://www.gingerich.net/SFBT/research/Default.htm

Goldstein, H. (2002). The literary and moral foundations of the strengths perspective. In D. Saleebey (Ed.), *The strengths perspective in social work practice* (3rd ed., pp. 23–47). Boston: Allyn & Bacon.

Goolishian, H. A., & Anderson, H. (1991). An essay on changing theory and changing ethics: Some historical and post structural views. *American Family Therapy Association Newsletter, 46,* 6–10.

Gray, S. W., Zide, M. R., & Wilker, H. (2000). Using the solution focused brief therapy model with bereavement groups in rural communities: Resiliency at its best. *Hospice Journal, 15,* 13–30.

Greene, R. R. (2007). *Social work practice: A risk and resilience perspective.* Belmont, CA: Thomson Brooks/Cole.

Guest, J. (1976). *Ordinary people.* New York: Ballantine.

Haley, J. (1973). *Uncommon therapy.* New York: Norton.

Haley, J. (1987). *Problem-solving therapy.* San Francisco: Jossey-Bass.

Hall, D. (2003). *Criminal law and procedure.* Albany, NY: Delmar.

Hartman, C., & Reynolds, D. (1987). Resistant clients: Confrontation, interpretation, and alliance. *Social Casework, 68,* 205–213.

Hepworth, D. H., Rooney, R. H. & Larsen, J. A. (2002). *Direct social work practice: Theory and skills* (6th ed.). Pacific Grove, CA: Brooks/Cole.

Hiebert-Murphy, D., & Richert, M. (2000). A parenting group for women dealing with child sexual abuse and substance abuse. *International Journal of Group Psychotherapy, 50,* 397–405.

Hoffman, L. (1990). Constructing realities: An art of lenses. *Family Process, 29,* 1–12.

Hopwood, L., & de Shazer, S. (1994). From here to there and who knows where: The continuing evolution of solution-focused brief therapy. In M. Elkaim (Ed.), *Therapies familiales: Les approches principaux* (pp. 555–576). Paris: Editions de Seuil.

Hwoschinsky, C. (2001). *Listening with the heart: A guide for compassionate listening.* Indianola, WA: The Compassionate Listening Project.

Ivanoff, A., Blythe, B. J., & Tripodi, T. (1994). *Involuntary clients in social work practice: A research-based approach.* New York: Aldine de Gruyter.

Ivey, A. E., & Ivey, M. B. (2007). *Intentional interviewing and counseling: Facilitating client development in a multicultural society* (6th ed.). Belmont, CA: Thomson Brooks/Cole.

Jackson, P. Z., & McKergow, M. (2002). *The solutions focus: The simple way to positive change.* London: Nicholas Brealey.

James, H. (Ed.). (1920). *The letters of William James (Vol. 2).* Boston: Atlantic Monthly Press.

James, R. K., & Gilliland, B. E. (2005). *Crisis intervention strategies* (5th ed.). Pacific Grove, CA: Brooks/Cole.

Kadushin, A. (1990). *The social work interview.* New York: Columbia University Press.

Kagle, J. D. (1991). *Social work records* (2nd ed.). Belmont, CA: Wadsworth.

Keefe, T. (1976). Empathy: The critical skill. *Social Work, 21,* 10–14.

Kendall, P. C., Holmbeck, G., & Verduin, T. (2004). Methodology, design, and evaluation in psychotherapy research. In M. J. Lambert (Ed.), *Bergin and Garfield's handbook of psychotherapy and behavior change* (5th ed., pp. 16–43). New York: Wiley.

Kennedy, J., Eberthart, R., & Shi, Y. (2001). *Swarm intelligence.* San Francisco: Morgan Kaufmann.

Kim, J. (2006). *Examining the effects of solution-focused brief therapy: A meta-analysis using random effects modeling.* Unpublished doctoral dissertation, University of Texas, Austin.

Kiser, D. (1988). *A follow-up study conducted at the Brief Family Therapy Center.* Unpublished manuscript.

Kiser, D. & Nunally, E. (1990). *The relationship between treatment length and goal achievement in solution-focused therapy.* Unpublished manuscript.

Kiser, D., Piercy, F. P., & Lipchik, E. (1993). The integration of emotion in solution-focused therapy. *Journal of Marital and Family Therapy, 19,* 233–242.

Kuhn, T. S. (1962). *The structure of scientific revolutions.* Chicago: University of Chicago Press.

LaFountain, R. M., & Garner, N. E. (1996). Solution-focused counseling groups: The results are in. *The Journal for Specialists in Group Work, 21*, 128–143.

LaFrance, M. (1992). Questioning knowledge acquisition. In T. W. Lauer, E. Peacock, & A. C. Graesser (Eds.), *Questions and information systems* (pp. 11–28). Hillsdale, NJ: Lawrence Erlbaum.

Laird, J. (1993). Family-centered practice: Cultural and constructionist reflections. In J. Laird (Ed.), *Revisioning social work education: A social constructionist approach* (pp. 77–109). New York: Haworth.

Lambert, M. J., & Bergin, A. E. (1994). The effectiveness of psychotherapy. In A. E. Bergin & S. L. Garfield (Eds.), *Handbook of psychotherapy and behavior change* (4th ed., pp. 143–189). New York: Wiley.

Lange, S. M. (2001). Solution-focused group psychotherapy for incarcerated fathers. *Journal of Family Psychotherapy, 12*, 1–21.

Lee, M. Y., Greene, G. J., & Rheinscheld, J. (1999). A model for short-term solution-focused group treatment of male domestic violence offenders. *Journal of Family Social Work, 3*, 39 57.

Lee, M. Y., Sebold, J., & Uken, A. (2003). *Solution-focused treatment of domestic violence offenders: Accountability for change.* New York: Oxford University Press.

Lee, M. Y., Sebold, J., & Uken, A. (2004). Accountability for change: Solution-focused treatment with domestic violence offenders. *Families in Society: The Journal of Contemporary Human Services, 85*, 463–476.

Lewis, J. A., Dana, R. Q., & Blevins, G. A. (2002). *Substance abuse counseling: An individualized approach* (3rd ed.). Pacific Grove, CA: Brooks/Cole.

Lindforss, L., & Magnusson, D. (1997). Solution-focused therapy in prison. *Contemporary Family Therapy: An International Journal, 19*, 89–103.

Lipchik, E. (1999). Theoretical and practical thoughts about expanding the solution-focused approach to include emotions. In W. R. Ray & S. de Shazer (Eds.), *Evolving brief therapy: In honor of John Weakland* (pp. 157–177). Galena, IL, and Iowa City, IA: Geist & Russell.

Lipchik, E. (2002). *Beyond technique in solution-focused therapy.* New York: Guilford.

Lukas, S. (1993). *Where to start and what to ask: An assessment handbook.* New York: Norton.

Lum, D. (2004). *Social work practice and people of color: A process-stage approach* (5th ed.). Pacific Grove, CA: Brooks/Cole.

Macdonald, A. J. (2006). Solution-focused brief therapy evaluation list. Retrieved August 1, 2006, from http://www.psychsft.freeserve.co.uk/sfb.html

MacDonald, C., Ricci, N., & Stewart, M. (1998). *Solution-focused therapy.* Unpublished manuscript, University of Victoria, Victoria, British Columbia, Canada.

Martin, D. G., & Moore, A. D. (1995). *First steps in the art of intervention: A guidebook for trainees in the helping professions.* Pacific Grove, CA: Brooks/Cole.

Maslow, A. (1970). *Motivation and personality* (2nd ed.). New York: Harper & Row.

McClam, T., & Woodside, M. (1994). *Problem solving in the helping professions.* Pacific Grove, CA: Brooks/Cole

McCollum, E. E., Trepper, T. S., & Smock, S. (2003). Solution-focused group therapy for substance abuse: Extending competency-based models. *Journal of Family Psychotherapy, 14*, 27–43.

McGee, D. R. (1999). *Constructive questions: How do therapeutic questions work?* Unpublished doctoral dissertation, University of Victoria, Victoria, British Columbia, Canada.

McGee, D. R., Del Vento, A., & Bavelas, J. B. (2005). An interactional model of questions as therapeutic interventions. *Journal of Marital and Family Therapy, 31,* 371–384.

McKeel, A. J. (1996). A clinician's guide to research on solution-focused brief therapy. In S. D. Miller, M. A. Hubble, & B. L. Duncan, *Handbook of solution-focused brief therapy* (pp. 251–271). San Francisco: Jossey-Bass.

McKeel, A. J. (1999). A selected review of research of solution-focused brief therapy. Retrieved August 1, 2006, from http://www.ebta.nu

McMahon, M. O. (1996). *The general method of social work practice: A problem-solving approach* (3rd ed.). Boston: Allyn & Bacon.

Mead, G. H. (1934). *Mind, self and society.* Chicago: University of Chicago Press.

Metcalf, L. (1995). *Counseling toward solutions: A practical solution-focused program for working with students, teachers, and parents.* West Nyack, NY: Center for Applied Research in Education.

Metcalf, L. (1998). *Solution-focused group therapy: Ideas for groups in private practice, schools, agencies, and treatment programs.* New York: Free Press.

Miley, K. K., O'Melia, M., & DuBois, B. (2007). *Generalist social work practice: An empowering approach* (5th ed.). Boston: Allyn & Bacon.

Miller, G. (1991). *Enforcing the work ethic: Rhetoric and everyday life in a work incentive program.* Albany, NY: SUNY Press.

Miller, G. (1997). *Becoming miracle workers: Language and meaning in brief therapy.* New York: Aldine de Gruyter.

Miller, G., & de Shazer, S. (2000). Emotions in solution-focused therapy: A re-examination. *Family Process, 39,* 5–23.

Miller, S. D., & Berg, I. K. (1995). *The miracle method: A radically new approach to problem drinking.* New York: Norton.

Miller, S. D., Hubble, M. A., & Duncan, B. L. (Eds.). (1996). *Handbook of solution-focused brief therapy.* San Francisco: Jossey-Bass.

Miller, W. R., & Rollnick, S. (2002). *Motivational interviewing* (2nd ed.). New York: Guilford.

Modcrin, M., Rapp, C. A., & Poertner, J. (1988). The evaluation of case management services with the chronically mentally ill. *Evaluation and Program Planning, 11,* 307–314.

Nelson, T. (Ed.). (2005). *Education and training in solution-focused brief therapy.* New York: Haworth.

Neufeldt, V., & Guralnik, D. (Eds.). (1988). *Webster's new world dictionary of the American language* (3rd college ed.). New York: Simon & Schuster.

O'Hanlon, W. H., & Weiner-Davis, M. (1989). *In search of solutions.* New York: Norton.

Okun, B. F. (1997). *Effective helping: Interviewing and counseling techniques* (5th ed.). Pacific Grove, CA: Brooks/Cole.

Okun, B. F., Fried, J., & Okun, M. L. (1999). *Understanding diversity: A learning-as-practice primer.* Pacific Grove, CA: Brooks/Cole.

Parad, H. J. (1971). Crisis intervention. In R. Morris (Ed.), *Encyclopedia of social work* (Vol. 1, pp. 196–202). New York: National Association of Social Workers.

Parton, N., & O'Byrne, P. (2000). *Constructive social work: Towards a new practice.* London: Macmillan.

Pichot, T., & Dolan, Y. M. (2003). *Solution-focused brief therapy: Its effective use in agency settings.* Binghamton, NY: Haworth Press.

Pincus, A., & Minahan, A. (1973). *Social work practice: Model and method.* Itasca, IL: Peacock.

Rapp, C. A. (1998). *The strengths model: Case management with people suffering from severe and persistent mental illness.* New York: Oxford.

Rappaport, J. (1981). In praise of paradox: A social policy of empowerment over prevention. *American Journal of Community Psychology, 9,* 1–25.

Rappaport, J. (1990). Research methods and the empowerment social agenda. In P. Tolan, C. Keys, F. Chertak, & L. Jason (Eds.). *Researching community psychology* (pp. 51–63). Washington, DC: American Psychological Association.

Rita, E. S. (1998). Solution-focused supervision. *The Clinical Supervisor, 17,* 127–139.

Roberts, A. R. (1990). *Crisis intervention handbook: Assessment, treatment, and research.* Belmont, CA: Wadsworth.

Rogers, C. R. (1957). The necessary and sufficient conditions for therapeutic personality change. *Journal of Counseling Psychology, 21,* 95–103.

Rogers, C. R. (1961). *On becoming a person: A therapist's view of psychotherapy.* Boston: Houghton Mifflin.

Rooney, R. H. (1992). *Strategies for work with involuntary clients.* New York: Columbia University Press.

Rudes, J., Shilts, L., & Berg, I. K. (1997). Focused supervision seen through a recursive frame of analysis. *Journal of Marital and Family Therapy, 23,* 203–215.

Saari, C. (1991). *The creation of meaning in clinical social work.* New York: Guilford.

Saleebey, D. (Ed.). (1992). *The strengths perspective in social work practice.* New York: Longman.

Saleebey, D. (1994). Culture, theory, and narrative: The intersection of meanings in practice. *Social Work, 39,* 351–359.

Saleebey, D. (Ed.). (2007). *The strengths perspective in social work practice* (4th ed.). Boston: Allyn & Bacon.

Satir, V. (1982). The therapist and family therapy: Process model In A. M. Horne & M. M. Ohlsen (Eds.), *Family counseling and therapy* (pp. 12–42). Itasca, IL: Peacock.

Schon, D. A. (1983). *The reflective practitioner.* New York: Basic Books.

Schorr, M. (1995). Finding solutions in a relaxation group. *Journal of Systemic Therapies, 14,* 55–63.

Selekman, M. D. (1991). The solution-oriented parenting group: A treatment alternative that works. *Journal of Strategic and Systemic Therapies, 10,* 36–49.

Selekman, M. D. (1993). *Pathways to change: Brief therapy solutions with difficult adolescents.* New York: Guilford.

Selekman, M. D. (1997). *Solution-focused therapy with children: Harnessing family strengths for systemic change.* New York: Guilford.

Selekman, M. D. (2002). *Living on the razor's edge: Solution-oriented brief therapy with self-harming adolescents.* New York: Norton.

Sharry, J. (2001). *Solution-focused groupwork*. London: Sage.

Sharry, J., Madden, B., Darmody, M., & Miller, S. D. (2001). Giving our clients the break: Applications of client-directed, outcome-informed clinical work. *Journal of Systemic Therapies, 20*, 68–76.

Sheafor, B. W., & Horejsi, C. R. (2007). *Techniques and guidelines for social work practice* (7th ed.). Boston: Allyn & Bacon.

Sparks, P. M. (1989). Organizational tasking: A case report. *Organizational Development Journal, 7*, 51–57.

Stam, P. (2004, September). *Building a Large Solution Focused Organization*. Paper presented at the meeting of the European Brief Therapy Association, Amsterdam, The Netherlands.

Stancer, M., Sreety, D., & Britton, I. (2006, May). *Solution-focused brief therapy in a statutory social work setting*. Paper presented at the meeting of Solutions with Children and Adolescents, London, United Kingdom.

Sue, D. W., & Sue, D. (1999). *Counseling the culturally different: Theory and practice* (3rd ed.). New York: Wiley.

Sundstrom, S. M. (1993). *Single-session psychotherapy for depression: Is it better to be problem-focused or solution-focused?* Unpublished doctoral dissertation, University of South Dakota.

Talmon, M. (1990). *Single session therapy*. San Francisco: Jossey-Bass.

Thomas, F. (1995). Genograms and competence: Fashioning meaning through an alternate use. *News of the Difference, IV*, 9–11.

Timberlake, E. M., Farber, M. Z., & Sabatino, C. A. (2002). *The general method of social work practice: McMahon's generalist perspective* (4th ed.). Boston: Allyn & Bacon.

Triantafillou, N. (1997). A solution-focused approach to mental health supervision. *Journal of Systemic Therapies, 16*, 305–328.

Trotter, C. (1999). *Working with involuntary clients: A guide to practice*. London: Sage.

Turnell, A., & Edwards, S. (1999). *Signs of safety: A solution and safety oriented approach to child protection*. New York: Norton.

Uken, A., & Sebold, J. (1996). The Plumas project: A solution-focused goal directed domestic violence diversion program. *Journal of Collaborative Therapies, 4*, 10–17.

Vaughn, K., Hastings-Guerrero, S., & Kassner, C. (1996). Solution-oriented inpatient group therapy. *Journal of Systemic Therapies, 15*, 1–14.

Vinter, R. (1985). Components of social work practice. In M. Sundel, P. Glasser, R. Sarri, & R. Vinter (Eds.), *Individual change through small groups* (2nd ed., pp. 11–34). New York: Free Press.

Wade, A. (1997). Small acts of living: Everyday resistance to violence and other forms of oppression. *Contemporary Family Therapy: An International Journal, 19*, 23–39.

Walker, L. (2004). Pono Kaulike: A pilot restorative justice program. *Hawaii Bar Journal, 8*, 4–15.

Walter, J. L., & Peller, J. E. (1992). *Becoming solution-focused in brief therapy*. New York: Brunner/Mazel.

Walter, J. L., & Peller, J. E. (2000). *Recreating brief therapy: Preferences and possibilities*. New York: Brunner/Mazel.

Watzlawick, P. (Ed.). (1984). *The invented reality*. New York: Norton.

Weakland, J. H., Fisch, R., Watzlawick, P., & Bodin, A. (1974). Brief therapy: Focused problem resolution. *Family Process, 13*, 141–168.

Weick, A. (1992). Building a strengths perspective for social work. In D. Saleebey (Ed.), *The strengths perspective in social work practice* (pp. 18–26). New York: Longman.

Weick, A. (1993). Reconstructing social work education. In J. Laird (Ed.), *Revisioning social work education: A social constructionist approach* (pp. 11–30). New York: Haworth.

Weick, A., Rapp, C., Sullivan, W. P., & Kishardt, W. (1989). A strengths perspective for social work practice. *Social Work, 34*, 350–354.

Weiner-Davis, M. (1993). *Divorce busting: A revolutionary and rapid program for staying together.* New York: Simon & Schuster.

Weiner-Davis, M. (1995). *Change your life and everyone in it.* New York: Simon & Schuster.

Weiner-Davis, M., de Shazer, S., & Gingerich, W. J. (1987). Building on pretreatment change to construct the therapeutic solution: An exploratory study. *Journal of Marital and Family Therapy, 13*, 359–363.

White, M., & Epston, D. (1990). *Narrative means to therapeutic ends.* New York: Norton.

Witkin, S. L. (1999). Questions [Editorial]. *Social Work, 44*, 197–200.

Witkin, S. L. (2000). Noticing [Editorial]. *Social Work, 45*, 101–104.

Young, S. (2002). *Solutions to bullying.* Tamworth, UK: Nasen.

Young, S., & Holdorf, G. (2002). Using solution-focused brief therapy in individual referrals for bullying. *Educational Psychology in Practice, 19*, 271–282.

Zehr, H. (2002). *The little book of restorative justice.* Intercourse: PA: Good Books.

Zeig, J. K., & Lankton, S. R. (Eds.). (1988). *Developing Ericksonian therapy: State of the art.* New York: Brunner/Mazel.

Zimmerman, T. S., Jacobsen, R. B., MacIntyre, M., & Watson, C. (1996). Solution-focused parenting groups: An empirical study. *Journal of Systemic Therapies, 15*, 12–25.

Zimmerman, T. S., Prest, L. A., & Wetzel, B. E. (1997). Solution-focused couples therapy groups: An empirical study. *Journal of Family Therapy, 19*, 125–144.

Index